Cyber Law in Israel

Cyber Law in Israel

Gabriel Hallevy

This book was originally published as a monograph in the International Encyclopaedia of Laws/Cyber Law.

Founding Editor: Roger Blanpain
General Editor: Frank Hendrickx
Volume Editor: Jos Dumortier, Pieter Gryffroy, Ruben Roex &
Yung Shin Van Der Sype

Wolters Kluwer

Published by:
Kluwer Law International B.V.
PO Box 316
2400 AH Alphen aan den Rijn
The Netherlands
E-mail: international-sales@wolterskluwer.com
Website: www.wolterskluwer.com/en/solutions/kluwerlawinternational

Sold and distributed by:
Wolters Kluwer Legal & Regulatory U.S.
7201 McKinney Circle
Frederick, MD 21704
United States of America
E-mail: customer.service@wolterskluwer.com

ISBN 978-94-035-4235-5

e-Book: ISBN 978-94-035-4240-9
web-PDF: ISBN 978-94-035-4241-6

The Author

Professor Dr Gabriel Hallevy is a Full Professor at the Faculty of Law, Ono Academic College, Israel, which is the largest faculty of law in Israel. He lectures Criminal Law, Criminal Justice, Evidence Law, Conflict of Laws, Bankruptcy Law, Game Theory and the Law, and Robo-Ethics.

He has an LLB *magna cum laude* from Tel Aviv University, Israel, an LLM *magna cum laude* from Tel Aviv University, and a PhD *summa cum laude* from the University of Haifa, Israel.

By 2021, he has published over forty books and dozens of academic articles around the world, and many of them are cited by the Israeli Supreme Court, besides hundreds of citations in academic articles and books. Some of his famous publications were translated and published in various languages around the world, such as Chinese and Turkish. His book *When Robots Kill* is considered the fundamental source for any regulation of artificial intelligence technology around the world. In 2013, he was chosen as one of the forty most promising persons under the age of 40 by *Globes* magazine in Israel, and he is a prominent speaker in many international popular events, such as TEDx and BBB.

The Author

Table of Contents

List of Abbreviations

ADR	Alternative Dispute Resolutions
ADSL	Asymmetric Digital Subscriber Line
AI	Artificial Intelligence
Anon.	Anonymous Party in Civil or Criminal Proceedings
ATM	Asynchronous Transfer Mode
Civ. App.	Civil Appeal in the Israeli Supreme Court
Civ. App. Req.	Civil Appeal Request in the Israeli Supreme Court
Civ. Cer.	Civil Certiorari in the Israeli Supreme Court
citizens and the government (C2G)	
Civ. Serv. App.	Civil Service Appeal in the Israeli Supreme Court
Cri. App.	Criminal Appeal in the Israeli Supreme Court
Cri. App. Req.	Criminal Appeal Request in the Israeli Supreme Court
Cri. Cas.	Criminal Case
Cri. Req.	Criminal Request in the Israeli Supreme Court
Cri. Ret.	Criminal Retrial Request in the Israeli Supreme Court
DDEC	Department of Defence Export Controls
DECA	Defence Export Controls Agency
DHCP	Dynamic Host Configuration Protocol
DSL	Digital Subscriber Line
DVB	Digital Video Broadcasting
FTTH	Fibre to the Home
G2B	Government and Businesses
G2C	Government and Citizens
G2E	Government and Employees
G2G	Government and Other Government

List of Abbreviations

GDP	Gross Domestic Product
HCJ	High Court of Justice Petition in the Israeli Supreme Court
ICT	Information and Communications Technology
IDF	Israel Defense Forces
IDN	Internationalized Domain Names
IETV	Israeli Educational Television
IIX	Israeli Internet Exchange
IP	Intellectual Property
ISPs	Internet Service Providers
IT	Information Technology
IUCC	Inter-University Computation Centre
LTE	Long Term Evolution
MVNE	Mobile Virtual Network Enabler
MVNO	Mobile Virtual Network Operator
NCU	National Cyber Unit
NFV	Network Functions Virtualization
NGN	Next Generation Network
OECD	Organisation for Economic Co-operation and Development
PAL	Phase Alternating Line
PD	Published Decisions of the Israeli Supreme Court
SAR	Specific Absorption Rate
UN	United Nations
US	United States
VPNs	Virtual Private Networks

General Introduction

Chapter 1. General Background of Israel

§1. Geography and Climate

1. The state of Israel is located in the Middle East at the eastern side of the Mediterranean Sea, bounded by Lebanon and Syria to the north, the kingdom of Jordan to the east, and Egypt to the south. The sovereign territory of Israel is approximately 22,072 square kilometres. Israel is home to a variety of geographic features, from the Judea desert in the east, the Negev desert in the south to the mountain ranges in the north. About 70% of Israel's population is concentrated in the coastal plain on the shore of the Mediterranean Sea. The Jordan River runs along the Jordan Rift Valley, from Mount Chermon to the Dead Sea, the lowest land point on Earth. In the south is the Arava, ending with the Gulf of Eilat, part of the Red Sea.

Temperatures in Israel vary widely, especially during the winter. The more mountainous regions can be windy, cold, and sometimes snowy. Jerusalem usually receives one snowfall every decade. However, coastal cities, such as Tel Aviv and Haifa, have a typical Mediterranean climate with cool rainy winters and long HOT summers. The area of Beer-Sheba and the Northern Negev has a semi-arid climate with HOT summers and cool winter, but with fewer rainy than the Mediterranean climate. The Southern Negev and the Arava areas have a Desert climate with very HOT and dry summers and mild winters with few days of rain. The highest temperature in the continent of Asia (53.7°C) was recorded in 1942 at Tirat Zvi kibbutz. From May to September, rain in Israel is rare.

§2. Population, Languages and Religions

2. Israel is defined as Jewish and democratic state, and as the homeland of the Jewish people.[1] In 2021, Israel's population was an estimated 9.4 million, of whom 74.2% are Jews and 21% are Arabs.[2] Israel has one official language, the Hebrew language, which was spoken by Jews since the second millennium BC. In 2018, Arabic was classified as having a 'special status in the state' with its use by state

1. Basic Law: Israel – the Nation State of the Jewish People.
2. https://www.cbs.gov.il/en/subjects/Pages/Population.aspx (accessed 23 Jul. 2021).

institutions to be set in law.[3] Hebrew is the primary language of the state and is spoken by the majority of the population.[4] Arabic is spoken mostly by the Arab population. As a country of refugees and immigrants, many languages are occasionally spoken by its inhabitants in addition to Hebrew and Arabic.

Retention of Israel's population since 1948 is about even or greater, when compared to other countries with mass immigration. Emigration from Israel to other countries, primarily the United States (US) and Canada, is described by demographers as modest. Approximately 80% of Israeli Jews are Israeli-born, 14% are immigrants from Europe and the Americas, and 5% are immigrants from Asia and Africa (including the Arab countries).[5] Jews who were refugees of the Arab and Muslim lands and their descendants constitute approximately 50% of Jewish Israelis.[6]

About 18% of the population is Sunni Muslim.[7] The Muslims constitute Israel's largest religious minority. About 2% of the population is Christian and 1.5% is Druze.[8] The Christian population includes both Arab Christians, Post-Soviet immigrants and the foreign workers of multi-national origins. Members of many other religious groups, including Buddhists and Hindus, maintain a presence in Israel, but in small numbers.

§3. Economy, Science, Technology and Energy

3. Israel is considered one of the most advanced countries in the Middle East in economic and industrial development. In 2010, it joined the Organisation for Economic Co-operation and Development (OECD). Intensive development of the agricultural and industrial sectors in Israel over the past decades has made Israel largely self-sufficient in food production, apart from grains and beef. Imports to Israel, totalling USD 66.76 billion in 2017, include raw materials, military equipment, investment goods, rough diamonds, fuels, grain, and consumer goods. Leading exports include machinery and equipment, software, cut diamonds, agricultural products, chemicals, and textiles and apparel.[9] In 2017, Israeli exports reached USD 60.6 billion.[10] Israel has the second-largest number of start-up companies in the world (after the US) and the largest number of NASDAQ-listed companies after the US and China.

Working days in Israel are Sunday through Thursday (for a five-day workweek), or Friday (for a six-day workweek). In observance of Saturday, in places where Friday is a workday and the majority of the population is Jewish, Friday is a short

3. Section 4(b) of the Basic Law: Israel – the Nation State of the Jewish People.
4. Section 4(a) of the Basic Law: Israel – the Nation State of the Jewish People.
5. https://www.cbs.gov.il/en/subjects/Pages/Population.aspx (accessed 23 Jul. 2021).
6. *Ibid.*
7. *Ibid.*
8. *Ibid.*
9. https://www.cbs.gov.il/en/subjects/Pages/Imports-and-Exports-in-Goods-and-Services.aspx (accessed 23 Jul. 2021).
10. *Ibid.*

working day, usually lasting until 14:00 in the winter, or 16:00 in the summer.[11] Several proposals have been raised to adjust the work week with the majority of the world, and make Sunday a non-working day, while extending working time of other days or replacing Friday with Sunday as a workday.

Israel's development of cutting-edge technologies in software, communications, and the life sciences has evoked comparisons with Silicon Valley. Israel ranks tenth in the Bloomberg Innovation Index and is first in the world in expenditure on research and development as a percentage of Gross Domestic Product (GDP). Israel boasts 140 scientists, technicians, and engineers per 10,000 employees, the highest number in the world (in comparison, the same is 85 for the US).[12]

As of 2021, Israel has produced six Nobel Prize-winning scientists since 2004 and has been frequently ranked as one of the countries with the highest ratios of scientific papers per capita in the world. Israel has led the world in stem-cell research papers per capita since 2000. Israeli universities are ranked among the top fifty world universities in computer science, mathematics, and chemistry.

In 2012, Israel was ranked ninth in the world by the Futron's Space Competitiveness Index.[13] The Israel Space Agency coordinates all Israeli space research programmes with scientific and commercial goals and has indigenously designed and built thirteen commercial, research and spy satellites. Some of Israel's satellites are ranked among the world's most advanced space systems.

The ongoing shortage of water in the country has spurred innovation in water conservation techniques, and a substantial agricultural modernization, drip irrigation, was invented in Israel. Israel is also at the technological forefront of desalination and water recycling. The Sorek desalination plant is the largest seawater reverse osmosis (SWRO) desalination facility in the world. By 2015, Israel's desalination programmes provided roughly 40% of Israel's drinking water and it is expected to supply 70% by 2050.[14]

As of 2021, more than 50% of the water for Israeli households, agriculture, and industry is artificially produced.[15] The country hosts an annual Water Technology and Environmental Control Exhibition and Conference (WATEC) that attracts thousands of people from across the world. In 2011, Israel's water technology industry was worth around USD 2 billion a year with annual exports of products and services in the tens of millions of dollars.[16] As a result of innovations in reverse osmosis technology, Israel is set to become a net exporter of water in the coming years.

Israel has embraced solar energy. Its engineers are on the cutting edge of solar energy technology, and its solar companies work on projects around the world. Over 90% of Israeli homes use solar energy for hot water, the highest per capita in the world.[17] According to government figures, the country saves 8% of its electricity consumption per year because of its solar energy use in heating. The high annual

11. Working Hours and Rest Act, 1951.
12. https://www.cbs.gov.il/en/subjects/Pages/Labour-Market.aspx (accessed 23 Jul. 2021).
13. https://en.wikipedia.org/wiki/Space_Competitiveness_Index (accessed 23 Jul. 2021).
14. https://www.water-technology.net/projects/israel/ (accessed 23 Jul. 2021).
15. http://watec-israel.com/ (accessed 23 Jul. 2021).
16. *Ibid.*
17. *Ibid.*

incident solar irradiance at its geographic latitude creates ideal conditions for what is an internationally renowned solar research and development industry.

Israel began producing natural gas from its own offshore gas fields in 2004.[18] Between 2005 and 2012, Israel had imported gas from Egypt, but this was terminated due to Egyptian political crisis of 2011. In 2009, a natural gas reserve was found near the coast of Israel. A second natural gas reserve was discovered in 2010.[19] The natural gas reserves in these two fields could make Israel's energy secure for more than fifty years. As of 2014, Israel produced over 7.5 billion cubic meters of natural gas a year.[20] In early 2017, Israel began exporting natural gas to the Kingdom of Jordan.[21]

§4. Government

4. Israel operates under a parliamentary system as a democratic republic with universal suffrage.[22] The President of Israel is the head of state, but his duties are limited and largely ceremonial.[23] A Parliament Member supported by a majority in parliament becomes the Prime Minister, usually the chairman of the largest party. The Prime Minister is the head of government and head of the Cabinet. Israel is governed by a 120-member parliament, known as the Knesset. Membership of the Knesset is based on proportional representation of political parties, with a 3.25% electoral threshold, which commonly results in coalition governments.[24] Parliamentary elections are scheduled every four years, but unstable coalitions or a no-confidence vote by the Knesset often dissolves governments earlier.

The State of Israel is divided into six main administrative districts: Jerusalem, Centre, Haifa, North, South, and Tel Aviv Districts. Districts are further divided into fifteen sub-districts, which are themselves partitioned into fifty natural regions. For statistical purposes, the country is divided into three metropolitan areas: Tel Aviv metropolitan area, Haifa metropolitan area, and Beer-Sheba metropolitan area. Israel's largest municipality, both in population and area, is Jerusalem in an area of 126 square kilometres. Tel Aviv and Haifa rank as Israel's next most populous cities. Above the government, the parliament and the legal system is the president of the state of Israel. The presidential function is mostly representative, but it also includes the power of amnesty over convicted defendants.

18. https://en.wikipedia.org/wiki/Natural_gas_in_Israel (accessed 23 Jul. 2021).
19. *Ibid.*
20. *Ibid.*
21. *Ibid.*
22. Basic Law: The Government.
23. Basic Law: The President.
24. Basic Law: The Knesset.

§5. Legal System

5. Israel has a three-instance court system.[25] At the lowest level are Magistrates' Courts ('Shalom Courts'), situated in most cities across the country. Above them are District Courts, serving both as appellate courts and courts of first instance. They are situated in Israel's six districts. In general, in criminal matters, the jurisdiction of the magistrate's courts includes offences of up to seven years' imprisonment, and the jurisdiction of the District Courts includes the other offences. In civil matters, the jurisdiction of the Magistrates' Courts includes suits of up to NIS 2.5 million and real estate suits of possession, and the jurisdiction of the District Courts include all other civil matters.

The third and highest tier in Israel is the Supreme Court, seated in Jerusalem. It serves a dual role as the highest Court of Appeals and the High Court of Justice. In the latter role, the Supreme Court rules as a Court of First Instance, allowing individuals, both citizens and non-citizens, to petition against decisions of state authorities. Although Israel supports the goals of the International Criminal Court, it has not ratified the Rome Statute, citing concerns about the ability of the court to remain politically impartial.

In addition to the three-instances court system described above, Israel has also a system of specialized Courts (the Labour Courts, the Military Courts, besides the specialized departments of the general court system (Juvenile Court, Family Court, Transportation Court, Sea Affairs Court, etc.). The Labour Courts, for example, have unique jurisdiction over labour matters (both in the individual and collective spheres) as well as social welfare matters (e.g., lawsuits related to pensions, social security benefits, healthcare).

Most matters in Labour Courts are adjudicated by a three-panel court consisting of one professional judge, and two lay representatives nominated to the court with the consent of the largest employees and employers unions (one representative termed as 'Employees Representative' and the other as 'Employers Representative'). Some matters (e.g., criminal cases related to labour law) are adjudicated by a professional judge only. The National Labour Court, situated in Jerusalem, serves as an appeal court as well as a first instance court for matters with national importance (e.g., collective bargaining disputes, on a national level, between employees and employers unions).

Israel's legal system combines English Common Law, civil law, and Hebrew law. It is based on the principle of stare decisis (precedent). The binding precedent in Israel is limited. Only the Supreme Court of Israel is authorized to create binding precedents. All courts, both in the general system and the specialized systems are bound to the Supreme Court's binding precedents. The Supreme Court itself is not bound to its precedents, and previous precedents may be replaced by new ones.

Israel's legal system is also an adversarial system, where the parties in the lawsuit bring evidence before the court. Court cases are decided by professional judges rather than juries. Marriage and divorce are under the jurisdiction of the religious courts: Rabbinical, Muslim, Druze, and Christian. A committee of Knesset members, Supreme Court justices, and Israeli Bar members carries out the election of

25. The Courts [Combined Version] Act, 1984.

judges. Administration of Israel's courts (both the general courts and the Labour Courts) is carried by the Administration of Courts, situated in Jerusalem. Both the general and Labour courts are paperless courts, that is, storage of court files, as well as court decisions, are carried out electronically.

§6. The Justice System

I. The Israeli Police

6. The Israeli police is the primary legitimate power of law enforcement.[26] It is authorized to accept complaints and to investigate all types of offences, including crimes. In addition, with respect to some offences, which are not crimes, the police is authorized to prosecute the accused in the magistrate's courts. In most transportation offences, the police is the most professional prosecution, and only the police is competent to prosecute. In complicated investigations, district prosecutors are accompanying the investigation, although it is managed by the police.

II. The Prosecution

7. The prosecution in Israel is divided into various departments, which all are subordinated to the prosecutor general's office.[27] As aforesaid, the police is authorized to function as a prosecution in some offences which are not crimes. The district prosecutors are authorized to prosecute in all offences within their local jurisdiction. Beyond that, there are professional specific departments which are authorized to prosecute specific offences (e.g., tax offences, securities offences, and money laundering offences) or specific parts of the population (e.g., offences committed by youth or policemen). All departments are always subordinated to the attorney general of Israel.

III. Prison System and Probation Service

8. The prison system in Israel is independent from the police, and it is bound not only for the holding of the prisoner within one of its devices, but also for the rehabilitation of the prisoner.[28] The rehabilitation within the prison system is expressed by enabling the prisoners to study and complete their education, by teaching the prisoners professional skills for life, and by enabling the prisoners to work inside or outside the prison.

The probation service in Israel is part of the welfare ministry, and it is aimed to identify the defendants who have a plausible potential of rehabilitation, and to execute rehabilitation programmes for these defendants. In some cases it might be

26. The Police [New Version] Ordinance, 1971.
27. The Criminal Procedure Act [Combined Version], 1982.
28. The Prison [New Version] Ordinance, 1971.

expressed by abolition of the conviction of the defendants, but in most cases, it is expressed by recommendations to the court of how to combine the rehabilitation programme within the sentencing.

IV. The Israeli Bar

9. All Israeli attorneys are members of the Israeli bar.[29] A member of the Israeli bar may be any person who has successfully accomplished LLB degree in the Israeli academy, eighteen months of apprenticeship, and passed the bar exam. The bar exam is a written exam that was reformed in 2017. Since 2017, the Israeli bar exam contains questions regarding substantive law areas, procedural law, and formation of legal documents.

The Israeli bar suggests professional courses for the benefit of its members, and it is authorized to prosecute its members for offences of ethics within their professional occupation. The Israeli bar protects the occupation from various threats, private (private corporations or people that wish to represent people in legal affairs) or others (regulatory restraints performed by the governments, limitations posed by courts).

§7. Education

10. Education is highly valued in the Israeli culture and was viewed as a fundamental block of ancient Israelites. Jewish communities in the Levant were the first to introduce compulsory education for which the organized community, not less than the parents, were responsible. Many international business leaders have praised Israel for its high quality of education in helping spur Israel's economic development and technological boom. In 2015, the country ranked third among OECD members (after Canada and Japan) for the percentage of 25–64-year-olds that have attained tertiary education with 49% compared with the OECD average of 35%. In 2012, the country ranked third in the world in the number of academic degrees per capita (20% of the population).

Israel has a school life expectancy of sixteen years and a literacy rate of 97.8%. The Public Education Act, passed in 1953, established five types of schools: state secular, state religious, ultra-orthodox, communal settlement schools, and Arab schools.[30] The public secular is the largest school group and is attended by the majority of Jewish and non-Arab pupils in Israel. Most Arabs send their children to schools where Arabic is the language of instruction. Education is compulsory in Israel for children between the ages of three and eighteen. Schooling is divided into three tiers – primary school (grades 1–6), middle school (grades 7–9), and high school (grades 10–12) – culminating with matriculation exams.

Proficiency in core subjects such as mathematics, the Hebrew language, Hebrew and general literature, the English language, history, Biblical scripture, and civics is

29. The Israeli Bar Act, 1961.
30. The Public Education Act, 1953.

necessary to receive a matriculation certificate. Israel's Jewish population maintains a relatively high level of educational attainment where just under half of all Israeli Jews (46%) hold post-secondary degrees. This figure has remained stable in their already high levels of educational attainment over recent generations. Israeli Jews (among those ages 25 and older) have an average of 11.6 years of schooling, making them one of the most highly educated of all major religious groups in the world. In Arab, Christian, and Druze schools, the exam on Biblical studies is replaced by an exam on Muslim, Christian, or Druze heritage.

Israel has a tradition of higher education where its quality university education has been largely responsible in spurring the nation's modern economic development. Israel has nine public universities that are subsidized by the state and 49 private and public colleges.[31] The Hebrew University of Jerusalem, Israel's second-oldest university after the Technion, houses the National Library of Israel, the world's largest repository of Judaica and Hebraica. The Technion and the Hebrew University consistently ranked among the world's 100 top universities by the ARWU academic ranking.

Other major universities in the country include the Weizmann Institute of Science, Tel Aviv University, University of Haifa, the Open University of Israel, Ben-Gurion University of the Negev, Bar-Ilan University, and Ariel University. Ariel University is the newest university institution, upgraded from college status, and the first in over thirty years. The largest private college in Israel is Ono Academic College, which hosts the faculties of law, business administration, healthcare professions, computer science, music, social sciences, and humanities in four campuses in the cities of Kiryat Ono, Jerusalem, Haifa, and Or-Yehuda.

§8. Brief Historical Background of Israel

11. Israel is a modern democracy in the Middle East, known for its hi-tech achievements around the world. But Israel has a very long history, which still influences the people, the industry, the politics, and the law. It is much easier to understand Israeli law due to the historical background of Israel.

I. Ancient History

12. The exact beginning of the history of Israel is uncertain, but it is indisputable that around the middle of the second millennium BC, Israeli tribes were already permanent inhabitants in the area called 'Canaan'.[32] Canaan was a province in the

31. *See* https://che.org.il/en/ (accessed 23 Jul. 2021).
32. The ancient history of Israel until 538 BC is based mostly on the following resources: Oded Bustenay, *The History of Israel During the First Temple Period* vol. I (2nd ed., Open University Press 2007); Oded Bustenay, *The History of Israel During the First Temple Period* vol. II (2nd ed., Open University Press 2007); Oded Bustenay, *The History of Israel During the First Temple Period* vol. III (2nd ed., Open University Press 2007); Oded Bustenay, *The History of Israel During the First Temple Period* vol. IV (2nd ed., Open University Press 2007).

Egyptian empire. By the end of the millennium, the new Egyptian empire had collapsed, and the area was reorganized under the Hebrew kings David and Solomon who established the Hebrew United Kingdom around 1000 BC. The capital of the kingdom was Jerusalem.

However, internal struggles led to the split of the kingdom into two kingdoms in 928 BC. The northern kingdom was called 'Israel', and the southern kingdom was called 'Judea'. The northern kingdom was a regional power, and it was centred in Samaria. Under the rule of King Ahab, peace and prosperity were brought to the region. Peace treaties were achieved with the Phoenician kingdoms, with Judea, and with the kingdoms of the east bank of the Jordan River. When the Assyrian empire attempted to conquer the region, King Ahab established a twelve-king coalition to block thc Assyrians. In 853 BC, during the battle of Qarqar, the Assyrians were defeated by Ahab's coalition.

Queen Athaliah, Ahab's daughter, became the queen of Judea (842–836 BC) and was the first Jewish Queen. About 130 years after King Ahab's death, the Assyrian empire occupied the region in 722 BC, and the Israeli kingdom was destroyed. Many Israelis were exiled to Mesopotamia, and tribes from Mesopotamia were brought by the Assyrians to Israel. These tribes are known today as 'Samaritans'. Many Israelis preferred a shelter in the southern kingdom of Judea. Judea, for its weakness, preferred to surrender to the Assyrians; therefore, it was not destroyed. The Assyrians were defeated by the Babylonians, who occupied the Assyrian empire.

Judea gathered a coalition against the Babylonians, but the rebel was failure. In 586 BC Jerusalem was destroyed, Solomon's temple was burned, and the Jews were exiled to Babylon. After the Persian king Cyrus conquered Babylon, he granted the Jews in 538 BC the right to return to Judea.[33] The Jewish royal dynasty was expelled by the Persians from the reign. Judea became a Persian province with a limited religious autonomy. A second temple was built, but not all Jews came back to their homeland for various reasons. This situation lasts up to this day, and these Jews form the Jewish diaspora.

In 333 BC, Alexander the Great has conquered Judea, and in 200 BC, Judea came under the rule of the Seleucid Empire.[34] The Hellenic and Greek culture influence on the local inhabitants was wide, but when the Seleucid king Antiochus IV Epiphanes prohibited in 167 BC any Jewish religious tradition, the Maccabean revolt begun. In 141 BC, the rebels defeated the Seleucid Empire and established the independent Judea. Judea was reorganized as a kingdom, and under the reign of Alexander Jannaeus (103–76 BC), it became a regional power.

Under the Jewish Queen Salome Alexandra (76–67 BC), many of the predemocratic political institutes were finalized, and peace between Judea and its neighbours was established. This era was known as an era of prosperity. Unfortunately, this era did not last for long. After only seventy-eight years of independence, Judea was conquered by the Romans in 63 BC. For the first sixty-nine years under

---

33. Uriel Rappaport, *From Cyrus to Alexander: The Jews under Persian Rule* (Open University Press 2004).
34. The ancient history of Israel until the second century AD is based mostly on Uriel Rappaport, *A History of Israel in the Period of the Second Temple* (3rd ed., Amichai 1984).

the reign of the Roman Empire, Judea was granted certain political autonomy under local rulers. Herod (from 37 BC until 4 AD) was one of them, and he is known especially as the 'builder' for re-building the country.

The Roman Empire had no tolerance to rebels or to potential rebels, and many Jews were executed by crucifixion. Thus, when a Jewish Rabbi, called Jesus from Nazareth, was suspected as a rebel, the Romans executed him by crucifixion around 30 AD. In 6 AD, the Romans abolished the Jewish autonomy and ruled directly in Judea. Judea became a Roman province, and the population was suffering from the Roman regime. In 67 AD, the Great Revolt of the Jews against the Roman Empire had begun.

After six years, the revolt was suppressed, the second Temple was destroyed (70 AD), and many Jews were exiled out of Judea. The Roman Empire increased the oppression against the Jews in Judea, and the Jews rebelled against it. Fifty-nine years after the failure of the Great Revolt, a new revolt has occurred, which is considered to be the last of the great revolts. After Hadrian, the Roman Emperor withdrew his promise to let the Jews rebuild the temple and restore the country, the Roman foreign policy was meant to expel them from the country, and Jewish religious traditions were prohibited, the Bar-Kokhba revolt (132–135) has begun.

The consequences of the revolt were catastrophic. Using one-third of the Roman Empire army (28 fully armed legions) against the Jewish rebels, and after three years, about 600,000 Jews were killed, many of the rest were exiled as slaves, and the Jewish majority was lost for the first time in history. Afraid from losing their ancient tradition, all traditional data and literature were recorded by the survivors of the revolt.

Severe sanctions were taken against the survivors in order to weaken the connection to the country. The name 'Judea' was replaced by 'Palestine', the name 'Jerusalem' was replaced by 'Aelia Capitolina', the Jews were not allowed to enter Jerusalem, all Jewish religious ceremonies were prohibited, it was prohibited to read any of the ancient literature, and many more sanctions. The punishment was a collective death of the person and his family, and sometimes of the whole village. Jewish children were often taken to slavery or prostitution. The Christians and the Samaritans supported the Roman Empire against the Jews and often participated in these sanctions.

II. From the Middle Ages to the State of Israel

13. In the Middle Ages, major powers occupied the country, and their policy was to weaken the connection of the Jews to the country in order to strengthen their connection to the country.[35] In the fourth century, the country was ruled by the Byzantine Empire, who gave rise to Christianity. Some Jews were forced to convert to Christianity under the rule of Justinian (527–565). Jewish Holydays were not allowed, and reading the holy Jewish scripts was prohibited. The temple mount was converted to garbage dump in order to humiliate the Jews. In 627, the Byzantine

35. The Middle Ages history of Israel is based mostly on Haim Hillel Ben Sason, *Israel History in Middle Ages* (Dvir 1972).

Empire expelled the Persians from the country, and as part of the celebrations, the Christians were allowed to perform a massacre in the Jews.

In 641, the Arabs have conquered the country and expelled the Byzantine troops. The Christian conquest was replaced by the Muslim conquest. As a result, massive immigration of Arabs into the country has occurred. In 1071, the Muslims allowed the Jews to enter Jerusalem for the first time since 135, but this situation has lasted only until 1099.

In 1099, after killing Jews in Europe and taking their property, the first Crusade arrived in Jerusalem and conquered it. A common phrase among the Crusaders was 'If you can't kill a Turk, kill a Jew'.[36] The country was ruled due to the feudal system, and it was divided into small principalities. This conquest had lasted until 1291, when the country was conquered by the Mamluks, former slaves of the Muslims. The Mamluk conquest had lasted until 1517, when the Ottoman Empire took over the country.

For 400 years, the Ottomans have ruled the country from Turkey.[37] However, in 1831, Ibrahim Pasha, an Egyptian officer, has rebelled against the Ottoman Empire and took over major cities. In order to establish a stable regime of his own, he brought tens of thousands of Egyptian Muslim Arab peasants to settle the country. In addition, he brought thousands of Egyptian Muslim Arab former-soldiers to settle in the country. These new immigrants have integrated into the Muslim population and became part of it. The demographic change was tremendous. In the beginning of the twentieth century, they embraced the title 'Palestinians' as a contradiction to the Jewish Zionists. The Ottomans have re-conquered the country, but the new Arab population was allowed to stay.

When the national movements in Europe flourished in the nineteenth century, the antisemitism against the Jews became massive, and the Zionist movement called the Jews to return to their homeland. But the Ottomans prohibited any Jewish immigration into the country, besides small numbers of immigrants out of religious purposes; therefore, the Jews still could not return.

During the First World War, the Ottoman Empire joined Germany and Austro-Hungary against Britain and France. The British foreign minister, Lord Balfour, has promised in 1917 that the British Empire would allow the Jews to rebuild their ancient homeland, in which they were not allowed to return to it since the days of the Roman Empire. Nevertheless, after defeating the Ottoman Empire, Britain has delayed its promise.

Due to Versailles Treaties, after the end of the First World War, the British Mandate was established in the country.[38] Traditional Jewish regions were given to others due to British political considerations. On the regions left by the British Mandate, only a small number of Jewish immigrants were allowed to settle. The Arab inhabitants massacred the Jews under the British Mandate especially in 1921,

---

36. Jack L. Arnold, *Church History (1073-1517)* (1999). *See*: http://www.thirdmill.org/newfiles/jac_arnold/CH.Arnold.CH.19.html (accessed 23 Jul. 2021).
37. The history of Israel under the Ottoman Empire is based mostly on Shmuel Etinger, *Israel History in the New Age* (Dvir 1969).
38. The history of Israel under the British Mandate is based mostly on Mordechai Naor and Dan Giladi, *Eretz Israel in the 20th Century* (Ministry of Defence Press 1990).

1929, and 1936–1939. The British Mandate has reacted by restricting the Jewish immigration to very small numbers in order to satisfy the Arabs.

During the Second World War many Muslims, under the command of Muhammed Amin Al-Husseini, the British-appointed leader of the Muslims under the Mandate regime, joined the SS Nazi troops in Europe in order to help the extermination of the Jews.[39] Many Jews joined the British army against Nazi Germany. Six million Jews were exterminated during the Second World War, and this era is known in the Jewish history as the 'Holocaust'. A third of the Jewish people was wiped out, and many of the survivors were refugees. Many of them were not allowed to return to their homeland by the British Mandate.

The British mandate refused to enable the Jewish refugees to seek a shelter in their homeland, and attempts resulted in imprisonment of the refugees. The Jews began a revolt against the British Mandate in 1946. Consequently, on 29 November 1947, the United Nations (UN) assembly has confirmed an offer to divide the country into a Jewish state and an Arab state. The Jews accepted the offer, but the Arabs refused, and on the following day, they began to fight against the Jewish settlements with some support from the British Mandate.

III. The State of Israel

14. The British Mandate has expired on 15 May 1948, and the Jewish inhabitants have declared the establishment of a new democracy named 'Israel' on 14 May 1948.[40] The Arabs, who refused the two-states solutions, have fought against the new state. In order to assist in the elimination of Israel and the extermination of the Jewish population, Arab armies and militias have joined the war against Israel (from Lebanon, Syria, Iraq, Jordan, and Egypt). Jordan has illegally conquered Samaria, Judea, and Eastern Jerusalem, and Egypt has illegally conquered Gaza, but the state of Israel has survived. The fighting stopped in March 1949, but Israel was still under occasional military attacks.

Israel has granted equality to all its citizens, regardless of their religion, gender, sex, ethnic origin, or language.[41] The lessons from the holocaust made the Israeli Parliament enact in 1950 a statute which allows the Jews to return to their homeland.[42] For being a small state with a small population, the priority of resources was given to education. Education between the ages of 4 and 18 is compulsory in Israel and free of charge. However, higher education is not compulsory and fully paid by the students. The priority of education gave rise to the high-technology industry and scientific achievements in Israel.

The Arab states around Israel kept attacking it and refused to accept its very existence. The Egyptian, Jordanian, and Syrian threat on Israel in 1967, supported by the

39. Jenny Lebl, *Haj Amin and Berlin* (Cigoya Stampa 1996).
40. The history of the state of Israel is based mostly on mostly on Mordechai Naor and Dan Giladi, *Eretz Israel in the 20th Century* (Ministry of Defence Press 1990).
41. The Israeli Declaration of Independence.
42. The Return Act, 1950.

Soviet Union, has resulted in the six days war. Samaria, Judea, and Eastern Jerusalem, which were illegally conquered by Jordan, were returned to Israel. Syria has lost the Golan, an ancient Jewish area. Egypt has lost the Sinai. In 1973, in order to eliminate Israel, a combined Egyptian-Syrian attack was launched on Israel. Although suffering from thousands of casualties, Israel survived and defeated both armies.

Israel tried to achieve peace with its neighbours, but only after their defeat in 1973, they began to realize that elimination of Israel and extermination of the Jews would not be easily achieved; therefore, they have agreed to consider peace with Israel. The large Arab states wanted territories, whereas the small state of Israel was seeking normalization. In 1979, a peace treaty with Egypt was signed, only after Israel gave up the vast territory of Sinai. But still after the treaty was signed, normalization was not achieved, in spite of continuous Israeli attempts.

In 1994, a peace treaty with Jordan was achieved, but normalization was not achieved, in spite of continuous Israeli attempts. In 1993, the Israeli government had signed some agreements with the Arab leadership in Samaria and Judea, meant to establish an Arab autonomy in these territories. However, Arab terrorist attacks against innocent Israeli citizens were continued. These agreements are considered a failure. The Arab leadership in Samaria and Judea refuses to recognize the state of Israel. In order to defend itself from terrorist attacks, Israel has to develop highly sophisticated measures, and this is an incentive for many hi-tech industries in Israel.

Chapter 2. Telecommunications Infrastructure

15. The telecommunication infrastructure in Israel is one of the most developed in the Western world. Many international corporations prefer to test many of their new products in the Israeli market, mostly based on the developed infrastructure. Israel's basic telecommunications infrastructure consists of coaxial cables, optical fibres, and microwave radio relay. The Israeli telecom industry has been among global leaders in technology development, pioneering developments of protocols such as Worldwide Interoperability for Microwave Access (WiMAX), voice over Internet protocol (VoIP), and Time Division Multiplexing over IP (TDMoIP). During the 2000s, Israel emerged as a leading supplier for the global telecommunications industry and a global leader in technological research.

§1. Telephone

16. By the mid-1990s, most Israelis were using only landline telephones, and mobile phones were far beyond their economic capabilities. However, by the end of the second decade of the new millennium, most Israelis use mobile phones and only a few still have landline telephones in their homes, but rarely use them. However, the landline telephones in most residential homes are analogue, in which the speaker's voice directly determines the signal's voltage.

Although short-distance calls may be handled from end-to-end as analogue signals, increasingly telephone service providers are transparently converting the signals to digital signals for transmission. The advantage of this technology is that digitized voice data can travel side-by-side with data from the Internet and can be perfectly reproduced in long-distance communication. However, the new infrastructure of landline telephones is mostly digital in Israel, at least since 2010.

Mobile phones have had a significant impact on telephone networks in Israel since the mid-1990s. Mobile phone subscriptions outnumber fixed-line subscriptions. Increasingly these phones are being serviced by systems where the voice content is transmitted digitally using GSM and W-CDMA. As of 2021, most operators use the 4G and 5G technology due to the increasing use of smartphones, not just as telephones, but also as mini-tablets. As of 2021, there is no market in Israel for analogue systems such as AMPS.

Deep changes in telephone communication infrastructure occurred in Israel starting in the mid-1990s by the adoption of systems based on optical fibres. The benefit of communicating with optic fibres is that they offer a drastic increase in data capacity. That has increased data capacity, because optic fibres were physically much smaller than competing technologies, and they did not suffer from crosstalk (several hundreds of them can be easily bundled together in a single cable).

In addition, improvements in multiplexing have led to an exponential growth in the data capacity of a single fibre. ATM protocol is also used in Israel (ATM is an assisting communication across many modern optic fibre networks is a protocol known as Asynchronous Transfer Mode). However, there are competitors to ATM protocol, such as Multiprotocol Label Switching (MPLS), that perform similar tasks and are expected to supplant ATM protocol in the future.

§2. Internet

17. It is estimated that 98% of the information flowing through two-way telecommunications networks in Israel are flowing through the Internet. Most of the rest through mobile phones.[43] Almost all Israeli population has access to the Internet via personal computers, mobile phones, and other devices. Most Israelis use wireless connection to the Internet, using cellular infrastructure or Wi-Fi connection.

In November 1990, the undersea cable Eastern Mediterranean Optical System (EMOS-1), connecting Israel with Turkey, Greece, and Italy, was deployed. This was the first Israeli-built undersea cable and was augmented by Cyprus-Israel Optical System (CIOS) in April 1994. Since then, other cables have been laid which have provided large capacity links between Israel and abroad. Until 1997, most domestic Internet traffic was routed either directly between Internet Service Providers (ISPs) or through the Israeli universities' academic network operated by the Inter-University Computation Centre (IUCC). Since 1997, the Israel Internet Association has been responsible for operating the Israeli Internet Exchange (IIX) through which much of the domestic Internet traffic is routed.

Broadband Internet has been available in Israel via asymmetric digital subscriber line (ADSL) since the late 1990s, in theory, but it only became practical to an average residential customer in 2001. This was enabled by a significant upgrade to the Internet infrastructure in 1999, at the cost of over a billion NIS. Since then prices have dropped considerably. In 2001, the Communications Act, 1982 was amended to allow the provision of broadband Internet through the cable infrastructure.

As of 2021, the average download speed in household broadband connections in Israel is 51Mbit/s, while upload speeds average at 5.2Mbit/s. Maximum speeds via the cable modem provider's connection are 200Mbit/s down and 10Mbit/s up for consumers (and 500Mbit/s down and 20Mbit/s up for business customers in select markets) over DOCSIS 3.0, a service started in October 2009. All ADSL services require and use the Point-to-Point Protocol over Ethernet (PPPoE) protocol, and cable modem connections generally operate over dynamic host configuration protocol (DHCP). For speed under 30Mbit/sec, a cable user can select to use virtual private networks (VPNs) using the PPTP/L2TP protocol.

Bezeq, the major local exchange carrier, began rolling out their Next Generation Network (NGN) in 2009 with theoretical speeds up to 100Mbit/s by using a combination of fibre to the curb (FTTC) and ADSL2+/VDSL2 technologies. Initial product offerings of their NGN were 10Mbit/s and 15Mbit/s download and 800kbit/s upload speeds over ADSL2+, with a best effort package of up to 100Mbit/s were available since 2010. According to Bezeq, NGN has reached 90% of the households in Israel since 2011, and offerings of 100Mbit/s are provided since 2012. Its main cable competitor, HOT, is using DOCSIS 3.0 infrastructure, which allows higher bandwidths.

The three largest mobile phone carriers, Pelephone, Partner, and Cellcom, offer High-Speed Downlink Packet Access (HSDPA) service, typically 24Mbit/s, over

43. This paragraph is based mostly on the Israeli Internet Association reports. *See* https://en.isoc.org.il/ (accessed 23 Jul. 2021).

their respective 4G networks as well. Partner was the first provider to operate a consumer 4G and 5G (Long Term Evolution (LTE)) network, reaching a theoretical symmetrical speed of 100Mbit/s. As of 2021, all major mobile carriers offer 5G and 4G LTE Advanced connectivity in the 1,800 MHz and 2,600 MHz frequencies, available in most populated regions in Israel; however, these services are limited to about 20% of their maximum speeds since the Israeli Ministry of Communications has not completed allocating the full spectrum of the required frequencies.

Israel is connected abroad by three undersea cables: MedNautilus, owned by Telecom Italia, the Bezeq International Optical System, and Tamares Telecom's submarine cable. Domestic connectivity is provided by the IIX, a central meeting point of the ISPs in Israel.

Due to Israeli competition law, any Digital Subscriber Line (DSL) or cable Internet user has to pay separately to the infrastructure provider and to the ISP. Infrastructure is provided by Bezeq (via dial-up and DSL) and HOT (cable Internet). All cellular companies provide wireless Internet infrastructure and also serve as ISPs. The three main ISPs are Partner, 013 Netvision, and Bezeq International. In 2006, the companies held market shares of 34%, 33%, and 30%, respectively, although these numbers include international phone calls. In all, as of August 2019, there were forty-three companies with ISP licenses given by the Ministry of Communications.

In Israel, Gilat Satellite Networks provides multi-gigabit per second broadband access to consumers and the defence industry by means of high throughput satellites.

A third of landline Internet infrastructure is being built by the Israel Electric Corporation, which will provide fibre to the home access in the country. This follows a 2011 communications ministry approval. The network is called 'Unlimited' and will provide up to 1 Gbit/s access to Israeli homes. After the network is laid, speeds above 1 Gbit/s are possible. Bezeq is also set to conduct a similar pilot, paving the way for fibre to the home (FTTH) connections in Israel. By 2021, the 160 tbps Quantum Cable will be added to the array of submarine communication cables that land in Israel.

§3. Radio and Television

18. The broadcast media industry in Israel was at a critical turning point in its development between 2009 and 2011, with the move from analogue to digital broadcasts. This move was made possible by the production of cheaper, faster, and more capable integrated circuits. The chief advantage of digital broadcasts is that they prevent a number of complaints common to traditional analogue broadcasts. For television, this includes the elimination of problems such as snowy pictures, ghosting, and other distortion.

Digital transmission overcomes this problem because digital signals are reduced to discrete values upon reception, and hence, small perturbations do not affect the final output. In August 2009, Israel launched digital terrestrial broadcasts with the intention to phase out the analogue broadcast. Israel shut down analogue television services on 13 June 2011. The first nation in the Middle East to abandon analogue over-the-air broadcasting.

In the early stage, there was only single mux broadcast in single-frequency network (SFN) with five channels, and later on a sixth TV channel was added and also a selection of public and regional radio stations. In digital television broadcasting, there are three competing families of standards that have been adopted worldwide. These are the Advanced Television Systems Committee (ATSC), Digital Video Broadcasting (DVB), and Integrated Services Digital Broadcasting (ISDB) standards. Most television distribution channels in Israel utilize the European DVB family of standards. DVB has no standard for audio compression but typically uses MPEG-1 Part 3 Layer 2.

By mid-2017, an additional mux was introduced with five new TV channels in DVB-T2 standard, including Israeli Public Broadcasting Corporation's (IPBC's) Hebrew channel 'Kan 11' channel in HD. The Israeli cable TV provider, HOT, uses DVB-C. The Israeli satellite TV provider, Yes, uses DVB-S and DVB-S2. Digital terrestrial television is transmitted using DVB-T (with MPEG-4 compression) with DVB-T2 in experimental transmissions since 2015 mainly in Tel Aviv area and central Israel including IBA-1 HD. The date of regular introduction of HDTV services under the Idan Plus service is still unknown. Analogue terrestrial television transmissions were switched off between 30 March 2011 and 13 June 2011. They have been operated using the Phase Alternating Line (PAL) colour standard. The Israeli TV Company uses Over the Top (OTT).

For analogue radio, the switch to digital radio is made more difficult by the higher cost of digital receivers. The choice of modulation for analogue radio is typically between amplitude (AM) or frequency modulation (FM). To achieve stereo playback, an amplitude modulated subcarrier is used for stereo FM, and quadrature AM is used for stereo AM or C-QUAM.

Chapter 3. The Information and Communications Technology Market

19. One of the most growing markets in Israel since the 1990s is the communications technology market. The catalyst for this growth was both the entrance of the Internet for private and commercial use and the mobile phones. A full list of operating corporations in the Israeli telecommunications market and general information may be found on the official website of the ministry of communication.[44]

§1. Telephone

I. Development and Activity Inside Israel

20. Telephones were first introduced by the British Mandate authorities in the 1920s. The Israeli Ministry of Posts (later the Ministry of Communications) took over the telephone infrastructure after independence, and in 1950 introduced international calls. In that same year, the first-ever Hebrew telephone directory was published. In 1955 inter-urban dialling enabled phone calls between Israeli cities without contacting local exchanges and by 1963 all Israel's exchanges were automated. By 1977, it was estimated that half of Israel's homes had a phone, the millionth Israeli line was installed several months before the establishment of Bezeq in 1984.

The scope of Israel's telecommunications infrastructure today is particularly remarkable, when one considers that in the early 1980s, the average waiting time for a new telephone was over three years, and existing lines could not cope with demand during peak hours. Since then a combination of high-tech innovation and economic re-organization has transformed the situation. This transformation began in 1984 when Bezeq, the Israel Telecommunication Corporation Ltd., was formed as a government-owned enterprise working on a profit and loss basis.

Previously, telephones had been issued by a department within the Ministry of Communications which worked on an allocated annual budget. Subject to the forces of the market, Bezeq set about satisfying a waiting list of 250,000 subscriber requests. By 1990, it had fulfilled all requests and was even subsequently able to launch a marketing campaign to persuade homeowners to install a second line. Today Israel has 40 lines per 100 people with a fixed-line network of 2.55 million.

Bezeq also set about upgrading Israel's telecommunications infrastructure. Complete digitalization has meant that subscribers can enjoy a range of state-of-the-art services from call waiting and call forwarding to voice-mail recordings, caller identification and dial-back to missed calls. Most inter-urban links and much of the urban infrastructure are underground fibre optic lines to Israel's cable television network. Subscribers can dial directly to any country in the world via underwater fibre optic lines connecting Israel to Europe, or via satellite link-ups.

---

44. https://www.science.co.il/companies/Telecom.php (accessed 23 Jul. 2021).

In the mid-1980s, the first mobile phone company made its appearance in Israel. At first prohibitively expensive, market penetration became substantial by the 1990s and soared when the second company began operations in 1994 using new digital technology and a revolutionary marketing strategy of extremely low tariffs. A third cellular communications company has begun operating during the following year.

Phone use has also proliferated in Israel due to extensive use of data communications facilities. Any business and institution and many homes have facsimile machines and are linked to electronic mail and the Internet. Many companies are installing Integrated Services Digital Networks (ISDN) for a wider range of voice, data, and video services.

Since 2016, Bezeq, HOT, 012 Smile, and Cellcom offer landline telephony services. Bezeq is the oldest of all of them and is reputed to have a monopoly in the field. HOT uses its cable infrastructure in order to provide telephony services. The cable infrastructure is not yet spread throughout the entire country and therefore not all houses in Israel are equipped to be members of HOT.

In comparison, Bezeq has landline infrastructure in all towns and villages in the country. The strategy of 012 Smile and Cellcom is different from the former two in that they did not rush to establish a new physical infrastructure, rather, they provide telephone services which are based on the infrastructure of Bezeq and HOT, by means of Internet telephony technologies and additional technologies.

In 2021, seven operators, 012 Smile, NetVision, Bezeq International, Golan Telecom, HOT Mobile, Exphone, and Telzar provided international telephony. All the companies offer membership services which usually offer their customers cheaper rates. Membership might include some benefits such as billing, and dialling the default 00 prefix instead of the need to dial the specific prefix of the company (as it was done in the past, when Bezeq had a monopoly in this field). Because these companies have an extensive infrastructure of links abroad, the majority of them also provide Internet services. Incoming calls are distributed through the companies relative to market share.

In 2018, there were five major network operators in Israel which offer cellular communication services: Pelephone, Cellcom, Partner, HOT Mobile, and Golan Telecom. There are also several Mobile Virtual Network Operator (MVNO):[45] Rami Levy, Home Cellular, 019 Telzar, and Cellact. The services which these companies provide have passed the boundaries of voice conversations long ago, and currently, they provide also SMS text messaging, videoconferencing, and broadband Internet access.

---

45. An MVNO is a wireless communications services provider that does not own the wireless network infrastructure over which it provides services to its customers. An MVNO enters into a business agreement with a mobile network operator to obtain bulk access to network services at wholesale rates, then sets retail prices independently. An MVNO may use its own customer service, billing support systems, marketing, and sales personnel, or it could employ the services of a mobile virtual network enabler (MVNE).

II. Israeli Overseas Activity

21. Israeli corporations are active in developing conventional and mobile phone infrastructure overseas, as well as operating and maintaining them. Some of the overseas projects are a satellite station that has been installed in Alma-Ata, Kazakhstan, and a similar facility is being constructed in neighbouring Uzbekistan. In southern Hungary, a joint venture between Israeli and local partners is developing a telecommunications infrastructure comprising 108,000 lines with digital switching. In Poland, Israeli companies and the Polish telecommunications company RP Telecom are installing 81,000 lines near Warsaw. In India, Bezeq is setting up a cellular phone network in three southern states. Motorola Israel is developing a cellular phone network for Accra, Ghana.

In addition to developing basic infrastructure, Israeli companies have also entered high-tech niche markets. Systems developed in Israel can increase the capacity of digital satellite and fibre optic cable telecommunications links by five times. Customers include Deutsche Telecom and the Chinese national telephone corporation. Local wireless loops and small rural switch systems, which are very popular in Eastern Europe and the former Soviet Union, have also been developed in Israel.

§2. Internet

22. Due to Israeli competition law, any DSL or cable Internet user has to pay separately to the infrastructure provider and to the ISP. Infrastructure is provided by Bezeq (via dial-up and DSL) and HOT (cable Internet). All cellular companies provide wireless Internet infrastructure, and also serve as ISPs. The three main ISPs are Partner, 013 Netvision, and Bezeq International. In 2006, the companies held market shares of 34%, 33%, and 30%, respectively, although these numbers include international phone calls. In all, as of August 2019, there were forty-three companies with ISP licenses given by the Ministry of Communications.

A third of landline Internet infrastructure is being built by the Israel Electric Corporation, which will provide fibre to the home access in the country. This follows a 2011 communications ministry approval. The network is called ‘Unlimited’ and will provide up to 1 Gbit/s access to Israeli homes. After the network is laid, speeds above 1 Gbit/s are possible. Bezeq is also set to conduct a similar pilot, paving the way for FTTH connections in Israel. By 2021, the 160 tbps Quantum Cable will be added to the array of submarine communication cables that land in Israel.

Israel’s telecommunications providers are currently installing ‘intelligent networks’ to facilitate the expansion of the global information highway. These include VPNs, premium service rates, and toll-free calling. Experimental pilot projects include video-on-demand, ATM, transmission technology, smart cards, digital broadcasting services, and the development of metropolitan area networks (MANs).

Intelligent network services will enable mobile phone subscribers to use data transmissions by facsimile or computer, voice-activated dialling, and call filtering and identification, all through their personal phone service anywhere in the world. By 2020, the 160 tbps Quantum Cable will be added to the array of submarine communication cables that land in Israel.

§3. RADIO AND TELEVISION

I. Early Developments of Israeli Broadcasting

23. In 1948, Israel had one radio station, run directly by the government, which was a continuation of the British Mandate's Hebrew radio station.[46] The early governments did not favour the establishment of TV stations. Nevertheless, the Israeli government discussed the idea of using television as an instructional and educational tool in 1952 and 1955. In 1961 the Israeli government asked United Nations Educational, Scientific and Cultural Organization (UNESCO) to offer its opinion, which was in favour of using television for educational purposes.

In the early 1960s, television broadcasts from neighbouring Egypt, Lebanon, and Cyprus gradually became available to Israelis through TV sets which were placed in public places, like cafés. Since they were mainly in Arabic, these broadcasts were popular among Israeli Arabs. This raised the government's concern about anti-Israel propaganda that might be included in them.

In 1963, the government started to promote the establishment of an Israeli TV channel. In 1964, it invited a team of experts from the European Broadcasting Union to submit their recommendations. In 1965, the Israeli Broadcasting Authority (IBA) was established in order to distant the government from the everyday management and editorial decisions of the state-owned radio station. The government also passed a resolution stating that this new body will start TV broadcasts within two years.

Television in Israel was finally introduced on 24 March 1966, though not by the IBA, but rather by the Israeli Educational Television (IETV), which was funded by the Rothschild Foundation and acted as part of the Ministry of Education. The first transmissions were lessons to school students in various subjects, filmed in black and white, and intended to be received by thirty-two schools across the country. The IBA launched regular public transmissions on 2 May 1968, on the occasion of Israeli Independence Day.

Israeli television began operations when American and European stations were switching to full-scale colour transmissions, but Israel's state-controlled stations broadcast only in black and white. The IBA had the equipment for filming and broadcasting in colour for nearly a decade before putting it into use, and the introduction of colour transmissions was halted due to political pressure.

Newscasts and other regular productions were filmed using black and white cameras. However, many special productions ordered from private Israeli studios were filmed and taped in colour. Furthermore, Israeli television bought the rights to many American and British TV series and movies (broadcast with Hebrew-Arabic subtitles). The result was a mixture of colour and black and white broadcasts, which encouraged traders to import colour TV sets, especially as TV stations in neighbouring Jordan and Egypt started colour transmissions in 1974.

46. Section [A] is based mostly on Dana Vinkler, *Making an Israeli Television – Discussions Prior to the Establishment of Television in Israel, 1948–1968* (2006).

The Israeli new right-wing government considered the import of colour televisions as a frivolous luxury that would increase social gaps. Therefore, the government ordered IBA and IETV to erase the colour from colour-taped telecasts by erasing the 'burst phase' signal. The 'damaged' signal triggered the 'colour killer' mechanism, installed in colour TV sets to prevent the appearance of incidental colour spots on the screen when black-and-white films are broadcast or when the reception is disturbed.

The Israeli government allowed colour transmissions by the IBA in November 1977 when IBA provided live colour coverage of the historical visit of the Egyptian president in Israel. This transmission was sent via satellite to stations around the world. In March 1979, the IBA hosted the annual Eurovision Song Contest, and once again sent the transmission live in colour to stations around the world.

Public pressure on the issue of colour transmissions mounted, and in 1981, IBA and IETV were allowed to film their own regular productions in colour. This process took more than two years and reached the last stretch on 16 February 1983 when the main daily newscast was broadcast in colour for the first time. The IBA stopped filming in black and white on 10 May 1983.

II. The Multi-channel Broadcasting Era

24. In 1978, the Israeli government appointed a special committee to explore the establishment of a second channel that would not be under the IBA supervision and would be financed by advertising; however, the idea of commercial television was rejected by some parties in the ruling coalition. On 7 October 1986, the Minister of Communications ordered the beginning of 'experimental transmissions' on a second channel, claiming that unless these transmissions had started, the frequencies would have been used by TV networks in neighbouring countries.

First transmissions were aired on UHF channel 21 from Jerusalem. These transmissions, which initially included two to three hours of video clips every evening and broadcast from a private TV studio in Jerusalem, expanded gradually to include a full programme lineup. At this stage, the IBA was legally responsible for the channel, but in fact it saw it as an unexpected competition, tried to prevent its inauguration, and was reluctant to take responsibility for its broadcasts.

In 1986, the Knesset started discussing the law forming the Second IBA, which was finally approved in 1990. This new body took responsibility for the second channel from this year onwards. From 1990 to 1993, the Second Broadcasting Authority reviewed bids from commercial companies to establish the regular commercial broadcasts of the second channel, which started on 4 November 1993. The second channel was officially handed to three concessionaires, starting the first commercial broadcasts in Israel, with IETV as the fourth broadcaster which was entitled, by law, for additional hours on this channel as a commercial entity.

Pirated television broadcasts via cables became very popular in the major cities of Israel during the late 1980s. These were usually local cable television stations broadcasting illegally from private houses to subscribers, mainly films released on videotapes. These local stations vanished with the introduction of regulated cable television in 1989. By mid-1994, some 720,000 Israeli households were hooked up to cable television. Satellite television was introduced to Israel in 2000.

Israeli television broadcasts mainly in Hebrew and English. While Hebrew is the common language of communication, numerous shows and series of different genres are bought from English-speaking countries. Unless the target audience is preschool children, subtitling in Hebrew is preferred over dubbing, not only for economic considerations. Subtitling is often bilingual, the secondary language being either Arabic or Russian.

The state-owned Israel Broadcasting Authority (IBA) has an Arabic department which broadcasts news, talk shows, educational programmes for children, and Egyptian films on IBA's Channel 33. From May 2017, the Arabic channel is operated by the IPBC. IBA's English department broadcasts a daily locally produced newscast. Commercial channels are obligated to broadcast a portion of their programmes in Arabic and Russian, or alternatively translate programmes into these languages. There is also a legal obligation on all channels to translate some of their newscasts into the Israeli Sign Language.

In 2002, an Israeli Russian-speaking commercial channel was launched, named Israel Plus. A similar Arabic-speaking channel started broadcasting in March 2012, after several attempts to establish it earlier failed. The first bid for the establishment of this channel was published in 1995 but cancelled for formal legal problems. In January 2003, a new bid was published, but the winning company failed to fulfil its financial obligations. A final modified bid was published on 14 April 2010, for which eight companies competed. The Halla TV Company was selected in September 2011.

The public non-commercial main channels in Israel are Kan 11 (replaced Channel 1 and Channel 1 HD since 15 May 2017), Makan 33 (replaced Channel 33 since 15 May 2017), Kan Hinuchit (Educational Channel, Channel 23), and Knesset Channel (The Parliament Channel, and its operations are outsourced to private companies via competitive tender).

The public commercial main channels in Israel are Keshet 12 (replaced Channel 2 since November 2017), Reshet 13 (replaced Channel 2 since November 2017), Channel 10 (merged with Reshet 13 on 15 January 2019), Channel 20, Music 24 (Israeli music and video clips), available only via Yes (satellite TV), and HOT (cable TV), both pay TV systems, Israel Plus, in Russian, available only via Yes (satellite TV) and HOT (cable TV), both pay TV systems, Israel Plus International, in Russian, export version of the local channel, Hala TV (Israeli Arabic language channel), available only via Yes (satellite TV) and HOT (cable TV), both pay TV systems. A full list of broadcasting channels in Israel may be found on the Internet.[47]

In contrast with the state which exists in the television field, in the radio field, IBA is allowed to produce earnings from advertising. The radio section of IBA is called Kol Israel ('Voice of Israel'). Reshet Bet ('Second Channel') is the leading radio station in Israel. Two additional radio stations belong to the Israeli defence forces: Israel Defence Forces Radio and Galgalatz (music and traffic reports). In

---

47. For example at https://en.wikipedia.org/wiki/List_of_television_channels_in_Israel (accessed 23 Jul. 2021).

addition to the main radio stations which could be received throughout the country, there are also regional commercial radio stations broadcasting under the auspices of the Second Authority for Television and Radio.

Chapter 4. E-Commerce: Facts and Figures

§1. Products and Services

25. The electronic commerce (e-commerce), sometimes called the 'digital commerce', in Israel has similar characteristics as the e-commerce in most OECD countries. E-commerce in Israel is not limited to Israeli-located business. Many transactions made through the Internet by Israelis are with business outside Israel. E-commerce in Israel is concentrated on tangible goods (mostly electronics, books, food, clothing, and jewellery), on digital content (mostly text, pictures, music, and video) and on services (mostly tourism, consulting, dating, and financial services).[48]

As to tangible goods, in 2017, electronics was 18% of e-commerce in tangible goods, clothing and jewellery were 17%, books were 10%, software and games were 7%, cosmetics was 6%, children toys were 5%, sports devices were 3%, mechanical parts for transportation were 3%, medications were 2%, and furniture was 1% of e-commerce in tangible goods. The business model of e-commerce in tangible goods is not different than the classic commerce, as the consumer pays directly to the merchant for the goods. The payment is through international credit cards, which are very common in Israel, especially MasterCard, Visa, and American Express. The websites of Ali Express, Amazon, and E-bay are highly used for this purpose in Israel.

As to digital content, e-commerce is concentrated on intellectual property (IP). The consumer purchases the rights of use in the digital content. However, there are two basic business models of e-commerce in digital content. The first is the direct model, of which the consumer pays the merchant directly for using the digital content ('pay per use' or 'pay per download'). The second is the indirect model, of which the consumer does not pay for the digital content, and thus the number of consumers entering the website is higher. The high 'rating' of the website enables the merchant to be attractive for advertising. Other businesses thus pay the website to be advertised by the website. The direct model is more common in e-commerce in Israel.

As to services, this is the most growing e-commerce market in Israel. Most Israelis prefer to manage their daily life through the Internet rather than through human interactions. For example, banking services in Israel are rarely given by bankers face-to-face. Since the 1990s, most Israelis preferred banking services through the telephone, and since the beginning of the new millennium, most Israelis prefer their banking services through the Internet. That allowed the banks in Israel to reduce manpower in customer services to a minimum, but it has also motivated them to find sophisticated solutions for security of the data and accessibility of the banking services on the Internet.

The services on the Internet are widely spread among Israelis, both as consumers and as business. Most Israelis find the services on the Internet much more comfortable for them than face-to-face or telephone services. As of 2019, most of the daily

48. https://e-conomy.co.il/ (accessed 23 Jul. 2021).

services are consumed in Israel through the Internet, and that includes banking services, other financial services (pension, for example), tourism services, insurance services, transportation services (order train, bus or taxi, for example), information services, food services, leisure services, and many more. Many international companies which service Israelis keep operating a website in Hebrew, knowing the Israelis prefer using it. Alitalia, Iberia, and Crowne Plaza are examples in the tourism area.

It is expected that due to COVID-19 pandemic, which arrived to Israel on 27 February 2020, the usage of e-commerce inside Israel and from outside of Israel has been increased. However, once discovered the convenience of e-commerce, most Israelis prefer to continue using it regardless of the pandemic.

§2. Statistical Figures

I. E-Commerce Market

26. In statistical figures, the e-commerce market in Israel is defined narrowly. The e-commerce market in Israel encompasses the sale of physical goods via a digital channel to a private end-user (B2C – Business to Customer). Incorporated in this definition are purchases via desktop computer (including notebooks and laptops) as well as purchases via mobile devices such as smartphones and tablets. The following are not included in the e-commerce market: digitally distributed services (as they are statistically defined as e-services), digital media downloads or streams, digitally distributed goods in B2B (Business to Business) markets nor digital purchase or resale of used, defective or repaired goods (re-commerce and C2C – Customer to Customer).

Revenue in the e-commerce market in Israel amounts to USD 3,355 million in 2018.[49] Revenue is expected to show an annual growth rate (CAGR 2018–2023) of 10.8%, resulting in a market volume of USD 5,614 million by 2023. The market's largest segment is Toys, Hobby, and DIY (Do It Yourself) with a market volume of USD 1,158 million in 2018. User penetration is 64.6% in 2018 and is expected to hit 70.8% by 2023. The average revenue per user (ARPU) currently amounts to USD 587.93. All monetary figures refer to the annual gross revenue and do not factor in shipping costs.

Revenue in the Food and Personal Care segment amounts to USD 208 million in 2018.[50] Revenue is expected to show an annual growth rate (CAGR 2018–2023) of 13.2%, resulting in a market volume of USD 387 million by 2023. The market's largest segment is Personal Care with a market volume of USD 138 million in 2018. In global comparison, most revenue is generated in the US (USD 64,117 million in 2018).

Revenue in the Furniture and Appliances segment amounts to USD 211 million in 2018.[51] Revenue is expected to show an annual growth rate (CAGR 2018–2023)

49. https://www.statista.com/outlook/243/111/ecommerce/Israel (accessed 23 Jul. 2021).
50. https://www.statista.com/outlook/246/111/food-personal-care/Israel (accessed 23 Jul. 2021).
51. https://www.statista.com/outlook/247/111/furniture-appliances/Israel (accessed 23 Jul. 2021).

of 15.7%, resulting in a market volume of USD 436 million by 2023. The market's largest segment is Furniture and Homeware with a market volume of USD 142 million in 2018. In global comparison, most revenue is generated in China (USD 95,015 million in 2018).

Revenue in the Toys, Hobby, and DIY segment amounts to USD 1,158 million in 2018.[52] Revenue is expected to show an annual growth rate (CAGR 2018–2023) of 9.1%, resulting in a market volume of USD 1,788 million by 2023. The market's largest segment is Hobby and Stationery with a market volume of USD 692 million in 2018. In global comparison, most revenue is generated in the US (USD 152,912 million in 2018).

Revenue in the Electronics and Media segment amounts to USD 954 million in 2018.[53] Revenue is expected to show an annual growth rate (CAGR 2018–2023) of 8.4%, resulting in a market volume of USD 1,429 million by 2023. The market's largest segment is Consumer Electronics with a market volume of USD 707 million in 2018. In global comparison, most revenue is generated in China (USD 136,111 million in 2018).

Revenue in the Fashion segment amounts to USD 823 million in 2018.[54] Revenue is expected to show an annual growth rate (CAGR 2018–2023) of 13.8%, resulting in a market volume of USD 1,574 million by 2023. The market's largest segment is Apparel with a market volume of USD 557 million in 2018. In global comparison, most revenue is generated in China (USD 246,877 million in 2018).

II. E-Services Market

27. In statistical figures, the e-services market in Israel is defined by the sale of online services and digital goods via the Internet. The definition includes event tickets (sport events, music events, and cinema tickets), fitness apps and wearables, dating services (matchmaking, online dating, casual dating) as well as online food delivery (restaurant-to-consumer and platform-to-consumer delivery). The tickets reservation or purchase can be completed on a desktop PC or via mobile devices (smartphones or tablets).

For statistical reasons, the definition of e-services does not include media content acquired online (Digital Media) or the online sale of physical goods (e-commerce). Furthermore, no business-to-business segments are included, neither are revenues from online gambling, software downloads and services, or commission fees of price/product comparison websites.

Revenue in the e-services market amounts to USD 232 million in 2018.[55] Revenue is expected to show an annual growth rate (CAGR 2018–2023) of 13.5%, resulting in a market volume of USD 437 million by 2023. The market's largest segment is Event Tickets with a market volume of USD 104 million in 2018. In global comparison, most revenue is generated in the US (USD 50,047 million in 2018).

52. https://www.statista.com/outlook/248/111/toys-hobby-diy/Israel (accessed 23 Jul. 2021).
53. https://www.statista.com/outlook/245/111/electronics-media/Israel (accessed 23 Jul. 2021).
54. https://www.statista.com/outlook/244/111/fashion/Israel (accessed 23 Jul. 2021).
55. https://www.statista.com/outlook/261/111/eservices/Israel (accessed 23 Jul. 2021).

Revenue in the Online Food Delivery segment amounts to USD 89 million in 2018.[56] Revenue is expected to show an annual growth rate (CAGR 2018–2023) of 19.5%, resulting in a market volume of USD 216 million by 2023. The market's largest segment is restaurant-to-consumer delivery with a market volume of USD 85 million in 2018. In global comparison, most revenue is generated in China (USD 32,908 million in 2018).

Revenue in the Event Tickets segment amounts to USD 104 million in 2018.[57] Revenue is expected to show an annual growth rate (CAGR 2018–2023) of 10.0%, resulting in a market volume of USD 167 million by 2023. The market's largest segment is Sport Events with a market volume of USD 40 million in 2018. In global comparison, most revenue is generated in the US (USD 28,079 million in 2018).

Revenue in the Fitness segment amounts to USD 31 million in 2018.[58] Revenue is expected to show an annual growth rate (CAGR 2018–2023) of 7.5%, resulting in a market volume of USD 45 million by 2023. The market's largest segment is wearables with a market volume of USD 27 million in 2018. In global comparison, most revenue is generated in China (USD 4,825 million in 2018).

Revenue in the Dating Services segment amounts to USD 8 million in 2018.[59] Revenue is expected to show an annual growth rate (CAGR 2018–2023) of 2.6%, resulting in a market volume of USD 9 million by 2023. The market's largest segment is Matchmaking with a market volume of USD 5 million in 2018. In global comparison, most revenue is generated in the US (USD 1,513 million in 2018).

III. E-Travel Market

28. In statistical figures, the e-travel market is defined by the sale of online services and digital goods via the Internet. The definition includes online travel bookings (package holidays, HOTels, and vacation rentals) and mobility tickets for services such as flights, long-distance bus tickets, train travel, car rentals, and ride hailing services. The ticket reservation or purchase can be completed on a desktop PC or via mobile devices (Smartphones or Tablets).

The definition of e-travel does not include price comparison and recommendation websites without a check-out process, offline and telephone bookings, non-commercial air traffic and tickets for public transport, for within the city, or other local travel. Furthermore, no business-to-business segments are included.

Revenue in the e-travel market amounts to USD 2,021 million in 2018.[60] Revenue is expected to show an annual growth rate (CAGR 2018–2023) of 4.2%, resulting in a market volume of USD 2,488 million by 2023. The market's largest segment is Online Travel Booking with a market volume of USD 1,015 million in 2018. In global comparison, most revenue is generated in the US (USD 217,136 million in 2018).

---

56. https://www.statista.com/outlook/374/111/online-food-delivery/Israel (accessed 23 Jul. 2021).
57. https://www.statista.com/outlook/264/111/event-tickets/Israel (accessed 23 Jul. 2021).
58. https://www.statista.com/outlook/313/111/fitness/Israel (accessed 23 Jul. 2021).
59. https://www.statista.com/outlook/370/111/dating-services/Israel (accessed 23 Jul. 2021).
60. https://www.statista.com/outlook/359/111/etravel/Israel (accessed 23 Jul. 2021).

Revenue in the Online Travel Booking segment amounts to USD 1,015 million in 2018.[61] Revenue is expected to show an annual growth rate (CAGR 2018–2023) of 3.9%, resulting in a market volume of USD 1,229 million by 2023. The market's largest segment is Package Holiday with a market volume of USD 445 million in 2018. In global comparison, most revenue is generated in the US (USD 93,679 million in 2018).

Revenue in the Online Mobility Services segment amounts to USD 1,006 million in 2018.[62] Revenue is expected to show an annual growth rate (CAGR 2018–2023) of 4.6%, resulting in a market volume of USD 1,259 million by 2023. The market's largest segment is Flights with a market volume of USD 726 million in 2018. In global comparison, most revenue is generated in the US (USD 123,457 million in 2018).

IV. Financial Technology

29. In statistical figures, financial technology is the central concept of structural change and digitization within the financial services industry. Under the collective name financial technology (which still lacks a clear definition even within the industry), financial services are understood within the framework of the Digital Market Outlook, digital infrastructures allowing the establishment of new types of agreements and procedures in the classic areas of banking such as lending, investment strategies, and payments.

The characteristics of the digitization process of financial services include: simplified access for end users via the Internet or mobile Apps, an increase in the processing speed of automated processes, reduction in costs, a stronger focus on customer service, more convenience, higher transparency, and the exploitation of network effects.

The financial technology market is characterized by a rapidly growing number of start-ups and businesses without bank licenses (non-banks). For an overview of the total potential of the financial technology market, a split between classic banks and non-banks is not sensible, because consolidation processes, cooperation, and white label solutions mean that there will be no clear differentiation in the future. Therefore, a functions-oriented segmentation is preferred, based on an access- or business model-based split of the market. Financial technology start-ups tend to focus on selected parts of the financial value chain and try to unbundle traditional bank business models.

All monetary information in the financial technology section of the Digital Market Outlook refers to the potential transaction volumes of the respective segments and not corporate revenue. The following are not included in the current market definition: agency commissions via metasearch engines, for example, in the credit and insurance sector, business-to-business payments, application programming

61. https://www.statista.com/outlook/262/111/online-travel-booking/Israel (accessed 23 Jul. 2021).
62. https://www.statista.com/outlook/263/111/online-mobility-services/Israel (accessed 23 Jul. 2021).

interface (API) management, agencies and external credit scoring, crypto currencies (including Bitcoin), and complementary services such as online identification or account management.

The market's largest segment is Digital Payments with a total transaction value of USD 7,049 million in 2018.[63] Total Transaction Value is expected to show an annual growth rate (CAGR 2018–2023) of 17.5% resulting in the total amount of USD 15,756 million by 2023.

Total Transaction Value in the Digital Payments segment amounts to USD 7,049 million in 2018.[64] Total Transaction Value is expected to show an annual growth rate (CAGR 2018–2023) of 17.5% resulting in the total amount of USD 15,756 million by 2023. The market's largest segment is Digital Commerce with a total transaction value of USD 5,787 million in 2018. From a global comparison perspective, it is shown that the highest cumulated transaction value is reached in China (USD 1,269,792 million in 2018).

Total Transaction Value in the Personal Finance segment amounts to USD 1,260 million in 2018.[65] Total Transaction Value is expected to show an annual growth rate (CAGR 2018–2023) of 22.8% resulting in the total amount of USD 3,519 million by 2023. The market's largest segment is P2P (Peer to Peer) Money Transfers with a total transaction value of USD 843 million in 2018. From a global comparison perspective, it is shown that the highest cumulated transaction value is reached in the US (USD 440,934 million in 2018).

Total Transaction Value in the Alternative Lending segment amounts to USD 48 million in 2018.[66] Total Transaction Value is expected to show an annual growth rate (CAGR 2018–2023) of 4.7% resulting in the total amount of USD 60.7 million by 2023. The market's largest segment is Marketplace Lending (Personal) with a total transaction value of USD 37.0 million in 2018. From a global comparison perspective it is shown that the highest cumulated transaction value is reached in China (USD 178,888 million in 2018).

Total Transaction Value in the Alternative Financing segment amounts to USD 576 million in 2018.[67] Total Transaction Value is expected to show an annual growth rate (CAGR 2018–2023) of 19.2% resulting in the total amount of USD 1,385.5 million by 2023. The market's largest segment is Crowd-investing with a total transaction value of USD 569.6 million in 2018. From a global comparison perspective, it is shown that the highest cumulated transaction value is reached in China (USD 4,778 million in 2018).

---

63. https://www.statista.com/outlook/295/111/fintech/Israel (accessed 23 Jul. 2021).
64. https://www.statista.com/outlook/296/111/digital-payments/Israel (accessed 23 Jul. 2021).
65. https://www.statista.com/outlook/298/111/personal-finance/Israel (accessed 23 Jul. 2021).
66. https://www.statista.com/outlook/399/111/alternative-lending/Israel (accessed 23 Jul. 2021).
67. https://www.statista.com/outlook/297/111/alternative-financing/Israel (accessed 23 Jul. 2021).

V. Digital Advertising

30. In statistical figures, digital advertising uses the Internet to deliver marketing messages via various formats to Internet users. This includes banners (e.g., Skyscrapers, Overlays, Rich media formats), video pre-rolls or mid-rolls, search engine advertising as well as online classifieds and social media advertising. Furthermore, the digital advertising market is segmented into desktop and mobile revenues depending on the delivery method such as desktop computers or mobile devices (smartphones and tablet PCs). E-mail marketing, audio ads, influencer sponsorships, and commission-based affiliate systems are not considered here. All figures refer to gross values.

Revenue in the Digital Advertising market amounts to USD 622 million in 2018.[68] The market's largest segment is Search Advertising with a market volume of USD 284 million in 2018. The retail industry accounts for the largest revenue share, i.e., 13.5% of Display Advertising revenues in 2018.

Revenue in the Banner Advertising segment amounts to USD 154 million in 2018.[69] Revenue is expected to show an annual growth rate (CAGR 2018–2023) of 2.6%, resulting in a market volume of USD 175 million by 2023. The average revenue per Internet user currently amounts to USD 24.49. The revenue in the Banner Advertising segment currently corresponds to 0 of the country's GDP.

Revenue in the Video Advertising segment amounts to USD 36 million in 2018.[70] Revenue is expected to show an annual growth rate (CAGR 2018–2023) of 6.2%, resulting in a market volume of USD 48 million by 2023. The average revenue per Internet user currently amounts to USD 5.68. The revenue in the Video Advertising segment currently corresponds to 0 of the country's GDP.

Revenue in the Search Advertising segment amounts to USD 284 million in 2018.[71] Revenue is expected to show an annual growth rate (CAGR 2018–2023) of 0.8%, resulting in a market volume of USD 295 million by 2023. The average revenue per Internet user currently amounts to USD 45.03. The revenue in the Search Advertising segment currently corresponds to 0 of the country's GDP

Revenue in the Social Media Advertising segment amounts to USD 85 million in 2018.[72] Revenue is expected to show an annual growth rate (CAGR 2018–2023) of 29.9%, resulting in a market volume of USD 315 million by 2023. The average revenue per Internet user currently amounts to USD 13.54. The revenue in the Social Media Advertising segment currently corresponds to 0 of the country's GDP.

Revenue in the Classifieds segment amounts to USD 63 million in 2018.[73] Revenue is expected to show an annual growth rate (CAGR 2018–2023) of 7.8%, resulting in a market volume of USD 92 million by 2023. The average revenue per Internet user currently amounts to USD 10.06. The revenue in the Classifieds segment currently corresponds to 0 of the country's GDP.

---

68. https://www.statista.com/outlook/216/111/digital-advertising/Israel (accessed 23 Jul. 2021).
69. https://www.statista.com/outlook/217/111/banner-advertising/Israel (accessed 23 Jul. 2021).
70. https://www.statista.com/outlook/218/111/video-advertising/Israel (accessed 23 Jul. 2021).
71. https://www.statista.com/outlook/219/111/search-advertising/Israel (accessed 23 Jul. 2021).
72. https://www.statista.com/outlook/220/111/social-media-advertising/Israel (accessed 23 Jul. 2021).
73. https://www.statista.com/outlook/221/111/classifieds/Israel (accessed 23 Jul. 2021).

VI. E-Education

31. On 8 March 2020, the Israeli government has decided to restrict education due to the COVID-19 pandemic. The restriction included prohibition on gathering within the lectures' halls inside the higher education institutes and within classes in schools all over the state.

A few days later, all education institutions in Israel continued the routine of education by using the Internet via some popular applications. However, by July 2021, almost all lessons and lectures which were not frontal were being given through a specific application called ZOOM.[74]

Using this application, a tremendous increase has been recorded in the number of beginner students in all higher education institutes. Accurate statistics is not available yet. Young Israelis have figured out that it would be beneficial to start their academic studies during the pandemic time via ZOOM, which would enable them comfort and efficient usage of time. Moreover, this has enabled higher education institutes to get to far-distance audience, such as Israelis who live outside Israel and willing to study in an Israeli institute.

On 4 April 2021, the Israeli government has decided to reopen all education institutes due to the low rates of pandemic in Israel. Most new students have discovered the clear advantages of frontal lectures and preferred to abandon e-education.

However, as long as the COVID-19 pandemic has not been over, e-education is still running on, and new types of audience join its relative advantages.

§3. Trends of Israeli E-Commerce

32. Two major trends of e-commerce in Israel may be indicated.[75] The first trend is the increasing rates of e-commerce. Most Israelis find e-commerce much more comfortable than any other platform of commerce. The international market is much more open for the Israeli consumer through the Internet, and cheaper products and services may be found using e-commerce rather than using any other platform of commerce. Moreover, the government has reduced taxes and customs dramatically during 2018 for importing products by individuals for personal use.

E-commerce is also considered in Israel as encouraging competition. The Israeli manufacturer must compete for the price and quality of products imported from outside Israel through the e-commerce platform. As e-commerce dramatically reduces the expenses of the transaction for the merchant, most Israeli commercial corporations prefer to sell their products through the e-commerce platform rather than in the traditional shops face-to-face. As aforesaid, the trend is increasing rates of e-commerce among other platforms of commerce in Israel. The increasing usage of smartphones in Israel has also contributed to this trend.

The second trend is mistrust in e-commerce. This trend balances the first, but it is in much lower rates in comparison to the first trend. Some Israelis prefer to use

74. https://zoom.us (accessed 18 Jul. 2021).
75. *See* more at Amal Jabareen, *The Law of Business to Consumer Electronic Commerce* vol. I 256–263 (Bursi Publishing House 2015).

the Internet just to get the information on the product and buy it from a shop face-to-face. This phenomenon is known also outside Israel as ROPO (research online, purchase offline). However, this trend relates only to tangible products that may be purchased physically in Israel. According to this trend, the use of the Internet is for comparison of prices between different merchants, comparison of services, and comparison of reviews on the products and on the merchant.

This trend is generally motivated by unsuccessful experiences of individuals with the e-commerce platform (e.g., unsuccessful delivery, unsecured financial data, mistakes in products). However, this trend is dramatically decreasing as businesses make efforts to increase the reliability of e-commerce with them. It may be predicted that this trend is likely to disappear within a few years. Most of the customers' reviews relate to this issue, and there are Israeli websites that even rate the reliability of e-commerce between different businesses.[76]

In sum, the first trend (increasing rates of e-commerce) is likely to characterize the Israeli e-commerce and markets. The consumer's experience using e-commerce platforms is often described as reliable, worthy (in relation to the price and the service), and easy. Due to the growth of use of smartphones among Israelis, this trend is likely to be the dominant trend.

76. *See*, for example: https://www.zap.co.il/ (accessed 23 Jul. 2021).

Chapter 5. E-Government Initiatives

§1. General Background

33. E-government in Israel is considered as one of the most developed in the world. In 2014, a UN survey has ranked Israel 12th (out of 193 countries) in the quality of the digital services granted to its citizens. The government's initiatives have begun in the late 1980s in order to facilitate the government services, make them more accessible for citizens and reduce bureaucracy to minimum. A public committee has been appointed to check feasibility of the initiative.

In 1989, the public committee published its conclusions and recommendations.[77] The conclusions were positive, and the recommendations were to prepare the necessary infrastructure as soon as possible. The Israeli government has embraced the committee's recommendations immediately. The prime minister and the minister of finance have appointed some officials to initiate the process in the public service and in the domestic authorities (at the beginning in the main cities). The main purpose was to make information be more accessible to the citizens with the technology that was in use then (mostly by phone).

In 1991, the ministries of the Israeli government have started gradually to implement this initiative. Basic official information has been accessible to the citizens by phone. In 1996, it has been understood that the growing use of Internet in Israel opens up new opportunities to expand the initiative, not only to make official information accessible but also to enable performance of actions by the citizens (e.g., completion of transactions, payments of bills, submission of tax reports, requesting services and submission of complaints).

As technology advanced, the e-government in Israel became more developed and more accessible. In 1997, a new unit was established, which was called 'Available Government', and it was under the direct responsibility of the Prime Minister. This unit was defined as responsible for the development of the e-government in Israel. This unit includes today about 400 employees, and it is the Israeli ICT (Information and communications technology) authority.

The first project of combining all government services in one electronic platform was 'Tehila' project in 1997. This project was developed in 2002 into 'Gov.il', which was accessible to citizens through the Gov.il portal, with a familiar logo, and operated in Hebrew, English, Arabic, Russian, Spanish and French.[78] The new 'Gov.il' website was launched in 2015 with an open access and compatibility to all browsers in use. As of 2019, almost all e-government initiatives are developed through the 'Gov.il' platform.

§2. E-Government Services in Israel

34. Through the 'Gov.il' platform all ministries of the Israeli government are accessible to any applicant. The 'Gov.il' project vision is to replace bureaucracy by

77. http://www.knesset.gov.il/docs/heb/infocom/final103.htm#Heading28 (accessed 23 Jul. 2021).
78. For the platform in English *see*: https://www.gov.il/en (accessed 23 Jul. 2021).

one accessible government, which poses the citizen at the centre of its activity, acts transparently and efficiently, develops innovations, and uses advanced technologies in favour of the public.

The main activities of the e-government in Israel are divided between the departments of the 'Available Government' unit in the Prime Minister's office. The main departments are the applications department (developing accessible applications for public services), the business clients department (concentrating the commercial affairs related to the e-government projects), the IT department (Information Technology department which is responsible for operating the project and grants customer services twenty-four hours a day), the cyber protection department, the developments and review department, and the digital identity department.

The main services of the e-government in Israel relate to the digital interactions between citizens and the government (C2G), between the government and other government agencies (G2G), between government and citizens (G2C), between government and employees (G2E) and between government and businesses (G2B). The main products of the e-government in Israel consist on developments of accessible applications in all available media, on cloud products, on Internet infrastructure development for private and public needs, and on secured communication C2G, G2C, G2G, G2E, and G2B.

The 'Gov.il' platform enables variable services including the forms service (enables the citizen to find the required form for any activity C2G), the payments service (enables to pay via credit cards any bill and to pay for any service offered by the government through a secure website), the Data Gov service (offers access to any of the Israeli government publications), the service-point service (enables access to the digital service from public points for citizens who lack access to the Internet), the mobile application's service (enables communication with the government services via smartphones), the bid service (enables unique service for potential private business which are interested in participating in public bids), and the licenses service (enables all required activities of bureaucracy related to formal licenses given by the Israeli government, e.g., driving license).

For educational purposes, the 'Gov.il' platform offers a digital platform unique for children.[79] This platform offers several educational activities for children designed by the government ministries. These activities include the ministry of finance activity for financial education (e.g., how to invest? what is pension?), the communication ministry for awareness of dangers using the Internet, the Israeli police activity for legal education (mostly on criminal law issues), the ministry of health activity for healthy life education (mostly on sports and nutrition), and the ministry of energies activity for saving energy and many more activities.

Besides the 'Gov.il' platform there are many more governmental digital platforms which are designed for specific services. The 'Net-Hamishpat' (the network of the legal service) is one of them.[80] All papers submitted to the Israeli court may be submitted electronically through this platform, with no necessity of paper or physically to appear in court. This platform is used mostly by advocates, but also

---

79. http://kids.gov.il/ (accessed 23 Jul. 2021).
80. https://www.court.gov.il/ngcs.web.site/homepage.aspx (accessed 23 Jul. 2021).

by the parties. This platform also offers information on ongoing court files, including court decisions in real time. Moreover, under the 2018 civil procedure regulations in Israel, in several sorts of civil proceedings, the electronic submission is the preferred submission both to court and to the counterparty.

In a 2014 UN survey, Israel was ranked in the highest-ranking class for the provision of digital services. The UN report measured the development of e-government in UN Member States, focusing on three main indexes: online public services index, human capital index, and infrastructure and communications index. The online public services index measures the development of e-government in each Member State according to the E-GOV 4 stage model, the provision of information services, interaction services, transaction services, and connected services, to the public. In the public involvement index Israel was ranked 12th.

In 2018, a report of the ICT authority in Israel had pointed out several tasks for the future e-government:[81] development of sophisticated digital services, increasing the quality of the service given to the citizens, efficient cyber protection in all government units, increasing the rate of using digital services among citizens and embracing new technologies in favour of the digital service (e.g., big data, data warehouse, data mining, business intelligence, public cloud, open source, and Agile).

Due to the COVID-19 pandemic influence in Israel, most Israeli governmental organizations had to make their e-services become more accessible, as this was the only way to fulfil their function and grant relevant services to Israelis. Moreover, even though the governmental services were reopened a few times during the pandemic, most Israelis preferred to consume governmental services as e-services rather than frontal. Statistics is not available yet.

81. https://www.gov.il/BlobFolder/news/mabat2018/he/Tikshuv_Activity_06_singles.pdf (accessed 23 Jul. 2021).

Part I. Regulation of the ICT Market

Chapter 1. Regulatory Framework of the Telecommunications Sector

35. The regulatory framework of the telecommunications sector is concentrated on the Communication (Telecommunication and Broadcasting) Act, 1982, which is amended regularly due to the changing realm of telecommunications in Israel. The main issues regulated are the licensing and the operating of telecommunication services.

§1. Licensing Telecommunication Services

36. Telecommunication activity is defined in Israeli law as transmitting, transferring, or receiving any sign, voice, or information using wires or not using wires, electronically, optically, or using any electromagnetic system.[82] By the law, all telecommunication activities are under the responsibility of the state, but the state has the right to grant licenses to activate telecommunication services to other entities.[83] As a result, no person is allowed to activate telecommunication services unless licensed to do so by the state.[84] Nevertheless, a few telecommunication activities are allowed to be activated without any license from the state. These activities include self-transmission on a private territory, manufacturing telecommunication devices, operating traffic lights, electronic data processing, and some other activities.[85]

The government is responsible for licensing telecommunication activities under the direct responsibility of the minister of communications. For licensing any type of telecommunication activity, the minister of communications is required to determine specific conditions and publish them through regulations.[86] However, granting any telecommunication license is required to be only after the major considerations have been considered. These major considerations consist of the government policy

82. The definition of 'Telecommunication' in s. 1 of the Communication (Telecommunication and Broadcasting) Act, 1982.
83. Section 2(a) of the Communication (Telecommunication and Broadcasting) Act, 1982.
84. Section 2(b) of the Communication (Telecommunication and Broadcasting) Act, 1982.
85. Section 3 of the Communication (Telecommunication and Broadcasting) Act, 1982.
86. Section 4(a) of the Communication (Telecommunication and Broadcasting) Act, 1982.

as published, the public welfare, the compatibility of the licensee to activate the specifics telecommunication service, and increasing the competition and the quality of the service.[87]

The request for license is submitted to the minister of communications, and the minister may approve it, dismiss it, or approve it under certain conditions. The minister is allowed to consult technical experts in order to evaluate correctly the request. The technical experts may also be required for the evaluation of the compatibility of the devices that may be used if the request is approved. If the request for license is approved and the license is granted, the license is not transferrable, but it is personal.[88]

After the license is granted, the ministry of communications is allowed to require any information on the telecommunication activity operated by the licensee.[89] If the specific telecommunication activity is defined by the government as essential service, the license is much more limited, and the government would supervise the operation of the activity much more carefully in favour of the public.[90] If an essential service is malfunctioned and unsuccessfully operated by the licensee, the government may abolish the license and operate the service through a commissioner (a public servant).[91]

The minister of communications is allowed to determine what are the basic telecommunication services that all Israeli citizens are entitled to have.[92] The list is published, and it may affect the terms of the license of any licensee. Thus, licensees may be required to supply telecommunication services of certain sorts although it is not profitable, as part of the license conditions. It is prohibited that any licensee would require the customers, directly or indirectly, to purchase one type of service as a condition to supply a different type of service.[93]

When the telecommunication activity is related to the Internet, the license inherently includes certain duties posed on the licensee. One of these duties is the duty to notify the customers of dangers using the Internet and dangerous websites.[94] Dangerous websites include websites that incite to perpetrate criminal offences, websites with humiliating sexual content, racism or violence and websites of gambling.

When the telecommunication activity is related to mobile communication, the license inherently includes certain duties posed on the licensee.[95] The licensee must permit the customer to move to a competing licensee with the same dialling number. The licensee must block SMS services free of charge, if the customer asks for it, and that includes also receiving commercial SMS.[96] The licensee must let private

87. Section 4(b) of the Communication (Telecommunication and Broadcasting) Act, 1982.
88. Section 4(d1) of the Communication (Telecommunication and Broadcasting) Act, 1982.
89. Section 4C1 of the Communication (Telecommunication and Broadcasting) Act, 1982.
90. Section 4D of the Communication (Telecommunication and Broadcasting) Act, 1982.
91. Section 4E of the Communication (Telecommunication and Broadcasting) Act, 1982.
92. Section 4F of the Communication (Telecommunication and Broadcasting) Act, 1982.
93. Section 4G of the Communication (Telecommunication and Broadcasting) Act, 1982.
94. Section 4I of the Communication (Telecommunication and Broadcasting) Act, 1982.
95. Section 5A of the Communication (Telecommunication and Broadcasting) Act, 1982.
96. Section 5B of the Communication (Telecommunication and Broadcasting) Act, 1982.

operators (other new licensees) use the licensee's infrastructure, if it is necessary for the quality of the services given by the private operator, but not necessarily free of charge.[97]

After the license is granted, the minister of communications may amend it or abolish it, if the licensee has asked for that, if not all conditions of the license were fulfilled, if the licensee has still not begun to operate the service, if the licensee has stopped the service, if the licensee has begun bankruptcy proceedings, if the quality of the service is insufficient or out of public welfare reasons.[98]

In 2012, the licensing proceedings of transmissions through digital transmission stations was legally separated from the general licensing procedures.[99] The reason for the separation was the difference between the content of the transmission and the technical act of transmission. As the content of transmission is licensed, as described above, the licensing of the technical transmission may be focused on technical requirements. In general, the operators of the digital transmission stations are appointed by the ministry of communications through a public bid.[100] The operator is required to transmit a minimum list of channels, and it may transmit more channels if the quality of the transmission is not damaged.[101] The operator may enable transmission through the Internet, if required by the channels.[102]

§2. Operating Telecommunication Services

37. The licensee is bound to service the customers with a high quality of service and according to the specific conditions determined in the license.[103] The minister of communications is responsible for supervising the licensees. If the minister suspects that a licensee operates telecommunication services of low quality, endangers the competition in the specific field of telecommunication, or unable to ensure regular service, the minister may order specific orders to the licensee to meet the requirements. The orders may be given after the licensee would be given a fair chance to explain the act or omission.

Nevertheless, if immediate actions are required, the minister may order the orders without enabling the licensee to explain. Such orders would be compulsory only after two days, and the licensee may comment within these two days. After the orders became compulsory, the licensee must be given a fair chance to explain the act or omission as soon as possible. The orders would be compulsory up to six months.

When a licensee disconnects a customer from a phone service for unpaid bills, the licensee must enable the customer the use of the service to call emergency centres operated in Israel for at least two months from the date of disconnection, free

97. Section 5C of the Communication (Telecommunication and Broadcasting) Act, 1982.
98. Section 6 of the Communication (Telecommunication and Broadcasting) Act, 1982.
99. The Transmission through Digital Transmission Stations Act, 2012.
100. Section 2 of the Transmission through Digital Transmission Stations Act, 2012.
101. Sections 6–7 of the Transmission through Digital Transmission Stations Act, 2012.
102. Section 13C of the Transmission through Digital Transmission Stations Act, 2012.
103. Section 11 of the Communication (Telecommunication and Broadcasting) Act, 1982.

of charge.[104] However, any call to any emergency centre in Israel must be free of charge from any supporting device (e.g., mobile phones and landline telephones). Due to privacy reasons, any calls for emergency centres would not be included in the customer bills and no information upon them would be given to *any* third party.[105]

Emergency centres in Israel include not only the police, the fire department, and the medical services (Magen David Adom – the red star of David), but assisting centres for women sexually attacked, mental first aid centres, and other assisting centres as well.[106]

In times of war or other emergency situations, including communications crisis (i.e., fatal harm to civil communication infrastructure), the minister of communications or the prime minister may license a public unit (e.g., communications unit of the Israeli police or communications unit of the Israeli Defence Forces) to operate telecommunications services in favour of the civil population in addition to the private licensees who fail to operate these services at full or in high quality.[107] However, when the emergency situation is over, the license automatically expires.

If no emergency situation has been declared, but the minister of communications realizes that the private licensee fails to operate the telecommunication services due to objective reasons or difficulties, the minister may temporarily license a public unit to operate these services in favour of the public.[108] However, public units should be licensed to operate telecommunication services only in extremely rare circumstances and only as the last resort.

Any licensee is allowed to determine operative rules for customers, as long as these rules are not contradicted with the law, and that they are certified by the minister of communications.[109] The minister may demand amendments of the rules in favour of the public, and if the licensee did not amend them within ninety days, the minister may amend them in lieu of the licensee.

Licensees are required to charge the customers fair fares. The minister is allowed to determine maximum fares for any telecommunication service.[110] However, the competition in the Israeli telecommunication market is considered to be developed enough for not intervening in the market fares. The ongoing trend of the fares in the Israeli market is lowering the fares and guarantee of high quality. For example, in 2019, Internet services of 100 Mb (download) were proposed for NIS 15 per month (approximately EUR 3.5 or USD 4), whereas in 2015, these very services were proposed for NIS 30. Debt for any private licensee is considered civil debt, and the licensee may submit a lawsuit against the customers who fail to pay the bills.

Licensee is allowed to build any infrastructure in order to ensure the telecommunication services only if it matches the legal requirement of the ministry of environmental protection.[111] In spite of the increasing use of mobile phones by Israelis,

104. Section 12 of the Communication (Telecommunication and Broadcasting) Act, 1982.
105. Section 12A of the Communication (Telecommunication and Broadcasting) Act, 1982.
106. Section 12A(e) of the Communication (Telecommunication and Broadcasting) Act, 1982.
107. Section 13(b) of the Communication (Telecommunication and Broadcasting) Act, 1982.
108. Section 13B of the Communication (Telecommunication and Broadcasting) Act, 1982.
109. Section 14 of the Communication (Telecommunication and Broadcasting) Act, 1982.
110. Section 15 of the Communication (Telecommunication and Broadcasting) Act, 1982.
111. Section 27B of the Communication (Telecommunication and Broadcasting) Act, 1982.

cellular radiation is not welcome in cities' centres. Therefore, mobile services companies are challenged to ensure high-quality services without relying on massive infrastructure in cities' centres. However, any cellular transmitting device (e.g., antenna) is restricted in radiation rates and physical dimensions, for reasons of public health.

Most breaches of the license conditions are protected through criminal offences.[112] Regardless of this type of protection, at any time after the license is granted to the licensee, the minister of communications may amend it or abolish it, if the licensee has asked for that, if not all conditions of the license were fulfilled, if the licensee has still not begun to operate the service, if the licensee has stopped the service, if the licensee has begun bankruptcy proceedings, if the quality of the service is insufficient or out of public welfare reasons.[113]

Specific regulations towards the operation of telecommunication services are enacted frequently in order to optimize the quality of the services for the benefit of specific groups in Israeli society or in favour of the whole public. For example, all television transmissions are required to add written translation, subtitles, or translation into sign language to certain part of the transmissions in favour of people who are hard of hearing.[114]

112. Chapter 7 of the Communication (Telecommunication and Broadcasting) Act, 1982.
113. Section 6 of the Communication (Telecommunication and Broadcasting) Act, 1982.
114. The Television Transmissions (Subtitles and Sign Language) Act, 2005.

Chapter 2. Regulation of Competition in the ICT Market

38. There are two main branches of the Israeli regulation of competition. The traditional branch is the antitrust law. A newer branch emerged in 2014, apart from antitrust law, and it is the competition encouragement and reduction of centralization law. The competition in the ICT market in Israel is not considered as requiring different or special regulation; therefore, it has been incorporated into the general regulation of competition. However, the Israeli ministry of communications prefers to encourage competition in the ICT market using economic motivations rather than regulation, and let the efficiency considerations in the market initiate the competition.

§1. ANTITRUST LAW

39. The Israeli ICT market is subordinated to the antitrust law, and a few significant transactions in the Israeli ICT market were prevented due to the antitrust law. The law distinguishes between four main forms of antitrust: restrictive arrangements (cartels), mergers of corporations, monopolies, and concentration groups. All of these forms of antitrust were already relevant to the Israeli ICT market in specific cases, and the involvement of the regulator, and sometimes the involvement of the court as well, were required.

I. The Regulator, the Antitrust Tribunal and the Court

40. The antitrust law in Israel is under the supervision of both administrative authorities and the judiciary. The minister of economics is directly responsible in the Israeli government for the applicability of antitrust law in Israel. The government appoints the inspector of antitrust law by the suggestion of the minister.[115] The inspector is the chairman of the Israeli Antitrust Authority, which functions as the regulator in any of the antitrust matters in Israel. The regulator is authorized to determine whether any transaction is legal in the aspect of antitrust law. The regulator acts only in specific cases and not generally, as the standards for antitrust are determined by the law.

In order to make appropriate decisions, the regulator is allowed to inspect the Israeli market, perform surveys and detect suspicious transactions or other activities. If a suspicious activity is detected, the regulator may initiate an inquiry and decide whether a breach of the law has occurred. If so, the regulator may prevent the activity, impose administrative fines and charge the parties in criminal proceedings.[116] The maximum punishment for antitrust offences is five years imprisonment, and the maximum administrative fine is approximately EUR 6 million.

The Antitrust Tribunal functions as supervisory authority in relation to the regulator. The tribunal consists of seventeen members, and the president of the tribunal

115. Section 41 of the Antitrust Act, 1988.
116. Chapter 7 and Chapter 7A of the Antitrust Act, 1988.

and the vice president are judges of one of the District Courts in Israel, appointed by the minister of justice after consulting the chief justice of the Supreme Court.[117] In general, the tribunal sessions are of three members. The tribunal is authorized to overrule the regulator's decisions and to confirm in advance transactions that may be suspicious in the aspect of antitrust law. The procedures of the tribunal are determined in specific regulations.[118]

However, the Antitrust Tribunal is an administrative authority as well as the regulator. As a result, according to the Israeli administrative law, its decisions should also be supervised, but by the judiciary. Thus, any party may appeal on the tribunal decisions. Appeals on the tribunal's decisions are submitted to the Israeli Supreme Court.[119] The Supreme Court may change, abolish, or confirm the tribunal's decisions.

II. Restrictive Arrangements (Cartels)

41. A restrictive arrangement is defined as any arrangement, in which at least one of the parties restrict itself to actions or omissions that may endanger the competition between the parties or between a third party and the parties.[120] For example, parties in the mobile communication market who restrict themselves to a certain minimum price for their services. However, regardless the specific content of the arrangement, any arrangement between competing parties in the ICT market is considered to be restrictive, if the arrangement related to the price of any service, to the profit, to the market distribution, to the number of the proposed services or to the quality of the proposed services.

Functioning as a party of a restrictive arrangement is considered to be a criminal offence. However, the Antitrust Tribunal is authorized to confirm a restrictive arrangement in advance, if the tribunal is convinced that the restrictive arrangement does not endanger the competition between the parties and that it is for the benefit of the consumers.[121] The tribunal's decision must take into consideration the balance between any damage or danger to the public and the total benefit of the consumers, including the aspects of sufficient amount of supplies or quality of services proposed to the public, efficiency considerations, prevention of damage to ICT market and to the customers, reduction of unemployment and domestic considerations.[122]

The tribunal's confirmation should determine the period for the validity of the confirmation. If the tribunal has not determined any period, the default period is the shorter of three years and the period the parties determined in the confirmed arrangement.[123] However, the tribunal is authorized to amend the confirmation after

117. Section 32 of the Antitrust Act, 1988.
118. Section 40 of the Antitrust Act, 1988.
119. Section 39 of the Antitrust Act, 1988.
120. Section 2 of the Antitrust Act, 1988.
121. Section 9 of the Antitrust Act, 1988.
122. Section 10 of the Antitrust Act, 1988.
123. Section 11 of the Antitrust Act, 1988.

it has been given, if the regulator has asked for amending it, due to changing circumstances. Although confirmation of restrictive arrangements is under the tribunal's authority, in clear cases of the public benefit, the regulator may exempt the parties from the requirement of the tribunal's confirmation.[124] If the parties to a confirmed restrictive arrangement changed one of its details, it is considered to be a new restrictive arrangement which requires a new confirmation. However, in recent years, no restrictive arrangement has been detected in the Israeli ICT market.

III. Mergers of Corporations

42. The reasons for corporations to merger may be various and different in different cases, and it is directed mostly out of efficiency reasons, but any merger of corporations endangers competition as the number of competitors reduces. In the Israeli ICT market, this is the most common type of antitrust, and most interventions of the regulators were towards the prohibition to merge. In 2018, two commercial television companies in Israel ('Channel 10' and 'Reshet') were not allowed to merge, although without their merger, at least one of them was about to begin bankruptcy proceedings within a short time.[125] Eventually, in December 2018, they had submitted a new application to the merger, the merger was approved and came into force on 15 January 2019.

Not all mergers of companies are relevant to antitrust law, but any merger between companies requires a confirmation from the regulator in the aspect of antitrust law.[126] The merger of companies is suspicious if, after the merger, the merged companies would control at least half of the relevant market, and in some cases even below that, if the mutual financial turnover of the companies, prior to the merger, was above a certain sum (approximately EUR 35 million) or if at least one of the companies fulfils the definition of monopoly.[127] However, if the company has businesses outside Israel, only its businesses in Israel would be taken into consideration.

The companies are required to notify the regulator of their intent to merge. The regulator is required to respond within thirty days, and the response may be confirmation, rejection, or confirmation under certain conditions. If after thirty days the regulator did not respond, the merger is considered to be confirmed.[128] The process of confirmation begins with the above notification, but the regulator is required to notify all relevant government ministries for their opinion. The regulator's discretion is independent, but it may consider the ministries' opinions.

---

124. Section 14 of the Antitrust Act, 1988.
125. *See* at https://en.wikipedia.org/wiki/Channel_10_(Israeli_TV_channel) (accessed 23 Jul. 2021) and https://en.wikipedia.org/wiki/Reshet (accessed 23 Jul. 2021).
126. Section 19 of the Antitrust Act, 1988.
127. Section 17 of the Antitrust Act, 1988. For the definition of monopoly *See* below at s. [IV]: Monopolies.
128. Section 20 of the Antitrust Act, 1988.

The regulator must consider the impact of the merger on the competition in the Israeli ICT market in relation to the prices, the quality and the quantity of the services.[129] The regulator's decision must be published in at least two different newspapers and in the official gazette. The merging companies may object the regulator's decision by applying to the Antitrust Tribunal. Nevertheless, the exempt committee in the ministry of economics is authorized to exempt sorts of mergers between companies, but not specific cases.[130] As a supervisory act, if the regulator intends to confirm a merger between companies, the confirmation of the committee is required.[131]

A general remedy in case of unlawful merger of corporations is separation of the merged corporation into several corporations. However, only the Antitrust Tribunal is authorized to order such separation.[132] As aforesaid, in the Israeli ICT market, this is the most common type of antitrust, and most interventions of the regulators were towards the prohibition to merge. However, in most cases when the regulator has intervened, another solution was found without endangering the competition in the ICT market. For example, in the mobile communication market in 2016, the regulator has rejected the request of 'Cellcom' and 'Golan Telecom' to merge due to financial difficulties of the latter. In 2017, 'Electra', an Israeli company outside the ICT market has purchased 'Golan Telecom' and increased competition in the mobile communication market in Israel.[133]

IV. Monopolies

43. A monopoly is considered devastative to competition in the Israeli market, as Israel is relatively a small country. The legal definition of monopoly is the control over at least half of the assets, half of the given services or half of the accepted services in any part of the ICT market.[134] However, the regulator may consider a monopoly not only in the national level but also in a domestic level, or restricted to certain geographical area.[135] Such considerations are affected by the relevant type of ICT service and infrastructure.

The first and most important step of the regulator is to declare the entity as monopoly. This declaration is public, and the regulator is required to publish it in the official gazette. However, the minister of economics is authorized to declare monopoly on entity even if it does not fulfil the above requirement, if it has a decisive control in the relevant market, and due to the recommendation of the regulator.

The regulator may restrict the monopoly to market only products or services that meet the requirements of standardization law, even if these requirements are not

129. Section 21 of the Antitrust Act, 1988.
130. Section 23 of the Antitrust Act, 1988.
131. Section 24 of the Antitrust Act, 1988.
132. Section 25 of the Antitrust Act, 1988.
133. *See* more at https://en.wikipedia.org/wiki/Golan_Telecom (accessed 23 Jul. 2021).
134. Section 26(a) of the Antitrust Act, 1988.
135. Section 26(b) of the Antitrust Act, 1988.

compulsory.[136] The monopoly is not allowed to reject any request to purchase products or services by potential customers, unless the rejection is reasonable.[137] The monopoly is not allowed to take unfair advantage over its competitors.[138] The regulator is granted a discretion towards the fairness of the advantage taken; however, in certain types of cases, the advantage is presumed to be unfair. These types of cases include determination of unfair fares for the products or services, reduction of quantity or quality of services, determination of different conditions for similar transactions, or conditioning the terms of one transaction in commitment to perform another transaction.

If the regulator detects endangerment of the competition in the ICT market related to the monopoly's certain conduct, it may order the monopoly to take the required steps to eliminate its effect or reduce it.[139] However, it is presumed that any danger to the quality, quantity, price, or availability of any of the services supplied by the monopoly is considered to be an endangerment of the competition in the ICT market. It is also presumed that limitation or creation of difficulties to customers who wish to move to the competitors is considered endangerment of the competition. However, worthy proposals to the customer in order to make them change their mind are allowed, as they are considered part of fair competition.

Although a monopoly is not necessarily an outcome of a merger, the remedy of separation may still be relevant. The Antitrust Tribunal is authorized to order the separation of the monopoly, if, due to the regulator's opinion and supporting evidence, it has been convinced that the monopoly damages the public welfare, and the damage may be prevented efficiently only through separation of the monopoly.[140] The separation of the monopoly may be executed by the establishment of a new entity or by transferring some of the control in the certain activity to an existing entity.[141]

The ongoing trend in the Israeli ICT market since the 1990s is the dismantling of monopolies that have dominated the market for decades. The most significant example is the monopoly of Bezeq. Bezeq was founded in 1984 as a government-owned corporation, taking over the provision of telephony services in Israel, which were previously run directly by the ministry of communications. The motivation for creating the company was the highly bureaucratic and inefficient nature of the government run service, requiring customers to wait several years until they got a phone line installed. In 1994, Bezeq acquired 50% ownership of Pelephone, Israel's first mobile communication company; in 2004, it acquired full ownership of the company from its co-owner Motorola. In 1998, Bezeq co-founded Yes, a direct-broadcast satellite provider, which began broadcasting in July 2000.

However, in 1994, Cellcom, a new mobile communication company, was founded, breaking Pelephone's monopoly in this area. In 1999, a third competitor, Partner Communications Company, was established. In 1997, two new competitors

136. Section 27(a)(2) of the Antitrust Act, 1988.
137. Section 29 of the Antitrust Act, 1988.
138. Section 29A of the Antitrust Act, 1988.
139. Section 30 of the Antitrust Act, 1988.
140. Section 31(a) of the Antitrust Act, 1988.
141. Section 31(b) of the Antitrust Act, 1988.

were introduced in international calling services, and Bezeq was obliged to establish a new subsidiarity to compete with them named Bezeq International. Until the mid-first decade of the twenty-first century when it was owned by the Israeli government, Bezeq had a monopoly on landline telephony and Internet access infrastructure. Though still the most dominant provider of telephone services, it has had competition from the sole cable provider in the country (since September 2006), HOT, which offers a cable-based telephone and Internet access services as of 2005, and with 012 Smile and more recently 013 Netvision and Orange corporations.

V. Concentration Groups

44. A relatively new form of antitrust was introduced to the Israeli antitrust law in 2011, the concentration groups.[142] In fact, the concentration group is a wider definition of monopoly. Accordingly, a concentration group is a group of persons (including legal entities), who control more than half of all services or assets in the specified market, and that there is very little competition between the members of the group, if any.[143] The regulator may declare these persons concentrating group, if, in addition, there are some administrative actions that may be taken in order to increase competition and reduce damages to the public's welfare.

If a concentration group has been declared, the regulator is authorized to order all members of the concentration group various administrative measures in order to increase competition and reduce damages to the public's welfare. These measures include the reduction or abolition of limitation of consumers to move to other competitors, the reduction or abolition of limitation of suppliers to supply products and services to the competitors, the order to stop any activity by members of the group which makes the concentration group be efficient in damaging the competition and prohibition of transferring information between members of the group.[144]

The Antitrust Tribunal is authorized, if required to by the regulator, to order members of the group to sell their holdings to a third party in favour of fair competition in the specified market.[145] Such an order given by the Antitrust Tribunal is considered as the last resort, and may be given only if no other administrative order of the regulator is efficient under the specific circumstances of the case. However, regulating concentration groups in Israel is not only through antitrust law but also through the competition encouragement and reduction of centralization law.

§2. Competition Encouragement and Reduction of Centralization Law

45. By the 1990s, the Israeli society has become aware of the centralization problem in the ICT market in Israel. A small group of persons and corporations dominated the ICT market in various manners. The Knesset has begun to collect

142. Chapter D1 of the Antitrust Act, 1988.
143. Section 31B(a) of the Antitrust Act, 1988.
144. Section 31C(a) of the Antitrust Act, 1988.
145. Section 31C(b) of the Antitrust Act, 1988.

data upon this subject, and several reports were published.[146] However, most cases of centralization were treated through the antitrust law and specific initiatives of the ministry of communications to encourage competition in the specific field. In order to determine a modern standard in this issue, in 2013, the Competition Encouragement and Reduction of Centralization Act, 2013 has been enacted, and it includes specific provisions in relation to the ICT market.

The main measures that the law uses to encourage competition and to reduce centralization are towards granting rights to private entities. In relation to the ICT market it is very significant, as any ICT activity requires licensing, as discussed above.[147] A committee for the reduction of centralization has been established which includes the inspector of antitrust (chairman), the general manager of the ministry of finance, and the chairman of the national committee of economics.[148] The committee is authorized to summon any person (including legal entities) to deliver any document or information relevant to the centralization in the ICT market in Israel.[149]

According to the information held by the committee, the committee is specifically authorized to publish a list of significantly affecting entities in the Israeli ICT market.[150] It is authorized to publish such list regarding other markets, but the legislator has specifically authorized it regarding the ICT market. The list is updated occasionally, and it may be accessed through the website of the ministry of finance.[151] As of 2021, the list includes twenty-eight entities (including groups) regarding the ICT market in Israel. However, the list should not include the state, any statutory corporation, or any authority.[152]

Significantly affecting entity in the ICT market is defined as a daily newspaper published nationally, a publisher of such a newspaper, a licensed television channel that may be received nationally, a news producer, a licensed cable television transmitter, a licensed satellite television transmitter, or an international news television channel.[153]

Any authority in Israel is authorized not to license any entity from the above list, if it has been found out that it is likely that no damage would be caused to the public welfare or the relevant ICT field in Israel.[154] Thus, even if no damage is likely to occur if that entity is licensed, the authority is still authorized not to license that entity. The rationale behind this legal provision is that the very act of licensing that entity contributes to the centralization of the ICT market in Israel, damages the competition in that field, and indirectly (or directly) damages the public welfare.

---

146. *See, e.g.*, from 2013: https://fs.knesset.gov.il/globaldocs/MMM/5cf36d8d-f1f7-e411-80c8-00155d01107c/2_5cf36d8d-f1f7-e411-80c8-00155d01107c_11_8014.pdf (accessed 23 Jul. 2021).
147. Above at s. §1: Licensing Telecommunication Services, in Part I.
148. Section 40 of the Competition Encouragement and Reduction of Centralization Act, 2013.
149. Section 42 of the Competition Encouragement and Reduction of Centralization Act, 2013.
150. Section 4(a)(1)(a)(3) of the Competition Encouragement and Reduction of Centralization Act, 2013.
151. https://mof.gov.il/Committees/Pages/CentralizationDecreaseCommittee.aspx (accessed 23 Jul. 2021). *See also* http://www.antitrust.gov.il/subject/241/item/35278.aspx (accessed 23 Jul. 2021).
152. Section 4(c) of the Competition Encouragement and Reduction of Centralization Act, 2013.
153. Section 4(f) of the Competition Encouragement and Reduction of Centralization Act, 2013.
154. Section 5(a) of the Competition Encouragement and Reduction of Centralization Act, 2013.

Moreover, granting any additional license to an entity from the above list requires the relevant ICT authority to consult the committee for the reduction of centralization and consider the relevant considerations towards the competition in that ICT field.[155] The considerations may be regarding the competition in the specific ICT field, but they may also be regarding the competition at the national level, whether it is related to the ICT market or not.[156] For example, when the entity controls significant resources or services in different fields, but ICT is not one of them, it may affect granting this entity a license in the ICT market. The rationale behind this legal provision is that centralization may also be achieved through small pieces from different fields.

Any renewal of license in the ICT market is subordinated to the Competition Encouragement and Reduction of Centralization Act, 2013, if the expiring license has been granted more than ten years before the renewal or that the centralization rate of that entity has not been examined in the past ten years.[157] This legal provision is meant to ensure examination of the centralization rate of such entities at least once in ten years.

The competition encouragement and reduction of centralization law also prohibit opposite control in corporations of pyramid structure in order to reduce bypassing the law's restrictions through using different corporations.[158] The major prohibition is that if one corporation is controlling a second corporation, the second corporation is prohibited from controlling the first corporation. Thus, a mother company may not be controlled by one of its daughter companies. In the Israeli ICT market, this prohibition is considered to be very significant. 'Control' in this manner is defined as the real potential to direct the corporation.[159]

If such structure of control is detected, the District Court in the district where one of the corporations is registered should appoint a trustee.[160] The trustee would be given the problematic control and would act to eliminate it through sale or other reasonable measures. In addition, the competition encouragement and reduction of centralization law prohibit dual-function entities, in which one of the functions is financial (e.g., banking services, credit services, or financial investments services) and the other is within the ICT market.[161]

155. Section 5(b) of the Competition Encouragement and Reduction of Centralization Act, 2013.
156. Section 11 of the Competition Encouragement and Reduction of Centralization Act, 2013.
157. Section 18(b) of the Competition Encouragement and Reduction of Centralization Act, 2013.
158. Section 21 of the Competition Encouragement and Reduction of Centralization Act, 2013.
159. Section 1 of the Securities' Act, 1968, which is applicable through s. 1 of the Companies' Act, 1999, which is applicable through s. 20(a) of the Competition Encouragement and Reduction of Centralization Act, 2013.
160. Section 22 of the Competition Encouragement and Reduction of Centralization Act, 2013.
161. Sections 28–31 and 39 of the Competition Encouragement and Reduction of Centralization Act, 2013.

Chapter 3. Regulation of Cryptography and Other Dual-Use Goods

§1. Encryption Controls

46. The state of Israel regulates the use of encryption items through the Ordinance Governing the Control of Commodities and Services (Engagement in Encryption Items).[162] In order to regulate engagement in this field, the ministry of defence has instituted a system of control and licensing for items of encryption. The purpose of regulating engagement in items of encryption is to enable the Israeli encryption industry, one of the most advanced in the world, to develop, produce, sell and export its products while at the same time safeguarding the national security interests of Israel.[163]

Commercial encryption and related technologies are regarded in most countries as 'Dual Use' in nature and are therefore subject to control. This relates to technologies, products, and information which, though as a rule used for (commercial or private) civilian purposes, can also be used for military and security purposes. There is always the concern that in case such technologies fall into the wrong hands (states recognized as supporting terrorism, terrorist organizations, or criminal elements) they might be used for harmful purposes.

The Israeli ministry of defence recognizes that commercial encryption developed by commercial elements for commercial purposes is not a military product. For this reason, control over such commercial encryption items is different than that relating to defence exports. The amendment of the Encryption Ordinance, among certain other things, excluded encryption items from the Ordinance of Regulating Defence Exports. The definition of encryption items as items of combat that come under the system of control over defence exports was duly amended. Other countries also have similar regulations.

The Encryption Ordinance provides for the establishment of an advisory committee on engagement in encryption items. The advisory committee is chaired by a senior official of the ministry of defence, who is appointed by the general manager. The chairman of the advisory committee is the director of the department of defence export controls (DDEC). A representative of the public serves on the advisory committee. The office within the DDEC that deals with encryption control and regulation handles liaisons with the encryption industry, deals with all license requests as well as policy enforcement and outreach.

Following the amendment of the Encryption Ordinance and transfer of responsibility for regulation of engagement in encryption items to the ministry of defence, several reforms were instituted: authority over licensing and regulation was transferred from a military to a civilian licensing authority, i.e., from the Israel Defense Forces (IDF) to the ministry of defence; commercial means of encryption were exempted from the Defence Export Ordinance; three categories of licenses for engagement in encryption were defined: a general license, a special license and a

162. Ordinance Governing the Control of Commodities and Services (Engagement in Encryption Items), 1974.

163. *See* more at http://www.mod.gov.il/English/Encryption_Controls/Pages/default.aspx (accessed 23 Jul. 2021).

restricted license (these different categories of licenses are intended to provide particular solutions for different types of application); the authority to define an item of encryption as a 'free means' and thereby exempt it from further regulation; and an advisory committee to the general manager of the ministry of defence was set up (among its members is a representative of the public).

Furthermore, updated policy statements were announced, which included a comprehensive reform of regulation over commercial encryption export policy (issued in November 1999). A new policy, including reform of controls within Israel, including easing of the restrictions pertaining to aspects such as use, import, and distribution within Israel (announced in February 2000), and an additional reform eased restrictions on importers of computer and communications equipment incorporating commercial encryption items (introduced in July 2001).

Introduction of the new policy led to a substantial reduction in the number of applications for export licenses, since following the reform, an exporter now has to apply for a license to export a specific commercial encryption item only once a year, whereas in the past, there was a necessity to apply separately for any sales transaction.

Three categories of licenses for engaging in encryption items were determined. A 'restricted license' is a license that imposes restrictions on engagement in encryption items. These restrictions may also apply to permissible forms of engagement in encryption items, or to the nature of permissible sales (e.g., restriction on selling to certain countries and sectors). In general, a restricted license is valid for one year. A 'special license' is a license for specific engagement, generally involving sale to clients who do not fall under the restrictions imposed on an applicant for a restricted license. In general, a special license is valid for one year.

A 'general license' is a license for a particular encryption item which allows the license-holder free use of that item (other than modifications or integration that essentially create a new item for which a separate license is required). The sale of such items of encryption is decontrolled and not subject to reporting procedures. Such general licenses are issued with no time limit to their validity.

The definition of 'free means' is a means of encryption for which a general license has been granted or which the general manager of the ministry of defence has declared to be decontrolled. Once an encryption item is defined as a free means, it is free of the licensing restrictions. A periodically revised list of encryption items which have been declared 'decontrolled' is published in the official gazette as well as on the ministry of defence's website.

The legal framework of this issue mostly consists of the Ordinance regarding Regulating Engagement in Encryption Items was issued in 1974 and signed by the minister of defence in accordance with the Control of Commodities and Services Act.[164] A declaration on control of means of encryption was attached to the ordinance, affirming that engagement in encryption items is a service that is subject to control. In 1998, the original ordinance was amended, and under the amended ordinance, authority over controlling encryption items was transferred from the chief communications officer of the IDF to the general manager of the ministry of

164. The Supervision on Commodities and Services Act, 1957.

defence. The ordinance also includes a comprehensive definition of the term 'engaging in encryption items' which *inter alia* includes development, production, integration, sale, import and export of encryption items.

The granting of a license to engage in encryption items does not exempt the applicant from the obligation to comply with any other legal requirement, including the need to obtain other permits or licenses required under other legislation. The application form consists of a checklist enabling the applicant to obtain a license for engagement in commercial encryption. The form is suitable for filing applications for all types of engagement in commercial encryption. The review of encryption items is performed pursuant to the authority of the general manager of the ministry of defence in the framework of the order regarding the engagement in encryption items.

The information submitted by the applicant serves the purpose of the review of the encryption items in the course of the licensing process. The review is performed by a small team of authorized personnel acting under non-disclosure obligations with regard to the information provided.

§2. Export of Dual-Use Equipment

47. The supervision of defence exports from the State of Israel is based on the Defence Export Control Act (DECA),[165] and on the regulations and decrees under it. Due to this legislation, the system that supervises the export of defence equipment, defence know-how, and defence services from Israel is structured and based on that legislation, control lists that define the controlled equipment, know-how and services which require marketing licenses and export licenses were published.

The purpose of the primary and secondary legislation in this matter, as defined under the law, is 'to regulate state control of the export of defence equipment, the transfer of defence know-how and the provision of defence services, for reasons of national security considerations, foreign relations considerations, international obligations and other vital interests of the state'. This law also relates to controlling the export of defined defence equipment and the export of dual-use equipment sold for defence uses.

Materials and equipment which were intended for civil uses and are also suitable for defence uses are defined under the law as 'dual-use equipment'. It may be noticed, that this wide definition could include a wide variety of materials and equipment, that even when intended for civilian uses, could be suitable for use by defence forces such as armed forces or state police entities, intelligence entities.

'Controlled dual-use equipment' is defined under the law as dual-use equipment that is included in the list of dual-use goods and technologies defined by the Wassenaar Arrangement and is intended for defence uses, or other dual-use equipment defined by the minister of defence's decree.

The law refers to the Wassenaar Arrangement of 1996, which includes a list of dual-use equipment that is classified into nine categories: advance materials, processed materials, electronics, computers, telecommunications, IT, sensors and

165. The Defence Export Control Act, 2007.

lasers, navigation and avionics (aviation electronics), and naval and ignition. The export of goods which are detailed in one of these categories and which are intended for defence forces requires the obtainment of a license from the DECA in the ministry of defence.

Dual-use equipment which is not intended for defence forces, is exempt from obtaining a license issued by the ministry of defence, but is subject to the supervision of another government ministry, the ministry of economics. The Import and Export Decree (Control of Dual-Purpose Goods, Services and Technology Exports),[166] which came into force on January 2007, states that an individual may not export goods or technology detailed in the Wassenaar list, except with a license from the Chemistry and Environment Administration in the ministry of economics.

The decree excludes the supervised dual-use equipment, the export of which is supervised by the ministry of Defence as mentioned above. In other words, dual-use equipment intended for defence uses is subject to the supervision of the ministry of defence, and 'regular' dual-use equipment is subject to the supervision of the ministry of economics. The responsibility of any exporter is to examine carefully and determine whether the exported goods or technology appear in the Wassenaar list.

If the export-designated goods appear in the list, the exporter must turn to the appropriate authority (according to the end user) in order to receive an export license. If the goods are intended to be exported to a defence user, the exporter should turn to the DECA in the ministry of defence, and if the goods are intended to be exported to a civilian user, the exporter should turn to the Chemistry and Environment Administration in the ministry of economics, in order to obtain an exporter license.

For example, if the exporter receives an order for mobile and personal communications systems which can be used either by civilians (such as by travellers while navigating), or by military or police entities; these are dual-use goods, therefore, the exporter must determine who the end users are. If the end user is, for example, a travelling agency, then the export license will be issued by the ministry of economics, and if the end user is a military or police entity, the license is obtained through the DECA.

Another example, an exporter exports a computer or navigation software which is used to remotely control small aircrafts. On the one hand, it is plausible that this software is designated for the civilian use of navigating model airplanes and small aircrafts, used and classified as toys. On the other hand, in light of the wide interpretation of the objects detailed in the Wassenaar Arrangement, which also includes the possible uses of the product and is not satisfied by its primary function, name and verbal description while being marketed, even when it is a seemingly 'innocent' product, one could claim that the software could be used for military uses such as navigating 'suicide model airplanes', navigating unmanned aerial vehicles for the collection of intelligence and assisting combat units in the field in real time and so on.

---

166. The Import and Export (Control of Dual-Purpose Goods, Services and Technology Exports) Decree, 2006.

Accordingly, it is reasonable that such a product is included in the 'dual-use goods' definition, as defined in the statute and decrees. In this case, it is an export which requires obtaining a relevant license, regardless of the identity of the end user to which the goods are exported, and failing to obtain a license accordingly is considered criminal offence of up to twelve months imprisonment, fines of up to NIS 250,000 (approximately EUR 60,000) per case and confiscation of the goods.[167]

A request for a license to export dual-use equipment must be filed, as previously stated, with the Chemistry and Environment Administration in the ministry of economics, while stating who the end user of the equipment is. The Administration is authorized to demand documents or additional details required to examine the request within ten working days from the day of receiving the request. The Administration should transfer the request to the ministry of defence and the ministry of foreign affairs in order to receive their opinions within fifteen days from the day of receiving the request. Within twenty days, at the most, from the day of receiving the request, or within ten days at the most, from the time it received the additional details, the Administration should reply to the request.

If there is a conflict between the opinions of the Administration and the ministry of defence or the ministry of foreign affairs, the request is decided by a committee of general managers, whose members include the general managers of the ministry of economics, of the ministry of foreign affairs and the ministry of defence. If a decision is not taken by the committee, the matter is brought to the decision of the Prime Minister. The applicant can appeal the Administration's decision before the above committee within fourteen working days.

An individual who exports defence items without a defence export license or exports not in accordance with the license's terms, as opposed to the instructions of the law, may be sentenced to three years imprisonment or a fine of up to NIS 6 million (approximately EUR 1.5 million), and the goods and all objects used for their shipment are confiscated.

167. Chapter B of the Import and Export (Control of Dual-Purpose Goods, Services and Technology Exports) Decree, 2006.

Chapter 4. Legal Status of Standardization

48. Standardization in Israel is directed by the Standards Institution of Israel. Significant part of the institute's activity is dedicated to the standardization of ICT in Israel. Although not all standards are mandatory, the Israeli ICT market prefers to embrace these standards due to the competition in this market, in favour of the quality of products and services marketed to the customers.

§1. The Standards Institution of Israel

49. The Standards Institution of Israel, mandated by the Israeli Government, is Israel's national standards authority, preparing and publishing Israeli standards as well as representing Israel in the international standards organizations, International Organization for Standardization (ISO) and International Electrotechnical Commission (IEC). The institute was established in 1953 by a statute.[168] The Standardization Division coordinates the preparation of Israeli standards through hundreds of committees, comprising thousands of representatives from all the sectors of the Israeli economy and society.

Standards are prepared, revised, and published by the Standardization Division of the Standards Institution of Israel according to the rules for preparing standards approved by the minister of economics. As of 2021, more than 3,150 Israeli standards have been published. Standardization activities are divided into 17 different areas, each of which is directed by a central committee.[169] Actual preparation is carried out by approximately 600 technical committees and working groups, where experts representing all the diverse sectors of the economy operate together.[170]

The Standards Institution of Israel follows a policy of standards harmonization, whenever possible. The Technical Committees are encouraged to adopt existing, accepted international standards as Israeli standards, as long as there is no compelling local reason for not doing so. Occasionally, originally created Israeli standards have been adopted by the international community. One of the areas in which the Israeli standard is regarded as a basic standard for international reference is irrigation equipment, in which Israel is considered as a world leader.

After being approved within the institute's committees, a new standard is published in the official gazette.[171] It is recommended by the law to approve standards which match the international standards in most developed countries, if possible.[172] If an international standard has been amended, the institute has the duty to re-examine the Israeli standard on the same issue and decide whether it should be changed following the amendment of the standard.[173]

---

168. Section 2 of the Standards Act, 1953.
169. Section 3M of the Standards Act, 1953.
170. Section 3P of the Standards Act, 1953.
171. Section 6 of the Standards Act, 1953.
172. Section 7 of the Standards Act, 1953.
173. Section 8A of the Standards Act, 1953.

Most Israeli standards are voluntary. However, they may be converted into mandatory standards if they are vital for the protection of public safety or public health or quality of the environment. For example, voluntary standards for machine-readable passports, telecommunications traffic, and network functions were converted into mandatory standards in 2009 and 2011.[174] The procedure to convert standards into mandatory standards is performed either by a declaration by the minister of economics, proclaiming the standards as official standards, or by publishing a decree or regulation on behalf of the minister in charge of the particular area.

If a standard becomes mandatory, the institute is authorized to enforce it. The institute's officials are authorized to enter any place, in which they suspect a product is manufactured there not under the mandatory standard or a service is given there not under the mandatory standard.[175] If the suspicion is verified, the standardization inspector is authorized to order to stop the manufactory or the service. Moreover, such an activity may be considered as a criminal offence,[176] or at least, an administrative offence.[177] Any manufacturer or services giver may apply the institute voluntarily to be examined and certified as matching the official relevant standard.[178] After being certified, the institute would inspect the products and services occasionally in order to verify the justification for the certification.

§2. Standardization of ICT in Israel

50. Standards of ICT are prepared, revised, and published by the Standardization Division of the Standards Institution of Israel according to the rules for preparing standards approved by the minister of economics. In general, standardization activities are divided into seventeen different areas, each of which is directed by a central committee.[179] The relevant central committee issuing ICT is the ICT Standardization Central Committee (8100).[180] Actual preparation is carried out by eleven technical committees.

The technical committee of Accessibility on the Internet (8101) deals mostly with accessibility of Israeli websites and smart cards.[181] Two of its most significant standards are 'web contents accessibility guidelines' (IS 5568, i.e., Israeli Standard no. 5568) from 2013 and 'management and website life cycle' (IS 23026) from 2007.

The technical committee of Information Industry Documentation (8102) deals mostly with the processing of information in Israel.[182] Two of its most significant standards are 'development documentation' (IS 1096) from 1979 and 'cycle processes' (IS 12207) from 2008.

---

174. IS 7501, (i.e., Israeli Standard no. 7501, IS 11671 and IS 21158).
175. Section 10 of the Standards Act, 1953.
176. Section 17–17B of the Standards Act, 1953.
177. Section 16A–16B of the Standards Act, 1953.
178. Section 12 of the Standards Act, 1953.
179. Section 3M of the Standards Act, 1953.
180. *See* at https://portal.sii.org.il/heb/standardization/vaadapage/?vid=8100 (accessed 23 Jul. 2021).
181. https://portal.sii.org.il/heb/standardization/vaadatekens/?vid=8101 (accessed 23 Jul. 2021).
182. https://portal.sii.org.il/heb/standardization/vaadatekens/?vid=8102 (accessed 23 Jul. 2021).

The technical committee of Data Units (8103) deals mostly with software codes in Israel.[183] Two of its most significant standards are 'interchange representation of date and time' (IS 1111) from 1999 and 'information transfer relating non-population entities' (IS 4186) from 2016.

The technical committee of Radio and Television Broadcasting (8104) deals mostly with the quality of radio and television broadcasts in Israel.[184] Two of its most significant standards are 'guidelines for DAB standards' (IS 11495) from 2017 and 'specification for electronic programme guide (EPG)' (IS 12371) from 2017.

The technical committee of Hebrew in Computer Systems and on the Internet (8109) deals mostly with the representation of graphs and formulas in the Hebrew environment and with Hebrew keyboards for different applications.[185] Two of its most significant standards are 'improved Hebrew keyboards' (IS 1452) from 2018 and 'operating systems interface (POSIX)' (IS 1478) from 2014.

The technical committee of Terminology (8110) deals mostly with definitions and adaptation of Hebrew terminology to the developing technology.[186] Two of its most significant standards are 'information technology vocabulary: biometrics' (IS 1080-38) from 2015 and 'information technology vocabulary: networking' (IS 1080-35) from 2012.

The technical committee of Applicability of Information Technology in Medicine Sciences (8111) deals mostly with the growing usage and needs of IT in hospitals, healthcare authorities, and healthcare private organizations.[187] Two of its most significant standards are 'standard key characteristics' (IS 5537) from 2004 and 'structure and high-level indicators' (IS 5536) from 2004.

The technical committee of Cyber Security (8114) deals mostly with security issues on the web, including digital signature, Supervisory control and data acquisition (SCADA), servers' security, and analysis of cyber threats.[188] Two of its most significant standards are 'guidelines to cyber security for ICT organizations based on ISO/IEC 27002' (IS 27011) from 2018 and 'cyber security for inter-organizational communications' (IS 27010) from 2018.

The technical committee of ICT Products and Services (8120) deals mostly with ICT infrastructure and customer services in the ICT market.[189] Two of its most significant standards are 'due diligence in ICT services bills' (IS 5262) from 2005 and 'wire-tapping requirements for the law enforcement authorities' (IS 11331) from 2011.

The technical committee of Geographical Information Systems (8130) deals mostly with Global Positioning System (GPS) systems and mapping systems.[190] One of its most significant standards is 'geographic information meta-data' (IS 19115) from 2009.

---

183. https://portal.sii.org.il/heb/standardization/vaadatekens/?vid=8103 (accessed 23 Jul. 2021).
184. https://portal.sii.org.il/heb/standardization/vaadatekens/?vid=8104 (accessed 23 Jul. 2021).
185. https://portal.sii.org.il/heb/standardization/vaadatekens/?vid=8109 (accessed 23 Jul. 2021).
186. https://portal.sii.org.il/heb/standardization/vaadatekens/?vid=8110 (accessed 23 Jul. 2021).
187. https://portal.sii.org.il/heb/standardization/vaadatekens/?vid=8111 (accessed 23 Jul. 2021).
188. https://portal.sii.org.il/heb/standardization/vaadatekens/?vid=8114 (accessed 23 Jul. 2021).
189. https://portal.sii.org.il/heb/standardization/vaadatekens/?vid=8120 (accessed 23 Jul. 2021).
190. https://portal.sii.org.il/heb/standardization/vaadatekens/?vid=8130 (accessed 23 Jul. 2021).

The technical committee of Biometrics (8140) deals mostly with the use of biometric data throughout various services in Israel.[191] Two of its most significant standards are ‘interchange formats of DNA data’ (IS 19794) from 2015 and ‘technology and scenario evaluation’ (IS 19795) from 2018.

As aforesaid, most of these technical committees’ standards are voluntary; however, they may be converted into mandatory standards if they are vital for the protection of public safety or public health or quality of the environment. The procedure to convert standards into mandatory standards is performed either by a declaration by the minister of economics, proclaiming the standards as official standards, or by publishing a decree or regulation on behalf of the minister in charge of the particular area.

191. https://portal.sii.org.il/heb/standardization/vaadatekens/?vid=8140 (accessed 23 Jul. 2021).

Chapter 5. Legal Status of Out-of-Court Dispute Settlement in the ICT Sector

§1. Alternative Dispute Resolutions Philosophy in Israel

I. Background and Development

51. Since the 1960s, the Israeli civil procedure gave some priority to parties who wish to end the dispute between them using alternative dispute resolutions (ADR). The first ADR legal pattern in Israel was arbitration.[192] The parties were not ordered by the court (or by any other entity) to settle the dispute through arbitration, but it was absolutely voluntary. Since the parties can control the applicable substantive law and the applicable procedure within arbitration, arbitration was highly preferred to settle civil disputes which involve professional issues.

Moreover, the parties can decide who would be their arbitrator, and they may select a professional arbitrator who has the necessary professional background in the dispute field. Thus, the ICT sector preferred gradually the settlements by arbitrations rather than resolutions by courts. Most arbitrators were former communications persons who retired a few years before, and they were considered to be objective and impartial.

In ongoing contracts between private parties in the ICT market, most parties prefer a compulsory arbitration clause, which prevents them and, of course, the counterparty to apply to court in case of disagreement towards the contract. In most of these contracts, the parties note specifically the name of the arbitrator, which is a former communications person. However, some parties prefer a retired judge for impartial reasons, especially when the parties are large commercial corporations within the Israeli ICT market.

The Israeli legislator has preferred not to intervene in arbitration settlements, unless in extreme cases, as discussed below.[193] However, not all parties prefer arbitration as they believe that their interests would be maximized within the court as the judge is impartial and has no interest in the results of the process. The main disadvantages of civil proceedings in court are the time and complexity. Civil proceedings take long months before they are prepared for the court's resolutions, and they involve complicated analysis of the evidence. For these reasons, the Israeli legislator has embraced two more basic patterns of settlement.

When the parties prefer the court resolution due to its impartiality, the judge may offer the parties a judicial decision that would be based on compromise settlement in court, as discussed below.[194] This pattern of settlement enables the judge to be the person who makes the final decision in the case, but not under the long and complicated civil procedure.

Another pattern embraced by the Israeli legislator is mediation. At first, mediation was an absolutely voluntary settlements, that could only be recommended by the court, if the court has found out that the parties experience some difficulties in

192. The Arbitration Act, 1968.
193. Below at s. [II]: Arbitration.
194. Below at s. [I]: Compromise Settlement.

compromising or even participating in the civil proceedings in a fair manner. However, as the experience with mediation settlements grew up and was generally positive, the Israeli legislator has expanded this settlement within the Civil Procedure Regulations, 2018, and made it a mandatory stage within regular civil procedure.

The parties are not forced to settle their dispute within mediation process, but they are forced to participate in such a process. However, the default process is civil process in court. Any party at any time may return back to the court. Most disputes in the Israeli ICT sector are settled through ADR patterns. Most parties prefer to be out of the formal framework of civil proceedings in court, if possible, as ICT market evolves rapidly, and they prefer fast and proper solutions on thorough solutions.

Thus, ADR philosophy is considered developed in Israel, especially within the ICT sector. Even in criminal proceedings most parties prefer ADR on courts resolutions, which are mostly achieved through plea bargains,[195] and in some cases through mediation.[196] The most significant expression of the positive appeal of ADR philosophy in Israel is its incorporation into the Israeli Civil Procedure Regulations, 2018.

II. Incorporation of ADR Philosophy into the Israeli Civil Procedure Regulations, 2018

52. In September 2018, new civil procedure regulations were published (replacing the 1984 civil procedure regulations), and they were supposed to be applied gradually until September 2019. After two-years disputes among jurists and three embedded amendments, they were eventually applied on 1 January 2021. Under these regulations, ADR philosophy is an integral part of the formal civil proceedings in court, and the discretion of both court and parties towards it has been reduced. The main assumption is that by the name of efficiency, the legislator may impose on the parties at least several attempts to settle their disputes in frameworks outside the court.

The first point under the 2018 regulations where the ADR philosophy becomes relevant is immediately after the lawsuit is submitted to the court. Within fourteen days after all statements of the parties have been submitted to the court, all parties must appoint a meeting outside the court, based on all of the documents they possess, and examine possible settlements of the dispute between them outside the court.[197] Only if the party is not represented by an attorney of law, the meeting is not compulsory. The reason for this exempt is an attempt to prevent taking advantages on such party.

195. *See* Gabriel Hallevy, *Is ADR (Alternative Dispute Resolution) Philosophy Relevant to Criminal Justice? – Plea Bargains as Mediation Process Between the Accused and the Prosecution*, 6 Orig. L. Rev. 1 (2009).

196. *See* Gabriel Hallevy, *Therapeutic Victim-Offender Mediation within the Criminal Justice Process – Sharpening the Evaluation of Personal Potential for Rehabilitation while Righting Wrongs under the Alternative-Dispute-Resolution (ADR) Philosophy*, 16 Harvard Nego. L. Rev. 65 (2011).

197. Regulation 35 of the Civil Procedure Regulations, 2018.

If one of the parties has refused to participate in this meeting, or the meeting did not take place at all due to one of the parties' refusal, the court may use several procedural sanctions towards that party. These sanctions include the suspension of the lawsuit (if the refusing party is the plaintiff), erasure of all party's statements (if the refusing party is the plaintiff or the defendant) and impose expenses on the refusing party in favour of the counterparty.[198] If the meeting has taken place, both parties are requested to report its consequences to the court.[199]

The second point under the 2018 regulations where the ADR philosophy becomes relevant is the compulsory mediation. If the dispute is evaluated in more than NIS 40,000 (approximately EUR 10,000), within twenty days after all statements of the parties have been submitted to the court, a mediator is appointed in the lawsuit.[200] It has no importance in this context, whether the parties are represented by attorneys at law, or not. The parties' statements are sent to the mediator in order to prepare the mediation meeting.

No later than thirty days after the mediator is appointed, the first meeting within the mediation process should take place. The parties are not charged for this meeting.[201] The mediator is required to explain the parties the principles of mediation and that settling the dispute through mediation is not compulsory.[202] If the parties have agreed on settling their dispute through mediation, the mediator should notify the court on their decision within fourteen days.[203]

Although settling the dispute through mediation is not compulsory, the participation in the first meeting of the mediation process is compulsory, as aforesaid. If one of the parties has refused to participate in this meeting, or the meeting did not take place at all due to one of the parties' refusal, the court may use several procedural sanctions towards that party. These sanctions include the suspension of the lawsuit (if the refusing party is the plaintiff), erasure of all party's statements (if the refusing party is the plaintiff or the defendant) and impose expenses on the refusing party in favour of the counterparty.[204]

§2. The Main Out-of-Court Civil Dispute Settlements in Israel

53. There are three main out-of-court civil dispute settlements under Israeli law: compromise settlement, arbitration, and mediation. All out-of-court dispute settlements are not compulsory, but in various sectors, they are preferred in comparison to the civil proceedings in court. Within the Israeli ICT sector, the most preferred type of settlement is the arbitration. The three main out-of-court civil dispute settlements under Israeli law are discussed below.

198. Regulation 38 of the Civil Procedure Regulations, 2018.
199. Regulation 36 of the Civil Procedure Regulations, 2018.
200. Regulation 37(b) of the Civil Procedure Regulations, 2018.
201. Regulation 37(d) of the Civil Procedure Regulations, 2018.
202. Regulation 37(e) of the Civil Procedure Regulations, 2018.
203. Regulation 37(f) of the Civil Procedure Regulations, 2018.
204. Regulations 37(k) and 38 of the Civil Procedure Regulations, 2018.

I. Compromise Settlement

54. Sometimes parties of civil dispute agree on several points but disagree on other points. Procedurally, the agreement between the parties on certain points is achieved through admission within the parties' statements. The derivative outcome of these admissions is that the dispute between the parties is reduced to certain points, and the court is not required to decide on the agreed points. The civil process is assumed to continue from this stage and on towards the points, in which no agreements between the parties were achieved.

If a certain point is factual, the civil procedure is required to continue into the evidence stage, where each of the parties may prove the required facts. If a certain point is legal (e.g., interpretation of the law concerning the facts), no evidence is required, and the parties may conclude their legal arguments. No evidence is required in Israel as to non-factual versions.[205] When the redefined dispute between the parties requires efforts that the dispute does not justify or that makes the dispute resolution become inefficient, the parties may choose a compromise settlement.

The parties may also choose the compromise settlement when they wish to minimize their risk or limit it between certain limits. The initiative for compromise settlement may be the parties' of the court's, and it is not limited on time, unless the lawsuit has already been over. If the parties have agreed between themselves on the final settlement in the particular case, they may apply the court to confirm the settlement and make it to be considered as a judgment.[206]

However, in most cases, the parties do not agree on the final settlement between them, and they wish to authorize the court to figure out a settlement between them, with or without posing limitations on the court's decision. For example, the parties may authorize the court to figure out a settlement in which the defendant would pay the plaintiff not less than NIS 100,000, but not more than NIS 200,000. Thus, the risk for both parties is reduced in comparison to possible judgments.

If the parties agree so, they may authorize the court to make a judgment on this pattern of compromise settlement.[207] The initiative may be both the parties' and the court's, but the parties must agree to authorize the court to act this way. The authorization may relate to the whole lawsuit or to portions of it, but authorizing the court in regard to the whole lawsuit is considered more efficient. The court's judgment in compromise settlement functions as any other judgment, and in rare cases, it may be reversed in appeal proceedings.[208]

205. Section 57B of the Evidence [New Version] Ordinance, 1971.
206. Section 79A(b) of the Courts [Combined Version] Act, 1984.
207. Section 79A(a) of the Courts [Combined Version] Act, 1984.
208. *See* Gabriel Hallevy, *Theory of Civil Procedure* vol. III 659–721 (Bursi Publishing House 2019) and Civ. App. 2346/06 *Oren v. Tapuzit Ltd.* (14 May 2007).

II. Arbitration

55. As aforesaid, the ICT sector in Israel has preferred the settlements gradually by arbitrations rather than resolutions by courts. Arbitration may become the dispute's resolution in two main patterns. The first is *ex ante*, i.e., the parties agree that any of their disputes would be settled through arbitration. The second is *ex post*, i.e., a lawsuit has been submitted to the court, and the parties accept the court's offer to settle the dispute through arbitration.

The second pattern (*ex post*) is rare as to Israeli ICT sector. However, the court is authorized to offer the parties to settle their dispute outside the court through arbitration. Only if all parties agree to this offer, the court is authorized to deliver it.[209] The parties may agree to deliver portions of the dispute or the whole dispute, and they may determine the terms of arbitration, by themselves or let the court determine the terms. The arbitrator is appointed by the parties, or if the parties have difficulties to agree on the arbitrator's identity, they may authorize the court to appoint an arbitrator.[210]

On both patterns of arbitrations, the general law governing arbitrations applies.[211] Arbitration requires the parties' agreement, and the default in case of disagreement is settling the dispute in court. The parties may agree on the applicable law and on the applicable procedure. They may also agree that the arbitrator may decide regardless of the law, unless the decision contradicts the public policy. There may be more than one arbitrator, as long as the number of the arbitrators is odd.

The arbitrator is authorized to summon witnesses to testify, and any witness may apply the court in order to cancel the summon.[212] The arbitrator has been granted a wide discretion towards the most efficient procedure for the particular case, but the parties may agree on other procedures. The arbitrator is authorized to apply the court in any legal question required for settling the dispute. The parties may also agree on the maximum period for the end of the arbitration.

At the end of the process, the arbitrator is required to deliver a written judgment.[213] The judgment functions as res judicata between the parties, as if it were the court's judgment.[214] Only if the parties agreed on a possibility to appeal to another arbitrator, they may submit an appeal.[215] However, if the parties have agreed on the applicability of the law, they may submit to the court a request to appeal for the reason of mistakes in law within the arbitrator's judgment.[216]

If the parties wish to enforce the judgment they have to submit to the court a request to approve the judgment.[217] If approved, it functions as any of the court's judgment. However, the parties may plea for cancellation of the judgment, namely for procedural reasons (e.g., the judgment has been given after the maximum period

209. Section 79B(a) of the Courts [Combined Version] Act, 1984.
210. Section 79B(b) of the Courts [Combined Version] Act, 1984.
211. Section 79B(c) of the Courts [Combined Version] Act, 1984.
212. Section 13 of the Arbitration Act, 1968.
213. Section 20 of the Arbitration Act, 1968.
214. Section 21 of the Arbitration Act, 1968.
215. Section 21A of the Arbitration Act, 1968.
216. Section 29B of the Arbitration Act, 1968.
217. Section 23 of the Arbitration Act, 1968.

agreed between the parties),[218] but also for substantive reasons (e.g., the judgment is in contrast with public policy).[219] The court may also decide to return the case back to the arbitrator to amend the judgment or to complete the arbitration properly.[220] Arbitration is not unique for private parties, and the state in civil dispute may agree with its counterparty on arbitration.

III. Mediation

56. Mediation as an alternative dispute resolution in Israeli ICT sector is rare. Most disputes in ICT sector do not involve emotional aspects; therefore, the mediation is not necessarily suitable for the dispute resolution more than settling in court or through arbitration. Mediation in Israel is more common in other legal fields (e.g., family law and labour law). However, in rare cases, some emotional aspects are involved in the dispute. For example, disputes within a partnership in the ICT sector may require mediation for some emotional aspects between the partners are involved.[221]

However, mediation may become part of the dispute's resolution in two main patterns. One is compulsory at the beginning of the civil proceedings in court, and the other is voluntary all along the proceedings. If the dispute is evaluated in more than NIS 40,000 (approximately EUR 10,000), within twenty days after all statements of the parties have been submitted to the court, a mediator is appointed in the lawsuit.[222] It has no importance in this context, whether the parties are represented by attorneys at law, or not. The parties' statements are sent to the mediator in order to prepare the mediation meeting.

No later than thirty days after the mediator is appointed, the first meeting within the mediation process should take place. The parties are not charged for this meeting.[223] The mediator is required to explain the parties the principles of mediation and that settling the dispute through mediation is not compulsory.[224] If the parties have agreed on settling their dispute through mediation, the mediator should notify the court on their decision within fourteen days.[225]

Although settling the dispute through mediation is not compulsory, the participation in the first meeting of the mediation process is compulsory. If one of the parties has refused to participate in this meeting, or the meeting did not take place at all due to one of the parties' refusal, the court may use several procedural sanctions towards that party. These sanctions include the suspension of the lawsuit (if the

218. Section 24(8) of the Arbitration Act, 1968.
219. Section 24(9) of the Arbitration Act, 1968.
220. Section 25 of the Arbitration Act, 1968.
221. *See, e.g.*, Civ. App. 8420/14 *Morel v. Zur* (22 Feb. 2015).
222. Regulation 37(b) of the Civil Procedure Regulations, 2018.
223. Regulation 37(d) of the Civil Procedure Regulations, 2018.
224. Regulation 37(e) of the Civil Procedure Regulations, 2018.
225. Regulation 37(f) of the Civil Procedure Regulations, 2018.

refusing party is the plaintiff), erasure of all party's statements (if the refusing party is the plaintiff or the defendant) and impose expenses on the refusing party in favour of the counterparty.[226]

However, all along the civil proceedings, the court is authorized to offer the parties to participate in mediation process in order to make them come closer to a consensual resolution for the dispute. Only if all parties have agreed, the court is authorized to deliver the case to a mediator and suspend the lawsuit proceedings until the parties inform what the results of the mediation were.[227] Mediation is designed to make the parties understand each other and communicate with each other, directly or through the mediator, in cases where civil proceedings in court fail to do so.

In order to obtain open communication between the parties, confidentiality within mediation is ensured, and it includes both verbal statements and documents or other evidence.[228] The mediator is authorized to meet parties together and meet each of them separately as well. If necessary for the dispute resolution, the mediator is also authorized to meet the third party.[229] As mediation process is running, the lawsuit is suspended, and the court is required to determine the final date for which the mediation process should terminate.

The mediator may offer the parties a compromise, and if the parties agree, the compromise agreement is submitted to the court for approval. The approved agreement functions as a compromise settlement, as discussed above.[230] The approval of the agreement is a judgment.[231] However, the mediator is not authorized to impose a settlement, but only to offer one. If the parties did not accept the offer, the mediation is terminated, and the dispute returns to the court.[232]

The parties may also initiate mediation process between them before any lawsuit is submitted to the court. In such cases, the court is not involved in the voluntary mediation process. However, if due to the mediation process, the parties have agreed on a certain resolution for their dispute, they may submit the detailed settlement to the court and ask the court to approve it. If approved, the settlement is considered as if it were a court's judgment, even though no lawsuit has been submitted.[233] However, as aforesaid, mediation as an alternative dispute resolution in Israeli ICT sector is rare.

---

226. Regulations 37(k) and 38 of the Civil Procedure Regulations, 2018.
227. Section 79C(b) of the Courts [Combined Version] Act, 1984.
228. Section 79C(d) of the Courts [Combined Version] Act, 1984.
229. Section 79C(c) of the Courts [Combined Version] Act, 1984.
230. Above at s. [I]: Compromise Settlement.
231. Section 79C(g) of the Courts [Combined Version] Act, 1984.
232. Section 79C(e) of the Courts [Combined Version] Act, 1984.
233. Section 79C(h) of the Courts [Combined Version] Act, 1984.

Part II. Protection of IP in the ICT Sector

Chapter 1. Application of Copyright in the Area of ICT

57. Copyright in the area of ICT in Israel is applicable through both Israeli law of copyright and international and foreign law. Particular provisions of Israeli copyright law are dedicated to software, broadcasters and performers, but most subjects in the ICT area are protected through the general law of copyright.

§1. ICT Copyright under Israeli Law

58. In 2007, the Israeli legislator enacted the Copyright Act, 2007, which has replaced the former British-originated law.[234] Accordingly, copyright may be relevant to any ICT product or service if they are original and they have been published or activated first in Israel or their creators are Israelis at the time they were published or activated.[235] However, mere idea, mere process, performance method, mere fact or daily news are not subject to copyright,[236] although credit is generally given to the original source or creator. Official publications are neither subject to copyright.[237]

The copyright protection is the default protection for ICT products and services, and if certain products or services are protected under specific law (e.g., under the Patents Act, 1967), the specific law governs (*lex specialis derogat generali*).[238] As a result, many ICT products and services are protected not through the Israeli copyright law.

Copyright includes the exclusive rights to copy, publish, perform, broadcast, publicize, translate, process, or rent the copyright's subject.[239] As a result, copyright includes direct rights, derivative rights,[240] and indirect rights.[241] However, copyright does not include fair use for research purposes, criticism, review, report, or

234. The Copyright Ordinance, 1924.
235. Sections 4 and 8 of the Copyright Act, 2007.
236. Section 5 of the Copyright Act, 2007.
237. Section 6 of the Copyright Act, 2007.
238. Section 7 of the Copyright Act, 2007.
239. Section 11 of the Copyright Act, 2007.
240. Section 16 of the Copyright Act, 2007.
241. Section 48 of the Copyright Act, 2007.

education.[242] Fairness of the use is examined due to the use's purpose, to the type of products or services, to the influence of the use on the value of the product or the service, and to the extent of use.[243]

Copyright neither includes use of the products and services in judicial processes or administrative processes, if the particular process justifies the use.[244] Copying the ICT product for preservation purposes in public libraries or archives is not protected under Israeli copyright law, if no legal copy is available for purchase.[245]

In general, the copyright is granted to the creator, unless otherwise agreed.[246] The creator's employer owns the copyright, if the copyright's subject has been created within the creator's employment and the creation is related to the field of that employment.[247] If the creator is a public servant, the owner of the copyright is the state.[248] However, the copyright's owner has the right to grant rights to others, exclusively or unexclusively, in the whole copyright's subject or in portions of it.[249] The proper way to grant such rights is through a license.

In general, copyright is granted for the life-being of the creator and seventy years after the creator's death.[250] If the creator's identity is unknown, the copyright is granted for seventy years from the date of first publication.[251] If the creator is the state, the copyright is granted for fifty years.[252]

The original creator has in addition a personal 'moral right' in the creation, regardless the ownership of the copyright. The 'moral right' is *not* applicable to software,[253] and it includes relating the creation to the name of the creator and not changing the creation in a manner that damages the creator's reputation.[254]

Infringement of copyright or 'moral right' is considered tort, and if the plaintiff fails to prove the damage, a compensation of up to NIS 100,000 (approximately EUR 25,000) is granted.[255] The most significant defence in copyright lawsuits in the ICT area is the bona fide defence. If the defendant proves that the infringement was done under bona fide with no harmful intent, the defendant is exempt from compensating the plaintiff.[256] This defence is relevant to both copyright and 'moral right'.

Certain type of infringements of copyright may also be considered criminal offence. Copying a creation illegally or importing into Israel an illegal copy of a creation for commercial purposes are considered a criminal offence of up to five years

242. Section 19(a) of the Copyright Act, 2007.
243. Section 19(b) of the Copyright Act, 2007.
244. Section 20 of the Copyright Act, 2007.
245. Section 30 of the Copyright Act, 2007.
246. Section 33 of the Copyright Act, 2007.
247. Section 34 of the Copyright Act, 2007.
248. Section 36 of the Copyright Act, 2007.
249. Section 37 of the Copyright Act, 2007.
250. Section 38 of the Copyright Act, 2007.
251. Section 40 of the Copyright Act, 2007.
252. Section 42 of the Copyright Act, 2007.
253. Section 45(a) of the Copyright Act, 2007.
254. Section 46 of the Copyright Act, 2007.
255. Section 56(a) of the Copyright Act, 2007.
256. Section 58 of the Copyright Act, 2007.

imprisonment.[257] However, possession, selling, or renting of an illegal copy of a creation for commercial purposes are considered a criminal offence of up to three years imprisonment.[258] All offences are *mens rea* offences, i.e., imposition of criminal liability requires awareness of the factual element of these offences, and negligence is insufficient for criminal liability.

§2. ICT Copyright under International Law and Foreign Law in Israel

59. If a bilateral covenant on copyright between Israel and another country is signed or if Israel has joined a multilateral covenant on copyright, the question is whether the covenant's provisions are directly applicable in Israel. In general, if the covenant is ratified in the Knesset, the covenant's provisions are not different than any other Israeli statute. However, the minister of justice is authorized to determine in a decree that the covenant's provisions are applicable in Israel, even though the Knesset did not ratify the covenant.[259]

However, any protection on copyright due to such a decree would not exceed the protection granted by Israeli law, unless explicitly otherwise agreed within the covenant. If the minister of justice has found out that the covenant's provisions are not adhered by another country, member in the multilateral covenant, or the counterparty in the bilateral covenant, the minister is authorized, under the government's approval, to restrict the copyright of that country's subjects in Israel, according to the principle of reciprocity.[260]

The Israeli minister of justice has exercised this authority several times. The most known covenants, in which the minister of justice has included in such decrees, are the Universal Covenant (Geneva, 6 September 1952) in 1955,[261] the Bern Covenant in 1953,[262] the Geneva Covenant (Geneva, 29 October 1971) in 1978,[263] and the TRIPS Covenant (Agreement on Trade-Related Aspects of Intellectual Property Rights Including Trade in Counterfeit Goods) in 1999.[264] In addition, the minister of justice has equalized the protection on copyright of any US citizen as if it is the copyright of an Israeli citizen in 1953.[265]

---

257. Section 62(a) of the Copyright Act, 2007.
258. Section 62(b) of the Copyright Act, 2007.
259. Section 9 of the Copyright Act, 2007.
260. Section 10 of the Copyright Act, 2007.
261. Copyright Decree (the Universal Covenant), 1955.
262. Copyright Decree (Bern Covenant), 1953.
263. Copyright Decree (Geneva Covenant), 1978.
264. Copyright Decree (TRIPS Covenant), 1999.
265. Copyright Decree (United States), 1953.

Chapter 2. Legal Protection of Software

§1. Legal Protection of Software under Israeli Law

60. In general, software is protected under copyright law in Israel. However, particular provisions have been enacted and specified in this issue. Software includes in this context any type of software,[266] including operating systems. Accordingly, copyright may be relevant to any software if it is original and it has been released, published, or activated first in Israel or its creators are Israelis at the time it has been released, published, or activated.[267] The copyright protection is the default protection for software, and if a certain software is protected under specific law (e.g., under the Patents Act, 1967), the specific law governs (*lex specialis derogat generali*).[268]

Copyright includes the exclusive rights to copy, publish, perform, broadcast, publicize, translate, process, or rent the software.[269] As a result, copyright includes direct rights, derivative rights,[270] and indirect rights.[271] Original fonts used by the software are also protected, but the use of such font is allowed, even if the software has made an illegal use of it (i.e., although the software illegally copied an original protected font, the users of that software are allowed to use that font).[272] Copying a software is allowed only to a person who possesses a legal copy of the software,[273] even for backup purposes,[274] or maintenance purposes.[275]

However, copying software for fixing problems within the software or for adapting it to a different operating system or computer is allowed if performed in favour of the legal possessor of a copy.[276] Copying software for security checks is also allowed, if the checks are performed in favour of the legal possessor of a copy.[277] In addition, software copyright does not include fair use for research purposes, criticism, review, report, or education.[278] Fairness of the use is examined due to the use's purpose, to the type of software, to the influence of the use on the value of the software, and to the extent of use.[279]

Copyright neither includes use of the software in judicial processes or administrative processes, if the particular process justifies the use.[280] Copying the software

266. *See* the definition of the term 'software' under s. 1 of the Copyright Act, 2007.
267. Sections 4 and 8 of the Copyright Act, 2007.
268. Section 7 of the Copyright Act, 2007.
269. Section 11 of the Copyright Act, 2007.
270. Section 16 of the Copyright Act, 2007.
271. Section 48 of the Copyright Act, 2007.
272. Section 28B of the Copyright Act, 2007.
273. Section 24(c) of the Copyright Act, 2007.
274. Section 24(a) of the Copyright Act, 2007.
275. Section 24(b) of the Copyright Act, 2007.
276. Section 24(c)(1) of the Copyright Act, 2007.
277. Section 24(c)(2) of the Copyright Act, 2007.
278. Section 19(a) of the Copyright Act, 2007.
279. Section 19(b) of the Copyright Act, 2007.
280. Section 20 of the Copyright Act, 2007.

for preservation purposes in public libraries or archives is not protected under Israeli copyright law, if no legal copy is available for purchase.[281]

In general, the copyright is granted to the creator, unless otherwise agreed.[282] The creator's employer owns the copyright, if the copyright's subject has been created within the creator's employment and the software is related to the field of that employment.[283] If the creator is a public servant, the owner of the copyright is the state.[284] However, the copyright's owner has the right to grant rights to others, exclusively or unexclusively, in the whole software or in portions of it.[285] The proper way to grant such rights is through a license.

In general, copyright is granted for the life-being of the creator and seventy years after the creator's death.[286] If the creator's identity is unknown, the copyright is granted for seventy years from the date of first publication of the software.[287] If the creator is the state, the copyright is granted for fifty years.[288] Although in other ICT products, the original creator has, in addition, a personal 'moral right' in the creation, regardless the ownership of the copyright, the 'moral right' is *not* applicable on software.[289]

Infringement of copyright of software is considered tort, and if the plaintiff fails to prove the damage, a compensation of up to NIS 100,000 (approximately EUR 25,000) is granted.[290] The most significant defence in copyright lawsuits in the ICT area, including as to software, is the bona fide defence. If the defendant proves that the infringement was done under bona fide with no harmful intent, the defendant is exempt from compensating the plaintiff.[291]

Certain type of infringements of copyright may also be considered criminal offence. Copying software illegally or importing into Israel an illegal copy of software for commercial purposes are considered a criminal offence of up to five years imprisonment.[292] However, possession, selling, or renting of an illegal copy of software for commercial purposes is considered a criminal offence and include a penalty of up to three years imprisonment.[293] All offences are *mens rea* offences, i.e., imposition of criminal liability requires awareness of the factual element of these offences, and negligence is insufficient for criminal liability.

281. Section 30 of the Copyright Act, 2007.
282. Section 33 of the Copyright Act, 2007.
283. Section 34 of the Copyright Act, 2007.
284. Section 36 of the Copyright Act, 2007.
285. Section 37 of the Copyright Act, 2007.
286. Section 38 of the Copyright Act, 2007.
287. Section 40 of the Copyright Act, 2007.
288. Section 42 of the Copyright Act, 2007.
289. Section 45(a) of the Copyright Act, 2007.
290. Section 56(a) of the Copyright Act, 2007.
291. Section 58 of the Copyright Act, 2007.
292. Section 62(a) of the Copyright Act, 2007.
293. Section 62(b) of the Copyright Act, 2007.

§2. Legal Protection of Software under International Law and Foreign Law in Israel

61. If a bilateral covenant on copyright between Israel and another country is signed or if Israel has joined a multilateral covenant on copyright, the question is whether the covenant's provisions are directly applicable in Israel. In general, if the covenant is ratified in the Knesset, the covenant's provisions are not different than any other Israeli statute. However, the minister of justice is authorized to determine in a decree that the covenant's provisions are applicable in Israel, even though the Knesset did not ratify the covenant.[294]

However, any legal protection on software due to such a decree would not exceed the protection granted by Israeli law, unless explicitly otherwise agreed within the covenant. If the minister of justice has found out that the covenant's provisions are not adhered by another country, member in the multilateral covenant, or the counterparty in the bilateral covenant, the minister is authorized, under the government's approval, to restrict the copyright of that country's subjects in Israel, according to the principle of reciprocity.[295]

The Israeli minister of justice has exercised this authority several times. The most known covenants, in which the minister of justice has included in such decrees are the Universal Covenant (Geneva, 6 September 1952) in 1955,[296] the Bern Covenant in 1953,[297] the Geneva Covenant (Geneva, 29 October 1971) in 1978,[298] and the TRIPS Covenant (Agreement on Trade-Related Aspects of Intellectual Property Rights Including Trade in Counterfeit Goods) in 1999.[299] In addition, the minister of justice has equalized the protection on copyright of any US citizen as if it is the copyright of an Israeli citizen in 1953.[300]

294. Section 9 of the Copyright Act, 2007.
295. Section 10 of the Copyright Act, 2007.
296. Copyright Decree (the Universal Covenant), 1955.
297. Copyright Decree (Bern Covenant), 1953.
298. Copyright Decree (Geneva Covenant), 1978.
299. Copyright Decree (TRIPS Covenant), 1999.
300. Copyright Decree (United States), 1953.

Chapter 3. Legal Protection of Database

§1. Legal Protection of Database under Israeli Law

62. In general, databases are protected under copyright law in Israel. However, particular provisions have been enacted and specified in this issue. A database is considered a 'creation' protected through copyright law.[301] The originality of the database is defined in relation to the selection and organization of the data within the specific database.[302] Accordingly, copyright may be relevant to any database if it is original and its creators are Israelis.[303] Database which is part of any official publication is not subject to copyright.[304]

Copyright includes the exclusive rights to copy, publish, perform, broadcast, publicize, translate, process, or rent the database.[305] As a result, copyright includes direct rights, derivative rights,[306] and indirect rights.[307] However, copyright does not include fair use for research purposes, criticism, review, report or education.[308] Fairness of the use is examined due to the use's purpose, to the type of database, to the influence of the use on the value of the database, and to the extent of use.[309] Copyright neither includes use of the database in judicial processes or administrative processes, if the particular process justifies the use.[310]

In general, the copyright in database is granted to the creator, unless otherwise agreed.[311] The creator's employer owns the copyright, if the database has been created within the creator's employment and the database is related to the field of that employment.[312] If the creator is a public servant, the owner of the copyright is the state.[313] However, the copyright's owner has the right to grant rights to others, exclusively or unexclusively, in the whole database or in portions of it.[314] The proper way to grant such rights is through a license.

In general, copyright is granted for the life-being of the creator and seventy years after the creator's death.[315] If the creator's identity is unknown, the copyright is granted for seventy years from the date of creation of the database.[316] If the creator is the state, the copyright is granted for fifty years.[317] The original creator has in

301. *See* the definition of the term 'collection' under s. 1 of the Copyright Act, 2007, which includes 'database'. 'Collection' is part of the term 'creation' under this section. Therefore, 'database' is a type of 'creation', in this context.
302. Section 4(b) of the Copyright Act, 2007.
303. Sections 4 and 8 of the Copyright Act, 2007.
304. Section 6 of the Copyright Act, 2007.
305. Section 11 of the Copyright Act, 2007.
306. Section 16 of the Copyright Act, 2007.
307. Section 48 of the Copyright Act, 2007.
308. Section 19(a) of the Copyright Act, 2007.
309. Section 19(b) of the Copyright Act, 2007.
310. Section 20 of the Copyright Act, 2007.
311. Section 33 of the Copyright Act, 2007.
312. Section 34 of the Copyright Act, 2007.
313. Section 36 of the Copyright Act, 2007.
314. Section 37 of the Copyright Act, 2007.
315. Section 38 of the Copyright Act, 2007.
316. Section 40 of the Copyright Act, 2007.
317. Section 42 of the Copyright Act, 2007.

addition a personal 'moral right' in the database, regardless the ownership of the copyright. The 'moral right' includes relating the database to the name of the creator and not changing the database in a manner that damages the creator's reputation.[318]

Infringement of copyright or 'moral right' is considered tort, and if the plaintiff fails to prove the damage, a compensation of up to NIS 100,000 (approximately EUR 25,000) is granted.[319] The most significant defence in copyright lawsuits is the bona fide defence. If the defendant proves that the infringement was done under bona fide with no harmful intent, the defendant is exempt from compensating the plaintiff.[320] This defence is relevant to both copyright and 'moral right'.

Certain type of infringements of copyright may also be considered criminal offence. Copying a database illegally or importing into Israel an illegal copy of a database for commercial purposes are considered a criminal offence of up to five years imprisonment.[321] However, possession, selling, or renting of an illegal copy of a database for commercial purposes is considered a criminal offence of up to three years imprisonment.[322] All offences are *mens rea* offences, i.e., imposition of criminal liability requires awareness of the factual element of these offences, and negligence is insufficient for criminal liability.

§2. Legal Protection of Database under International Law and Foreign Law in Israel

63. If a bilateral covenant on copyright between Israel and another country is signed or if Israel has joined a multilateral covenant on copyright, the question is whether the covenant's provisions are directly applicable in Israel. In general, if the covenant is ratified in the Knesset, the covenant's provisions are not different than any other Israeli statute. However, the minister of justice is authorized to determine in a decree that the covenant's provisions are applicable in Israel, even though the Knesset did not ratify the covenant.[323]

However, any legal protection on database due to such a decree would not exceed the protection granted by Israeli law to a similar database, unless explicitly otherwise agreed within the covenant. If the minister of justice has found out that the covenant's provisions are not adhered by another country, member in the multilateral covenant, or the counterparty in the bilateral covenant, the minister is authorized, under the government's approval, to restrict the copyright of that country's subjects in Israel, according to the principle of reciprocity.[324]

The Israeli minister of justice has exercised this authority several times. The most known covenants, in which the minister of justice has included in such decrees are

318. Section 46 of the Copyright Act, 2007.
319. Section 56(a) of the Copyright Act, 2007.
320. Section 58 of the Copyright Act, 2007.
321. Section 62(a) of the Copyright Act, 2007.
322. Section 62(b) of the Copyright Act, 2007.
323. Section 9 of the Copyright Act, 2007.
324. Section 10 of the Copyright Act, 2007.

the Universal Covenant (Geneva, 6 September 1952) in 1955,[325] the Bern Covenant in 1953,[326] the Geneva Covenant (Geneva, 29 October 1971) in 1978,[327] and the TRIPS Covenant (Agreement on Trade-Related Aspects of Intellectual Property Rights Including Trade in Counterfeit Goods) in 1999.[328] In addition, the minister of justice has equalized the protection on copyright of any US citizen as if it is the copyright of an Israeli citizen in 1953.[329]

325. Copyright Decree (the Universal Covenant), 1955.
326. Copyright Decree (Bern Covenant), 1953.
327. Copyright Decree (Geneva Covenant), 1978.
328. Copyright Decree (TRIPS Covenant), 1999.
329. Copyright Decree (United States), 1953.

Chapter 4. Legal Protection of Computer Chips

64. Legal protection of computer chips in Israel is applicable through both Israeli law and international and foreign law. Israeli law has not only specified legal provisions on this issue in 1999 but has also incorporated provisions from the international law into the Israeli applicable law.

§1. Legal Protection of Computer Chips under Israeli Law

65. In 2000, the Israeli legislator enacted the Protection of Computer Chips Act, 2000. A 'computer chip' is defined as a product which is designed for electronic activities and that its components are built within one or more layers of material.[330] However, the most significant term in the protection of computer chips is 'topography'. 'Topography', in this context, is defined as the three-dimensional array of layers and components of the computer chip.[331] The subject of the legal protection, in fact, is the topography.

An original topography is a topography which has been independently developed by its creator, and that at the time of creation, it was not common for use among topographies' creators or computer chips' manufacturers.[332] Either is considered an original topography a topography which includes components that are already in use among topographies' creators or computer chips' manufacturers, but that the combinations between these components were, at the time of creation, not common for use among topographies' creators or computer chips' manufacturers.[333]

The legal protection is granted to topographies in which their creator is Israeli or an entity (physical or legal) which had an active factory in Israel for the creation of topographies or for manufacturing of computer chips.[334] The creation time of the topography is defined as the time of which the topography has been expressed in writing for the first time or got its current tangible form for the first time.[335]

The owner of the topography's IP rights is its creator (the topography's owner),[336] unless the creator is an employee, and the topography has been created within the employment, in which the employer would be the owner of the topography's IP rights.[337] However, the employer and the employee are allowed to agree otherwise.[338] Any agreement on the topography's IP rights must be in writing, otherwise it is considered invalid.[339] The writing requirement is fulfilled both in traditional writing (an agreement written on a paper) or electronically. However, an agreement *viva voce* is invalid.

330. Section 1 of the Protection of Computer Chips Act, 1999.
331. *Ibid.*
332. Section 3(1) of the Protection of Computer Chips Act, 1999.
333. Section 3(2) of the Protection of Computer Chips Act, 1999.
334. Section 2 of the Protection of Computer Chips Act, 1999.
335. Section 1 of the Protection of Computer Chips Act, 1999.
336. Section 4(a) of the Protection of Computer Chips Act, 1999.
337. Section 4(b) of the Protection of Computer Chips Act, 1999.
338. *Ibid.*
339. Section 5 of the Protection of Computer Chips Act, 1999.

The topography's owner has the exclusive right to copy the topography (including within another topography), to import it for commercial purposes, to distribute is and to sell it.[340] This right includes not only the topography itself but also any product which contains that topography.[341] Nevertheless, the topography's owner has no IP right in another original topography created by another creator, independently, even if it is identical.[342] The topography's owner has no IP right in another original topography which has been created due to analysis of the first.[343]

The IP rights in the topography are related to their owner from the time of the creation of the topography.[344] These rights would expire after fifteen years from that date or after ten years from the first commercial use of the topography, by the earlier date of them.[345] Certain types of actions are not considered infringement of the IP rights in the topography. These actions include copying the topography for research purposes, copying the topography for private purposes, creation of new and original topography based on that topography, and any other action onto the unoriginal parts of the topography.[346]

Infringement of IP rights in the topography is considered tort, and general provisions of the Israeli tort law are applicable.[347] However, if the defendant has not known that the topography is protected, and that defendant could not have known about that, the plaintiff is not entitled to damages or any other remedy.[348] If the plaintiff has notified the defendant on the protection of the topography, the plaintiff is entitled to royalties from the date of the notification.[349] Since 2017, the court is authorized to determine that the owner of the products manufactured as a result of the infringement would be the plaintiff's or to destroy these products.[350]

Regardless the provisions of the Protection of Computer Chips Act, 2000, the creator of the topography may register a patent relating to the topography. The patents registrar in Israel may order in this case, that the topography may be used for certain usages, although a patent is registered.[351] The minister of justice may also order that the topography may be used in favour of the state under certain and defined conditions.[352]

340. Section 6 of the Protection of Computer Chips Act, 1999.
341. Section 6(2) of the Protection of Computer Chips Act, 1999.
342. Section 7(2) of the Protection of Computer Chips Act, 1999.
343. Section 7(1) of the Protection of Computer Chips Act, 1999.
344. Section 9(a) of the Protection of Computer Chips Act, 1999.
345. Section 9(b) of the Protection of Computer Chips Act, 1999.
346. Section 11 of the Protection of Computer Chips Act, 1999.
347. Section 10(b) of the Protection of Computer Chips Act, 1999.
348. Section 12(a) of the Protection of Computer Chips Act, 1999.
349. Section 12(b) of the Protection of Computer Chips Act, 1999.
350. Section 12A of the Protection of Computer Chips Act, 1999.
351. Section 13(a) of the Protection of Computer Chips Act, 1999.
352. Section 13(b) of the Protection of Computer Chips Act, 1999.

§2. Legal Protection of Computer Chips under International Law and Foreign Law in Israel

If a bilateral covenant on the legal protection of computer chips between Israel and another country is signed or if Israel has joined a multilateral covenant on the legal protection of computer chips, the question is whether the covenant's provisions are directly applicable in Israel. In general, if the covenant is ratified in the Knesset, the covenant's provisions are not different than any other Israeli statute. However, the minister of justice is authorized to determine in a decree that the covenant's provisions are applicable in Israel, even though the Knesset did not ratify the covenant.[353]

Moreover, the minister of justice is authorized to make the provisions of the Protection of Computer Chips Act, 2000 become applicable on original topographies which are not related to Israel, if it has been agreed within an international covenant.[354] However, any protection on computer chips due to such a decree would not exceed the protection granted by Israeli law, unless explicitly otherwise agreed within the covenant.

The Israeli minister of justice has exercised this authority one time explicitly in relation to the protection of computer chips and a few times implicitly. In 1999, the minister of justice had embraced the provisions of the TRIPS covenant (Agreement on Trade-Related Aspects of Intellectual Property Rights Including Trade in Counterfeit Goods) regarding computer chips.[355] Accordingly, the legal protection is granted to topographies in which their creator is a citizen of a Member State or an entity (physical or legal) which had an active factory in the territory of a Member State for the creation of topographies or for manufacturing of computer chips. In addition, the minister of justice has equalized the protection on copyright of any US citizen as if it is the copyright of an Israeli citizen in 1953.[356]

---

353. Section 2(b) of the Protection of Computer Chips Act, 1999.
354. *Ibid.*
355. Protection on Computer Chips Decree (TRIPS Covenant), 1999.
356. Copyright Decree (United States), 1953.

Chapter 5. Other Intellectual Property Rights in the ICT Sector

66. Besides the protections of IP discussed above, in Chapters 1–4, there are several more types of IP protections that may be relevant in the ICT sector.

§1. Broadcasters' and Performers' Rights

I. Broadcasters' and Performers' Rights under Israeli Law

67. Particular provisions within the Israeli copyright law are dedicated to the IP rights of broadcasters and performers, which have a significant role in the area of ICT. The performer is unnecessarily the creator; therefore, the general copyright law is generally irrelevant. Accordingly, the performer is granted that no record or reproduction of the creation is done without the performer's consent.[357] Broadcasting the creation without the performer's consent is not allowed as well, unless the broadcast is within an uncommercial channel (in radio or television).[358] No consent is required if the purpose of the use is research, review, criticism, or non-profit purpose.[359]

The consent, if achieved, is delivered by the performer or through a representing organization which represents the performer.[360] The performer is granted royalties for any use of the performance; however, the royalties would be paid to the largest royalties' organization in Israel, which distributes the royalties among all performers of that kind in Israel.[361] This arrangement is social for the benefit of the unsuccessful or unfruitful performers.

The performer is also granted a 'moral right'. Accordingly, the performer's name would be related to the performance and on any copy or reproduction of the performance.[362] The performer's 'moral right' includes in addition that no change within the original performance is made in a manner that damages the performer's reputation.[363]

All performer's rights are valid for seventy years from the date of the original performance.[364] Infringement of the performer's rights is considered tort equivalent to the torts under the Copyright Act, 2007.[365] In addition, it may be considered criminal offence of up to three years imprisonment.[366] The offence is classified as *mens rea* offence, i.e., imposition of criminal liability requires awareness of the factual element of this offence, and negligence is insufficient for criminal liability.

357. Section 2(1) and 2(2) of the Performers' and Broadcasters' Rights Act, 1984.
358. Section 2(3) of the Performers' and Broadcasters' Rights Act, 1984.
359. Section 4 of the Performers' and Broadcasters' Rights Act, 1984.
360. Section 3 of the Performers' and Broadcasters' Rights Act, 1984.
361. Section 3A of the Performers' and Broadcasters' Rights Act, 1984.
362. Section 4A(a) of the Performers' and Broadcasters' Rights Act, 1984.
363. Section 4A(b) of the Performers' and Broadcasters' Rights Act, 1984.
364. Section 10 of the Performers' and Broadcasters' Rights Act, 1984.
365. Section 5 of the Performers' and Broadcasters' Rights Act, 1984.
366. Section 6 of the Performers' and Broadcasters' Rights Act, 1984.

The broadcaster is granted that no copy, reproduction, broadcasting, sell, rent or distribution of the broadcast would be done, unless explicitly consented by the broadcaster.[367] This broadcaster's right is valid for twenty-five years.[368] Infringement of this right is considered a criminal offence of up to six months imprisonment.[369]

II. Broadcasters' and Performers' Rights under International Law and Foreign Law in Israel

68. If a bilateral covenant on broadcasters' and performers' rights between Israel and another country is signed or if Israel has joined a multilateral covenant on broadcasters' and performers' rights, the question is whether the covenant's provisions are directly applicable in Israel. In general, if the covenant is ratified in the Knesset, the covenant's provisions are not different than any other Israeli statute. However, the minister of justice is authorized to determine in a decree that the covenant's provisions are applicable in Israel, even though the Knesset did not ratify the covenant.[370]

In general, the Israeli broadcasters' and performers' rights are not applicable on broadcasts and performances outside Israel, unless explicitly defined in a covenant, and a decree given by the Israeli minister of justice determines that the covenant's provisions are applicable in Israel, even though the Knesset did not ratify the covenant. The Israeli minister of justice has exercised this authority several times. The most known covenants in which the minister of justice has included in such decrees are the TRIPS Covenant (Agreement on Trade-Related Aspects of Intellectual Property Rights Including Trade in Counterfeit Goods) in 1999,[371] and the Rome Covenant (Rome, 1961) in 2002.[372]

§2. Other Types of Protection

I. Patents Law

69. An invention may be registered as patent in Israel if it is a product or a process in any technological area and it is new, useful, innovative and may have an industrial use.[373] This definition may be suitable for many products in the ICT sector, including some of the products that have been mentioned above in Chapters 1–4 (e.g., computer chips). The innovation condition is satisfied if, for an expert in this field, the invention is not trivial due to the current knowledge in this field.[374]

367. Section 4A1 of the Performers' and Broadcasters' Rights Act, 1984.
368. Section 10A of the Performers' and Broadcasters' Rights Act, 1984.
369. Section 6(a3) of the Performers' and Broadcasters' Rights Act, 1984.
370. Section 13(b) of the Performers' and Broadcasters' Rights Act, 1984.
371. Performers' and Broadcasters' Rights Decree (TRIPS Covenant), 1999.
372. Performers' and Broadcasters' Rights Decree (Rome Covenant), 2002.
373. Section 3 of the Patents Act, 1967.
374. Section 5 of the Patents Act, 1967.

The first applicant of patent registration on a specific invention has the right for the patent registration.[375] The patents registrar is authorized to examine the patent, to publish the request for registration and decide on any objection. If the request is accepted, the invention is registered as a patent.[376] The patent is valid for twenty years from the date of the submission of the request,[377] and in rare cases, it may be extended up to five more years.[378] Infringement of a patent is considered tort or civil wrong.[379]

The Washington Covenant of 1970 has been incorporated within Israeli law through ratification by the Knesset.[380] As a result, the covenant provisions, including its amendments from 1979 and 1984, and the regulations of the covenant are directly applicable in Israel.

II. Trademarks Law

70. Logos, significant words, or other marks in the ICT market may be considered subjects to IP legal protection through trademarks law. Trademark is defined as any mark used in any manner in relation to the products produced by a certain person (physical or legal) or in relation to the services given by a certain person.[381] Any trademark may be registered in the trademark registry, and the trademark registrar is subordinated to the Israeli ministry of justice.[382]

Any person may request the registry of a trademark for an exclusive use if the trademark identifies the product or the service as that person's.[383] Nevertheless, if the trademark might deceive the public, hurt the public's feelings, or be related to one of the state's symbols, the registrar may reject the request.[384] The registrar is also authorized to order the applicant to make some changes in the trademark for the above reasons. If the applicant does not agree with the registrar decision, an appeal may be submitted to the District Court within thirty days from the date the decision has been given.[385]

If the registrar regards no reason to reject the request, the request is published, and any person may object that request within three months from the date of publication.[386] If the trademark is not restricted to certain colours, the registry includes

375. Section 9 of the Patents Act, 1967.
376. Section 36 of the Patents Act, 1967.
377. Section 52 of the Patents Act, 1967.
378. Section 64J of the Patents Act, 1967.
379. Section 183 of the Patents Act, 1967.
380. Chapter C1 of the Patents Act, 1967.
381. The definition of the terms 'trademark' and 'service mark' in s. 1 of the Trademark Ordinance [New Version], 1972.
382. Section 5 of the Trademark Ordinance [New Version], 1972.
383. Section 8 of the Trademark Ordinance [New Version], 1972.
384. Section 11 of the Trademark Ordinance [New Version], 1972.
385. Section 25 of the Trademark Ordinance [New Version], 1972.
386. Section 24 of the Trademark Ordinance [New Version], 1972.

all colours.[387] The registry of a trademark is valid for ten years, and it may be prolonged if an official fee is paid.[388] The registry of a trademark grants an exclusive use, of any kind, of that trademark.[389]

Infringement of that exclusive use is considered tort, and the remedies may be both damages and an injunction that prohibits any further use of that trademark by the defendant.[390] In addition the court is authorized to order the defendant to destroy any infringing product, sell the infringing products to the plaintiff or make any other action with them.[391] Infringement may also be considered a criminal offence of up to three years imprisonment, if the infringement was intended to deceive the public.[392]

The Madrid Protocol of 1989 and the Nice Covenant of 1957 (as amended in Stockholm in 1967 and in Geneva in 1997) are incorporated within Israeli law through ratification by the Knesset.[393] Special regulations were added by the minister of justice for the implementation of both the protocol and covenant in 2007.[394] As a result, both protocol and covenant provisions, including their amendments, are directly applicable in Israel.

III. Commercial Torts Law

71. Trade secrets and commercial confidential information in the ICT market may be considered subjects to IP legal protection through commercial torts law. Trade secret is defined as *any* commercial information, which is not known to the public, not easily discovered using legal means, its owner takes reasonable measures to prevent its discovery and it grants a commercial advantage to its owner in comparison to the competitors.[395]

In fact, this very definition of trade secret embodies the IP meaning of it, but the commercial torts law relates to cases of using the trade secret by an unauthorized person. Unlawful taking of trade secret is defined as one of three options.[396] The first is taking or using the information without the owner's consent using unlawful means. The second is using contractual relations (e.g., employee and employer) to unlawfully use the trade secret. The third is using the trade secret while knowing it is without the owner's consent.

Nevertheless, in some cases, the use of the trade secret may be allowed, even if one of the above options is fulfilled. If the employer's trade secret has been discovered to an employee while at work for that employer, the employee has used it, and the trade secret became part of the employee professional skills, such use of the

387. Section 9 of the Trademark Ordinance [New Version], 1972.
388. Sections 31–35 of the Trademark Ordinance [New Version], 1972.
389. Section 46 of the Trademark Ordinance [New Version], 1972.
390. Section 59 of the Trademark Ordinance [New Version], 1972.
391. Section 59A of the Trademark Ordinance [New Version], 1972.
392. Section 60 of the Trademark Ordinance [New Version], 1972.
393. Chapter H1 of the Trademark Ordinance [New Version], 1972.
394. The Trademark Regulations (Implementation of Madrid Protocol), 2007.
395. The definition of the term 'trade secret' in s. 5 of the Commercial Torts Act, 1999.
396. Section 6(b) of the Commercial Torts Act, 1999.

trade secret by the employee is allowed.[397] In addition, if the use of the trade secret is considered to be justified for public policy reasons, that use is considered allowed.[398] Moreover, according to the Israeli market overt doctrine, if a person has purchased the information within the trade secret in full price and under bona fide, the use of the information is allowed.[399]

It makes no difference whether the use is in the original information or in any generic information produced from the original information, as long as the similarities between them are dominant.[400] Any person is presumed to be using a trade secret if the information was accessible to that person and the use is in information which is similar to the trade secret in major points.[401]

Unlawful use of trade secret is considered tort, and the plaintiff is entitled to any remedy known within the Israeli tort law.[402] In addition, if the plaintiff fails to prove any damage, the court is authorized to grant the plaintiff damages of up to NIS 100,000 (approximately EUR 25,000).[403] The court is also authorized to order that the defendant would present accounts in order to assess the damages, and it is authorized to order receivership of all products produced due to the use of the trade secret.[404] In addition, unlawful discovery of trade secret may be considered a criminal offence of up to six months imprisonment.[405]

IV. Designs Law

72. Designs in the ICT market may be considered subjects to IP legal protection through designs law. Design is defined as the appearance of a product, or part of a product, including structure, colour, shape, decoration, or substance.[406] A design may be protected under IP law if the design is new and unique.[407] Unique design is defined as a design that the objective impression out of it is that it is not similar to any other design.[408]

In general, the designer is the owner of the design, unless otherwise determined in a specific agreement or in law.[409] For example, the employer is considered to be the owner of the design, if the employee has designed it while working for the employer and while using the employer's resources, unless otherwise agreed.[410]

397. Section 7(a)(1) of the Commercial Torts Act, 1999. *See* more HCJ 1683/93 *Yavin Plast Ltd. v. The National Labour Court*, 47(4) PD 702 (1993).
398. Section 7(a)(1) of the Commercial Torts Act, 1999. For the Israeli public policy *see* Gabriel Hallevy, *Theory of the Conflict of Laws* vol. I 287–297 (Bursi Publishing House 2014).
399. Section 8 of the Commercial Torts Act, 1999.
400. Section 9 of the Commercial Torts Act, 1999.
401. Section 10 of the Commercial Torts Act, 1999.
402. Section 11 of the Commercial Torts Act, 1999.
403. Section 13 of the Commercial Torts Act, 1999.
404. Sections 15–16 of the Commercial Torts Act, 1999.
405. Section 496 of the Israeli Penal Code, 1977.
406. The definition of the term 'design' in s. 1 of the Designs Act, 2017.
407. Section 2 of the Designs Act, 2017.
408. Section 7 of the Designs Act, 2017.
409. Section 11 of the Designs Act, 2017.
410. Section 12 of the Designs Act, 2017.

Similarly, if a design has been ordered, the ordering person (the client) is the owner of the design, unless otherwise agreed.[411]

The design's owner may request registration of the design within the designs' registration, managed by the ministry of justice.[412] After examined as compatible for registration, the design is registered, and the details of the design are published, *inter alia*, on the ministry of justice website.[413] The registry grants the owner an exclusive right to manufacture, sell, rent, import, or export, for commercial purposes, any product designed within the registered design.[414] The registration is valid for twenty-five years.[415]

Infringement of the registered design is considered tort, and the plaintiff is entitled to any remedy known within the Israeli tort law.[416] In addition, if the plaintiff fails to prove any damage, the court is authorized to grant the plaintiff damages of up to NIS 100,000 (approximately EUR 25,000).[417] The court is also authorized to grant an injunction that prohibits any further use of that design by the defendant.[418] The court is also authorized to order that the defendant would present accounts in order to assess the damages, and it is authorized to order receivership of all products produced due to the use of the design.[419] In addition, infringement of the registered design may be considered a criminal offence of up to NIS 226,000 (approximately EUR 56,500) fine.[420]

The Hague Covenant of 1960 (as amended in Geneva in 1999) is incorporated within Israeli law through ratification by the Knesset.[421] As a result, the covenant provisions, including its amendments, are directly applicable in Israel.

411. Section 13 of the Designs Act, 2017.
412. Section 18 of the Designs Act, 2017.
413. Section 31 of the Designs Act, 2017. *See* at https://www.justice.gov.il/En/Units/ILPO/Departments/Designs/Pages/default.aspx (accessed 23 Jul. 2021).
414. Section 37 of the Designs Act, 2017.
415. Section 39 of the Designs Act, 2017.
416. Section 73 of the Designs Act, 2017.
417. Section 75 of the Designs Act, 2017.
418. Section 74 of the Designs Act, 2017.
419. Section 77 of the Designs Act, 2017.
420. Section 92 of the Designs Act, 2017.
421. Chapter H of the Designs Act, 2017.

Chapter 6. Internet Domain Name Registration

73. The Internet domain names are registered by registrars accredited by the Israel Internet Association.

§1. The Israeli Internet Association

74. The Israel Internet Association was established in 1994 as an independent entity that acts in order to promote the Internet and its integration into Israel's technological, research, educational, social, and business infrastructure.[422] The Association is managed by nine board members, all volunteers, and acts within this framework towards developing and advancing infrastructure services vital for the existence of the Internet in Israel, narrowing the country's digital divide, and representing Israel in international forums that are significant in determining the future of the Internet.

The Israel Internet Association operates the registry for domain names ending with Israel's national suffix, il. The Domain Name Registry has been managed by the Association since 1997. The Association is currently labouring to change Israel's existing domain name registration process to one based on registration by certified registrars. This change in the domain registration process is expected to further improve the level of service the local Internet community receives in this field.

The Israel Internet Association establishes and operates the IIX, which directs all Israeli internal Internet traffic between the various Internet providers in the most effective manner and serves as the Israeli Internet's backbone. The Internet Association hosts a domain name system (DNS) Root Server duplicate at its facilities. Global DNS Root Servers function as the base for the process of decoding domain names across the entire Internet network. Deployment of a DNS Root Server adjacent to the Israeli Internet Exchange contributes to the surfing experience of Israeli users by carrying out decoding of domain names in their immediate environment, without the need for access to remote servers or navigators, in a way that improves response time and the surfing experience.

§2. Domain Name Registration

75. Registration of Domain Names under.co.il,.org.il, ac.il, muni.il, net.il is available via accredited registrars. The accredited registrars are companies or organizations which have been accredited by Israeli Internet Association (ISOC-IL) after meeting technological and service criteria. Thus, accredited registrars are companies or organizations that meet technological and service criteria set forth by ISOC-IL, and with whom ISOC-IL has signed an accreditation agreement.

422. *See* https://en.isoc.org.il/ (accessed 23 Jul. 2021).

There exists free competition among Accredited Registrars. ISOC-IL recommends comparing the Accredited Registrars and the services offered by them, prior to choosing a particular one.

The registration of domain names containing Hebrew characters is available since 26 December 2010. The registration of Hebrew domain names is an expansion of the existing domain name registration service and is done subject to the registration rules.[423] In general, Hebrew domain names use the IDN (Internationalized Domain Names) suite of standards.

When a Hebrew domain name is typed in an IDN-aware browser (or another application), the domain name is automatically translated into a 'traditional' domain name comprising of Latin characters, digits, and hyphens. The translated domain name is resolved in the global DNS. Most of the modern browsers today already have IDN support.

Technically, the ISOC-IL REG-REG system introduces an interface between ISOC-IL, the.il ccTLD domain name registry, and accredited registrars. The system allows accredited registrars to programmatically perform registration acts against the domain name registry (new name registration, modifications and deletion of names, etc.) in a secure and authenticated manner. The system is available exclusively to registrars that have been accredited by ISOC-IL.

Disputes regarding the allocation of Domain Names under the.IL ccTLD are generally resolved by the IL-DRP. The IL-DRP is an alternative dispute resolution procedure intended to provide expedited resolution to disputes regarding the allocation of domain names under the.IL ccTLD in accordance with the Rules for Allocation of Domain Names under.IL.[424]

The IL-DRP is not intended to create or replace judicial precedence or jurisprudence. Further, agreeing to dispute resolution under the IL-DRP procedures does not constitute an arbitration agreement as defined by the arbitration law of Israel.

Under the IL-DRP, any case of which a third-party challenge to an existing allocation of a domain name by ISOC-IL to a holder is reviewed. Each dispute is determined on a case-by-case basis. Disputes that are not reviewed under the IL-DRP are any request to disallow, in advance, the allocation of a domain name, disputes such that the allocation of a domain name was carried out prior to 1 January 1999 (prior to adoption of the Domain Name Registration Rules) unless the holder of the domain name under dispute has agreed to such dispute resolution in writing and disputes between the holder and an accredited registrar regarding allocation of domain name based on the quality of service or breach of contract or other commercial disputes, denial by ISOC-IL of a request to allocate a domain name, cancellation by ISOC-IL of an allocation of a domain name and disputes challenging allocation to a holder, based on ISOC-IL's malfeasance in the allocation of a domain name. Challenges based on ISOC-IL's actions or omissions may be brought to an Israeli Court within a civil lawsuit.

---

423. The registration rules in English are available at https://www.isoc.org.il/files/docs/ISOC-IL_Registration_Rules_v1.6_ENGLISH_-_18.12.2017.pdf (accessed 23 Jul. 2021).
424. The rules and procedure are available at https://en.isoc.org.il/domains/ildrp_rules.html (accessed 23 Jul. 2021).

Part III. ICT Contracts

76. In general, all contracts under Israeli law are subject to the general law of contracts. Nevertheless, particular legal provisions regulate special contracts, including ICT contracts. These provisions relate not only to substantive issues, but they may also relate to formal aspects of the contract (e.g., contracts concerning computer chips are required to be in writing).[425]

425. Section 5 of the Protection of Computer Chips Act, 1999.

Chapter 1. Hardware Contracts

§1. General Legal Framework and the Applicable Law

77. Hardware contracts are basically agreements relating to hardware components, physical devices, and other tangible objects in use at the ICT market. There are three basic layers of the law relating to ICT hardware contracts. The first layer is the general law of contracts, the second layer is the consumption law, and the third layer is the ICT law. The interpretation rule between these layers is *lex specialis derogat generali*. Therefore, legal provisions from ICT law derogate legal provisions from consumption law, which derogate legal provisions from the general law of contracts.

However, most issues in hardware contracts are covered by the general law of contracts. The common hardware contracts are between merchants and consumers (e.g., purchasing a laptop from a virtual store on the web), and Israeli law prefers to classify these contracts as consumption contracts rather than contracts regarding technology. As a result, certain legal duties are imposed on the merchants regardless the type of 'merchandise'. Only in rare types of hardware contracts the law dictates specific relevant legal arrangements.

Hardware contracts are subject to the Israeli conflict of laws rules, and in particular to the rules of choice-of-law in contracts. The general rule in Israel is that the law which governs the hardware contract is the law that both parties agreed on, explicitly or implicitly. If no such law has been agreed on, the applicable law is the law which has the closest and most real connection to the contract.[426] Particular rules of choice-of-law in contracts are deduced from the English Common Law through case laws.

Hardware may be described as movable object, therefore, if no specific law has been agreed on within the hardware contract, the applicable law (i.e., the law which has the closest and most real connection to the contract) is the law governing the domicile of the person who sold the hardware.[427] Nevertheless, if the particular hardware contract may be considered as consumption contract (e.g., when a customer buys a laptop from a computer store), even though the hardware is a movable object, the applicable law on that contract may be different.

Hardware contracts which are classified as consumption contracts are governed by the law that both parties agreed on, explicitly or implicitly, unless it deprives the consumer of rights granted by the alternative law (i.e., the applicable law that should have governed the contract without the parties' agreement). If no such law has been agreed on, or if the agreed law deprives the consumer of granted rights, the applicable law is the law which has the closest and most real connection to the contract. In general, this is the law that governs the consumer's domicile, unless another law has a closer and more real connection to the contract.[428]

426. Gabriel Hallevy, *Theory of the Conflict of Laws* vol. I 478–493 (Bursi Publishing House 2014); Civ. App. 165/60 *Onion Ltd. v. Moshe,* 17 PD 646 (1963); Civ. App. 352/87 *Greifin Corp. v. Cur Ltd.*, 44(3) PD 45 (1990).
427. Hallevy, *ibid.,* at pp. 549–552.
428. *Ibid.*, at pp. 589–595.

This situation may cause some ambiguity. Consequently, most written hardware contracts include a choice-of-law clause which defines in particular the applicable law of the contract. This clause is generally accompanied by an exclusive jurisdiction clause (i.e., a clause which grants the Israeli court an exclusive jurisdiction over any lawsuit regarding the contract). Nevertheless, the agreed law is not applicable if its content is contradicted to the Israeli public policy or to the Israeli criminal law (e.g., a contract that permits an action which is considered a criminal offence in Israel, but according to the foreign law, which has been defined as the applicable law, it is not forbidden).

§2. Substantive Legal Provisions under Israeli Law

78. If the hardware contract's applicable law is Israeli law, the general law of contracts is the basic layer that governs the hardware contract. The Israeli general law of contracts is highly inspired by the German law of contracts. Any hardware contract is considered formed, and its existence is inferred, if both factual element and mental element requirements are fulfilled. The factual element is expressed by an offer and an acceptance.[429] The acceptance may be by writing, orally (*viva voce*), or through consenting behaviour.[430]

The mental element requirement is expressed by awareness of the parties to the major terms of the contract and by an intention to create legal relations through the particular contract.[431] The negotiations between the parties prior to the agreement and the formation of the contract are subject to a wide bona fide requirement.[432] The bona fide requirement may, if not fulfilled, result in invalidation of the contract, even though all other formal requirements have been fulfilled. However, if both factual element and mental element requirements are fulfilled, the contract is allegedly considered formed.

Consideration, however, under Israeli law is not required. Gifts and presents given for free with no charge are considered valid contracts.[433] Certain types of disorders, which indirectly may be related to the mental element, might result in invalidation of the contract. Some types makes the contract become voidable (i.e., the court is required to declare that the contract is void), and other types automatically make the contract become void. Fictive contracts are, of course, void.[434]

Contracts may also be void on grounds of public policy or illegality (in contrast to the criminal law).[435] Thus, if the relevant hardware is forbidden in Israel by the criminal law, the hardware contract is void. Nevertheless, contracts which have been

429. Section 1 of the Contracts (General Part) Act, 1973.
430. Section 6 of the Contracts (General Part) Act, 1973.
431. Section 2 of the Contracts (General Part) Act, 1973.
432. Section 12 of the Contracts (General Part) Act, 1973.
433. The Gifts Act, 1968.
434. Section 13 of the Contracts (General Part) Act, 1973.
435. Section 30 of the Contracts (General Part) Act, 1973.

formed due to mistakes, misrepresentation, duress or threat, are voidable.[436] If the contract is void, a statement of cancellation of the contract by one of the parties, at least, is required.[437]

Form requirements of the contract are, in general, not required by the law and the parties have wide discretion towards it, unless a particular legal provision imposes specific form requirements.[438] For example, if the hardware contract relates to computer chips, it must be formed in writing, otherwise it is invalid and void, regardless of its content.[439] However, in certain cases, the court preferred to validate the contract, although the form requirements were not fulfilled, if its validation is coherent with bona fide.[440] Performance of the contract may be in favour of the parties or in favour of a third party.[441] However, any hardware contract must be performed under wide requirement of bona fide.[442]

In cases of breach of hardware contract, the court is authorized to impose on the violator a duty to perform the contract (specific performance or enforcement), unless the contract is not operative any more, the specific performance involves personal service, the specific performance requires unreasonable inspection by the court or the specific performance is unjust.[443] Thus, the primary remedy for breach of hardware contracts is specific performance.

Only if specific performance is inapplicable, the court may impose other remedies. One of these remedies is the cancellation of the contract together with restoration of resources (i.e., each party returns the other party any resources given prior to the breach, e.g., advances).[444] However, the common remedy is damages. The plaintiff is granted damages for the loss caused by the breach, and in some cases, even without proving any loss.[445] Nevertheless, if the breach was caused by force major, the plaintiff is discharged, as the doctrine of frustration has been accepted in Israel.[446]

Most hardware contracts in Israel are between merchants and consumers; therefore, they are subject to consumption law as well. Under Israeli consumption law, the general rule of *caveat emptor* is invalid or, at least, minimized. This attitude is expressed by imposition of wide duties on the merchant in favour of the consumer. Many of these duties are enforced through criminal law. The most significant duties are the full disclosure and due diligence duties.

Accordingly, any act or omission of any merchant is forbidden, if it *might* cause misrepresentation or mistake.[447] That includes the duty to let the consumer the full information on the hardware, the service regarding it, the time of performance, all relevant terms, the price and calculations of the price, the terms for cancellation, etc.

---

436. Sections 14–15 and 17–18 of the Contracts (General Part) Act, 1973.
437. Section 20 of the Contracts (General Part) Act, 1973.
438. Section 23 of the Contracts (General Part) Act, 1973.
439. Section 5 of the Protection of Computer Chips Act, 1999.
440. *See, e.g.*, Civ. App. 986/93 *Klemer v. Guy,* 50(1) PD 185 (1996).
441. Sections 34–38 of the Contracts (General Part) Act, 1973.
442. Section 39 of the Contracts (General Part) Act, 1973.
443. Section 3 of the Contracts (Remedies for Breach of Contract) Act, 1970.
444. Sections 6–9 of the Contracts (Remedies for Breach of Contract) Act, 1970.
445. Sections 10–11 of the Contracts (Remedies for Breach of Contract) Act, 1970.
446. Section 18 of the Contracts (Remedies for Breach of Contract) Act, 1970.
447. Section 2 of the Consumer's Protection Act, 1981.

It is forbidden for the merchant to limit the consumer's liberty to contact (or, more important, *not* to contact) with the merchant.[448] The merchant must disclose any possible damage in the hardware that may defect its performance.[449]

If the hardware is defective, the consumer has an unconditional right to return the hardware to the merchant and get back the money paid or another hardware instead, by the consumer's choice, within fourteen days from the consumer's announcement to the merchant.[450] If the hardware is not defective, the consumer has the right to return it to the merchant, for any reason, within seven days, unless the hardware was opened from its original pack or the hardware was designed according to specific and unusual order of the consumer.[451]

Imported hardware must include on its pack details identifying it, including the country of which the hardware was manufactured; the hardware's official name and commercial name; the manufacturer's name, ID, and address;, the importer's name, ID, and address; and the hardware-specific ingredients.[452]

If the hardware is mobile telephone or any other device that radiates non-ionizing radiation, the merchant must inform the costumer on the rate of radiation (SAR – Specific Absorption Rate) using 5cm x 5cm label on the device's pack and using clear brochure in Hebrew, Arabic and Russian regarding the SAR.[453] The brochure must also include information on the maximum permitted rate of radiation according to both the European and American standards and the Israeli Standard.

Any hardware contract must include clear and specific clauses on the warranty conditions, the service towards the hardware, and the relevant periods of warranty and service.[454] If the service requires a technician, the technician's visit would be appointed between 08.00 and 19.00 on Sunday until Thursday or between 08.00 and 13.00 on Friday. Waiting for a technician would not last more than two hours. A compensation of NIS 300 (approximately EUR 75) is granted for waiting beyond two hours, and of NIS 600 (approximately EUR 150) for waiting beyond three hours.[455]

Free-of-charge customer service must be granted by the merchant in any hardware contract.[456] The customer service agent must be identified at the beginning of the call by name, and the call would be from a line that may be reconnected by the customer easily by redialling.[457]

Enforcement of the consumption law provisions is under the responsibility of the Consumer's Protection Authority. This authority is authorized to enforce the law using administrative measures, and in particular through administrative fines of up

448. Section 3 of the Consumer's Protection Act, 1981.
449. Section 4 of the Consumer's Protection Act, 1981.
450. Section 14E of the Consumer's Protection Act, 1981.
451. Section 4C(d) of the Consumer's Protection Act, 1981.
452. Section 17 of the Consumer's Protection Act, 1981.
453. Regulations 1–3 of the Consumer's Protection (Information Regarding Non-Ionizing Radiation From Mobile Devices) Regulations, 2002.
454. Section 18A of the Consumer's Protection Act, 1981.
455. *Ibid.*
456. Section 18B of the Consumer's Protection Act, 1981.
457. Section 18C of the Consumer's Protection Act, 1981.

to NIS 45,000 (approximately EUR 11,000).[458] In addition, infringement of the consumption law may be considered criminal offence of up to three years imprisonment, confiscation of the hardware, and fines of up to NIS 4.5 million (approximately EUR 1.1 million).[459]

458. Chapter E1 of the Consumer's Protection Act, 1981.
459. Chapter F of the Consumer's Protection Act, 1981.

Chapter 2. Software Contracts

§1. General Legal Framework and the Applicable Law

79. Software contracts are basically agreements relating to the use of computer programs in compatible devices. The software may be obtained by purchasing a tangible media containing the software (e.g., disk containing word processor program) accompanied by a license or by purchasing a license to use a software of a downloaded software. However, the core of a software contract is the license to use the software. Sometimes, the license itself functions as a software contract, as it defines the conditions for the permitted use of the software and the consideration, if required, for that use.

There are three basic layers of the law relating to software contracts. The first layer is the general law of contracts, the second layer is the consumption law, and the third layer is the ICT law. The interpretation rule between these layers is *lex specialis derogat generali*. Therefore, legal provisions from ICT law derogate legal provisions from consumption law, which derogate legal provisions from the general law of contracts.

However, most issues in software contracts are covered by the general law of contracts. The common software contracts are between merchants and consumers (e.g., purchasing a license to use a word processor program from a virtual store on the web), and Israeli law prefers to classify these contracts as consumption contracts rather than contracts regarding technology. As a result, certain legal duties are imposed on the merchants regardless the type of 'merchandise'. Only in rare types of software contracts the law dictates specific relevant legal arrangements.

Software contracts are subject to the Israeli conflict of laws rules, and in particular to the rules of choice-of-law in contracts. The general rule in Israel is that the law which governs the software contract is the law that both parties agreed on, explicitly or implicitly. If no such law has been agreed on, the applicable law is the law which has the closest and most real connection to the contract.[460] Particular rules of choice-of-law in contracts are deduced from the English Common Law through case laws.

In many cases, software may be described as movable object (e.g., when the consumer purchases a disc containing the software, and the license is embodied within that disc), therefore if no specific law has been agreed on within the software contract, the applicable law (i.e., the law which has the closest and most real connection to the contract) is the law governing the domicile of the person who sold the software.[461] Nevertheless, if the particular software contract may be considered as consumption contract (e.g., when a customer purchases a license to use a software downloaded from a certain website), the applicable law on that contract may be different.

---

460. Gabriel Hallevy, *Theory of the Conflict of Laws* vol. I 478–493 (Bursi Publishing House 2014); Civ. App. 165/60 *Onion Ltd. v. Moshe,* 17 PD 646 (1963); Civ. App. 352/87 *Greifin Corp. v. Cur Ltd.*, 44(3) PD 45 (1990).

461. Hallevy, *ibid.*, at pp. 549–552.

Software contracts which are classified as consumption contracts are governed by the law that both parties agreed on, explicitly or implicitly, unless it deprives the consumer of rights granted by the alternative law (i.e., the applicable law that should have governed the contract without the parties' agreement). If no such law has been agreed on, or if the agreed law deprives the consumer of granted rights, the applicable law is the law which has the closest and most real connection to the contract. In general, this is the law that governs the consumer's domicile, unless another law has a closer and more real connection to the contract.[462]

This situation may cause some ambiguity. Consequently, most written software contracts (including licenses purchased from official websites) include a choice-of-law clause in which defines in particular the applicable law of the contract. This clause is generally accompanied by an exclusive jurisdiction clause (i.e., a clause which grants the Israeli court an exclusive jurisdiction over any lawsuit regarding the contract). Nevertheless, the agreed law is not applicable if its content is contradicted to the Israeli public policy or to the Israeli criminal law (e.g., a contract that permit an action which is considered criminal offence in Israel, but according the foreign law, which has been defined as the applicable law, it is not forbidden).

§2. Substantive Legal Provisions under Israeli Law

80. If the software contract's applicable law is Israeli law, the general law of contracts is the basic layer that governs the software contract. The Israeli general law of contracts is highly inspired by the German law of contracts. Any software contract is considered formed, and its existence is inferred, if both factual element and mental element requirements are fulfilled. The factual element is expressed by an offer and an acceptance.[463] The acceptance may be by writing, orally (*viva voce*), or through consenting behaviour.[464]

The mental element requirement is expressed by awareness of the parties to the major terms of the contract and by an intention to create legal relations through the particular contract.[465] The negotiations between the parties prior to the agreement and the formation of the contract are subject to a wide bona fide requirement.[466] The bona fide requirement may, if not fulfilled, result in invalidation of the contract, even though all other formal requirements have been fulfilled. However, if both factual element and mental element requirements are fulfilled, the contract is allegedly considered formed.

Consideration, however, under Israeli law is not required. Gifts and presents given for free with no charge are considered valid contracts.[467] Thus, a free-of-charge license to use software is considered a contract under Israeli law. For example, if the license grants the availability of the software for at least three months, and after two months the software is not available any more, the licensee

462. *Ibid.*, at pp. 589–595.
463. Section 1 of the Contracts (General Part) Act, 1973.
464. Section 6 of the Contracts (General Part) Act, 1973.
465. Section 2 of the Contracts (General Part) Act, 1973.
466. Section 12 of the Contracts (General Part) Act, 1973.
467. The Gifts Act, 1968.

is granted a remedy, if damages were caused by that change. Free-of-charge licenses to use a software do not reduce the licensor liability under Israeli contracts law.

Certain types of disorders, which indirectly may be related to the mental element of both parties of the contract, might result in invalidation of the contract. Some types make the contract become voidable (i.e., the court is required to declare that the contract is void), and other types automatically make the contract become void. Fictive contracts are, of course, void.[468]

Contracts may also be void on grounds of public policy or illegality (in contrast with the criminal law).[469] Thus, if the relevant software is forbidden for use in Israel by the criminal law (e.g., gambling software),[470] the software contract is void. Nevertheless, contracts which have been formed due to mistakes, misrepresentation, duress or threat, are voidable.[471] If the contract is void, a statement of cancellation of the contract by one of the parties, at least, is required.[472]

Form requirements of the contract are, in general, not required by the law, and the parties have wide discretion towards it, unless a particular legal provision imposes specific form requirements.[473] Moreover, in certain cases, the court preferred to validate contracts, although the form requirements were not fulfilled, if its validation is coherent with bona fide.[474] Performance of the contract may be in favour of the parties or in favour of a third party.[475] However, any software contract must be performed under wide requirement of bona fide.[476]

In cases of breach of software contract, either by the licensor or the licensee, the court is authorized to impose on the violator a duty to perform the contract (specific performance or enforcement), unless the contract is not operative any more, the specific performance involves personal service, the specific performance requires unreasonable inspection by the court or the specific performance is unjust.[477] Thus, the primary remedy for breach of software contracts is specific performance. For example, if the licensee has purchased the software and it was not supplied, the preferred remedy is to order the supplier to supply the software.

Only if specific performance is inapplicable, the court may impose other remedies. One of these remedies is the cancellation of the contract together with restoration of resources (i.e., each party returns the other party any resources given prior to the breach, e.g., advances).[478] However, the common remedy is damages. The plaintiff is granted damages for the loss caused by the breach, and in some

468. Section 13 of the Contracts (General Part) Act, 1973.
469. Section 30 of the Contracts (General Part) Act, 1973.
470. Sections 224–233 of the Israeli Penal Code, 1977.
471. Sections 14–15 and 17–18 of the Contracts (General Part) Act, 1973.
472. Section 20 of the Contracts (General Part) Act, 1973.
473. Section 23 of the Contracts (General Part) Act, 1973.
474. *See, e.g.*, Civ. App. 986/93 *Klemer v. Guy*, 50(1) PD 185 (1996).
475. Sections 34–38 of the Contracts (General Part) Act, 1973.
476. Section 39 of the Contracts (General Part) Act, 1973.
477. Section 3 of the Contracts (Remedies for Breach of Contract) Act, 1970.
478. Sections 6–9 of the Contracts (Remedies for Breach of Contract) Act, 1970.

cases, even without proving any loss.[479] Nevertheless, if the breach was caused by force major, the plaintiff is discharged, as the doctrine of frustration has been accepted in Israel.[480]

Most software contracts in Israel are between merchants and consumers; therefore, they are subject to consumption law as well. Under Israeli consumption law, the general rule of *caveat emptor* is invalid or, at least, minimized. This attitude is expressed by imposition of wide duties on the merchant in favour of the consumer. Many of these duties are enforced through criminal law. The most significant duties are the full disclosure and due diligence duties.

Accordingly, any act or omission of any merchant is forbidden, if it *might* cause misrepresentation or mistake.[481] That includes the duty to let the consumer the full information on the software, the service regarding it, the time of performance, all relevant terms, the price and calculations of the price, the terms for cancellation, etc. It is forbidden for the merchant to limit the consumer's liberty to contact (or, more important, *not* to contact) with the merchant.[482] The merchant must disclose any possible damage in the software that may defect its performance, including its incompatibility to certain devices, to certain operating systems, or to certain software in common use.[483]

If the software is defective, the consumer has an unconditional right to return the software to the merchant and get back the money paid or another software instead, by the consumer's choice, within fourteen days from the consumer's announcement to the merchant.[484] If the consumer has purchased a license, returning it means to inactivate it by the merchant, or by the consumer, if possible. If the software is not defective, the consumer has the right to return it to the merchant, for any reason, within seven days, unless the software was opened from its original pack (if thus purchased) or the software was designed according to specific and unusual order of the consumer.[485]

Imported software must include on its pack (if thus purchased) or in a visible and accessible place (e.g., on the webpage before its download) details identifying it, including the country of which the software was manufactured or written; the software's official name and commercial name; the manufacturer's name, ID, and address; the importer's name, ID, and address; and the software-specific ingredients.[486]

Any software contract must include clear and specific clauses on the warranty conditions, the service towards the software, and the relevant periods of warranty and service.[487] If the service requires a technician, the technician's visit would be appointed between 08.00 and 19.00 on Sunday until Thursday or between 08.00 and

479. Sections 10–11 of the Contracts (Remedies for Breach of Contract) Act, 1970.
480. Section 18 of the Contracts (Remedies for Breach of Contract) Act, 1970.
481. Section 2 of the Consumer's Protection Act, 1981.
482. Section 3 of the Consumer's Protection Act, 1981.
483. Section 4 of the Consumer's Protection Act, 1981.
484. Section 14E of the Consumer's Protection Act, 1981.
485. Section 4C(d) of the Consumer's Protection Act, 1981.
486. Section 17 of the Consumer's Protection Act, 1981.
487. Section 18A of the Consumer's Protection Act, 1981.

13.00 on Friday. Waiting to a technician would not last more than two hours. A compensation of NIS 300 (approximately EUR 75) is granted for waiting beyond two hours, and of NIS 600 (approximately EUR 150) for waiting beyond three hours.[488]

Free-of-charge customer service must be granted by the merchant in any software contract.[489] The customer service agent must be identified at the beginning of the call by name, and the call would be from a line that may be reconnected by the customer easily by redialling.[490]

Enforcement of the consumption law provisions is under the responsibility of the Consumer's Protection Authority. This authority is authorized to enforce the law using administrative measures, and in particular through administrative fines of up to NIS 45,000 (approximately EUR 11,000).[491] In addition, infringement of the consumption law may be considered criminal offence of up to three years imprisonment, confiscation of the software media, if any, and fines of up to NIS 4.5 million (approximately EUR 1.1 million).[492]

488. *Ibid.*
489. Section 18B of the Consumer's Protection Act, 1981.
490. Section 18C of the Consumer's Protection Act, 1981.
491. Chapter E1 of the Consumer's Protection Act, 1981.
492. Chapter F of the Consumer's Protection Act, 1981.

Chapter 3. Turnkey Contracts

81. In IT, a turnkey contract generally refers to a contract under which, when a computer system is delivered to the user, the user only has to 'turn a key' to have a fully operable computer system. Thus, a turnkey computer system is a complete computer including hardware, operating system, and application designed and sold to satisfy specific business requirements.

A turnkey product in ICT market is, in fact, a combination of both hardware and software, ready for use by the consumer. This type of products is mostly useful for non-expert customers, who need the functioning device without preparing it for use. This is the most common way to purchase computers, mobile phones, tablets, and other technological devices.

§1. General Legal Framework and the Applicable Law

82. There are three basic layers of the law relating to turnkey contracts. The first layer is the general law of contracts, the second layer is the consumption law, and the third layer is the ICT law. The interpretation rule between these layers is *lex specialis derogat generali*. Therefore, legal provisions from ICT law derogate legal provisions from consumption law, which derogate legal provisions from the general law of contracts.

However, most issues in turnkey contracts are covered by the general law of contracts. The common turnkey contracts are between merchants and consumers (e.g., purchasing a laptop from a virtual store on the web and the operating system and other applications are already installed on the laptop's hard drive), and Israeli law prefers to classify these contracts as consumption contracts rather than contracts regarding technology. As a result, certain legal duties are imposed on the merchants regardless of the type of 'merchandise'. Only in rare types of turnkey contracts, the law dictates specific relevant legal arrangements.

Turnkey contracts are subject to the Israeli conflict of laws rules, and in particular to the rules of choice-of-law in contracts. The general rule in Israel is that the law which governs the turnkey contract is the law that both parties agreed on, explicitly or implicitly. If no such law has been agreed on, the applicable law is the law that has the closest and most real connection to the contract.[493] Particular rules of choice-of-law in contracts are deduced from the English Common Law through case laws.

Turnkey product may be described as movable object; therefore, if no specific law has been agreed on within the turnkey contract, the applicable law (i.e., the law which has the closest and most real connection to the contract) is the law governing the domicile of the person who sold the turnkey product.[494] Nevertheless, if the particular turnkey contract may be considered as consumption contract (e.g., when a

493. Gabriel Hallevy, *Theory of the Conflict of Laws* vol. I 478–493 (Bursi Publishing House 2014); Civ. App. 165/60 *Onion Ltd. v. Moshe*, 17 PD 646 (1963); Civ. App. 352/87 *Greifin Corp. v. Cur Ltd.*, 44(3) PD 45 (1990).

494. Hallevy, *ibid.*, at pp. 549–552.

customer buys a laptop from a computer store and the operating system and other applications are already installed on the laptop's hard drive), even though the turnkey product is a movable object, the applicable law on that contract may be different.

Turnkey contracts which are classified as consumption contracts are governed by the law that both parties agreed on, explicitly or implicitly, unless it deprives the consumer of rights granted by the alternative law (i.e., the applicable law that should have governed the contract without the parties' agreement). If no such law has been agreed on, or if the agreed law deprives the consumer of granted rights, the applicable law is the law which has the closest and most real connection to the contract. In general, this is the law that governs the consumer's domicile, unless another law has a closer and more real connection to the contract.[495]

This situation may cause some ambiguity. Consequently, most written turnkey contracts include a choice-of-law clause which defines in particular the applicable law of the contract. This clause is generally accompanied by an exclusive jurisdiction clause (i.e., a clause which grants the Israeli court an exclusive jurisdiction over any lawsuit regarding the contract). Nevertheless, the agreed law is not applicable if its content is contradicted to the Israeli public policy or to the Israeli criminal law (e.g., a contract that permit an action which is considered a criminal offence in Israel, but according to the foreign law, which has been defined as the applicable law, it is not forbidden).

§2. Substantive Legal Provisions under Israeli Law

83. If the applicable law of the particular turnkey contract is Israeli law, the general law of contracts is the basic layer that governs the turnkey contract. The Israeli general law of contracts is highly inspired by the German law of contracts. Any turnkey contract is considered formed, and its existence is inferred, if both factual element and mental element requirements are fulfilled. The factual element is expressed by an offer and an acceptance.[496] The acceptance may be by writing, orally (*viva voce*), or through consenting behaviour.[497]

The mental element requirement is expressed by awareness of the parties to the major terms of the contract and by an intention to create legal relations through the particular contract.[498] The negotiations between the parties prior to the agreement and the formation of the contract are subject to a wide bona fide requirement.[499] The bona fide requirement may, if not fulfilled, result in invalidation of the contract, even though all other formal requirements have been fulfilled. However, if both factual element and mental element requirements are fulfilled, the contract is allegedly considered formed.

495. *Ibid.*, at pp. 589–595.
496. Section 1 of the Contracts (General Part) Act, 1973.
497. Section 6 of the Contracts (General Part) Act, 1973.
498. Section 2 of the Contracts (General Part) Act, 1973.
499. Section 12 of the Contracts (General Part) Act, 1973.

Consideration, however, under Israeli law is not required. Gifts and presents given for free with no charge are considered valid contracts.[500] Certain types of disorders, which indirectly may be related to the mental element, might result in invalidation of the contract. Some types make the contract become voidable (i.e., the court is required to declare that the contract is void), and other types automatically make the contract become void. Fictive contracts are, of course, void.[501]

Contracts may also be void on grounds of public policy or illegality (in contrast with the criminal law).[502] Thus, if the relevant turnkey product is forbidden in Israel by the criminal law, the turnkey contract is void. Nevertheless, contracts which have been formed due to mistakes, misrepresentation, duress or threat, are voidable.[503] If the contract is void, a statement of cancellation of the contract by one of the parties, at least, is required.[504]

Form requirements of the contract are, in general, not required by the law, and the parties have wide discretion towards it, unless a particular legal provision imposes specific form requirements.[505] Moreover, in certain cases, the court preferred to validate the contract, although the form requirements were not fulfilled, if its validation is coherent with bona fide.[506] Performance of the contract may be in favour of the parties or in favour of a third party.[507] However, any turnkey contract must be performed under wide requirement of bona fide.[508]

In cases of breach of turnkey contract, the court is authorized to impose on the violator a duty to perform the contract (specific performance or enforcement), unless the contract is not operative anymore, the specific performance involves personal service, the specific performance requires unreasonable inspection by the court or the specific performance is unjust.[509] Thus, the primary remedy for breach of turnkey contracts is specific performance. For example, if a computer with operating system and applications already installed on it was purchased, but not supplied, the court would prefer to order the merchant to supply that computer, if possible.

Only if specific performance is inapplicable, the court may impose other remedies. One of these remedies is the cancellation of the contract together with restoration of resources (i.e., each party returns the other party any resources given prior to the breach, e.g., advances).[510] However, the common remedy is damages. The plaintiff is granted damages for the loss caused by the breach, and in some

500. The Gifts Act, 1968.
501. Section 13 of the Contracts (General Part) Act, 1973.
502. Section 30 of the Contracts (General Part) Act, 1973.
503. Sections 14–15 and 17–18 of the Contracts (General Part) Act, 1973.
504. Section 20 of the Contracts (General Part) Act, 1973.
505. Section 23 of the Contracts (General Part) Act, 1973.
506. *See, e.g.*, Civ. App. 986/93 *Klemer v. Guy,* 50(1) PD 185 (1996).
507. Sections 34–38 of the Contracts (General Part) Act, 1973.
508. Section 39 of the Contracts (General Part) Act, 1973.
509. Section 3 of the Contracts (Remedies for Breach of Contract) Act, 1970.
510. Sections 6–9 of the Contracts (Remedies for Breach of Contract) Act, 1970.

cases, even without proving any loss.[511] Nevertheless, if the breach was caused by force major, the plaintiff is discharged, as the doctrine of frustration has been accepted in Israel.[512]

Most turnkey contracts in Israel are between merchants and consumers (e.g., purchasing a computer with an operating system installed in it from a computer store); therefore, they are subject to consumption law as well. Under Israeli consumption law, the general rule of *caveat emptor* is invalid or, at least, minimized. This attitude is expressed by imposition of wide duties on the merchant in favour of the consumer. Many of these duties are enforced through criminal law. The most significant duties are the full disclosure and due diligence duties.

Accordingly, any act or omission of any merchant is forbidden, if it *might* cause misrepresentation or mistake.[513] That includes the duty to let the consumer the full information on the turnkey product, the service regarding it, the time of performance, all relevant terms, the price and calculations of the price, the terms for cancellation, etc. It is forbidden for the merchant to limit the consumer's liberty to contact (or, more important, *not* to contact) with the merchant.[514] The merchant must disclose any possible damage in the turnkey product that may defect its performance (e.g., an installation of not the newest version of an operating system on a new computer).[515]

If the turnkey product is defective, the consumer has an unconditional right to return the turnkey product to the merchant and get back the money paid or another turnkey product instead, by the consumer's choice, within fourteen days from the consumer's announcement to the merchant.[516] If the turnkey product is not defective, the consumer has the right to return it to the merchant, for any reason, within seven days, unless the turnkey product was opened from its original pack or the turnkey product was designed according to specific and unusual order of the consumer.[517]

Imported turnkey product must include on its pack details identifying it, including the country of which the turnkey product was manufactured; the turnkey product's official name and commercial name; the manufacturer's name, ID, and address; the importer's name, ID, and address; and the turnkey product-specific ingredients, including both hardware and software ingredients.[518]

If the turnkey product is mobile telephone that an operating system is installed in it or any other device which includes an active operating system, but it radiates non-ionizing radiation, the merchant must inform the costumer on the rate of radiation (SAR) using 5cm x 5cm label on the device's pack and using clear brochure in Hebrew, Arabic and Russian regarding the SAR.[519] The brochure must also include

511. Sections 10–11 of the Contracts (Remedies for Breach of Contract) Act, 1970.
512. Section 18 of the Contracts (Remedies for Breach of Contract) Act, 1970.
513. Section 2 of the Consumer's Protection Act, 1981.
514. Section 3 of the Consumer's Protection Act, 1981.
515. Section 4 of the Consumer's Protection Act, 1981.
516. Section 14E of the Consumer's Protection Act, 1981.
517. Section 4C(d) of the Consumer's Protection Act, 1981.
518. Section 17 of the Consumer's Protection Act, 1981.
519. Regulations 1–3 of the Consumer's Protection (Information Regarding Non-Ionizing Radiation From Mobile Devices) Regulations, 2002.

information on the maximum permitted rate of radiation according to both the European and American standards and the Israeli Standard.

Any turnkey contract must include clear and specific clauses on the warranty conditions, the service towards the turnkey product, and the relevant periods of warranty and service for both hardware and software components of the product.[520] If the service requires a technician, the technician's visit would be appointed between 08.00 and 19.00 on Sunday until Thursday or between 08.00 and 13.00 on Friday. Waiting for a technician would not last more than two hours. A compensation of NIS 300 (approximately EUR 75) is granted for waiting beyond two hours, and of NIS 600 (approximately EUR 150) for waiting beyond three hours.[521]

Free-of-charge customer service must be granted by the merchant in any turnkey contract.[522] The customer service agent must be identified at the beginning of the call by name, and the call would be from a line that may be reconnected by the customer easily by redialling.[523]

Enforcement of the consumption law provisions is under the responsibility of the Consumer's Protection Authority. This authority is authorized to enforce the law using administrative measures, and in particular through administrative fines of up to NIS 45,000 (approximately EUR 11,000).[524] In addition, infringement of the consumption law may be considered a criminal offence of up to three years imprisonment, confiscation of the turnkey product, and fines of up to NIS 4.5 million (approximately EUR 1.1 million).[525]

520. Section 18A of the Consumer's Protection Act, 1981.
521. *Ibid.*
522. Section 18B of the Consumer's Protection Act, 1981.
523. Section 18C of the Consumer's Protection Act, 1981.
524. Chapter E1 of the Consumer's Protection Act, 1981.
525. Chapter F of the Consumer's Protection Act, 1981.

Chapter 4. Distribution Agreements

84. In the Israeli ICT market, distribution agreements are in general both franchise and distribution agreements. The object of these agreements may be both products and services within the ICT market. For example, an agreement between an international manufacturer of mobile phones and an Israeli franchisee towards marketing these mobile phones within the Israeli territory is a distribution agreement. Exclusive distribution rights within the agreement are optional, but in Israel they are considered rare.

Distribution agreements in the Israeli ICT market also refer to broadcasting and transmissions. Although broadcasting and transmissions in this context are classified as services, the distribution agreement itself does not refer to the service, but other agreements between the franchisee and the customers refer to the service.

§1. General Legal Framework and the Applicable Law

85. Basically, there are two basic layers of the law relating to distribution agreements. The first layer is the general law of contracts and the second layer is the ICT law. The interpretation rule between these two layers is *lex specialis derogat generali*. Therefore, legal provisions from ICT law derogate legal provisions from the general law of contracts. Although most issues in distribution agreements are covered by the general law of contracts, certain issues are covered particularly by the ICT law.

Distribution agreements are subject to the Israeli conflict of laws rules, and in particular to the rules of choice-of-law in contracts. The general rule in Israel is that the law which governs the distribution agreement is the law that both parties agreed on, explicitly or implicitly. If no such law has been agreed on, the applicable law is the law which has the closest and most real connection to the contract.[526] Particular rules of choice-of-law in contracts are deduced from the English Common Law through case laws.

The common interpretation in Israel of 'the law which has the closest and most real connection to the contract' is the law that governs franchisee's (distributer's) domicile, unless another law has a closer and more real connection to the contract.[527] However, most distribution agreements include a choice-of-law clause which defines in particular the applicable law of the contract.

The choice-of-law clause in distributive agreements is generally accompanied by an exclusive jurisdiction clause (i.e., a clause which grants the Israeli court an exclusive jurisdiction over any lawsuit regarding the contract). Nevertheless, the agreed law is not applicable if its content is contradicted to the Israeli public policy or to

526. Gabriel Hallevy, *Theory of the Conflict of Laws* vol. I 478–493 (Bursi Publishing House 2014); Civ. App. 165/60 *Onion Ltd. v. Moshe*, 17 PD 646 (1963); Civ. App. 352/87 *Greifin Corp. v. Cur Ltd.*, 44(3) PD 45 (1990).
527. Hallevy, *ibid.*, at pp. 558–561.

the Israeli criminal law (e.g., a contract that permit an action which is considered a criminal offence in Israel, but according the foreign law, which has been defined as the applicable law, it is not forbidden).

§2. Substantive Legal Provisions under Israeli Law

86. If the applicable law of the particular distribution agreement is Israeli law, the general law of agreements is the basic layer that governs the distribution agreement. However, only when both parties are Israelis, it is more common to find distribution agreements, in which Israeli law is the applicable law. In most distribution agreements between international corporations and Israeli franchisees, the applicable law is not Israeli law.

However, the Israeli general law of contracts is highly inspired by the German law of contracts. Under Israeli law, any distribution agreement is considered formed, and its existence is inferred, if both factual element and mental element requirements are fulfilled. The factual element is expressed by an offer and an acceptance.[528] The acceptance may be by writing, orally (*viva voce*), or through consenting behaviour.[529]

The mental element requirement is expressed by awareness of the parties to the major terms of the agreement and by an intention to create legal relations through the particular agreement.[530] The negotiations between the parties prior to the agreement and the formation of the agreement are subject to a wide bona fide requirement.[531] The bona fide requirement may, if not fulfilled, result in invalidation of the agreement, even though all other formal requirements have been fulfilled. However, if both factual element and mental element requirements are fulfilled, the agreement is allegedly considered formed.

Consideration, however, under Israeli law is not required. Gifts and presents given for free with no charge are considered valid agreements.[532] Certain types of disorders, which indirectly may be related to the mental element, might result in invalidation of the agreement. Some types make the agreement become voidable (i.e., the court is required to declare that the agreement is void), and other types automatically make the agreement become void. Fictive agreements are, of course, void.[533]

Agreements may also be void on grounds of public policy or illegality (in contrast with the criminal law).[534] Thus, if the relevant product or services, which are the object of the agreement, are forbidden in Israel by the criminal law (e.g., certain type of pornography content), the distribution agreement is void. Nevertheless, agreements which have been formed due to mistakes, misrepresentation, duress or

528. Section 1 of the Contracts (General Part) Act, 1973.
529. Section 6 of the Contracts (General Part) Act, 1973.
530. Section 2 of the Contracts (General Part) Act, 1973.
531. Section 12 of the Contracts (General Part) Act, 1973.
532. The Gifts Act, 1968.
533. Section 13 of the Contracts (General Part) Act, 1973.
534. Section 30 of the Contracts (General Part) Act, 1973.

threat, are voidable.[535] If the agreement is void, a statement of cancellation of the agreement by one of the parties, at least, is required.[536]

Form requirements of the agreement are, in general, not required by the law, and the parties have wide discretion towards it, unless a particular legal provision imposes specific form requirements.[537] Moreover, in certain cases, the court preferred to validate the agreement, although the form requirements were not fulfilled, if its validation is coherent with bona fide.[538] Performance of the agreement may be in favour of the parties or in favour of a third party.[539] However, any distribution agreement must be performed under wide requirement of bona fide.[540]

In cases of breach of distribution agreement, the court is authorized to impose on the violator a duty to perform the agreement (specific performance or enforcement), unless the agreement is not operative anymore (e.g., the broadcast relates to soccer games that have already terminated), the specific performance involves personal service, the specific performance requires unreasonable inspection by the court or the specific performance is unjust.[541] Thus, the primary remedy for breach of distribution agreements is specific performance.

Only if specific performance is inapplicable, the court may impose other remedies. One of these remedies is the cancellation of the agreement together with restoration of resources (i.e., each party returns the other party any resources given prior to the breach, e.g., advances).[542] However, the common remedy is damages. The plaintiff is granted damages for the loss caused by the breach, and in some cases, even without proving any loss.[543] Nevertheless, if the breach was caused by force major, the plaintiff is discharged, as the doctrine of frustration has been accepted in Israel.[544]

If distribution is carried out through the state's telecommunication facilities, a distribution fee is required. The fee is determined in particular regulations, and it is changed due to reasonable costs of maintenance.[545] In addition, there are particular regulations governing ICT franchisees towards the content, the products, or the services. For example, there are regulations which govern the broadcasting and production of radio programmes,[546] the broadcasting and production of television programmes,[547] and sectorial services in certain types of media.[548]

535. Sections 14–15 and 17–18 of the Contracts (General Part) Act, 1973.
536. Section 20 of the Contracts (General Part) Act, 1973.
537. Section 23 of the Contracts (General Part) Act, 1973.
538. *See, e.g.*, Civ. App. 986/93 *Klemer v. Guy,* 50(1) PD 185 (1996).
539. Sections 34–38 of the Contracts (General Part) Act, 1973.
540. Section 39 of the Contracts (General Part) Act, 1973.
541. Section 3 of the Contracts (Remedies for Breach of Contract) Act, 1970.
542. Sections 6–9 of the Contracts (Remedies for Breach of Contract) Act, 1970.
543. Sections 10–11 of the Contracts (Remedies for Breach of Contract) Act, 1970.
544. Section 18 of the Contracts (Remedies for Breach of Contract) Act, 1970.
545. The Second Authority for Television and Radio (Distribution Fees) Regulations, 2012.
546. The Second Authority for Television and Radio (Broadcasts of Radio Programs by a Franchisee) Rules, 1999.
547. The Second Authority for Television and Radio (Broadcasts of Television Programs by a Franchisee) Rules, 2009.
548. *See, e.g.*, the Second Authority for Television and Radio (Distribution of Radio Programs in Arabic) Regulations, 2002.

In relation to the broadcasting and production of television programmes, all distribution agreements must include the distributor's duty to broadcast at least eighteen hours a day, to broadcast in a variety of areas, to include educational content, to produce local and original television productions, to broadcast no more than 30% of entertaining content between 16:00 to 23:59, to sign the broadcast with common signs relating to the age limits (e.g., 8+, 14+, and 18+), and to avoid pop-up promos of certain programmes.[549] Other rules regulate the quality of signals, customer service, and administrative issues.

In relation to the broadcasting and production of radio programmes, all distribution agreements must include the distributor's duty to include news report every hour, to include short weather forecast in every news report, to consider holidays and holidays, to avoid broadcasts in Yom Kippur, to publish broadcasting schedule forty-five days in advance, and to consider children in certain types of broadcasts.[550] Other rules regulate the quality of signals, the customer service, and administrative issues.

549. The Second Authority for Television and Radio (Broadcasts of Television Programs by a Franchisee) Rules, 2009.

550. The Second Authority for Television and Radio (Broadcasts of Radio Programs by a Franchisee) Rules, 1999.

Chapter 5. Maintenance Contracts

87. Maintenance contracts in the ICT market basically refer to service contracts regarding technological equipment. The service contract is not necessarily between the customer and the merchant who supplied the equipment, but it may also be between the customer and a third party. Most of these contracts offer, out of warranty, maintenance services that help keep ICT equipment optimized for performance.

Thus, for example, most computer hardware equipment comes with a fixed warranty period of one or two years, under certain limitations. These warranties are often not as comprehensive as the consumer requires, and as a computer grows more prone to failures and problems as it ages and the common way to keep this equipment in shape is to perform routine maintenance.

The common hardware equipment that requires routine maintenance are PCs, laptops, workstations, printers and peripherals, data centres, servers, etc. Sometimes, a multi-vendor maintenance service is required, when different vendors and manufacturers have different maintenance requirements, as different components are embodied within the same hardware. Some of the maintenance contracts relate to the maintenance of ICT infrastructure at the domestic or national level.

However, as aforesaid, maintenance contracts are basically service contracts between the customer (private customer or public customer) and the service provider, whether the service provider has also supplied the equipment or not. The contract has no legal characteristics of hardware contracts,[551] but the legal characteristics of service contracts. The service is, of course, specified as maintenance service.

§1. General Legal Framework and the Applicable Law

88. ICT maintenance contracts are basically agreements relating to maintenance services of ICT equipment, as aforesaid. There are three basic layers of the law relating to ICT maintenance services contracts. The first layer is the general law of contracts, the second layer is the consumption law, and the third layer is the ICT law. The interpretation rule between these layers is *lex specialis derogat generali.* Therefore, legal provisions from ICT law derogate legal provisions from consumption law, which derogate legal provisions from the general law of contracts.

However, most issues in maintenance services contracts are covered by the general law of contracts. The common maintenance services contracts are between service providers and consumers (e.g., purchasing maintenance services for a period of twelve months), and Israeli law prefers to classify these contracts as consumption contracts rather than contracts regarding technology. As a result, certain legal duties are imposed on the service providers regardless the type of service. Only in rare types of maintenance services contracts, the law dictates specific relevant legal arrangements.

551. For hardware contracts *see* above at Chapter 1: Hardware Contracts.

Maintenance services contracts are subject to the Israeli conflict of laws rules, and in particular, to the rules of choice-of-law in contracts. The general rule in Israel is that the law which governs the maintenance services contract is the law that both parties agreed on, explicitly or implicitly. If no such law has been agreed on, the applicable law is the law that has the closest and most real connection to the contract.[552] Particular rules of choice-of-law in contracts are deduced from the English Common Law through case laws.

Maintenance services are 'services', therefore if no specific law has been agreed on within the maintenance services contract, the applicable law (i.e., the law which has the closest and most real connection to the contract) is the law governing the domicile of the services provider.[553] Nevertheless, if the particular maintenance services contract may be considered as consumption contract (e.g., when a customer purchases maintenance services for a period of twelve months), even though the maintenance services are 'services', the applicable law on that contract may be different.

Maintenance services contracts which are classified as consumption contracts are governed by the law that both parties agreed on, explicitly or implicitly, unless it deprives the consumer of rights granted by the alternative law (i.e., the applicable law that should have governed the contract without the parties' agreement). If no such law has been agreed on, or if the agreed law deprives the consumer of granted rights, the applicable law is the law that has the closest and most real connection to the contract. In general, this is the law that governs the consumer's domicile, unless another law has a closer and more real connection to the contract.[554]

This situation may cause some ambiguity. Consequently, most written maintenance services contracts include a choice-of-law clause which defines in particular the applicable law of the contract. This clause is generally accompanied by an exclusive jurisdiction clause (i.e., a clause which grants the Israeli court an exclusive jurisdiction over any lawsuit regarding the contract). Nevertheless, the agreed law is not applicable if its content is contradicted to the Israeli public policy or to the Israeli criminal law (e.g., a contract that permit an action which is considered criminal offence in Israel, but according to the foreign law, which has been defined as the applicable law, it is not forbidden).

§2. SUBSTANTIVE LEGAL PROVISIONS UNDER ISRAELI LAW

89. If the maintenance services contract's applicable law is Israeli law, the general law of contracts is the basic layer that governs the maintenance services contract. The Israeli general law of contracts is highly inspired by the German law of

552. Gabriel Hallevy, *Theory of the Conflict of Laws* vol. I 478–493 (Bursi Publishing House 2014); Civ. App. 165/60 *Onion Ltd. v. Moshe*, 17 PD 646 (1963); Civ. App. 352/87 *Greifin Corp. v. Cur Ltd.*, 44(3) PD 45 (1990).
553. Hallevy, *ibid.*, at pp. 561–570.
554. *Ibid.*, at pp. 589–595.

contracts. Any maintenance services contract is considered formed, and its existence is inferred, if both factual element and mental element requirements are fulfilled. The factual element is expressed by an offer and an acceptance.[555] The acceptance may be by writing, orally (*viva voce*), or through consenting behaviour.[556]

The mental element requirement is expressed by awareness of the parties to the major terms of the contract and by an intention to create legal relations through the particular contract.[557] The negotiations between the parties prior to the agreement and the formation of the contract are subject to a wide bona fide requirement.[558] The bona fide requirement may, if not fulfilled, result in invalidation of the contract, even though all other formal requirements have been fulfilled. However, if both factual element and mental element requirements are fulfilled, the contract is allegedly considered formed.

Consideration, however, under Israeli law is not required. Gifts and presents given for free with no charge are considered valid contracts.[559] Thus, free-of-charge maintenance services contracts are considered a valid contract under Israeli law. For example, if the services grant the availability of the maintenance services for at least three months, and after two months the maintenance services are not available anymore, the customer is granted a remedy, if damages were caused by that change. Free-of-charge maintenance services do not reduce the services provider liability under Israeli contracts law.

Certain types of disorders, which indirectly may be related to the mental element of both parties of the contract, might result in invalidation of the contract. Some types make the contract become voidable (i.e., the court is required to declare that the contract is void), and other types automatically make the contract become void. Fictive contracts are, of course, void.[560]

Contracts may also be void on grounds of public policy or illegality (in contrast with the criminal law).[561] Thus, if the relevant maintenance services are forbidden for use in Israel by the criminal law (e.g., game machines maintenance services),[562] the maintenance services contract is void. Nevertheless, contracts which have been formed due to mistakes, misrepresentation, duress or threat, are voidable.[563] If the contract is void, a statement of cancellation of the contract by one of the parties, at least, is required.[564]

Form requirements of the contract are, in general, not required by the law and the parties have wide discretion towards it, unless a particular legal provision imposes

555. Section 1 of the Contracts (General Part) Act, 1973.
556. Section 6 of the Contracts (General Part) Act, 1973.
557. Section 2 of the Contracts (General Part) Act, 1973.
558. Section 12 of the Contracts (General Part) Act, 1973.
559. The Gifts Act, 1968.
560. Section 13 of the Contracts (General Part) Act, 1973.
561. Section 30 of the Contracts (General Part) Act, 1973.
562. Sections 224–233 of the Israeli Penal Code, 1977.
563. Sections 14–15 and 17–18 of the Contracts (General Part) Act, 1973.
564. Section 20 of the Contracts (General Part) Act, 1973.

specific form requirements.[565] Moreover, in certain cases the court preferred to validate contracts, although the form requirements were not fulfilled, if its validation is coherent with bona fide.[566] Performance of the contract (i.e., supply the services) may be in favour of the parties or in favour of a third party.[567] However, any maintenance services contract must be performed under wide requirement of bona fide.[568]

In cases of breach of maintenance services contract, either by the services provider or the customer, the court is authorized to impose on the violator a duty to perform the contract (specific performance or enforcement), unless the contract is not operative anymore, the specific performance involves *personal* service (i.e., the maintenance services must be supplied by a particular technician), the specific performance requires unreasonable inspection by the court or the specific performance is unjust.[569] Thus, the primary remedy for breach of maintenance services contracts is specific performance. Consequently, if the customer has purchased the maintenance services and they were not supplied, the preferred remedy is to order the services provider to supply the maintenance services.

Only if specific performance is inapplicable, the court may impose other remedies. One of these remedies is the cancellation of the contract together with restoration of resources (i.e., each party returns the other party any resources given prior to the breach, e.g., advances).[570] However, the common remedy is damages. The plaintiff is granted damages for the loss caused by the breach, and in some cases, even without proving any loss.[571] Nevertheless, if the breach was caused by force major, the plaintiff is discharged, as the doctrine of frustration has been accepted in Israel.[572]

Most maintenance services contracts in Israel are between services providers and consumers; therefore, they are subject to consumption law as well. Under Israeli consumption law, the general rule of *caveat emptor* is invalid or, at least, minimized. This attitude is expressed by imposition of wide duties on the services provider in favour of the consumer. Many of these duties are enforced through criminal law. The most significant duties are the full disclosure and due diligence duties.

Accordingly, any act or omission of any services provider is forbidden, if it *might* cause misrepresentation or mistake.[573] That includes the duty to let the consumer the full information on the maintenance services, the service regarding it (e.g., how to contact the services provider), the time of supplying the services, all relevant terms, the price and calculations of the price, the terms for cancellation, etc. It is forbidden for the services provider to limit the consumer's liberty to contact

565. Section 23 of the Contracts (General Part) Act, 1973.
566. *See, e.g.*, Civ. App. 986/93 *Klemer v. Guy*, 50(1) PD 185 (1996).
567. Sections 34–38 of the Contracts (General Part) Act, 1973.
568. Section 39 of the Contracts (General Part) Act, 1973.
569. Section 3 of the Contracts (Remedies for Breach of Contract) Act, 1970.
570. Sections 6–9 of the Contracts (Remedies for Breach of Contract) Act, 1970.
571. Sections 10–11 of the Contracts (Remedies for Breach of Contract) Act, 1970.
572. Section 18 of the Contracts (Remedies for Breach of Contract) Act, 1970.
573. Section 2 of the Consumer's Protection Act, 1981.

(or, more important, *not* to contact) with the services provider.[574] The services provider must disclose any possible limitation in the maintenance services that may defect its performances, including its incompatibility to certain devices, to certain manufacturers, to certain operating systems, or to certain software in common use.[575]

If the maintenance services are not professional or insufficient for the consumer's needs, the consumer has an unconditional right to cancel the maintenance services and get back the money paid or be rewarded with other services instead, by the consumer's choice, within fourteen days from the consumer's announcement to the services provider.[576] If the maintenance services are not insufficient and they are professional, the consumer has the right to cancel them, for any reason, within seven days, unless the maintenance services were designed according to specific and unusual order of the consumer.[577]

Any maintenance services contract must include clear and specific clauses on the warranty conditions, the service towards the maintenance services, and the relevant periods of warranty and service.[578] If the service requires a technician, the technician's visit would be appointed between 08.00 and 19.00 on Sunday until Thursday or between 08.00 and 13.00 on Friday. Waiting for a technician would not last more than two hours. A compensation of NIS 300 (approximately EUR 75) is granted for waiting beyond two hours, and of NIS 600 (approximately EUR 150) for waiting beyond three hours.[579]

Free-of-charge customer service must be granted by the services provider in any maintenance services contract.[580] The customer service agent must be identified at the beginning of the call by name, and the call would be from a line that may be reconnected by the customer easily by redialling.[581]

Enforcement of the consumption law provisions is under the responsibility of the Consumer's Protection Authority. This authority is authorized to enforce the law using administrative measures, and in particular through administrative fines of up to NIS 45,000 (approximately EUR 11,000).[582] In addition, infringement of the consumption law may be considered a criminal offence of up to three years imprisonment, confiscation of the maintenance services media or measures, if any, and fines of up to NIS 4.5 million (approximately EUR 1.1 million).[583]

All ICT services corporations in Israel are required to supply maintenance services in order to ensure proper use and availability of its ICT services.[584] These services include customer services acting 24/7 (24 hours a day, 7 days a week),

574. Section 3 of the Consumer's Protection Act, 1981.
575. Section 4 of the Consumer's Protection Act, 1981.
576. Section 14E of the Consumer's Protection Act, 1981.
577. Section 4C(d) of the Consumer's Protection Act, 1981.
578. Section 18A of the Consumer's Protection Act, 1981.
579. *Ibid.*
580. Section 18B of the Consumer's Protection Act, 1981.
581. Section 18C of the Consumer's Protection Act, 1981.
582. Chapter E1 of the Consumer's Protection Act, 1981.
583. Chapter F of the Consumer's Protection Act, 1981.
584. Regulation 6 of the Intercommunications Services (Installation, Management and Maintenance) Regulations, 1985.

responsibility to fix any damage in infrastructure or devices supplied by the corporation within certain time (different maximum time periods were determined for different types of services), and responsibility to inform the consumer within 2 working days that the damage cannot be fixed.

Chapter 6. Facilities Management

90. Facilities management encompasses multiple disciplines to ensure functionality, comfort, safety, and efficiency of the built environment by integrating people, place, process, and technology. The ISO defined in April 2017 (ISO 41011) facilities management as the 'organizational function which integrates people, place and process within the built environment with the purpose of improving the quality of life of people and the productivity of the core business'.

In the ICT market context, facilities management refers to the 'soft' facilities management, which is a set of services, based on required technology, to ensure the functionality of infrastructure and devices in routine activity, relating to people and organizations. In Israel, this mostly refers to IT services and to accessibility of technology. Thus, facilities management contracts are service contracts. The relevant facilities refer to both infrastructure facilities and professional technological devices.

§1. General Legal Framework and the Applicable Law

91. Basically, there are three fundamental layers of the law relating to ICT facilities management services contracts. The first layer is the general law of contracts, the second layer is the consumption law, and the third layer is the ICT law. The interpretation rule between these layers is *lex specialis derogat generali*. Therefore, legal provisions from ICT law derogate legal provisions from consumption law, which derogate legal provisions from the general law of contracts.

However, most issues in facilities management services contracts are covered by the general law of contracts. The common facilities management services contracts are between service providers and consumers (e.g., purchasing facilities management services for a period of twenty-four months), and Israeli law prefers to classify these contracts as consumption contracts rather than contracts regarding technology. As a result, certain legal duties are imposed on the service providers regardless of the type of service. Only in rare types of facilities management services contracts, the law dictates specific relevant legal arrangements.

Facilities management services contracts are subject to the Israeli conflict of laws rules, and in particular to the rules of choice-of-law in contracts. The general rule in Israel is that the law which governs the facilities management services contract is the law that both parties agreed on, explicitly or implicitly. If no such law has been agreed on, the applicable law is the law that has the closest and most real connection to the contract.[585] Particular rules of choice-of-law in contracts are deduced from the English Common Law through case laws.

Facilities management services are 'services'; therefore, if no specific law has been agreed on within the facilities management services contract, the applicable law (i.e., the law which has the closest and most real connection to the contract) is

585. Gabriel Hallevy, *Theory of the Conflict of Laws* vol. I 478–493 (Bursi Publishing House 2014); Civ. App. 165/60 *Onion Ltd. v. Moshe,* 17 PD 646 (1963); Civ. App. 352/87 *Greifin Corp. v. Cur Ltd.*, 44(3) PD 45 (1990).

the law governing the domicile of the services provider.[586] Nevertheless, if the particular facilities management services contract may be considered as consumption contract (e.g., when a customer purchases facilities management services for a period of twenty-four months), even though the facilities management services are 'services', the applicable law on that contract may be different.

Facilities management services contracts which are classified as consumption contracts are governed by the law that both parties agreed on, explicitly or implicitly, unless it deprives the consumer of rights granted by the alternative law (i.e., the applicable law that should have governed the contract without the parties' agreement). If no such law has been agreed on, or if the agreed law deprives the consumer of granted rights, the applicable law is the law that has the closest and most real connection to the contract. In general, this is the law that governs the consumer's domicile, unless another law has a closer and more real connection to the contract.[587]

This situation may cause some ambiguity. Consequently, most written facilities management services contracts include a choice-of-law clause in which defines in particular the applicable law of the contract. This clause is generally accompanied by an exclusive jurisdiction clause (i.e., a clause which grants the Israeli court an exclusive jurisdiction over any lawsuit regarding the contract). Nevertheless, the agreed law is not applicable if its content is contradicted to the Israeli public policy or to the Israeli criminal law (e.g., a contract that permit an action which is considered criminal offence in Israel, but according to the foreign law, which has been defined as the applicable law, it is not forbidden).

§2. Substantive Legal Provisions under Israeli Law

92. If the facilities management services contract's applicable law is Israeli law, the general law of contracts is the basic layer that governs the facilities management services contract. The Israeli general law of contracts is highly inspired by the German law of contracts. Any facilities management services contract is considered formed, and its existence is inferred, if both factual element and mental element requirements are fulfilled. The factual element is expressed by an offer and an acceptance.[588] The acceptance may be by writing, orally (*viva voce*), or through consenting behaviour.[589]

The mental element requirement is expressed by awareness of the parties to the major terms of the contract and by an intention to create legal relations through the particular contract.[590] The negotiations between the parties prior to the agreement and the formation of the contract are subject to a wide bona fide requirement.[591] The bona fide requirement may, if not fulfilled, result in invalidation of the contract,

586. Hallevy, *ibid.*, at pp. 561–570.
587. *Ibid.*, at pp. 589–595.
588. Section 1 of the Contracts (General Part) Act, 1973.
589. Section 6 of the Contracts (General Part) Act, 1973.
590. Section 2 of the Contracts (General Part) Act, 1973.
591. Section 12 of the Contracts (General Part) Act, 1973.

even though all other formal requirements have been fulfilled. However, if both factual element and mental element requirements are fulfilled, the contract is allegedly considered formed.

Consideration, however, under Israeli law is not required. Gifts and presents given for free with no charge are considered valid contracts.[592] Thus, free-of-charge facilities management services contracts are considered a valid contract under Israeli law. For example, if the services grant the availability of the facilities management services for at least three months, and after two months the facilities management services are not available any more, the customer is granted a remedy, if damages were caused by that change. Free-of-charge facilities management services do not reduce the services provider liability under Israeli contracts law.

Certain types of disorders, which indirectly may be related to the mental element of both parties of the contract, might result in invalidation of the contract. Some types make the contract become voidable (i.e., the court is required to declare that the contract is void), and other types automatically make the contract become void. Fictive contracts are, of course, void.[593]

Contracts may also be void on grounds of public policy or illegality (in contrast with the criminal law).[594] Thus, if the relevant facilities management services are forbidden for use in Israel by the criminal law (e.g., facilities management services supplied to an illegal business), the facilities management services contract is void. Nevertheless, contracts which have been formed due to mistakes, misrepresentation, duress or threat, are voidable.[595] If the contract is void, a statement of cancellation of the contract by one of the parties, at least, is required.[596]

Form requirements of the contract are, in general, not required by the law, and the parties have wide discretion towards it, unless a particular legal provision imposes specific form requirements.[597] Moreover, in certain cases, the court preferred to validate contracts, although the form requirements were not fulfilled, if its validation is coherent with bona fide.[598] Performance of the contract (i.e., supply the services) may be in favour of the parties or in favour of a third party.[599] However, any facilities management services contract must be performed under wide requirement of bona fide.[600]

In cases of breach of facilities management services contract, either by the services provider or the customer, the court is authorized to impose on the violator a duty to perform the contract (specific performance or enforcement), unless the contract is not operative anymore, the specific performance involves *personal* service (i.e., the facilities management services must be supplied by a particular FM manager), the specific performance requires unreasonable inspection by the court or the

592. The Gifts Act, 1968.
593. Section 13 of the Contracts (General Part) Act, 1973.
594. Section 30 of the Contracts (General Part) Act, 1973.
595. Sections 14–15 and 17–18 of the Contracts (General Part) Act, 1973.
596. Section 20 of the Contracts (General Part) Act, 1973.
597. Section 23 of the Contracts (General Part) Act, 1973.
598. *See, e.g.*, Civ. App. 986/93 *Klemer v. Guy*, 50(1) PD 185 (1996).
599. Sections 34–38 of the Contracts (General Part) Act, 1973.
600. Section 39 of the Contracts (General Part) Act, 1973.

specific performance is unjust.[601] Thus, the primary remedy for breach of facilities management services contracts is specific performance. Consequently, if the customer has purchased the facilities management services and they were not supplied, the preferred remedy is to order the services provider to supply the facilities management services.

Only if specific performance is inapplicable, the court may impose other remedies. One of these remedies is the cancellation of the contract together with restoration of resources (i.e., each party returns the other party any resources given prior to the breach, e.g., advances).[602] However, the common remedy is damages. The plaintiff is granted damages for the loss caused by the breach, and in some cases, even without proving any loss.[603] Nevertheless, if the breach was caused by force major, the plaintiff is discharged, as the doctrine of frustration has been accepted in Israel.[604]

Most facilities management services contracts in Israel are between services providers and consumers; therefore, they are subject to consumption law as well. Under Israeli consumption law, the general rule of *caveat emptor* is invalid or, at least, minimized. This attitude is expressed by imposition of wide duties on the services provider in favour of the consumer. Many of these duties are enforced through criminal law. The most significant duties are the full disclosure and due diligence duties.

Accordingly, any act or omission of any services provider is forbidden, if it *might* cause misrepresentation or mistake.[605] That includes the duty to let the consumer the full information on the facilities management services, the service regarding it (e.g., how to contact the help desk), the times of supplying the services, all relevant terms, the price and calculations of the price, the terms for cancellation, etc. It is forbidden for the services provider to limit the consumer's liberty to contact (or, more important, *not* to contact) with the services provider.[606] The services provider must disclose any possible limitation in the facilities management services that may defect its performances, including its incompatibility to certain devices.[607]

If the facilities management services are not professional or insufficient for the consumer's needs, the consumer has an unconditional right to cancel the facilities management services and get back the money paid or be rewarded with other services instead, by the consumer's choice, within fourteen days from the consumer's announcement to the services provider.[608] If the facilities management services are not insufficient and they are professional, the consumer has the right to cancel them, for any reason, within seven days, unless the facilities management services were designed according to specific and unusual order of the consumer.[609]

601. Section 3 of the Contracts (Remedies for Breach of Contract) Act, 1970.
602. Sections 6–9 of the Contracts (Remedies for Breach of Contract) Act, 1970.
603. Sections 10–11 of the Contracts (Remedies for Breach of Contract) Act, 1970.
604. Section 18 of the Contracts (Remedies for Breach of Contract) Act, 1970.
605. Section 2 of the Consumer's Protection Act, 1981.
606. Section 3 of the Consumer's Protection Act, 1981.
607. Section 4 of the Consumer's Protection Act, 1981.
608. Section 14E of the Consumer's Protection Act, 1981.
609. Section 4C(d) of the Consumer's Protection Act, 1981.

Any facilities management services contract must include clear and specific clauses on the warranty conditions, the service towards the facilities management services, and the relevant periods of warranty and service.[610] If the service requires a technician, the technician's visit would be appointed between 08.00 and 19.00 on Sunday until Thursday or between 08.00 and 13.00 on Friday. Waiting for a technician would not last more than two hours. A compensation of NIS 300 (approximately EUR 75) is granted for waiting beyond two hours, and of NIS 600 (approximately EUR 150) for waiting beyond three hours.[611]

Free-of-charge customer service must be granted by the services provider in any facilities management services contract.[612] The customer service agent must be identified at the beginning of the call by name, and the call would be from a line that may be reconnected by the customer easily by redialling.[613]

Enforcement of the consumption law provisions is under the responsibility of the Consumer's Protection Authority. This authority is authorized to enforce the law using administrative measures, and in particular through administrative fines of up to NIS 45,000 (approximately EUR 11,000).[614] In addition, infringement of the consumption law may be considered a criminal offence of up to three years imprisonment, confiscation of the facilities management services measures, if any, and fines of up to NIS 4.5 million (approximately EUR 1.1 million).[615]

610. Section 18A of the Consumer's Protection Act, 1981.
611. *Ibid.*
612. Section 18B of the Consumer's Protection Act, 1981.
613. Section 18C of the Consumer's Protection Act, 1981.
614. Chapter E1 of the Consumer's Protection Act, 1981.
615. Chapter F of the Consumer's Protection Act, 1981.

Chapter 7. Network Services

93. In general, network service is a capability that facilitates a network operation. It is typically provided by a server (which can be running one or more services), based on network protocols running at the application layer in the open systems interconnection (OSI) model of the network. Some examples are DNS, DHCP, and VoIP.

As defined by Network Functions Virtualization (NFV) ETSI (European Telecommunications Standards Institute) industry specification group (ISG) in the NFV, Terminology for Main Concepts in NFV, a network service is a composition of network functions and defined by its functional and behavioural specification. E-mail, printing, and distributed (network) file system services are common services on local area networks (LAN). They require users to have permissions to access the shared resources.

The network service contributes to the behaviour of the higher layer service, which is characterized by at least performance, dependability, and security specifications. The end-to-end network service behaviour is the result of the combination of the individual network function behaviours as well as the behaviour of the network infrastructure composition mechanism. Network services contracts are basically services contracts, which are specified to certain types of services.

In most large organizations in Israel (e.g., companies, universities, and government units) most of the immediate network services are supplied internally by an IT department within the organization. However, not *all* network services are supplied internally, and some services are supplied to the IT department (in favour of the whole organization) externally by a network services provider outside the organization.

§1. General Legal Framework and the Applicable Law

94. There are three basic layers of the law relating to network services contracts. The first layer is the general law of contracts, the second layer is the consumption law, and the third layer is the ICT law. The interpretation rule between these layers is *lex specialis derogat generali*. Therefore, legal provisions from ICT law derogate legal provisions from consumption law, which derogate legal provisions from the general law of contracts.

However, most issues in network services contracts are covered by the general law of contracts. The common network services contracts are between service providers and consumers (e.g., purchasing network services for a certain period, and they include e-mail and printing services), and Israeli law prefers to classify these contracts as consumption contracts rather than contracts regarding technology. As a result, certain legal duties are imposed on the service providers regardless of the type of service. Only in rare types of network services contracts, the law dictates specific relevant legal arrangements.

Network services contracts are subject to the Israeli conflict of laws rules, and in particular to the rules of choice-of-law in contracts. The general rule in Israel is that the law which governs the network services contract is the law that both parties agreed on, explicitly or implicitly. If both parties are Israelis, the more comfortable option is, in general, to agree on Israeli law. Nevertheless, if no such law has been agreed on, the applicable law is the law which has the closest and most real connection to the contract.[616] Particular rules of choice-of-law in contracts are deduced from the English Common Law through case laws.

Network services, of course, are considered 'services'; therefore, if no specific law has been agreed on within the network services contract, the applicable law (i.e., the law which has the closest and most real connection to the contract) is the law governing the domicile of the services provider.[617] Nevertheless, if the particular network services contract may be considered as consumption contract (e.g., when a customer purchases network services for home use or for the organization), even though the network services are still 'services', the applicable law on that contract may be different.

Network services contracts which are classified as consumption contracts are governed by the law that both parties agreed on, explicitly or implicitly, unless it deprives the consumer of rights granted by the alternative law (i.e., the applicable law that should have governed the contract without the parties' agreement). If no such law has been agreed on, or if the agreed law deprives the consumer of granted rights, the applicable law is the law which has the closest and most real connection to the contract. In general, this is the law that governs the consumer's domicile, unless another law has a closer and more real connection to the contract.[618]

This situation may cause some ambiguity. Consequently, most written network services contracts include a choice-of-law clause in which defines in particular the applicable law of the contract. This clause is generally accompanied by an exclusive jurisdiction clause (i.e., a clause which grants the Israeli court an exclusive jurisdiction over any lawsuit regarding the contract). Nevertheless, the agreed law is not applicable if its content is contradicted to the Israeli public policy or to the Israeli criminal law (e.g., a contract that permit an action which is considered a criminal offence in Israel, but according to the foreign law, which has been defined as the applicable law, it is not forbidden).

§2. Substantive Legal Provisions under Israeli Law

95. If the network services contract's applicable law is Israeli law, the general law of contracts is the basic layer that governs the network services contract. The Israeli general law of contracts is highly inspired by the German law of contracts. Any network services contract is considered formed, and its existence is inferred, if

616. Gabriel Hallevy, *Theory of the Conflict of Laws* vol. I 478–493 (Bursi Publishing House 2014); Civ. App. 165/60 *Onion Ltd. v. Moshe,* 17 PD 646 (1963); Civ. App. 352/87 *Greifin Corp. v. Cur Ltd.*, 44(3) PD 45 (1990).
617. Hallevy, *ibid.,* at pp. 561–570.
618. *Ibid.*, at pp. 589–595.

both factual element and mental element requirements are fulfilled. The factual element is expressed by an offer and an acceptance.[619] The acceptance may be by writing, orally (*viva voce*), or through consenting behaviour.[620]

The mental element requirement is expressed by awareness of the parties to the major terms of the contract and by an intention to create legal relations through the particular contract.[621] The negotiations between the parties prior to the agreement and the formation of the contract are subject to a wide bona fide requirement.[622] The bona fide requirement may, if not fulfilled, result in invalidation of the contract, even though all other formal requirements have been fulfilled. However, if both factual element and mental element requirements are fulfilled, the contract is allegedly considered formed.

Consideration, however, under Israeli law is not required. Gifts and presents given for free with no charge are considered valid contracts.[623] Thus, free-of-charge network services contracts are considered a valid contract under Israeli law. For example, if the services grant the availability of the network services for an unlimited period, and after two months the network services are not available anymore, the customer is granted a remedy, if damages were caused by that change. Free-of-charge network services do not reduce the services provider liability under Israeli contracts law.

Certain types of disorders, which indirectly may be related to the mental element of both parties of the contract, might result in invalidation of the contract. Some types make the contract become voidable (i.e., the court is required to declare that the contract is void), and other types automatically make the contract become void. Fictive contracts are, of course, void.[624]

Contracts may also be void on grounds of public policy or illegality (in contrast with the criminal law).[625] Thus, if the relevant network services are forbidden for use in Israel by the criminal law (e.g., supplying network services to an illegal business which are required for money laundering), the network services contract is void through Israeli law of complicity. Nevertheless, contracts which have been formed due to mistakes, misrepresentation, duress or threat, are voidable.[626] If the contract is void, a statement of cancellation of the contract by one of the parties, at least, is required.[627]

Form requirements of the contract are, in general, not required by the law, and the parties have wide discretion towards it, unless a particular legal provision imposes specific form requirements.[628] Moreover, in certain cases, the court preferred to validate contracts, although the form requirements were not fulfilled, if its

619. Section 1 of the Contracts (General Part) Act, 1973.
620. Section 6 of the Contracts (General Part) Act, 1973.
621. Section 2 of the Contracts (General Part) Act, 1973.
622. Section 12 of the Contracts (General Part) Act, 1973.
623. The Gifts Act, 1968.
624. Section 13 of the Contracts (General Part) Act, 1973.
625. Section 30 of the Contracts (General Part) Act, 1973.
626. Sections 14–15 and 1718 of the Contracts (General Part) Act, 1973.
627. Section 20 of the Contracts (General Part) Act, 1973.
628. Section 23 of the Contracts (General Part) Act, 1973.

validation is coherent with bona fide.[629] Performance of the contract (i.e., supply the services according to the contract's terms) may be in favour of the parties or in favour of a third party.[630] However, any network services contract must be performed under wide requirement of bona fide.[631]

In cases of breach of network services contract, either by the services provider or the customer, the court is authorized to impose on the violator a duty to perform the contract (specific performance or enforcement), unless the contract is not operative anymore, the specific performance involves *personal* service (i.e., the specific network services must be supplied by a particular person), the specific performance requires unreasonable inspection by the court or the specific performance is unjust.[632] Thus, the primary remedy for breach of network services contracts is specific performance. Consequently, if the customer has purchased the network services and they were not supplied, the preferred remedy is to order the services provider to supply the network services.

Only if specific performance is inapplicable, the court may impose other remedies. One of these remedies is the cancellation of the contract together with restoration of resources (i.e., each party returns the other party any resources given prior to the breach, e.g., advances).[633] However, the common remedy is damages. The plaintiff is granted damages for the loss caused by the breach, and in some cases, even without proving any loss.[634] Nevertheless, if the breach was caused by force major, the plaintiff is discharged, as the doctrine of frustration has been accepted in Israel.[635]

Most network services contracts in Israel are between services providers and consumers; therefore, they are subject to consumption law as well. Under Israeli consumption law, the general rule of *caveat emptor* is invalid or, at least, minimized. This attitude is expressed by imposition of wide duties on the services provider in favour of the consumer. Many of these duties are enforced through criminal law. The most significant duties are the full disclosure and due diligence duties.

Accordingly, any act or omission of any services provider is forbidden, if it *might* cause misrepresentation or mistake.[636] That includes the duty to let the consumer the full information on the network services, the service regarding it (e.g., how to contact the help desk of the services provider), the time of supplying the services, all relevant terms, the price and calculations of the price, the terms for cancellation, etc. It is forbidden for the services provider to limit the consumer's liberty to contact (or, more important, *not* to contact) with the services provider.[637] The services provider must disclose any possible limitation in the network services that

629. *See, e.g.*, Civ. App. 986/93 *Klemer v. Guy,* 50(1) PD 185 (1996).
630. Sections 34–38 of the Contracts (General Part) Act, 1973.
631. Section 39 of the Contracts (General Part) Act, 1973.
632. Section 3 of the Contracts (Remedies for Breach of Contract) Act, 1970.
633. Sections 6–9 of the Contracts (Remedies for Breach of Contract) Act, 1970.
634. Sections 10–11 of the Contracts (Remedies for Breach of Contract) Act, 1970.
635. Section 18 of the Contracts (Remedies for Breach of Contract) Act, 1970.
636. Section 2 of the Consumer's Protection Act, 1981.
637. Section 3 of the Consumer's Protection Act, 1981.

may defect its performances, including its incompatibility to certain devices, to certain manufacturers, to certain operating systems, or to certain software in common use.[638]

If the network services are not professional or insufficient for the consumer's needs, the consumer has an unconditional right to cancel the network services and get back the money paid or be rewarded with other services instead, by the consumer's choice, within fourteen days from the consumer's announcement to the services provider.[639] If the network services are not insufficient and they are professional, the consumer has the right to cancel them, for any reason, within seven days, unless the network services were designed according to specific and unusual order of the consumer.[640]

Any network services contract must include clear and specific clauses on the warranty conditions, the service towards the network services, and the relevant periods of warranty and service.[641] If the service requires a technician, the technician's visit would be appointed between 08.00 and 19.00 on Sunday until Thursday or between 08.00 and 13.00 on Friday. Waiting for a technician would not last more than two hours. A compensation of NIS 300 (approximately EUR 75) is granted for waiting beyond two hours, and of NIS 600 (approximately EUR 150) for waiting beyond three hours.[642]

Free-of-charge customer service must be granted by the services provider in any network services contract.[643] The customer service agent must be identified at the beginning of the call by name, and the call would be from a line that may be reconnected by the customer easily by redialling.[644]

Enforcement of the consumption law provisions is under the responsibility of the Consumer's Protection Authority. This authority is authorized to enforce the law using administrative measures, and in particular through administrative fines of up to NIS 45,000 (approximately EUR 11,000).[645] In addition, infringement of the consumption law may be considered a criminal offence of up to three years imprisonment, confiscation of the network services media or measures, if any, and fines of up to NIS 4.5 million (approximately EUR 1.1 million).[646]

All network services corporations in Israel are required to supply customer services in order to ensure proper use and availability of its network services.[647] These customer services include services acting 24/7 (24 hours a day, 7 days a week),

638. Section 4 of the Consumer's Protection Act, 1981.
639. Section 14E of the Consumer's Protection Act, 1981.
640. Section 4C(d) of the Consumer's Protection Act, 1981.
641. Section 18A of the Consumer's Protection Act, 1981.
642. *Ibid.*
643. Section 18B of the Consumer's Protection Act, 1981.
644. Section 18C of the Consumer's Protection Act, 1981.
645. Chapter E1 of the Consumer's Protection Act, 1981.
646. Chapter F of the Consumer's Protection Act, 1981.
647. Regulation 6 of the Intercommunications Services (Installation, Management and Maintenance) Regulations, 1985.

responsibility to fix any damage in infrastructure or devices supplied by the corporation within certain time (different maximum time periods were determined for different types of services) and responsibility to inform the consumer within 2 working days that the damage cannot be fixed.

Chapter 8. Government Contracts

96. Government contracts, not necessarily in the ICT area, are agreements between any person and the government. In most of these agreements, the government functions as the client, whereas in some agreements, the government is the supplier of the products or the services. In the ICT area, in most government contracts, the government indeed functions as the client, and the counterparty functions as the service or product supplier. In other government contracts in the ICT area, the government generally functions as the licensor, and the counterparty functions as the licensee who purchases the license through that government contract.

§1. General Legal Framework: Contract Law Versus Administrative Law

97. The common legal perspective in Israel on government contracts is that these are hybrid institutions. On one hand, government contracts function as 'contracts'; therefore, the law of contracts is applicable to them. On the other hand, government contracts function as government act; therefore, the Israeli administrative law is applicable to them as well. If the law of contracts and the administrative law were identical in this context, no legal problem would have occurred. But, Israeli law of contracts and the Israeli administrative law are very different on this point.

The inevitable question is, of course, what is the applicable law on government contracts in those points where Israeli law of contracts is different than the Israeli administrative law. Most of the Israeli administrative law has not been enacted, but declared by the courts through judicial review of the government. Thus, most of the Israeli administrative law is actually case law.

In general, the administrative law includes wide duties imposed on the government, and consequently, the government's liberty to take actions is reduced. The government actions are restricted to legal and reasonable actions, otherwise they are invalid. For example, the government has no liberty in contracts to discriminate potential parties.[648] Although, today in Israel, discrimination by private business that services the public is not allowed as well, for the government, this prohibition is absolute. It generally requires a bid, prior to the contract, to adhere this prohibition.[649]

Nevertheless, administrative law may also grant a few liberties to the government within any contract. One of the most significant liberties granted to the government, and only to the government, in any contractual transaction is the liberty of breach of the contract whenever the public's good justifies.[650] This liberty is weaker than the *act of state* doctrine,[651] but it is still significant within contractual relations.

648. HCJ 262/62 *Perez v. Kfar Shmariahu*, 16 PD 2101 (1962).
649. HCJ 632/81 *Migda v. Minister of Health*, 36(2) PD 673 (1982).
650. HCJ 311/60 *Miller v. Minister of Transportation*, 15 PD 1989 (1961).
651. For the doctrine of *act of state* in Israel *see* Gabriel Hallevy, *Theory of the Conflict of Laws* vol. II 194–200 (Bursi Publishing House 2014).

The 'public's good' is a very vague term, and it grants the government and the court a wide discretion of interpretation. The private party of the contract has no such liberty.

However, administrative law does not include legal provisions which regulate contractual issues. Therefore, as aforesaid, the inevitable question is the question of the applicable law on government contracts in Israel. The common legal interpretation is that the general law governing government contracts is the law of contracts, whereas the administrative law is the specific law. Whenever there is a conflict of laws between the law of contracts and the administrative law, the administrative law provisions derogate the contracts' law provisions due to the interpretation principle of *lex specialis derogat generali.*[652]

Since the 1990s, the Israeli court used norms originated in the administrative law within the interpretation of contracts, regardless of the identity of the parties. Thus, even if it is not a government contract, a few norms from the administrative law have been applied. One of the most common norms that has been applied this way was the norm of reasonability.[653] Fairness has also been applied within the interpretation of private contracts. Consequently, the difference in interpretation of government contracts and private contracts is gradually decreased by the court.

§2. The Applicable Law under Israeli Conflict of Laws Rules

98. Regardless of the question of the applicability of administrative law within government contracts, the question of the conflict of laws still remains. Israeli law is not necessarily the applicable law in government contracts, especially when the counterpart is not Israeli. Government contracts are subject to the Israeli conflict of laws rules, and in particular, to the rules of choice-of-law in contracts. Thus, according to the Israeli rules of the conflict of laws, government contracts are classified as related to the legal sphere of 'contracts'.

The general conflict of laws rule in Israel is that the law which governs government contracts is the law that both parties agreed on, explicitly or implicitly. If no such law has been agreed on, the applicable law is the law which has the closest and most real connection to the contract.[654] Particular rules of choice-of-law in a contract are deduced from the English Common Law through case laws.

As aforesaid, in the ICT area, in most government contracts, the government functions as the client, and the counterparty functions as the service or product supplier. Thus, if the particular government contract may be considered as a consumption contract (e.g., when the government purchases technological service for a

---

652. *See, e.g.*, Gabriela Shalev, *Government Contracts: The Law and the Judge*, 11 Iyunei Mishpat 201 (1986). For the implementation of this principle in government contracts *see, e.g.*, Civ. App. 219/15 *Shkurei v. Hod Hasharon* (23 May 2016); Civ. App. 3313/13 *Nagar v. Rosh Haayin* (22 Nov. 2015); Civ. App. 7502/13 *Roded v. Eilat* (3 Jun. 2015).

653. *See, e.g.*, Civ. App. 9648/16 *Or-high-tech GIS v. Avitan Adv.* (28 Feb. 2018); Civ. App. 7728/14 *Avidor v. Netivei Israel* (11 Jul. 2016); Civ. App. 1691/11 *Leumi Bank v. Zuberi* (15 Dec. 2015).

654. Gabriel Hallevy, *Theory of the Conflict of Laws* vol. I 478–493 (Bursi Publishing House 2014); Civ. App. 165/60 *Onion Ltd. v. Moshe,* 17 PD 646 (1963); Civ. App. 352/87 *Greifin Corp. v. Cur Ltd.*, 44(3) PD 45 (1990).

certain period or technological equipment from a private supplier), the applicable law on that government contract may be different.

Government contracts which are classified as consumption contracts are governed by the law that both parties agreed on, explicitly or implicitly, unless it deprives the consumer of rights granted by the alternative law (i.e., the applicable law that should have governed the contract without the parties' agreement). This rule applies whether one of the parties is the government or not. If no such law has been agreed on, or if the agreed law deprives the consumer of granted rights, the applicable law is the law which has the closest and most real connection to the contract. In general, this is the law that governs the consumer's domicile, unless another law has a closer and more real connection to the contract.[655]

This situation may cause some ambiguity. Consequently, most government contracts include a choice-of-law clause which defines in particular the applicable law of the contract. This clause is generally accompanied by an exclusive jurisdiction clause (i.e., a clause which grants the Israeli court an exclusive jurisdiction over any lawsuit regarding the contract). Nevertheless, the agreed law is not applicable if its content is contradicted to the Israeli public policy or to the Israeli criminal law (e.g., a contract that permits an action which is considered criminal offence in Israel, but according to the foreign law, which has been defined as the applicable law, it is not forbidden).

Nevertheless, in some government contracts in the ICT area, the government generally functions as the licensor, and the counterparty functions as the licensee who purchases the license through that government contract. This kind of contracts is generally not classified as consumption contracts, but rather government acts using the government executive power within the ICT area. However, at any ICT license, there are some contractual aspects (e.g., the licensee is required to operate some services in a certain quality, otherwise the license is invalid). On these aspects, the law of contracts applies under the relevant limitations of the administrative law, as discussed above.

§3. Substantive Legal Provisions under Israeli Law

99. If the applicable law of the particular government contract is Israeli law, the general law of contracts is the basic layer that governs the government contract, under several limitations from the Israeli administrative law. The Israeli general law of contracts is highly inspired by the German law of contracts, but the Israeli administrative law is highly inspired by the English law. Any government contract is considered formed, and its existence is inferred, if both factual element and mental element requirements are fulfilled. If a bid preceded the contract, it is not part of the contract, unless explicitly determined otherwise in the contract.

The factual element is expressed by an offer and an acceptance.[656] The acceptance may be by writing, orally (*viva voce*), or through consenting behaviour.[657] The

655. Hallevy, *ibid.*, at pp. 589–595.
656. Section 1 of the Contracts (General Part) Act, 1973.
657. Section 6 of the Contracts (General Part) Act, 1973.

mental element requirement is expressed by awareness of the parties to the major terms of the contract and by an intention to create legal relations through the particular contract.[658] The negotiations between the parties prior to the agreement (whether through a bid or not) and the formation of the contract are subject to a wide bona fide requirement.[659] The bona fide requirement may, if not fulfilled, result in invalidation of the contract, even though all other formal requirements have been fulfilled. However, if both factual element and mental element requirements are fulfilled, the contract is allegedly considered formed.

Consideration, however, under Israeli law is not required. Gifts and presents given for free with no charge are considered valid contracts.[660] Thus, if the private party voluntarily grants services or products in favour of the government, it is considered a valid contract. In the opposite direction it is more difficult due to the administrative law. If the government grants anything free of charge to a private party, it should be justified under the administrative law. Consequently, it would be extremely rare, and possibly ground for police inquiry of bribery.

Certain types of disorders, which indirectly may be related to the mental element, might result in invalidation of the contract. Some types make the contract become voidable (i.e., the court is required to declare that the contract is void) and other types automatically make the contract become void. Fictive contracts are, of course, void.[661] Contracts may also be void on grounds of public policy or illegality (in contrast with the criminal law).[662] However, in some cases, the government had agreed to grant license to radio operators, even though they admitted in illegal operation of radio channels.[663]

Government contracts which have been formed due to mistakes, misrepresentation, duress or threat, are voidable.[664] If the contract is void, a statement of cancellation of the contract by one of the parties, at least, is required.[665] If the government cancels the contract, the cancellation statement must be published.

Form requirements of the contract are, in general, not required by the law, and the parties have wide discretion towards it, unless a particular legal provision imposes specific form requirements.[666] Moreover, in certain cases, the court preferred to validate the contract, although the form requirements were not fulfilled, if its validation is coherent with bona fide.[667] Performance of the contract may be in favour of the parties or in favour of a third party.[668] In most government contracts in the ICT area, the third party is the public. In some contracts, the services are supplied directly to the government (e.g., network services supplied to a certain ministry).

658. Section 2 of the Contracts (General Part) Act, 1973.
659. Section 12 of the Contracts (General Part) Act, 1973.
660. The Gifts Act, 1968.
661. Section 13 of the Contracts (General Part) Act, 1973.
662. Section 30 of the Contracts (General Part) Act, 1973.
663. *See, e.g.*, HCJ 2754/98 *Channel 7 v. the Ministry of Communications* (5 May 1998).
664. Sections 14–15 and 17–18 of the Contracts (General Part) Act, 1973.
665. Section 20 of the Contracts (General Part) Act, 1973.
666. Section 23 of the Contracts (General Part) Act, 1973.
667. *See, e.g.*, Civ. App. 986/93 *Klemer v. Guy*, 50(1) PD 185 (1996).
668. Sections 34–38 of the Contracts (General Part) Act, 1973.

Any government contract must be performed under wide requirement of bona fide,[669] in addition to the wide duties imposed on the government due to the applicability of administrative law. In cases of breach of a government contract, the court is authorized to impose on the violator a duty to perform the contract (specific performance or enforcement), unless the contract is not operative anymore, the specific performance involves personal service, the specific performance requires unreasonable inspection by the court or the specific performance is unjust.[670] Thus, the primary remedy for breach of government contracts is specific performance.

For example, if a computer with operating system and applications already installed on it was purchased by a governmental unit, but not supplied, the court would prefer to order the merchant to supply that computer to the government, if possible. This rule does not change when the violator is the government unit. If the government's violation of the contract is justified by the administrative law, the government may be exempt from any remedy. Exempt from administrative law applicability includes not only the remedy of specific performance, but all other remedies as well.

If the governmental unit is not exempt, all remedies may be applicable. Only if specific performance is inapplicable, the court may impose other remedies. One of these remedies is the cancellation of the contract together with restoration of resources (i.e., each party returns the other party any resources given prior to the breach, e.g., advances).[671] However, the common remedy is damages. The plaintiff is granted damages for the loss caused by the breach, and in some cases, even without proving any loss.[672] Nevertheless, if the breach was caused by force major, the plaintiff is discharged, as the doctrine of frustration has been accepted in Israel.[673]

As aforesaid, in the ICT area, in most government contracts the government functions as the client and the counterparty functions as the service or product supplier, therefore government contracts may be subject to consumption law as well as contracts law and administrative law. Under Israeli consumption law, the general rule of *caveat emptor* is invalid or, at least, minimized. This attitude is expressed by imposition of wide duties on the merchant in favour of the consumer. In these contracts, it is immaterial whether the government is the 'merchant' or the 'consumer', in the legal point of view, although in most of these contracts, the government functions as the consumer. Many of these duties are enforced through criminal law, if the violator is the private party, but not if the violator is the government. The most significant duties are the full disclosure and due diligence duties.

Accordingly, any act or omission of any merchant is forbidden, if it *might* cause misrepresentation or mistake.[674] That includes the duty to let the consumer the full information on the services or products, the service regarding it, the time of performance, all relevant terms, the price and calculations of the price, the terms for cancellation, etc. It is forbidden for the merchant to limit the consumer's liberty to

669. Section 39 of the Contracts (General Part) Act, 1973.
670. Section 3 of the Contracts (Remedies for Breach of Contract) Act, 1970.
671. Sections 6–9 of the Contracts (Remedies for Breach of Contract) Act, 1970.
672. Sections 10–11 of the Contracts (Remedies for Breach of Contract) Act, 1970.
673. Section 18 of the Contracts (Remedies for Breach of Contract) Act, 1970.
674. Section 2 of the Consumer's Protection Act, 1981.

contact (or, more important, *not* to contact) with the merchant.[675] The merchant must disclose any possible damage in the supplied services or products that may defect its performance.[676]

If the supplied product is defective, the government has an unconditional right to return it to the merchant and get back the money paid or another product instead, by the government's choice, within fourteen days from the government's announcement to the merchant.[677] If the product is not defective, the government has the right to return it to the merchant, for any reason, within seven days, unless the product was opened from its original pack or it was designed according to specific and unusual order of the government.[678]

If the product is a mobile telephone that an operating system is installed in it or any other device which includes an active operating system, but it radiates non-ionizing radiation (e.g., government contract in favour of the workers within the civil service), the merchant must inform the costumer on the rate of radiation (SAR) using 5cm x 5cm label on the device's pack and using clear brochure in Hebrew, Arabic and Russian regarding the SAR.[679] The brochure must also include information on the maximum permitted rate of radiation according to both the European and American standards and the Israeli Standard.

Free-of-charge customer service must be granted by the merchant in any government contract.[680] The customer service agent must be identified at the beginning of the call by name, and the call would be from a line that may be reconnected by the customer easily by redialling.[681]

675. Section 3 of the Consumer's Protection Act, 1981.
676. Section 4 of the Consumer's Protection Act, 1981.
677. Section 14E of the Consumer's Protection Act, 1981.
678. Section 4C(d) of the Consumer's Protection Act, 1981.
679. Regulations 1–3 of the Consumer's Protection (Information Regarding Non-Ionizing Radiation From Mobile Devices) Regulations, 2002.
680. Section 18B of the Consumer's Protection Act, 1981.
681. Section 18C of the Consumer's Protection Act, 1981.

Part IV. Electronic Transactions

Chapter 1. Legal Status of Electronic Transactions

100. Under Israeli law, electronic transactions function substantively as if they were any other type of transactions. The Israeli legislator was not convinced that there was a necessity to regulate electronic transactions through a particular substantive statute. The major difference between electronic transactions and other transactions is in questions of form and not in questions of substance. Nevertheless, form issues in electronic transactions were regulated in particular. The general legal framework, the applicable law and particular legal provisions regulating electronic transactions are discussed below.

§1. General Legal Framework and the Applicable Law

101. Electronic transactions have two basic legal aspects. One aspect is the contractual aspect and the other is the property aspect. Any electronic transaction is presumed to reflect an agreement between the parties. The agreement is achieved regardless the form, whether electronic or not. This is the contractual aspect of the transaction, and it is governed by the law of contracts. However, the transaction relates certain objects or services, and the completion of the transaction is dependent on any change in the property rights of these objects or on the full performance of the services. This is the property aspect of the transaction, and it is governed by the property law.

Nevertheless, the property aspect of electronic transactions is identical to the property aspect of any other transaction. For example, if the consumer orders a movable object via the Internet, in most cases, under Israeli law, the property rights within this object would be the consumer's after having physical possession over the object. But acquiring the physical possession over the object has nothing to do with the electronic form of the transaction. This property legal rule is identical in any other type of transactions, including physical purchase from a physical store.

Consequently, the property aspect is immaterial to the regulation of electronic transactions, and the contractual aspect may be the more significant legal aspect of electronic transactions. Nevertheless, the property aspect may affect, indirectly, the applicable law governing the electronic transaction. There are three basic layers of the law relating to electronic transactions. The first layer is the general law of contracts, the second layer is the consumption law, and the third layer is the ICT law.

The interpretation rule between these layers is *lex specialis derogat generali*. Therefore, legal provisions from ICT law derogate legal provisions from consumption law, which derogate legal provisions from the general law of contracts.

However, most issues in electronic transactions are covered by the general law of contracts. The common electronic transactions are between merchants and consumers (e.g., purchasing a laptop from a virtual store on the web), and Israeli law prefers to classify these contracts as consumption contracts rather than contracts regarding technology. As a result, certain legal duties are imposed on the merchants regardless of the form of contract or transaction. Only in rare types of electronic transactions, the law dictates specific relevant legal arrangements.

Electronic transactions are subject to the Israeli conflict of laws rules, and in particular to the rules of choice-of-law in contracts. The general rule in Israel is that the law which governs the electronic transaction is the law that both parties agreed on, explicitly or implicitly. If no such law has been agreed on, the applicable law is the law which has the closest and most real connection to the contract.[682] Particular rules of choice-of-law in contracts are deduced from the English Common Law through case laws.

The object of the electronic transaction may be a movable object, immovable object, intellectual property rights or services. If the object is a movable object, then if no specific law has been agreed on within the electronic transaction, the applicable law (i.e., the law which has the closest and most real connection to the contract) is the law governing the domicile of the person who sold the object.[683]

If the object is an immovable object, then if no specific law has been agreed on within the electronic transaction, the applicable law is the law governing the place where the object is situated (*lex situs*).[684] If the object is intellectual property rights (e.g., license for a downloaded software), then if no specific law has been agreed on within the electronic transaction, the applicable law is the law governing the place where the intellectual property rights are protected (*lex loci protectionis*).[685] If the object is services, then if no specific law has been agreed on within the electronic transaction, the applicable law is the law governing the domicile of the services provider.[686]

Nevertheless, if the particular electronic transaction may be considered as consumption contract (e.g., purchasing a laptop from a virtual store on the web), even though the object is a movable object, immovable object, intellectual property rights or services, the applicable law on that contract may be different.

Electronic transactions which are classified as consumption contracts are governed by the law that both parties agreed on, explicitly or implicitly, unless it deprives the consumer of rights granted by the alternative law (i.e., the applicable law that should have governed the contract without the parties' agreement). If no

682. Gabriel Hallevy, *Theory of the Conflict of Laws* vol. I 478–493 (Bursi Publishing House 2014); Civ. App. 165/60 *Onion Ltd. v. Moshe*, 17 PD 646 (1963); Civ. App. 352/87 *Greifin Corp. v. Cur Ltd.*, 44(3) PD 45 (1990).

683. Hallevy, *ibid.*, at pp. 549–552.

684. *Ibid.*, at pp. 555–558.

685. Gabriel Hallevy, *Theory of the Conflict of Laws* vol. II 328–333 (Bursi Publishing House 2014); HCJ 90/70 *Bacardi Ltd. v. The Patents' Registrar*, 25(2) PD 89 (1971).

686. Gabriel Hallevy, *Theory of the Conflict of Laws* vol. I 561–570 (Bursi Publishing House 2014).

such law has been agreed on, or if the agreed law deprives the consumer of granted rights, the applicable law is the law which has the closest and most real connection to the contract. In general, this is the law that governs the consumer's domicile, unless another law has a closer and more real connection to the contract.[687]

This situation may cause some ambiguity. Consequently, most written electronic transactions include a choice-of-law clause which defines in particular the applicable law of the contract. This clause is generally accompanied by an exclusive jurisdiction clause (i.e., a clause which grants the Israeli court an exclusive jurisdiction over any lawsuit regarding the contract). Nevertheless, the agreed law is not applicable if its content is contradicted to the Israeli public policy or to the Israeli criminal law (e.g., a contract that permits an action which is considered a criminal offence in Israel, but according to the foreign law, which has been defined as the applicable law, it is not forbidden).

§2. Particular Legal Provisions Regulating Electronic Transactions

102. Most electronic transactions may be characterized as consumption transactions, and the general law governing consumption transactions contains particular legal provisions regulating electronic transactions. These provisions impose certain duties on the merchant who offers the transaction within an electronic platform, namely the merchant's website. The electronic platforms are related to a wider set of platforms, in which are named as transaction of 'marketing by far'. These platforms are contradicted with face-to-face transactions.

However, 'marketing by far' transactions include not only electronic transactions, but also phone-transactions (i.e., marketing through the telephone), facsimile-transactions, postal-mail transactions, and so on. The definition of 'marketing by far' transaction is any transaction when not all of the parties are physically present at the transaction.[688] That includes electronic transactions, but some other types of transactions as well. Consequently, electronic transactions are regulated identically as all other 'marketing by far' transactions are regulated.

Accordingly, within an electronic transaction the merchant has the duty to disclose, prior to the final agreement with the consumer, the name, address, and ID number of the merchant in Israel and outside Israel,[689] the main quality characteristics of the products or services offered within that transaction,[690] the price and the payment conditions,[691] the time and way of supply (e.g., via postal mail),[692] the

687. *Ibid.*, at pp. 589–595.
688. Section 14C(f) of the Consumer's Protection Act, 1981.
689. Section 14C(a)(1) of the Consumer's Protection Act, 1981.
690. Section 14C(a)(2) of the Consumer's Protection Act, 1981.
691. Section 14C(a)(3) of the Consumer's Protection Act, 1981.
692. Section 14C(a)(4) of the Consumer's Protection Act, 1981.

period that the offer would be valid,[693] the warranty details,[694] and necessary details on the consumer's rights to cancel the transaction.[695] These details should be disclosed within the merchant's website.

After the transaction is formed, the merchant has the duty to supply the consumer, in writing, and no later than the date of the products' or services' supply, a statement that includes the name, address, and ID number of the merchant in Israel and outside Israel and the main quality characteristics of the products or services offered within that transaction,[696] the price and the final payment terms,[697] the necessary details on the consumer's rights to cancel the transaction,[698] the manufacturer's name and country,[699] the warranty details,[700] and any other terms which are relevant to the particular electronic transaction.[701]

In electronic transactions, the consumer has the right to cancel the transaction, if the transaction's object is a product, within fourteen days from the day the product has been physically accepted by the consumer or from the day of the above-written statement, by the latest of them.[702] If the transaction's object is a service, the consumer has the right to cancel the transaction within fourteen days from the day the transaction has been made or from the day of the above-written statement, by the latest of them.[703] It is insignificant if the service has already begun, if the transaction is continuous.

Nevertheless, the consumer has no right to cancel the electronic transaction if the products are expendable (e.g., fresh fruits),[704] if the products are designed especially for the consumer,[705] if the products are electronic media in which the consumer has already opened their pack,[706] if the product is mere information,[707] or if it is service relating to tourism or entertainment and the cancellation date has expired within seven working days prior to the supply of that service.[708]

If the consumer is a person with disabilities, a person aged 65 years or older, or a new immigrant (up to five years in Israel), the consumer has the right to cancel the electronic transaction within four months from the day the product has been physically accepted by the consumer, from the day of the above-written statement,

693. Section 14C(a)(5) of the Consumer's Protection Act, 1981.
694. Section 14C(a)(6) of the Consumer's Protection Act, 1981.
695. Section 14C(a)(7) of the Consumer's Protection Act, 1981.
696. Section 14C(b)(1) of the Consumer's Protection Act, 1981.
697. Section 14C(b)(2) of the Consumer's Protection Act, 1981.
698. Section 14C(b)(3) of the Consumer's Protection Act, 1981.
699. Section 14C(b)(4) of the Consumer's Protection Act, 1981.
700. Section 14C(b)(5) of the Consumer's Protection Act, 1981.
701. Section 14C(b)(6) of the Consumer's Protection Act, 1981.
702. Section 14C(c)(1) of the Consumer's Protection Act, 1981.
703. Section 14C(c)(2) of the Consumer's Protection Act, 1981.
704. Section 14C(d)(1) of the Consumer's Protection Act, 1981.
705. Section 14C(d)(4) of the Consumer's Protection Act, 1981.
706. Section 14C(d)(5) of the Consumer's Protection Act, 1981.
707. Section 14C(d)(3) of the Consumer's Protection Act, 1981.
708. Section 14C(d)(2) of the Consumer's Protection Act, 1981.

or from the day the transaction has been made, by the latest of them.[709] However, the merchant in these cases may demand an official proof for the consumer's above condition.[710]

Nevertheless, in spite of the consumer's condition, the consumer has no right to cancel the electronic transaction if the products are expendable (e.g., fresh fruits),[711] if the products are designed especially for the consumer,[712] if the products are electronic media in which the consumer has already opened their pack,[713] if the product is mere information,[714] or if it is service relating to tourism or entertainment and the cancellation date has expired within seven working days prior to the supply of that service.[715]

If the cancellation of any electronic transaction was due to the merchant's breach of the contract, the merchant has the duty to pay the consumer back any payment that has already been paid, to cancel the transaction, and to cancel any further charge, within fourteen days from the day the consumer's cancellation notification has been accepted.[716] The consumer has the duty to deliver the product to the merchant, including all products that have been given to the consumer due to the transaction, unless they were defined as gifts that are not dependent on the full performance of the transaction.[717]

Nevertheless, if the cancellation was not due to any breach of the contract, the merchant has the right to charge the consumer a cancellation fee of up to 5% of the transaction or NIS 100 (approximately EUR 25), by the lowest of them.[718] However, the merchant has the duty to pay the consumer back any payment that has already been paid, to cancel the transaction, and to cancel any further charge, within fourteen days from the day the consumer's cancellation notification has been accepted.[719] The consumer has the duty to deliver the product to the merchant, including all products that have been given to the consumer due to the transaction, unless they were defined as gifts that are not dependent on the full performance of the transaction.[720]

The consumer in an electronic transaction has the right that the cancellation notification would be possible telephonically, by postal mail, by e-mail, by facsimile, and through the Internet within the merchant's website.[721] For this purpose, the merchant is required to enable within the main page of the website an accessible form of cancellation notification.[722] The merchant is also required to publish within the

709. Section 14C1(c) of the Consumer's Protection Act, 1981.
710. Section 14C1(d) of the Consumer's Protection Act, 1981.
711. Section 14C(d)(1) of the Consumer's Protection Act, 1981.
712. Section 14C(d)(4) of the Consumer's Protection Act, 1981.
713. Section 14C(d)(5) of the Consumer's Protection Act, 1981.
714. Section 14C(d)(3) of the Consumer's Protection Act, 1981.
715. Section 14C(d)(2) of the Consumer's Protection Act, 1981.
716. Section 14E(a)(1) of the Consumer's Protection Act, 1981.
717. Section 14E(a)(2) of the Consumer's Protection Act, 1981.
718. Section 14E(b)(1) of the Consumer's Protection Act, 1981.
719. *Ibid.*
720. Section 14E(b)(2) of the Consumer's Protection Act, 1981.
721. Section 14I(a) of the Consumer's Protection Act, 1981.
722. Section 14I(b) of the Consumer's Protection Act, 1981.

main page of the website the above ways to communicate for the purpose of delivering a cancellation notification.[723] The consumer is required to include all details necessary to identify the transaction, including the consumer's name.[724]

In any other issue relating to the electronic transaction, the general law of contracts and the consumer's protection law apply. In general, any electronic transaction is considered formed, and its existence is inferred, if both factual element and mental element requirements are fulfilled. The factual element is expressed by an offer and an acceptance.[725] The acceptance may be by typing or clicking on the required buttons within the website, where the offer has been offered.[726]

The mental element requirement is expressed by awareness of the parties to the major terms of the transaction and by an intention to create legal relations through the particular transaction.[727] Consideration, however, under Israeli law is not required. Gifts and presents given for free with no charge are considered valid transactions.[728] Certain types of disorders, which indirectly may be related to the mental element, might result in invalidation of the transaction. Some types make the transaction become voidable (i.e., the court is required to declare that the transaction is void), and other types automatically make the transaction become void. Fictive transactions are, of course, void.[729]

Transactions may also be void on grounds of public policy or illegality (in contrast with the criminal law).[730] Thus, if the relevant product is forbidden in Israel by the criminal law, the electronic transaction is void. Nevertheless, transactions which have been formed due to mistakes, misrepresentation, duress or threat, are voidable.[731] If the transaction is void, a statement of cancellation of the transaction by one of the parties, at least, is required.[732] Performance of the transaction may be in favour of the parties or in favour of a third party.[733]

In cases of breach of electronic transaction, the court is authorized to impose on the violator a duty to perform the transaction (specific performance or enforcement), unless the transaction is not operative anymore, the specific performance involves personal service, the specific performance requires unreasonable inspection by the court or the specific performance is unjust.[734] Thus, the primary remedy for breach of electronic transactions is specific performance.

Only if specific performance is inapplicable, the court may impose other remedies. One of these remedies is the cancellation of the transaction together with restoration of resources (i.e., each party returns the other party any resources given prior to the breach, e.g., advances).[735] However, the common remedy is damages.

723. Section 14I(e)(2) of the Consumer's Protection Act, 1981.
724. Section 14I(c) of the Consumer's Protection Act, 1981.
725. Section 1 of the Contracts (General Part) Act, 1973.
726. Section 6 of the Contracts (General Part) Act, 1973.
727. Section 2 of the Contracts (General Part) Act, 1973.
728. The Gifts Act, 1968.
729. Section 13 of the Contracts (General Part) Act, 1973.
730. Section 30 of the Contracts (General Part) Act, 1973.
731. Sections 14–15 and 17–18 of the Contracts (General Part) Act, 1973.
732. Section 20 of the Contracts (General Part) Act, 1973.
733. Sections 34–38 of the Contracts (General Part) Act, 1973.
734. Section 3 of the Contracts (Remedies for Breach of Contract) Act, 1970.
735. Sections 6–9 of the Contracts (Remedies for Breach of Contract) Act, 1970.

The plaintiff is granted damages for the loss caused by the breach, and in some cases, even without proving any loss.[736] Nevertheless, if the breach was caused by force major, the plaintiff is discharged, as the doctrine of frustration has been accepted in Israel.[737]

As aforesaid, most electronic transactions in Israel are between merchants and consumers; therefore, they are subject to consumption law as well. Under Israeli consumption law, the general rule of *caveat emptor* is invalid or, at least, minimized. This attitude is expressed by imposition of wide duties on the merchant in favour of the consumer. Many of these duties are enforced through criminal law. The most significant duties are the full disclosure and due diligence duties.

Accordingly, any act or omission of any merchant is forbidden, if it *might* cause misrepresentation or mistake.[738] That includes the duty to let the consumer the full information on the product, the service regarding it, the time of performance, all relevant terms, the price and calculations of the price, the terms for cancellation, etc. It is forbidden for the merchant to limit the consumer's liberty to contact (or, more important, *not* to contact) with the merchant.[739] The merchant must disclose any possible damage in the product that may defect its performance.[740]

Free-of-charge customer service must be granted by the merchant in any electronic transaction.[741] The customer service agent must be identified at the beginning of the call by name, and the call would be from a line that may be reconnected by the customer easily by redialling.[742]

Enforcement of the consumption law provisions is under the responsibility of the Consumer's Protection Authority. This authority is authorized to enforce the law using administrative measures, and in particular through administrative fines of up to NIS 45,000 (approximately EUR 11,000).[743] In addition, infringement of the consumption law may be considered a criminal offence of up to three years imprisonment and fines of up to NIS 4.5 million (approximately EUR 1.1 million).[744]

736. Sections 10–11 of the Contracts (Remedies for Breach of Contract) Act, 1970.
737. Section 18 of the Contracts (Remedies for Breach of Contract) Act, 1970.
738. Section 2 of the Consumer's Protection Act, 1981.
739. Section 3 of the Consumer's Protection Act, 1981.
740. Section 4 of the Consumer's Protection Act, 1981.
741. Section 18B of the Consumer's Protection Act, 1981.
742. Section 18C of the Consumer's Protection Act, 1981.
743. Chapter E1 of the Consumer's Protection Act, 1981.
744. Chapter F of the Consumer's Protection Act, 1981.

Chapter 2. Regulation of Electronic Signatures and Certification Services

103. As electronic commerce and electronic transaction became popular, there emerged the necessity to adapt the requirement of signature from several legal areas (e.g., the law of evidence) to the electronic realm. Consequently, in 2001, the Electronic Signature Act was enacted in Israel. This statute relates both to electronic signature as a new type of signature and to certification services related to it. A law reform on this issue took place in 2018 in order to adapt the Israeli standards to both European and American standards. The validity of electronic signature as a new type of signature and the certification services related to it are discussed below.

§1. Validity of Electronic Signature

104. The legal definition of electronic signature is based on the definition of signature due to Israeli law of evidence. Accordingly, a signature is any sign that links the document with a certain person.[745] An electronic signature is defined as a signature, which is an electronic information or sign, that is attached or linked to any electronic message.[746] The electronic signature itself is not software, but electronic information or electronic sign(s), although the signature may be produced using a typical software.

There are two particular types of electronic signatures that may be accepted under Israeli law. The first type is the *secured electronic signature*. This type of electronic signature requires the fulfilment of four conditions. It should be unique to the signing person, it enables identification of the signing person, it is produced using a measure that is solely controlled by the signing person, and it enables to track any change made in the electronic message *after* being signed electronically.[747]

The second type of electronic signature is the *certified electronic signature*. The certified electronic signature is a secured electronic signature that has been certified by a certifying agent.[748] The certification is towards the measure that produces the electronic signature is actually controlled by the person who seems to be signing on the electronic message.

In general, under Israeli law, no signature is required on any document, unless specifically required by the law.[749] The law requires signature in particular cases where legal responsibility behind the document is required (e.g., bank cheques, certain types of contracts, promissory notes, or lawsuit statements). Accordingly, if the law requires signed document, an electronic signature may fulfil this requirement if

745. For the signature, the seal and the electronic signature under the Israeli law of evidence *see* Gabriel Hallevy, *Theory of the Law of Evidence* vol. III 464–470 (Bursi Publishing House 2013).
746. *See* the definition of the term 'electronic signature' in s. 1 of the Electronic Signature Act, 2001.
747. *See* the definition of the term 'secured electronic signature' in s. 1 of the Electronic Signature Act, 2001.
748. *See* the definition of the term 'certified electronic signature' in s. 1 of the Electronic Signature Act, 2001.
749. *See, e.g.*, Civ. App. 8837/05 *Marshud v. El Shorti* (11 Jan. 2009); Civ. App. Req. 5446/07 *Yahav v. Clal Ltd.* (23 Aug. 2007); Civ. App. Req. 4525/07 *Brill v. Moran Ltd.* (22 Nov. 2007).

the electronic signature is a *certified* electronic signature.[750] Nevertheless, if the electronic signature is not certified, but it fulfils the purposes of the particular law requiring signature (i.e., the signature fulfils the purpose of the particular signature's requirement), it may suffice.[751]

Wills under Israeli succession law require signatures of the witnesses who were present when the will was signed by the testator.[752] If the will has been signed by the testator in the presence of a judge, official registrar, or a notary, they are required to sign on the will as well.[753] The will of a dying person heard by witnesses should be written and signed by the witnesses.[754] In these particular cases from the law of succession, electronic signature may suffice only if it is *certified* electronic signature, and no other electronic signature substitute is valid.[755] However, if the will has been written in handwriting by the testator,[756] no electronic signature is valid, but only the handwriting signatures.[757]

The general rule in Israeli law of evidence is that in any legal proceeding, any signature is not inadmissible just because it is electronic signature,[758] unless specifically determined otherwise. However, the admissibility of the electronic signature does not necessarily reflect its reliability. In addition, secured electronic signature is admissible in any legal proceedings as an evidence that the electronic message has not been changed after it has been signed and that the message has been signed with an electronic signature produced using a measure that is solely controlled by the signing person.[759] If the electronic signature is certified, it is also an admissible evidence that the electronic message has actually been signed by the person who controls the measure.[760]

A party to a contract who wishes to use any electronic message of the counterparty, signed electronically and related to the contract (e.g., cancellation notification), has the duty to prove that the counterparty did sign (electronically) the message. Nevertheless, if the electronic signature is certified, it is presumed so, and the counterparty has the duty to refute it.[761]

An output of any electronic message which is signed by a certified electronic signature is not considered a copy but the original document in any legal proceedings.[762] Nevertheless, such an output is considered a copy and not the original document, if the message is an official judgment, a banknote, a promissory note, a physical share deed, or a report from the real estate registry.[763]

---

750. Section 2(a)(1) of the Electronic Signature Act, 2001.
751. Section 2(a)(2) of the Electronic Signature Act, 2001.
752. Section 20 of the Succession Act, 1965.
753. Section 22 of the Succession Act, 1965.
754. Section 23 of the Succession Act, 1965.
755. Section 2(b)(1) of the Electronic Signature Act, 2001.
756. Section 19 of the Succession Act, 1965.
757. Section 2(b)(2) of the Electronic Signature Act, 2001.
758. Section 3(a) of the Electronic Signature Act, 2001.
759. Section 3(b)(1) and 3(b)(2) of the Electronic Signature Act, 2001.
760. Section 3(b)(3) of the Electronic Signature Act, 2001.
761. Section 3A of the Electronic Signature Act, 2001.
762. Section 6(a) of the Electronic Signature Act, 2001.
763. Section 6(b) of the Electronic Signature Act, 2001.

Any person who possesses a measure to produce electronic signatures has the duty to take all reasonable steps to secure the access to that measure,[764] and to notify any person who may be affected, whenever the measure is insecure.[765] If the measure is used to produce certified electronic signatures, the possessing person has, in addition, the duty to notify the certifying agents that the measure is insecure.[766] If these duties are fulfilled, that person is not held liable for any damage which occurred due to misuse of the measure or due to unauthorized use of the measure.[767]

§2. Certification Services

105. The major function in certification services is the certifying agent. A certifying agent is authorized to produce a certificate which confirms that a certain measure producing electronic signature is in the possession of a particular person. The agent may produce such a certificate due to the request of any person,[768] but only after verifying that all required details are true and full.[769] The certifying agent has the duty to register all certifications produced and in addition to register all cancelled certifications.[770]

The certifying agent is required to use only reliable hardware and software, which grant reasonable protection from hackers, from malicious software and from malware, and ensure the availability and reliability of the computer system.[771] If this is not the only occupation of the certifying agent, all other occupations and activities must be separate from the occupation as a certifying agent.[772]

The certification is required to include the name and ID number of the person who requested the certification, confirmation that the measure producing electronic signature has been checked and found reliable, the serial number of the certification within the registry managed by the agent, the identification process of the person who requested the certification, the identification of the certifying agent, the secured electronic signature of the certifying agent, restrictions or limitations on the particular certification, if any, restrictions or limitations on the certifying agent, if any, and a clear reference to the cancelled certifications registry of that agent.[773]

The certifying agent is required to cancel any certification, if the person who requested the certification has asked for its cancellation, if the agent discovers wrong details within the certification, if the secured electronic signature has been damaged (e.g., due to malware activity), if the person who requested the certification is dead, if the corporation which requested the certification is liquidated, or if

764. Section 7(a)(1) of the Electronic Signature Act, 2001.
765. Section 7(a)(2) of the Electronic Signature Act, 2001.
766. Section 8(a) of the Electronic Signature Act, 2001.
767. Sections 7(b) and 8(b) of the Electronic Signature Act, 2001.
768. Section 18(a) of the Electronic Signature Act, 2001.
769. Section 18(b) of the Electronic Signature Act, 2001.
770. Section 18(c) of the Electronic Signature Act, 2001.
771. Section 18(d) of the Electronic Signature Act, 2001.
772. *Ibid.*
773. Section 19(a) of the Electronic Signature Act, 2001.

the agent's secured electronic signature has been damaged.[774] The cancellation should be notified immediately to the person who requested the certification, and it also should be published clearly.[775]

The certifying agent is not held liable for any damage caused by the certification, if proved that all reasonable measures were taken to fulfil all requirement determined by the law.[776] If restrictions or limitations on the particular certification have been imposed by the certifying agent, and they were breached, the certifying agent is not held liable for any damage caused by breaching the certificate.[777]

The government is authorized to produce certifications to any civil servant or if the identification of the person who requests the certification is based on biometric data.[778] Nevertheless, beginning in 2011, the government is authorized to produce certifications to any person, that the law requires such certification for legal or administrative proceedings, that the duty to supply the certification is imposed on that person.[779]

A foreign certifying agent may produce certificates in Israel, if that agent fulfils all requirements required from an Israeli certifying agent.[780] In that case, any certification produced by the foreign agent has the same legal status of any similar certification produced by an Israeli agent.[781]

All certifying agents are required to be registered. The registrar is required to be qualified as a judge of the Magistrates' Court.[782] The registrar is required to manage registry of Israeli and of foreign certifying agents and to inspect the agents' activity.[783] A person who wishes to be registered is required to submit an application to the registrar, which includes identification details, the occupation, the possessed facilities to produce certifications, the criminal record (if any), and bank securities (required to compensate for any damages caused by mistaken certification).[784]

After the application is submitted, its details are checked due to international standards,[785] and the registrar may add further requirements, if necessary, to ensure the legal and efficient of the certifying process.[786] If there is no prevention from registration, the registrar is required to register the applying person in the registry as one of the certifying agents.[787] The registration is published and may be accessed

774. Section 20(a) of the Electronic Signature Act, 2001.
775. Section 20(b) of the Electronic Signature Act, 2001.
776. Section 21(a) of the Electronic Signature Act, 2001.
777. Section 21(b) of the Electronic Signature Act, 2001.
778. Section 21A(a) of the Electronic Signature Act, 2001. For the procedure required *see* Electronic Signature (Registry of Governmental Agent or Statutory Corporation) Regulations, 2002.
779. Section 21A(b) of the Electronic Signature Act, 2001.
780. Section 22(a) of the Electronic Signature Act, 2001.
781. Section 22(c) of the Electronic Signature Act, 2001.
782. Section 9(a) of the Electronic Signature Act, 2001.
783. Section 9(b) of the Electronic Signature Act, 2001.
784. Sections 10–11 of the Electronic Signature Act, 2001.
785. The Electronic Signature (Secured Electronic Signature, Hardware, Software and Check of Applications) Regulations, 2001.
786. Section 11(b) of the Electronic Signature Act, 2001.
787. The Electronic Signature (Registry of Certifying Agent), 2001.

via the ministry of justice's official website.[788] If any change in the details of the application has occurred, the certifying agent is required to notify the registrar immediately.[789]

If the registrar finds out, after the certifying agent has been registered, that one of the requirements is not fulfilled, the registrar addresses the certifying agent a particular decree to fulfil it. If not fulfilled, the registrar may delete the agent from the registry after thirty days, if the agent had the chance to plea against the deletion.[790] In addition, if a requirement is not fulfilled, the registrar is authorized to impose an administrative fee of up to NIS 75,900 (approximately EUR 19,000) on the agent.[791] The fee is paid to the state's treasury.[792]

For the inspection of the activity of certifying agents, the registrar is authorized to require documents and information in regard to the agent's activity,[793] to enter any place and confiscate documents in regard to the agent's activity,[794] to enter any computer system and produce information in regard to the agent's activity,[795] and to confiscate any object required to ensure all requirements of the law are fulfilled.[796] These actions may be exercised by another agent, if skilled to perform them.[797]

788. *See* https://www.justice.gov.il/Units/ilita/subjects/HatimaElectronic/MeidaMeRashamCA/Pages/Gormim.aspx (accessed 23 Jul. 2021).
789. Section 13 of the Electronic Signature Act, 2001.
790. Section 14(a) of the Electronic Signature Act, 2001.
791. Section 14A of the Electronic Signature Act, 2001.
792. Section 14J of the Electronic Signature Act, 2001. For the required procedure *see* the Centre of Execution of Judgments and Fees (Fees under Electronic Signature Act, 2001) Regulations, 2018.
793. Section 17(a)(1) of the Electronic Signature Act, 2001.
794. Section 17(a)(2) of the Electronic Signature Act, 2001.
795. Section 17(a)(3) of the Electronic Signature Act, 2001.
796. Section 17(a)(4) of the Electronic Signature Act, 2001.
797. The Electronic Signature (Skills Required for the Inspection of Activities) Regulations, 2009.

Chapter 3. Legal Aspects of Electronic Banking

§1. The Duty to Offer Electronic Banking Services

106. Since the 1990s, Israeli banks have tried to reduce their operational costs through offering banking services by the phone. As more customers used these services, the banks could have reduced the number of the tellers at the bank's branches and reduce the hours of activity within the bank's branches. In the 1980s, most Israeli banks' branches were active with face-to-face service six days a week, as almost all banking activity was done through the bank's tellers. However, since the 1990s, the face-to-face services availability was reduced gradually.

Nevertheless, most Israeli customers have found banking services by the phone more comfortable, especially for business. When the Internet became more accessible for home users, the banking services evolved to the electronic platform, out of the same reasons (reduction of operational costs) and due to the same trend. For most customers, the bank website became a comfortable platform to watch the data of their bank account, and for some customers, it became a comfortable platform to perform banking actions (e.g., money transfers, investments, and currency services).

In the new millennium, almost all Israeli customers prefer electronic banking on any other service channel. As a result, this channel of service has been extremely developed and became user-friendly and available. All Israeli banks are using this channel as their primary channel of service. Although parts of the elderly population still prefer the face-to-face service, it is a minor part of the services' channels.

Due to this development, there was no necessity to regulate electronic banking services. Moreover, the competition between the banks on the young customers made them develop the electronic banking to become more secure, more available, more comfortable, and more reliable. This was a demonstration of the Israeli market forces in the field of electronic banking.

Nevertheless, in 2017, the legislator imposed a duty to offer electronic banking services, under certain conditions. For *all* Israeli banks, it was unnecessary, as all of them already operated advanced electronic banking services. Nevertheless, according to this legislation, any bank which holds at least 10% of all assets held by all Israeli banks is required to offer electronic banking services.[798] The bank is required to offer these banking services by itself or through external corporation which operates the infrastructure of these services.

However, in order to increase competition among the banks at this point, the minister of finances is authorized to support the banks to develop and operate the electronic banking services, if necessary, through generous grants.[799] As aforesaid, this regulatory provisions were not necessary, as all banks already operated developed electronic banking services in 2017.

Moreover, these legal provisions may be expanded by the minister of finance, and be applicable to credit corporations and other financial corporations which are not

798. Section 11C(c) of the Banking (Licensing) Act, 1981.
799. Section 11C(a)(2) of the Banking (Licensing) Act, 1981.

banks.[800] Nevertheless, most of these corporations do offer electronic services in regard to credit products. Consequently, although regulation of electronic banking services exists, it is unnecessary due to the banking market situation.

§2. General Legal Framework and the Applicable Law in Regard to Electronic Banking Transactions

107. Given the use of electronic banking services, one of the legal questions is the legal status of their outcomes, i.e., the legal status of electronic actions performed through the electronic banking services. These actions may be referred to as *electronic banking transactions*. For example, when a customer uses the bank's website to purchase some foreign currency, this is electronic banking transaction. The transaction is between the customer and the bank, and it may also be in favour of third party.

Electronic banking transactions have two basic legal aspects. One aspect is the contractual aspect, and the other is the property aspect. Any electronic banking transaction is presumed to reflect an agreement between the parties (the bank and the customer). The agreement is achieved regardless of the form, whether electronic or not. This is the contractual aspect of the transaction and it is governed by the law of contracts. However, the transaction relates to certain objects or services, and the completion of the transaction is dependent on any change in the property rights of these objects or the full performance of the services. This is the property aspect of the transaction, and it is governed by property law.

Nevertheless, the property aspect of electronic banking transactions is identical to the property aspect of any other transaction (e.g., banking activity through face-to-face service). For example, if the consumer orders foreign currency via the bank's website, in most cases, under Israeli law, the property rights within this currency would be the consumer's after having possession over it (within the customer's account or within physical possession). But acquiring the physical possession over the currency has nothing to do with the electronic form of the transaction. This property legal rule is identical in any other type of transactions, including the physical purchase through face-to-face service.

Consequently, the property aspect is immaterial to the regulation of electronic banking transactions, and the contractual aspect may be the more significant legal aspect of electronic banking transactions. Nevertheless, the property aspect may affect, indirectly, the applicable law governing the electronic banking transaction. There are three basic layers of the law relating to electronic banking transactions. The first layer is the general law of contracts, the second layer is the consumption law specified to banking, and the third layer is the ICT law. The interpretation rule between these layers is *lex specialis derogat generali*. Therefore, legal provisions from ICT law derogate legal provisions from consumption law, which derogate legal provisions from the general law of contracts.

However, most issues in electronic banking transactions are covered by the general law of contracts. These transactions are between the banks as merchants and

800. Section 11C(a) of the Banking (Licensing) Act, 1981.

their consumers (e.g., purchasing foreign currency, whereas it may be purchased outside the bank), and Israeli law prefers to classify these contracts as consumption contracts rather than contracts regarding technology. As a result, certain legal duties are imposed on the banks regardless of the form of contract or transaction. Only in rare types of electronic banking transactions, the law dictates specific relevant legal arrangements.

Electronic banking transactions are subject to the Israeli conflict of laws rules, and in particular to the rules of choice-of-law in contracts. The general rule in Israel is that the law which governs the electronic banking transaction is the law that both parties agreed on, explicitly or implicitly. If no such law has been agreed on, the applicable law is the law which has the closest and most real connection to the contract.[801] Particular rules of choice-of-law in contracts are deduced from the English Common Law through case laws.

Electronic banking transactions are classified as banking contracts. Therefore, these transactions are governed by the law that both parties agreed on, explicitly or implicitly, unless it deprives the consumer of rights granted by the alternative law (i.e., the applicable law that should have governed the contract without the parties' agreement). If no such law has been agreed on, or if the agreed law deprives the consumer of granted rights, the applicable law is the law which has the closest and most real connection to the contract. In general, this is the law that governs the bank's domicile (or the particular bank's branch domicile), unless another law has a closer and more real connection to the contract.[802]

Nevertheless, the particular electronic banking transaction may be considered as a consumption contract, in particular when the bank offers the customer certain services (e.g., a loan in 'attractive' conditions through the bank's website). Electronic banking transactions which are classified as consumption contracts are governed by the law that both parties agreed on, explicitly or implicitly, unless it deprives the consumer of rights granted by the alternative law (i.e., the applicable law that should have governed the contract without the parties' agreement). If no such law has been agreed on, or if the agreed law deprives the consumer of granted rights, the applicable law is the law which has the closest and most real connection to the contract. In general, this is the law that governs the consumer's domicile (and not the bank's domicile), unless another law has a closer and more real connection to the contract.[803]

This situation may cause some ambiguity. Consequently, most bank websites which offer electronic banking transactions include a choice-of-law clause which defines in particular the applicable law of the contract. This clause is generally accompanied by an exclusive jurisdiction clause (i.e., a clause which grants the Israeli court an exclusive jurisdiction over any lawsuit regarding the contract). Nevertheless, the agreed law is not applicable if its content is contradicted to the Israeli public policy or to the Israeli criminal law (e.g., a contract that permit an action

---

801. Gabriel Hallevy, *Theory of the Conflict of Laws* vol. I 478–493 (Bursi Publishing House 2014); Civ. App. 165/60 *Onion Ltd. v. Moshe*, 17 PD 646 (1963); Civ. App. 352/87 *Greifin Corp. v. Cur Ltd.*, 44(3) PD 45 (1990).
802. *Ibid.*, at pp. 603–609.
803. *Ibid.*, at pp. 589–595.

which is considered a criminal offence in Israel, but according to the foreign law, which has been defined as the applicable law, it is not forbidden, and in particular money laundering).

§3. Substantive Legal Provisions under Israeli Law

108. The bank's website may offer both services to manage the customer's account and 'marketing by far' banking services. For example, most banks offer their customers loans in certain conditions through their websites. The loan's conditions are already adapted to the customer's personal data, in regard to the customer's credit data. This offer is actually 'marketing by far' banking service, and it is subject to banking law. The consumption law has excluded its applicability on banking services,[804] and the banking law regulates electronic banking transactions, the same way it regulates other types of banking transactions (e.g., banking transactions through face-to-face service or phone service).

Accordingly, if the applicable law is Israeli law, the bank is not allowed to refuse to offer electronic banking services, unless the refusal is reasonable due to the customer's financial situation.[805] The bank is not allowed to act by a way that may deceive the client, including omission of details towards the transaction.[806] Consequently, the bank is required to disclose any relevant detail on the quality of the service, the time of service, the expected yield, the service's price, the warranty conditions (if any), and the identity of the service provider (if the service is supplied by an external entity).[807]

The bank must not abuse the inexperience of the client or affect the client unfairly in order to make the client accept unreasonable conditions within the transaction.[808] This duty obviously includes avoiding abuse of children, mentally retarded persons, or weaker-minded persons. Certain details must be noticed by the bank through the website before the electronic banking transaction is performed, and these details include all necessary data required for making a reasonable decision towards the bank's offer.

No lawsuit against any client would be submitted by the bank for any banking service, unless a written notice has been sent to the client, at least twenty-one days prior to any legal action.[809] Although the banking transaction was performed electronically, the notice must be in writing, and mailed to the client physically and not electronically.

Commercials within the bank's website (e.g., advertising banners) are subject to rules which are meant to minimize unfair influence, especially on minors.[810] The bank's website must not offer services that are conditioned on other services, so that

---

804. Section 39(1) of the Consumer's Protection Act, 1981.
805. Section 2 of the Banking (Client Service) Act, 1981.
806. Section 3 of the Banking (Client Service) Act, 1981.
807. *Ibid.*
808. Section 4 of the Banking (Client Service) Act, 1981.
809. Section 5A1 of the Banking (Client Service) Act, 1981.
810. Section 6A of the Banking (Client Service) Act, 1981; Banking (Client Service) (Commercials Addressed to Minors) Rules, 1995.

the client has to purchase both services, although only one is required.[811] All other duties imposed on the bank in any other type of banking (e.g., face-to-face, telephone, or facsimile) are imposed on the bank in electronic services. The client has no right to waive these rights, and any agreement in which the client waives these rights is void.[812]

Breach of these duties is considered criminal offences of up to NIS 1,500,000 (approximately EUR 350,000) and one-year imprisonment.[813] In addition, the client may submit a lawsuit against the bank for actual damages occurred due to the use of electronic banking services, as the breach of these duties is considered civil tort, and Israeli law of torts is applicable.[814] In such a lawsuit, it is no defence for the bank, if the bank did not intend to cause the damages or was not negligent towards the possibility that the damages would occur.

811. Section 7 of the Banking (Client Service) Act, 1981.
812. Section 17 of the Banking (Client Service) Act, 1981.
813. Sections 10, 11 and 11A of the Banking (Client Service) Act, 1981.
814. Section 15 of the Banking (Client Service) Act, 1981.

Chapter 4. Protection of Users of Electronic Services

§1. The Main Issues

109. In general, protection of users of electronic services may relate to privacy issues and consumption issues. The main privacy issues are the personal data processing and the telecommunications privacy. Thus, using electronic banking services might expose very sensitive data to the net, and if not well secured, it may leak outside. Without any proper protection on the user's privacy relating to the personal data, most users would probably prefer other platform rather than using electronic services. However, privacy issues are discussed in detail and separately below at Part VI: Privacy Protection.

The main consumption issues are towards unfair marketing through the electronic services, the required customer services if any problem occurs, and the responsibility for the consequences of using the electronic services. In general, any use of electronic services in the customary context creates a contract, explicitly or implicitly, between the user of the electronic services and the proposer of these services. The user is the 'consumer' and the services' proposer is the 'merchant'. Sometimes the services themselves are the object (e.g., using electronic banking for data), and sometimes the services are means to certain products (e.g., purchasing a product from a virtual store). The consumption issues are discussed below.

§2. Consumption Issues

110. As aforesaid, most electronic services may be characterized as consumption transactions accompanied by explicit or implicit contracts, and the general law governing consumption transactions contains particular legal provisions regulating electronic services. These provisions impose certain duties on the services' proposer who offers the services within an electronic platform, namely the services' proposer's website. The electronic platforms are related to a wider set of platforms, which are named as services of 'marketing by far'. These platforms are contradicted with face-to-face services.

However, 'marketing by far' services include not only electronic services, but also phone-services (i.e., marketing through the telephone) and some other services outside the Internet. The definition of 'marketing by far' service is any service when not all of the parties are physically present at the performance of the service.[815] That includes electronic services, but some other types of services as well. Consequently, electronic services are regulated identically the same way all other 'marketing by far' services are regulated.

815. Section 14C(f) of the Consumer's Protection Act, 1981.

Accordingly, within an electronic service, the services' proposer has the duty to disclose, prior to the final agreement with the user, the name, address, and ID number of the services' proposer in Israel and outside Israel,[816] the main quality characteristics of the products or services offered within that service,[817] the price and the payment conditions,[818] the time and way of supply (e.g., via postal mail),[819] the period that the offer would be valid,[820] the warranty details,[821] and necessary details on the user's rights to cancel the service.[822] These details should be disclosed within the services' proposer's website.

After the service is formed, the services' proposer has the duty to supply the user, in writing, and no later than the date of the products' or services' supply, the name, address, and ID number of the services' proposer in Israel and outside Israel and the main quality characteristics of the products or services offered within that service,[823] the price and the final payment terms,[824] the necessary details on the user's rights to cancel the service,[825] the manufacturer's name and country,[826] the warranty details,[827] and any other terms which are relevant to the particular electronic service.[828]

In electronic services the user has the right to cancel the service, if the service's object is a product, within fourteen days from the day the product has been physically accepted by the user or from the day of the above-written statement, by the latest of them.[829] If the service's object is a service, the user has the right to cancel the service within fourteen days from the day the service has been made or from the day of the above-written statement, by the latest of them.[830] It is insignificant if the service has already begun, if the service is continuous.

Nevertheless, the user has no right to cancel the contract or the transaction if the products purchased through the electronic service are expendable (e.g., fresh fruits),[831] if the products were designed especially for the user,[832] if the products are electronic media in which the user has already opened their pack,[833] if the product

816. Section 14C(a)(1) of the Consumer's Protection Act, 1981.
817. Section 14C(a)(2) of the Consumer's Protection Act, 1981.
818. Section 14C(a)(3) of the Consumer's Protection Act, 1981.
819. Section 14C(a)(4) of the Consumer's Protection Act, 1981.
820. Section 14C(a)(5) of the Consumer's Protection Act, 1981.
821. Section 14C(a)(6) of the Consumer's Protection Act, 1981.
822. Section 14C(a)(7) of the Consumer's Protection Act, 1981.
823. Section 14C(b)(1) of the Consumer's Protection Act, 1981.
824. Section 14C(b)(2) of the Consumer's Protection Act, 1981.
825. Section 14C(b)(3) of the Consumer's Protection Act, 1981.
826. Section 14C(b)(4) of the Consumer's Protection Act, 1981.
827. Section 14C(b)(5) of the Consumer's Protection Act, 1981.
828. Section 14C(b)(6) of the Consumer's Protection Act, 1981.
829. Section 14C(c)(1) of the Consumer's Protection Act, 1981.
830. Section 14C(c)(2) of the Consumer's Protection Act, 1981.
831. Section 14C(d)(1) of the Consumer's Protection Act, 1981.
832. Section 14C(d)(4) of the Consumer's Protection Act, 1981.
833. Section 14C(d)(5) of the Consumer's Protection Act, 1981.

is mere information,[834] or if it is service relating to tourism or entertainment and the cancellation date has expired within seven working days prior to the supply of that service.[835]

If the user of the electronic services is a person with disabilities, a person aged 65 years old or older, or a new immigrant (up to five years in Israel), the user has the right to cancel the contract or the transaction made through the electronic service within four months from the day the product has been physically accepted by the user, from the day of the above-written statement, or from the day the service has been used, by the latest of them.[836] However, the services' proposer in these cases may demand an official proof for the user's above condition.[837]

Nevertheless, in spite of the user's condition, the user has no right to cancel the contract or the transaction made through the electronic service, if the products are expendable (e.g., fresh fruits),[838] if the products were designed especially for the user,[839] if the products are electronic media in which the user has already opened their pack,[840] if the product is mere information,[841] or if it is service relating to tourism or entertainment and the cancellation date has expired within seven working days prior to the supply of that service.[842]

If the cancellation of any electronic service was due to the services' proposer's breach of the contract, the services' proposer has the duty to pay the user back any payment that has already been paid, to cancel the contract or the transaction made through the electronic service and to cancel any further charge, within fourteen days from the day the user's cancellation notification has been accepted.[843] The user has the duty to deliver the product to the services' proposer, including all products that have been given to the user due to the service, unless they were defined as gifts that are not dependent on the execution of the service.[844]

Nevertheless, if the cancellation was not due to any breach of the contract, the services' proposer has the right to charge the user a cancellation fee of up to 5% of the service or NIS 100 (approximately EUR 25), by the lowest of them.[845] However, the services' proposer has the duty to pay the user back any payment that has already been paid, to cancel the contract or the transaction made through the electronic service, and to cancel any further charge, within fourteen days from the day the user's cancellation notification has been accepted.[846] The user has the duty to deliver the product to the services' proposer, including all products that have been

834. Section 14C(d)(3) of the Consumer's Protection Act, 1981.
835. Section 14C(d)(2) of the Consumer's Protection Act, 1981.
836. Section 14C1(c) of the Consumer's Protection Act, 1981.
837. Section 14C1(d) of the Consumer's Protection Act, 1981.
838. Section 14C(d)(1) of the Consumer's Protection Act, 1981.
839. Section 14C(d)(4) of the Consumer's Protection Act, 1981.
840. Section 14C(d)(5) of the Consumer's Protection Act, 1981.
841. Section 14C(d)(3) of the Consumer's Protection Act, 1981.
842. Section 14C(d)(2) of the Consumer's Protection Act, 1981.
843. Section 14E(a)(1) of the Consumer's Protection Act, 1981.
844. Section 14E(a)(2) of the Consumer's Protection Act, 1981.
845. Section 14E(b)(1) of the Consumer's Protection Act, 1981.
846. *Ibid.*

given to the user due to the service, unless they were defined as gifts that are not dependent on the performance of the service's object.[847]

The user of an electronic service has the right that the cancellation notification would be possible telephonically, by postal mail, by e-mail, by facsimile, and through the Internet within the services' proposer's website.[848] For this purpose, the services' proposer is required to enable within the main page of the website an accessible form of cancellation notification.[849] The services' proposer is also required to publish within the main page of the website the above ways to communicate for the purpose of delivering a cancellation notification.[850] The user is required to include all details necessary to identify the service, including the user's name.[851]

In any other issue relating to the use of electronic services, the general law of contracts and the consumer's protection law apply. In general, any contract or transaction performed through electronic services is considered formed, and their existence is inferred, if both factual element and mental element requirements are fulfilled. The factual element is expressed by an offer and an acceptance.[852] The acceptance may be by typing or clicking on the required buttons within the website, where the offer has been offered.[853]

The mental element requirement is expressed by awareness of the parties to the major terms of the electronic service and by an intention to create legal relations through the particular electronic services.[854] Consideration, however, under Israeli law is not required. Gifts and presents given for free with no charge are considered valid contracts or transactions, even if formed through electronic services or if the electronic service itself is free of charge.[855] Certain types of disorders, which indirectly may be related to the mental element, might result in invalidation of the contract or transaction formed electronically. Some types make the contract or transaction become voidable (i.e., the court is required to declare that the service is void), and other types automatically make them become void. Fictive contracts or transactions formed electronically are void.[856]

Contracts or transactions formed electronically and the electronic services themselves may also be void on grounds of public policy or illegality (in contrast with the criminal law).[857] Thus, if the relevant electronic service is forbidden in Israel by the criminal law (e.g., prostitution services through the Internet), using the electronic service is illegal, and the contract is void. Nevertheless, contracts or transactions which have been formed electronically, due to mistakes, misrepresentation,

---

847. Section 14E(b)(2) of the Consumer's Protection Act, 1981.
848. Section 14I(a) of the Consumer's Protection Act, 1981.
849. Section 14I(b) of the Consumer's Protection Act, 1981.
850. Section 14I(e)(2) of the Consumer's Protection Act, 1981.
851. Section 14I(c) of the Consumer's Protection Act, 1981.
852. Section 1 of the Contracts (General Part) Act, 1973.
853. Section 6 of the Contracts (General Part) Act, 1973.
854. Section 2 of the Contracts (General Part) Act, 1973.
855. The Gifts Act, 1968.
856. Section 13 of the Contracts (General Part) Act, 1973.
857. Section 30 of the Contracts (General Part) Act, 1973.

duress or threat, are voidable.[858] If the contract or transaction is void, a statement of cancellation by one of the parties, at least, is required.[859] Use of the electronic service may be in favour of the parties or in favour of a third party.[860]

In cases of breach of contract or transaction formed by an electronic service or if the terms of the electronic service itself have been breached, the court is authorized to impose on the violator a duty to perform the obligations that have been violated (specific performance or enforcement), unless the service is not operative anymore, the specific performance involves personal service, the specific performance requires unreasonable inspection by the court or the specific performance is unjust.[861] Thus, the primary remedy for breach of obligations relating to electronic services is specific performance.

Only if specific performance is inapplicable, the court may impose other remedies. One of these remedies is the cancellation of the service, the contract or the transaction together with restoration of resources (i.e., each party returns the other party any resources given prior to the breach, e.g., advances).[862] However, the common remedy is damages. The plaintiff is granted damages for the loss caused by the breach, and in some cases, even without proving any loss.[863] Nevertheless, if the breach was caused by force major, the plaintiff is discharged, as the doctrine of frustration has been accepted in Israel.[864]

As aforesaid, most electronic services in Israel are between merchants (who function as services' proposers) and consumers (who function as users); therefore, they are subject to consumption law as well. Under Israeli consumption law, the general rule of *caveat emptor* is invalid or, at least, minimized. This attitude is expressed by imposition of wide duties on the services' proposer in favour of the user. Many of these duties are enforced through criminal law. The most significant duties are the full disclosure and due diligence duties.

Accordingly, any act or omission of any services' proposer is forbidden, if it *might* cause misrepresentation or mistake when using the electronic services.[865] That includes the duty to let the user the full information on the electronic service itself, the service regarding it (e.g., technical support by phone), the time of performance, all relevant terms, the price and calculations of the price, the terms for cancellation, etc. It is forbidden for the services' proposer to limit the user's liberty to contact (or, more important, *not* to contact) with the services' proposer.[866] The services' proposer must disclose any possible damage in the electronic service that may defect its performance (e.g., security problems within the website).[867]

858. Sections 14–15 and 17–18 of the Contracts (General Part) Act, 1973.
859. Section 20 of the Contracts (General Part) Act, 1973.
860. Sections 34–38 of the Contracts (General Part) Act, 1973.
861. Section 3 of the Contracts (Remedies for Breach of Contract) Act, 1970.
862. Sections 6–9 of the Contracts (Remedies for Breach of Contract) Act, 1970.
863. Sections 10–11 of the Contracts (Remedies for Breach of Contract) Act, 1970.
864. Section 18 of the Contracts (Remedies for Breach of Contract) Act, 1970.
865. Section 2 of the Consumer's Protection Act, 1981.
866. Section 3 of the Consumer's Protection Act, 1981.
867. Section 4 of the Consumer's Protection Act, 1981.

Free-of-charge customer service (including technical support to the electronic services) must be granted by the services' proposer in any electronic service.[868] The customer service agent must be identified at the beginning of the call by name, and the call would be from a line that may be reconnected by the customer easily by redialling.[869]

Enforcement of the consumption law provisions is under the responsibility of the Consumer's Protection Authority. This authority is authorized to enforce the law using administrative measures, and in particular through administrative fines of up to NIS 45,000 (approximately EUR 11,000).[870] In addition, infringement of the consumption law may be considered a criminal offence of up to three years imprisonment and fines of up to NIS 4.5 million (approximately EUR 1.1 million).[871]

868. Section 18B of the Consumer's Protection Act, 1981.
869. Section 18C of the Consumer's Protection Act, 1981.
870. Chapter E1 of the Consumer's Protection Act, 1981.
871. Chapter F of the Consumer's Protection Act, 1981.

Part V. Non-contractual Liability

111. Using modern platforms of commerce, government services, and other services exposes the users to dangers that have not been known before, not necessarily on a contractual basis. For example, when defamatory or libellous stuff is published on a certain person in the social media or in any other electronic platform, sometimes unanimously, the question is who is held liable for the damages. In these cases, the question of non-contractual liability is risen. However, as the use of electronic platforms increases, the involved parties try to reduce the effect of unexpected scenarios through contractual relations, but this is not always possible, and this does not necessarily cover third parties.

Chapter 1. Negligence

112. One of the most common and general legal grounds for the non-contractual liability is the tort of negligence, which is part of the law of torts. The tort of negligence functions both as particular tort and as legal framework for different types of acts and omissions that are relevant to the non-contractual liability related to cyber law. The general legal framework and the applicable law, and the substantive legal provisions under Israeli law are discussed below.

§1. General Legal Framework and the Applicable Law

113. Negligence is part of the law of torts, and in the context of ICT, there are three basic layers of the law relating to negligence within ICT situations. The first layer is the general law of torts, the second layer is particular negligence laws, and the third layer is the ICT law. The interpretation rule between these three layers is *lex specialis derogat generali*. Therefore, legal provisions from ICT law derogate legal provisions from particular negligence laws, which derogate legal provisions from the general law of torts.

Thus, even though in certain cases the general law of torts may determine one person as negligent, and therefore impose certain remedies, the ICT law may determine that negligence is not enough to impose any remedies or that the person was not negligent at all. As the ICT law in the context of negligence functions as the specific law, it derogates the general law of torts, which functions as the general law.

Particular negligence laws may relate to certain persons who may be negligent (e.g., the state) or to certain situations in which negligence may be involved (e.g., negligent deletion of software). As the general law of torts has been enacted in the 1940s, under the rule of the British Mandate, and the relevant provisions of the ICT law were enacted not before the 1990s, these laws are not always coherent, and the rules of interpretation are required.

Negligence is subject to the Israeli conflict of laws rules, and in particular to the rules of choice-of-law in torts. After sixty years of arguments towards the interpretation of choice-of-law rule in tort,[872] in 2004, inspired by the European and British rules, the Supreme Court has formulated the Israeli rule by case law. Accordingly, the applicable law on torts is the law of the place of occurrence of the tort (*lex loci delicti commissi*), and only if this law has absolutely no relevance to the case, the applicable law is the law which has the closest and most real connection to the tort.[873]

If negligence is through an omission, the place of occurrence of the tort is the place where the duty should have been fulfilled. If negligence is through an act, the

872. *See, e.g.*, Civ. App. 180/51 *Goldcorn v. Wissotzky*, 8(1) PD 262 (1954); Civ. App. 98/67 *Livhar v. Gazit and Shaham*, 21(2) PD 243 (1967); Civ. App. 750/79 *Klausner v. Berkowitz*, 37(4) PD 449 (1983).

873. Civ. App. 1432/03 *Yinon v. Karan*, 59(1) PD 345 (2004); Civ. Cer. 4655/09 *Scaler v. Ubiner* (25 Oct. 2011).

place of the occurrence of the tort is the place of its actual commission and not necessarily the place where the damage has occurred or has been discovered (*lex loci delicti commissi* and not *lex loci damni*). The second part of the rule grants the court wide discretion towards the interpretation of the law that has 'the closest and most real connection' to the tort.

However, some of the negligence cases in the ICT context are related to IP torts, i.e., torts which are defined within the IP law and involve an element of negligence. In these cases, the applicable law may be different. The applicable law in IP torts which involve an element of negligence is still the law of the place of occurrence of the tort (*lex loci delicti commissi*), but this place is the very place where the IP is protected (*lex loci protectionis*). Only if this law has absolutely no relevance to the case, the applicable law is the law which has the closest and most real connection to the IP tort.

The jurisdiction of the Israeli court over negligence cases in the ICT context is not different than its jurisdiction in any other case in torts, and it is determined by the general rules of the Israeli conflict of laws. Accordingly, if the law determines the Israeli court as the authorized forum, if both parties agreed on the court's jurisdiction over the particular case, if the lawsuit's documents have been accepted by the defendant or by the defendant's local representative or if the plaintiff was authorized to deliver the lawsuit's documents to the defendant outside Israel, the Israeli court has the jurisdiction over the case.

§2. Substantive Legal Provisions under Israeli Law

114. Given that the applicable law on the particular case is Israeli law, the case is governed by the legal provisions towards the tort of negligence and by the general law of torts, subject to particular negligent laws and ICT law. In addition, the special cases when the wrongdoer is the state were regulated separately under Israeli law. These legal provisions are discussed below.

I. The Tort of Negligence

115. The general tort of negligence, based on the English Common Law, functions in Israeli law as both particular tort and general legal framework of the required level of fault in most torts. As such, various cases in which damage has occurred may be governed by the tort of negligence. The general legal provisions regulating the tort of negligence are from 1944, when the British Mandate government has enacted the Torts Ordinance, and ever since then, the provisions regulating negligence in this ordinance have not been changed, besides officially translating them into Hebrew in 1968.[874]

The common interpretation of the tort of negligence in Israel is that it includes four basic elements that should be proven in order to grant any remedy. The first

874. Sections 35–36 of the Torts [New Version] Ordinance.

element is conceptual duty of prudence, the second element is concrete duty of prudence, the third is causation between the breach of the concrete duty of prudence and the damage, and the fourth is the damage element.[875] These elements are discussed below.

The first element of the tort of negligence is conceptual duty of prudence. This duty makes the court generalize the particular case in order to examine the entitlement for remedy. Accordingly, the court has to examine whether a reasonable person could have predicted that a person of the defendant's type in such situations has any duty towards persons of the plaintiff's type in such situations.[876]

For example, a technician makes a few reparations within a personal computer within a lab. During this process, a valuable information is deleted from the computer's hard disc, but not deliberately. The technician's explanation is that it was by accident. Under the examination of the first element, the court examines whether technicians in general have any professional duty towards their customers. Only if the answer is positive, the court continues to the examination of the second element.

However, particular legal provisions from the ICT law impose conceptual duties of prudence in certain situations. For example, hardware technicians are considered as having a conceptual duty of prudence towards both their clients and employers. The duty relates, of course, to professional aspects of the relations between the technician and the clients and employer. The question of conceptual duty of prudence between cellular companies and their clients towards radiation damages resulting from the use of the cellular devices has not been examined yet.

The second element of the tort of negligence is concrete duty of prudence. The main term within this element is foreseeability. Accordingly, the court has to examine whether the particular defendant could have foreseen that the breach of the conceptual duty of prudence (the first element) may cause any damage to the particular plaintiff within the concrete situation. This element is not examined abstractly, but due to the particular circumstances of the concrete case.[877]

The examination is due to standards of reasonability. If the defendant has actually foreseen the damage as a consequence of the breach of the duty, it is simple, and the second element is fulfilled. If the defendant has not actually foreseen that, but *could* have foreseen that, the second element is still fulfilled. Therefore, the court has to examine whether the defendant could have foreseen that. This is, basically, a hypothetical question; therefore, it is answered in accordance with reasonability standards.

Accordingly, the court examines whether a reasonable defendant within the particular case under the concrete circumstances could have foreseen the damage as a consequence of the breach of the duty. Of course, that type of examination grants the court wide discretion, which is expressed by shaping the characteristics of the reasonable person under the concrete circumstances ('the reasonable defendant').

---

875. *See, e.g.*, Civ. App. 243/83 *Jerusalem Municipality v. Gordon*, 39(1) PD 113 (1985); Civ. App. 3518/16 *Vogel v. Tiberias Municipality* (25 Oct. 2018).
876. *See, e.g.*, Civ. App. 145/80 *Vaknin v. Beit Shemesh Municipality*, 37(1) PD 113 (1982).
877. *See, e.g.*, Civ. App. 4/57 *Nadir v. Cahanovich*, 11(2) PD 1464 (1957).

The general trend in Israel in civil cases is to make this standard higher. That might serve potential plaintiffs, but it has its costs.

For example, A (technician) supplies e-mail services to small organizations, and these services are subject to a certain protocol (e.g., what actions are taken in case of malware attack). This protocol is designed to minimize malfunctions within the e-mail system. Of course, A has a conceptual duty of prudence towards the clients, as the service is professional and has implications on the clients' professional functioning. When A ignores the protocol while taking care of a certain problem that occurred at the e-mail system of one of the clients, that may raise the question of concrete duty of prudence.

In this example, the court examines whether A could have foreseen that the breach of the conceptual duty of prudence (the first element) may cause any damage to the client when ignoring the protocol. Accordingly, the court examines whether a reasonable technician within the particular case under the concrete circumstances could have foreseen the damage as a consequence of the breach of the duty (ignoring the protocol).

The third element of the tort of negligence is causation between the breach of the concrete duty of prudence and the damage. Causation in this context is interpreted as requiring two requirements: factual causation and legal causation. Factual causation consists of the basic standard of *causa sine qua non*, i.e., if the duty would have not been breached, the damage would not have been occurred. The examination is purely factual, and the court examines whether the damage is a factual consequence of the breach of the concrete duty.

However, factual causation may include many more consequences than the scope of negligence is meant to. Therefore, the second requirement of causation is meant to reduce the scope of causation into the necessary consequences under certain social attitude. The legal causation consists of the foreseeability of a reasonable person who examines the case from the outside. It is not parallel to the standard of the breach of the concrete duty (the second element), as it relates to 'the reasonable defendant', whereas this element relates to 'the reasonable *person*'.

The question within the third element is whether a reasonable person could have foreseen the factual causation, i.e., whether a reasonable person could have foreseen that the breach of the concrete duty would cause the damage, or at least, would be one of the major reasons for the damage.[878] The legal causation may be refuted easily in cases of *novus actus interveniens*,[879] if a third party interrupted the natural course of conduct. However, it should be emphasized that this standard of legal causation is completely different than the standard of legal causation in criminal law, which consists of the mental element (*mens rea*, negligence, or strict liability) in relation to the consequences.

The fourth element of the tort of negligence is damage. The term 'damage' is defined as loss or lack of life, of property, of comfort, of physical welfare or of reputation, and any loss or lack that derive from them.[880] This definition is wide, and it

---

878. *See, e.g.*, Civ. App. 735/75 *Reutman v. Aderet,* 30(3) PD 75 (1976); Civ. App. 732/80 *Arens v. Beit-El Zichron Yakov,* 38(2) PD 645 (1984).
879. Civ. App. 280/73 *Palimport v. Ciba*, 29(1) PD 597 (1974).
880. The definition of the term 'damage' in s. 2 of the Torts [New Version] Ordinance.

includes both physical and non-physical damages. The damage must be proven in court in relation to the remedy requested in the lawsuit. Thus, if the plaintiff sues for certain amount of money as compensation for the damages, the proofs should relate to the coherence between the damage and the amount of money.[881] However, if the remedy is mandatory injunction or prohibitory injunction, the quantitative assessment of the damage is not necessarily relevant.

The burden of proof regarding these four elements is the plaintiff's. Nevertheless, in certain types of cases, Israeli law determines that the burden of proof is the defendant's. In these cases, the defendant is presumed to be liable for negligence, unless this liability has been refuted. Of course, in case of equivalence in the parties' evidence, the plaintiff wins the case. In the ICT area, there are two main types of cases where the burden of proof in negligence lawsuits is the defendant's.

The first type of cases is where the damage is caused by a product that is considered (or proven) dangerous, and the defendant was its owner (or possessor). In these cases, the defendant has to prove that the use of the product was not negligent.[882] For example, when several types of mobile phones have exploded in 2016–2017 while being used and it was known in public, in lawsuits for negligence of the manufacturer, the defendants had to prove proper use, as these devices were proved as dangerous.

The second type of cases relates to control over the product. In these cases, if the court is convinced that the plaintiff did not know or could not have known, at the time when the damage occurred, what were the reasons for the damage, and the court is also convinced that the defendant had full control over the product that caused the damage, and it is more likely that the damage occurred due to the defendant's negligent behaviour, the court is authorized to impose the burden of proof on the defendant that no negligence was involved.[883]

For example, certain ICT devices or infrastructure are possessed by the client (plaintiff), but fully controlled and operated by the defendant (e.g., cable TV infrastructure or landline telephone infrastructure). In case of fire caused by overheating of the infrastructure, the plaintiff has no indication of the overheating, and the control over the infrastructure is the defendant's. In these cases, the court may impose the burden of proof on the defendant that no negligence was involved.

Nevertheless, these two types of cases may be relevant only if the lawsuit submitted to the court is for negligence (of the defendant). If the plaintiff chooses other torts, these particular provisions are inapplicable. Moreover, as discussed below, Israeli law offers wider liability in cases of product liability without any requirement of negligence.[884] Therefore, in cases of product liability, it is not likely that the plaintiffs choose negligence as the legal ground for their lawsuits.

In general, when all four elements of the tort of negligence are fulfilled and proven, the court may state that the defendant (the wrongdoer) is liable for the plaintiff's damages, and determine the remedies in favour of the plaintiff. Nevertheless, negligence is part of the general law of torts, both in the aspect of liability and in

881. *See, e.g.*, Civ. App. 4/57 *Nadir v. Cahanovich*, 11(2) PD 1464 (1957).
882. Section 38 of the Torts [New Version] Ordinance.
883. Section 41 of the Torts [New Version] Ordinance.
884. Below at Chapter 4: Product Liability.

the aspect of remedies, and therefore both liability and remedies for negligence are subject to the general law of torts. In the ICT area, this is significant, as many of these legal provisions are highly relevant in negligence lawsuits in the ICT area. Both liability and remedies aspects of the general law of torts in the ICT context are discussed below.

II. Applicability of the General Law of Torts: Liability

116. Liability for negligence in the ICT area is subject to a minimum damage proven by the plaintiff, and the mere proof of all elements of the tort is not enough in order to determine liability.[885] This resembles the general defence of *de minimis* in criminal law, as the minimum damage is presumed to have social interest. In the ICT area many lawsuits submitted by consumers are declined for this reason, even though negligence has been proven, especially if fair compensation has been offered before the lawsuit has been submitted.

If the plaintiff has been exposed to the negligence of the defendant knowingly or willingly, the plaintiff's right for any remedy is reduced or nullified.[886] However, if the lawsuit is based on infringement of any legal duty (i.e., determined by a particular statute), this is not a defence for the defendant. In any lawsuit besides negligence, if the defendant has acted according to a certain statute, no liability is imposed.[887] Nevertheless, in negligence lawsuits, even if the defendant has acted according to a certain statute, this defence is inapplicable, unless the defendant has proven that the act was not negligent (i.e., a reasonable person would have been acting similarly).[888]

If the wrongdoer is a public servant or any governmental entity in the ICT area, liability may be imposed only if the civil wrong has been committed intentionally or indifferently (i.e., the higher level of recklessness).[889] Consequently, if the plaintiff could have proven negligence of the public servant or of the governmental entity, but not more than negligence, no liability is imposed. In fact, this establishes an immunity for public servants and governmental entities in the ICT area from liability for negligence.

In the ICT area in Israel, some of the functions are fulfilled by tribunals. For example, the Antitrust Tribunal discussed above.[890] Sometimes, the tribunals' decisions may be civil wrong, and the reasons may be various (e.g., the examination was not thorough). In these situations, the elements of negligence may be fulfilled. Nevertheless, any lawsuit against the tribunal or against any of its members is declined, if it relates to the tribunal's functions.[891] This immunity has also been extended to arbitrations,[892] which are very common in the ICT area.

885. Section 4 of the Torts [New Version] Ordinance.
886. Section 5(a) of the Torts [New Version] Ordinance.
887. Section 5(b) of the Torts [New Version] Ordinance.
888. Section 6 of the Torts [New Version] Ordinance.
889. Section 7A and 7B of the Torts [New Version] Ordinance.
890. Above at s. [I]: The Regulator, the Antitrust Tribunal and the Court at Part I.
891. Section 8 of the Torts [New Version] Ordinance.
892. *Ibid.*

When there are more than one defendant within one lawsuit regarding the same tort or civil wrong, they would share the liability between them 'together and separately'.[893] That means that both of them are responsible for the whole damage, and the internal division of the responsibility between them is not the plaintiff's concern. Nevertheless, the court may determine the division between them. This arrangement is also applicable for accessories, inciters, solicitors, advisors, and other accomplices.[894] Of course, the accomplice's liability does not replace the perpetrator's, but it is additional.[895]

The employer may have vicarious liability for the negligent conduct of the employee. The conditions for vicarious liability are the confirmation of the employer to the employee's conduct and the commission of the conduct within the employment.[896] For this purpose, any of the employee's activities in favour of the employer is considered a commission of the conduct within the employment, even if the activity has been performed negligently (towards the employer).[897] However, the conduct may be either act or omission. The required fault in the civil wrong that has actually occurred through the agent would be attributed to the principal.[898] Of course, the employer's liability does not replace the employee's, but it is additional.[899]

Nevertheless, the employer is exempt from liability if the conduct has not been committed by one of the employees, but by a person who was authorized by an employee without the explicit or implicit consent of the employer.[900] In addition, if the employer has consented, but neither the employer nor the employee could have chosen any other person (e.g., when the person is a corporation who has a monopoly over the relevant services), both the employer and the employee are exempt from liability.[901] As aforesaid, in the Israeli ICT market, several corporations are monopolies in relation to certain services.[902] Thus, the opportunity to choose affects the liability.

In contractual relations between the parties, the contract itself is not an adequate ground for imposition of liability for any civil wrong, unless the contract is deliberately meant to authorize one of the parties to commit the civil wrong on behalf of the other.[903] Nevertheless, the contract may be an adequate ground for imposition

893. Section 11 of the Torts [New Version] Ordinance.
894. Section 12 of the Torts [New Version] Ordinance.
895. Section 16 of the Torts [New Version] Ordinance.
896. Sections 13(a)(1) and 13(a)(2) of the Torts [New Version] Ordinance.
897. Section 13(b) of the Torts [New Version] Ordinance.
898. Section 17 of the Torts [New Version] Ordinance.
899. Section 16 of the Torts [New Version] Ordinance.
900. Section 13(a)(2)(a) of the Torts [New Version] Ordinance.
901. Section 13(a)(2)(b) of the Torts [New Version] Ordinance.
902. Above at s. [IV]: Monopolies at Part I.
903. Section 15 of the Torts [New Version] Ordinance.

of liability on the relevant civil wrong if the choice of the counterparty was negligent,[904] if the damage has occurred due to intervention in the counterparty's conduct,[905] if the party permitted (*ex ante*) or ratified (*ex post*) the civil wrong,[906] if the party is personally liable due to the law,[907] or if the object of the contract is itself civil wrong.[908]

In general, in the ICT area, when there are agency relations between the parties, whether contractual or not (e.g., semi-contractual relations or fiduciary relations), the principal is liable for the agent's conduct.[909] The required fault in the civil wrong that has actually occurred through the agent would be attributed to the principal.[910] Of course, the principal's liability does not replace the agent's, but it is additional.[911] Nevertheless, being the spouse of the wrongdoer is not an adequate ground, itself, for liability.[912] In the Israeli ICT market, most corporations are held by families, and some of them by spouses; therefore, the liability of any of the spouses is examined separately.

In case of death of the plaintiff or of the defendant, all rights of the dead are reserved for the dead's estate.[913] Death itself does not form any exemption from liability. Nevertheless, if the dead person is the defendant, and the conduct is considered criminal offence as well, no criminal legal proceedings are allowed.[914] If the dead person was an insolvent defendant, the above legal arrangement is not different.[915] Any insolvent plaintiff has all rights to submit any lawsuit for any tort, and insolvency itself is neither defence nor barrier from submission of lawsuits.[916] However, the right for remedies for any tort is personal and may not be assigned, unless explicitly permitted by the law.[917]

The doctrine of contributory negligence has been accepted in Israeli tort law. Accordingly, if the damage has been caused solely by the plaintiff, the defendant is exempt from liability.[918] If the damage has been caused by the defendant, who was driven to act this way by the plaintiff (intentionally or not), the court is authorized to consider lower rate of remedies or even exemption for the defendant from remedies, dependent on the involvement of the plaintiff in the factual process that resulted in the particular damage.[919]

---

904. Section 15(1) of the Torts [New Version] Ordinance.
905. Section 15(2) of the Torts [New Version] Ordinance.
906. Section 15(3) of the Torts [New Version] Ordinance.
907. Section 15(4) of the Torts [New Version] Ordinance.
908. Section 15(5) of the Torts [New Version] Ordinance.
909. Section 14 of the Torts [New Version] Ordinance.
910. Section 17 of the Torts [New Version] Ordinance.
911. Section 16 of the Torts [New Version] Ordinance.
912. Section 18 of the Torts [New Version] Ordinance.
913. Section 19(a) of the Torts [New Version] Ordinance.
914. Section 236 of the Criminal Justice [Combined Version] Act, 1982.
915. Section 20 of the Torts [New Version] Ordinance.
916. Section 21 of the Torts [New Version] Ordinance.
917. Section 22 of the Torts [New Version] Ordinance.
918. Section 64 of the Torts [New Version] Ordinance.
919. Section 65 of the Torts [New Version] Ordinance.

If the plaintiff has negligently contributed to the occurrence of the damage, the court is required to reduce the rate of remedies in favour of the plaintiff to the defendant's contribution to the occurrence of the damage.[920] For example, if the plaintiff misused ICT equipment, but that equipment was defective regardless of the plaintiff's behaviour, it is more likely that the defendant is not considered liable for the whole damage. Thus, if the court is convinced that the plaintiff's contributory negligence is estimated by 30% of the damage, the defendant is regarded as liable for 70% of the damage, and the remedies in favour of the plaintiff are reduced accordingly.

Sometimes the civil wrong is considered a criminal offence. Negligence is one of the mental element requirements within the Israeli substantive criminal law, and a few dozens of offences may be committed under negligence. In such cases, the lawsuit regarding the civil wrong is not affected by any of the criminal proceedings and is not affected if no criminal proceedings have been taken.[921] Nevertheless, the court may order the parties to notify the police on the facts that might form a criminal offence.

However, the Israeli evidence law regards admissible in civil proceedings the judgment in criminal proceedings for the same facts,[922] and that may ease the plaintiff the burden of proof. In addition, the victim of any criminal offence may submit a civil lawsuit to the criminal court who has convicted the defendant,[923] and the court would function as if it were a civil court (i.e., authorized to grant any civil remedy in favour of the plaintiff).

III. Applicability of the General Law of Torts: Remedies

117. Any civil lawsuit is required to specify explicitly what is the requested remedy, regardless the legal cause for the lawsuit.[924] This requirement is relevant to any civil lawsuit, including lawsuits for negligence. In tort lawsuits, the Israeli court is authorized to grant the plaintiff any remedy within its jurisdiction and subject to any limitation determined explicitly by the law.[925]

The court is authorized to grant mandatory injunction or prohibitory injunction, whether permanent or temporary.[926] These injunctions may be given in addition to any other remedy and as sole remedies.[927] These injunctions do not necessarily derivate from other remedies, but they may be the sole object of the lawsuit. This is significant especially when the major object of the lawsuit is to prevent a future damage, as the damage already been occurred is immaterial. When the court is

920. Section 68 of the Torts [New Version] Ordinance.
921. Section 88 of the Torts [New Version] Ordinance.
922. Section 42A of the Evidence [New Version] Ordinance, 1971.
923. Section 77 of the Courts [Combined Version] Act, 1984.
924. Regulation 10(9) of the Civil Procedure Regulations, 2018.
925. Section 71 of the Torts [New Version] Ordinance.
926. Section 72 of the Torts [New Version] Ordinance.
927. Section 71 of the Torts [New Version] Ordinance.

authorized to grant injunctions in favour of the parties by other provisions of the law (e.g., by the Civil Procedure Regulations, 2018), the above provisions do not negate this authorization.[928]

Temporary injunction is an injunction which is valid until the judgment is given. When the plaintiff has reasonable causes to believe that the defendant might change the situation or the evidence so that the judgment would not be enforceable, temporary injunction to remain the situation as it is, is required. However, the court is authorized to grant a temporary injunction, only if the court is convinced that a real legal question occurs within the lawsuit, it is most probable that the plaintiff would win the case and justice would be prevented unless the injunction is granted.[929]

Nevertheless, the court has to consider hypothetically the balance of damages between the plaintiff and the defendant as a result of granting the injunction. Thus, if, as a result of granting the injunction in favour of the plaintiff, the defendant would probably be exposed to major damages, whereas the claimed damages by the plaintiff are relatively small and may be evaluated in certain sum of money, the court may refuse to grant the injunction, and it is authorized to grant other remedies in favour of the plaintiff, whether claimed or not.[930]

However, the common remedy in negligence lawsuits is damages. Damages are, basically, payment of money as compensation. The court is authorized to grant damages in favour of the plaintiff in addition to other remedies and as the sole remedy.[931] For example, in order to make the husband pay his wife and children regular payments, the court has ordered that the husband is not allowed to leave the country. However, the husband has escaped through Ben-Gurion airport. The state was sued by the wife and children for negligence in performing the court's order, and they were granted damages.[932]

Another example: a pedestrian has walked in the streets of Jerusalem at night, and has fallen into a pit of 4 meters in height. The pedestrian was severely injured, and it was found that he was hard of seeing and suffered from epilepsy before he fell. He sued the municipal authorities of Jerusalem for damages. The court has ignored his previous seeing problems and epilepsy, and ordered the defendant to pay him the whole damages and to ensure that no dangerous pits are existed in the streets of Jerusalem.[933] Under the 2018 regulations of civil procedure, the plaintiff is required to describe in detail the damage that the compensation is related to.[934]

The general objective of the damages is to compensate for the damage, and not to enrich the plaintiff. Therefore, the court is limited within the scope of the damage when calculating the damages. Moreover, damages for the same damage are granted only once, regardless of the identity of the plaintiff.[935] Thus, if the defendant has already compensated one plaintiff for a certain damage at full, i.e., the payment is

---

928. Section 75 of the Torts [New Version] Ordinance.
929. Section 73 of the Torts [New Version] Ordinance.
930. Section 74 of the Torts [New Version] Ordinance.
931. Section 76 of the Torts [New Version] Ordinance.
932. Civ. App. 429/82 *State v. Sohan*, 42(3) PD 733 (1988).
933. Civ. App. 1952/11 *Abu Alhawa v. Municipal Authorities of the City of Jerusalem* (6 Nov. 2012).
934. Regulation 10(9) of the Civil Procedure Regulations, 2018.
935. Section 77(a) of the Torts [New Version] Ordinance.

equivalent to the total damage, the defendant is not required to compensate any other party in any further lawsuit for the same damage.

Social security payment which is paid as a result of negligence of the defendant is reduced from the total sum of damages paid by the employer.[936] For example, if an employee suffers from non-ionizing radiation harm estimated 100, the Israeli social security institute determines 1% of functional disability and social security payment of 1 per annum, the employee is 60 years old, and the retirement age in Israel is 67, the employer is required to pay 93.[937]

However, any payment due to any insurance contract that is paid for any damage is *not* reduced from the damages payment granted by the court.[938] For example, ICT infrastructure has been overheated due to the defendant's negligence, and caused damage to the plaintiff's apartment. However, the apartment is insured by a contract for any damage, including such damage. When the court calculates the damages that the defendant is required to pay in favour of the plaintiff, the payment that has been paid by the insurance company due to the contract is not reduced from the payment that the defendant is required to pay as damages.

Lawsuits for death cases in the ICT area are rare in Israel, and most of them are related to labour law (e.g., an employee dies while at work for ICT company as a result of the company's negligence or third-party's negligence). Nevertheless, certain legal provisions are relevant in this issue. The plaintiffs are the dead's successors or estate and any other person who was financially dependent on the dead, and they are granted damages for the death and for any bodily harm involved.[939]

For example, in 2003, a technician of 'Bezeq' was called to the village of Baqa-el-Rarbia, populated by Arab inhabitants, to fix a telecommunication problem. He was brutally injured by one of the Arab habitants while at work, just for being a Jew. The Arab habitants refused to take care of the wounded technician. An Arab ambulance that has passed through this place has refused to take him to a hospital. The technician has been bleeding until he died, and no Arab habitant has assisted him. The murdered technician family has sued both Bezeq and the local authorities and damages were granted by the court.[940]

In addition, the successors and any other person who was financially dependent on the dead may sue for any future loss caused by the death.[941] That includes the relative loss of future earnings and any reasonable costs caused by the death (e.g., the funeral costs). Nevertheless, that does not include any payment due to insurance contract (e.g., life insurance or pension) or payment for the time of the grief, which are paid in addition.[942]

If the defendants acted as accomplices, the plaintiff may sue all of them within the same lawsuit, and all of them altogether would be required to pay the plaintiff

---

936. Section 82 of the Torts [New Version] Ordinance.
937. 100 – 1 (67 – 60) = 93.
938. Section 86 of the Torts [New Version] Ordinance.
939. Section 78 of the Torts [New Version] Ordinance.
940. Civ. App. 2144/13 *Late Mantin v. Bezeq* (6 Dec. 2017).
941. Section 80 of the Torts [New Version] Ordinance.
942. Section 81 of the Torts [New Version] Ordinance.

the total sum of payment.[943] However, if one of the accomplices has paid the damages, and the other accomplices have not, a lawsuit by the paying accomplice may be submitted against the other accomplices for their share (i.e., indemnity lawsuit).[944] The shares may be determined by the court due to the personal contribution to the damage or due to their actual function within the damage (e.g., perpetrators, joint-perpetrators, inciters, accessories, or advisors).[945]

If the plaintiff is a corporation, and the lawsuit relates to the ICT area, the corporation is not granted any payment for damages, unless actually proven the damages.[946] As many legal provisions in the ICT law and consumption law grant plaintiffs payments in lawsuits without any proof of damages, this legal provision towards corporations is very significant. However, it relates to corporations as plaintiffs and not as defendants. Thus, if a corporation is sued by a physical person, and the law grants payment for damages without any proof of damages, the corporation is required to pay.

When there are more than one defendant within one lawsuit regarding the same tort or civil wrong, they would share the responsibility for the remedies between them 'together and separately'.[947] That means that both of them are responsible for all of the damages, and the internal division of the responsibility between them towards the remedies is not the plaintiff's concern. Nevertheless, the court may determine the division between them. This arrangement is also applicable for the accessories, inciters, solicitors, advisors, and other accomplices.[948]

IV. Negligence by the State

118. As aforesaid, the state of Israel has major functions within the Israeli ICT market, not only as regulator and licensor, but also as services provider or customer. These functions may involve negligence, especially towards third parties, but not only. For example, when granting any license within the ICT area, third parties might be damaged (e.g., by radiation, by loss of the assets' value, or by environmental damage). If the license has been granted negligently, third parties may submit a lawsuit against the state (in addition or not to a lawsuit against the licensee). Moreover, when a licensee is negligently refused by the state to renew the license, it may submit a lawsuit against the state as well.

The British Mandate authorities granted themselves automatic full immunity from any civil lawsuit. However, four years after the declaration of the state of Israel, a special statute has been enacted by the Knesset, which abolished that immunity, inherited from the British Mandate.

Accordingly, the general rule is that the state functions, in relation to any lawsuit in tort law, as any corporation.[949] Thus, the state may be sued for negligence (or for

943. Section 83 of the Torts [New Version] Ordinance.
944. Section 84(a) of the Torts [New Version] Ordinance.
945. Section 84(b) of the Torts [New Version] Ordinance.
946. Section 10 of the Torts [New Version] Ordinance.
947. Section 11 of the Torts [New Version] Ordinance.
948. Section 12 of the Torts [New Version] Ordinance.
949. Section 2 of the Civil Torts (State's Liability) Act, 1952.

any other tort). If the state's conduct has been committed by the law (i.e., under explicit authorization by a particular legal provision), it is exempt from liability, unless the state has acted negligently.[950] Thus, if the state was negligent, although it had an explicit authorization by the law to commit the particular conduct, the state is held liable for any damage caused by its negligence and is required to compensate the plaintiffs.

The lawsuit against the state is submitted to any of the civil courts due to their jurisdiction determined by the law, as if the state were a private corporation. If the lawsuit relates to ICT issue regarding any of the state's estates (e.g., antennas, transmitters, or receivers), the state is liable for any damage, unless it had no physical possession over the estate (e.g., the estate has been granted to the state by the law, but the state has not physically possessed it yet).[951]

If the particular wrongdoer is a public servant or any governmental entity in the ICT area, liability may be imposed only if the civil wrong has been committed intentionally or indifferently (i.e., the higher level of recklessness).[952] Consequently, if the plaintiff could have proven negligence of the public servant or of the governmental entity, but not more than negligence, no liability is imposed. In fact, this establishes an immunity for public servants and governmental entities in the ICT area from liability for negligence.

In the ICT area in Israel, some of the functions are fulfilled by official tribunals activated by the state. For example, the Antitrust Tribunal discussed above.[953] Sometimes, the tribunals' decisions may be considered civil wrong, and the reasons may be various (e.g., the examination of the case, or of the request, was not thorough). In these situations, the elements of negligence may be fulfilled. Nevertheless, any lawsuit against the tribunal or against any of its members is declined, if it relates to the tribunal's functions.[954]

950. Section 3 of the Civil Torts (State's Liability) Act, 1952.
951. Section 8 of the Civil Torts (State's Liability) Act, 1952.
952. Section 7A and 7B of the Torts [New Version] Ordinance.
953. Above at s. [I] at Part I.
954. Section 8 of the Torts [New Version] Ordinance.

Chapter 2. Liability of Network Operators

119. A network operator in Israel is a licensee (the state is the licensor) who establishes and manages an ICT network within the Israeli territory. Most of the network operators in Israel function as service providers as well, but not all of them. Major network operators in Israel are Bezeq (landline telephony and Internet networks), HOT (cable TV, landline telephony and Internet networks), Pelephone (cellular network), and Cellcom (cellular network).

§1. General Legal Framework and the Applicable Law

120. Network operators usually have a dual system of legal relationships. One aspect of these relationships is contractual, and it relates to the network operators and the users of the network, whether they are service providers or private consumers. Within this aspect, the users of the network function as clients who 'consume' the network. This aspect of legal relationships has been discussed above.[955] The other aspect of these relationships is non-contractual. This aspect is discussed in this chapter.

The non-contractual aspect of the legal relationships of network operators may relate to the network operators and the users of the network or third parties. Both users and third parties might be damaged by any use of the network, malfunctioning of the network, unprofessional operating of the network, or unlawful operating of the network. For example, malfunctioning of a cellular network might cause severe damages to the users of the network as a result of the loss of communication channel. However, these users are not the network operator's direct clients, but the clients of the service providers using that network. Consequently, they have no contractual relations with the network operator, and they may sue the network operator only on non-contractual legal ground.

In this example, in most cases, the users have no legal ground to sue the service providers, as the network's malfunctioning was not under their control. Thus, the only potential wrongdoer is the network operator. The legal ground for these lawsuits is generally the law of torts. Although several particular civil wrongs have been enacted to protect the users and third parties and thus contributed to determine the liability of network operators, but in most cases, negligence is the wide and useful legal ground for these lawsuits.

In the context of network operators' liability, basically, there are two relevant basic layers of law. The first layer is the general law of torts, the second layer is particular laws which determine the network operators' liability (through particular torts or immunities) within the ICT law. The interpretation rule between these two layers is *lex specialis derogat generali*. Therefore, legal provisions from the particular laws determining network operators' liability derogate legal provisions from the general law of torts.

955. Above at Chapter 7 at Part III.

Thus, even though in certain cases the general law of torts may determine one network operator as liable, and therefore impose certain remedies, the ICT law may determine that liability is not enough to impose any remedies or that the network operator was not liable at all. As the ICT law, in the context of network operators' liability, functions as the specific law, it derogates the general law of torts, which functions as the general law.

Particular liability laws may relate to certain network operators who may be liable in tort law (e.g., cellular network operator) or to certain situations, in which liability may be involved (e.g., liability for malfunction of the network). As the general law of torts has been enacted in the 1940s, under the rule of the British Mandate, and the relevant provisions of the ICT law were enacted far later, these laws are not always coherent, and the rules of interpretation are required.

Liability in tort law is subject to the Israeli conflict of laws rules, and in particular to the rules of choice-of-law in torts. After sixty years of arguments towards the interpretation of choice-of-law rule in tort,[956] in 2004, inspired by the European and British rules, the Supreme Court has formulated the Israeli rule by case law. Accordingly, the applicable law on torts is the law of the place of occurrence of the tort (*lex loci delicti commissi*), and only if this law has absolutely no relevance to the case, the applicable law is the law that has the closest and most real connection to the tort.[957]

If the network operator's liability is through an omission, the place of occurrence of the tort is the place where the duty should have been fulfilled. If that liability is through an act, the place of the occurrence of the tort is the place of its actual commission and not necessarily the place where the damage has occurred or has been discovered (*lex loci delicti commissi* and not *lex loci damni*). The second part of the rule grants the court wide discretion towards the interpretation of the law that has 'the closest and most real connection' to the tort.

The jurisdiction of the Israeli court over network operators' liability in tort cases is not different than its jurisdiction in any other case in torts, and it is determined by the general rules of the Israeli conflict of laws. Accordingly, if the law determines the Israeli court as the authorized forum, if both parties agreed on the court's jurisdiction over the particular case, if the lawsuit's documents have been accepted by the defendant or by the defendant's local representative or if the plaintiff was authorized to deliver the lawsuit's documents to the defendant outside Israel, the Israeli court has the jurisdiction over the case.

956. *See, e.g.*, Civ. App. 180/51 *Goldcorn v. Wissotzky*, 8(1) PD 262 (1954); Civ. App. 98/67 *Livhar v. Gazit and Shaham*, 21(2) PD 243 (1967); Civ. App. 750/79 *Klausner v. Berkowitz*, 37(4) PD 449 (1983).

957. Civ. App. 1432/03 *Yinon v. Karan*, 59(1) PD 345 (2004); Civ. Cer. 4655/09 *Scaler v. Ubiner* (25 Oct. 2011).

§2. Liability, Immunities and Remedies

121. There are several civil wrongs which are in common use in the context of network operators. The civil wrong of trespass is usually used in cases of unauthorized use of land for infrastructure by the network operator (e.g., posing an antenna without authorization on private property).[958] A more general tort is nuisance (for the public or for a private person).[959] This tort is generally used in cases of misuse of infrastructure or devices by the network operator, and the lawsuits' objective is, in general, prohibitory injunction.

The general tort of fraud is generally used in cases where the network operator claims for certain characteristics, but they turn to be false.[960] For example, the network operator claims for certain speed of data transportation, but objective examinations do not support that. However, fraud is dependent on the network operator's awareness of the factual data and on the network operator's fraudulent intent (i.e., the network operator's intent to mislead the plaintiff by the false data).

However, the most common civil wrong that is used for the network operator's liability in torts is the tort of infringement of enacted duty.[961] In both civil and criminal statutes, several duties are imposed directly on network operators. If a certain duty enacted within a certain statute is infringed by the network operator, any person who experienced any damage as a result of the infringement has the right to submit a lawsuit on the ground of infringement of enacted duty. For example, the law prohibits network operators to enable annoying end users with commercial advertisements, unless previously agreed.[962] If this duty is infringed, a lawsuit against the network operator is submitted on the ground of infringement of enacted duty, regardless of a lawsuit against the advertiser.

As a result, the tort of infringement of enacted duty is used to enforce legal duties towards network operators. In this context, the network operator is bound to service the customers with a high quality of service and according to the specific conditions determined in the license which has licensed the network operator's activity.[963] The minister of communications is responsible for supervising the network operators. If the minister suspects that a network operator operates telecommunication services of low quality, endangers the competition in the specific field of telecommunication, or unable to ensure regular service, the minister may order specific orders to the network operator to meet the requirements. The orders may be given after the network operator is given a fair chance to explain the act or omission.

Nevertheless, if immediate actions are required, the minister may order the orders without enabling the network operator to explain. Such orders would be compulsory only after two days, and the network operator may comment within these two days. After the orders became compulsory, the network operator must be given a fair chance to explain the act or omission as soon as possible. The orders would be compulsory up to six months.

958. Sections 29–34 of the Torts [New Version] Ordinance.
959. Sections 42–47 of the Torts [New Version] Ordinance.
960. Section 63 of the Torts [New Version] Ordinance.
961. Sections 29–34 of the Torts [New Version] Ordinance.
962. Section 30A of the Communication (Telecommunication and Broadcasting) Act, 1982.
963. Section 11 of the Communication (Telecommunication and Broadcasting) Act, 1982.

When a network operator of telephony disconnects a customer from a phone service for unpaid bills, the network operator must enable the customer the use of the service to call emergency centres operated in Israel for at least two months from the date of disconnection, free of charge.[964] However, any call to any emergency centre in Israel must be free of charge from any supporting device (e.g., mobile phones and landline telephones). Due to privacy reasons, any calls for emergency centres would not be included in the customer bills and no information upon them would be given to *any* third party.[965] Emergency centres in Israel include not only the police, the fire department, and the medical services, but also assisting centres for women sexually attacked, mental first aid centres, and other assisting centres as well.[966]

In times of war or other emergency situations, including communications crisis (i.e., fatal harm to civil communication infrastructure), the minister of communications or the prime minister may license a public unit (e.g., communications unit of the Israeli police or communications unit of the Israeli Defence Forces) to operate telecommunications services as network operator in favour of the civil population in addition to the private network operators who fail to operate these services at full or in high quality.[967] However, when the emergency situation is over, the license automatically expires.

If no emergency situation has been declared, but the minister of communications realizes that the private network operator fails to operate the telecommunication services due to objective reasons or difficulties, the minister may temporarily license a public unit to operate these services as network operator in favour of the public.[968] However, public units should be licensed to operate telecommunication services as network operators only in extremely rare circumstances and only as a solution of the last resort.

Any network operator is allowed to determine operative rules for customers, as long as these rules are not contradicted with the law, and that they are certified by the minister of communications.[969] The minister may demand amendments of the rules in favour of the public, and if the network operator did not amend them within ninety days, the minister may amend them in lieu of the network operator.

Network operators are required to charge the customers fair fares. The minister is allowed to determine maximum fares for any telecommunication service.[970] However, the competition in the Israeli telecommunication market is considered to be developed enough for not intervening in the market fares. The ongoing trend of the fares in the Israeli market is lowering the fares and guarantee of high quality. For example, in 2019, Internet services of 100 Mb (download) were proposed for NIS 15 per month (approximately EUR 3.5 or USD 4), whereas in 2015, these very services were proposed for NIS 30. Debt for any private network operator is considered civil debt, and the network operator may submit a lawsuit against the customers who fail to pay the bills.

964. Section 12 of the Communication (Telecommunication and Broadcasting) Act, 1982.
965. Section 12A of the Communication (Telecommunication and Broadcasting) Act, 1982.
966. Section 12A(e) of the Communication (Telecommunication and Broadcasting) Act, 1982.
967. Section 13(b) of the Communication (Telecommunication and Broadcasting) Act, 1982.
968. Section 13B of the Communication (Telecommunication and Broadcasting) Act, 1982.
969. Section 14 of the Communication (Telecommunication and Broadcasting) Act, 1982.
970. Section 15 of the Communication (Telecommunication and Broadcasting) Act, 1982.

Network operator is allowed to build any infrastructure in order to ensure the telecommunication services only if it matches the legal requirement of the ministry of the environmental protection.[971] In spite of the increasing use of mobile phones by Israelis, cellular radiation is not welcome in cities' centres. Therefore, mobile services companies as network operators are challenged to ensure high-quality services without relying on massive infrastructure in cities' centres. However, any cellular transmitting device (e.g., antenna) is restricted in radiation rates and physical dimensions, for reasons of public's health.

Most breaches of the license conditions by network operators are protected through criminal offences.[972] Regardless of this type of protection, at any time after the license is granted to the network operator, the minister of communications may amend it or abolish it, if the network operator has asked for that, if not all conditions of the license were fulfilled, if the network operator has still not begun to operate the service, if the network operator has stopped the service, if the network operator has begun bankruptcy proceedings, if the quality of the service is insufficient or out of public welfare reasons.[973]

Network operators are also subject to particular standardization regarding the infrastructure and the quality of network. For example, cable TV network operators are bound to bandwidth of at least 400 MHz for ongoing data and of at least 20 MHz for incoming data.[974] In addition, the number of simultaneous channels should be at least 24,[975] and the signals should include receiving and transmitting capabilities of at least PAL/B and PAL/G systems.[976] Infringement of these enacted duties is considered civil wrong, as aforesaid, besides any other legal measures of enforcement (e.g., administrative and criminal measures).

However, network operator's liability in tort law is subject to a minimum damage proven by the plaintiff, and the mere proof of all elements of the tort is not enough in order to determine liability.[977] This resembles the general defence of *de minimis* in criminal law, as the minimum damage is presumed to have social interest. However, such a plea is rare in this sphere of law. Many lawsuits submitted by consumers against network operators are declined for this reason, even though liability has been proven, especially if fair compensation has been offered before the lawsuit has been submitted.

If the plaintiff has been exposed to the malfunction or negligence of the network operator knowingly or willingly, the plaintiff's right to any remedy is reduced or nullified.[978] However, if the lawsuit is based on infringement of any legal duty (i.e., determined by a particular statute), this is not a defence for the network operator. In

971. Section 27B of the Communication (Telecommunication and Broadcasting) Act, 1982.
972. Chapter 7 of the Communication (Telecommunication and Broadcasting) Act, 1982.
973. Section 6 of the Communication (Telecommunication and Broadcasting) Act, 1982.
974. Regulation 5 of the Communications (Telecommunication and Broadcasting) (Standards and Specification of Cable TV networks) Regulations, 1988.
975. Regulation 6 of the Communications (Telecommunication and Broadcasting) (Standards and Specification of Cable TV networks) Regulations, 1988.
976. Regulation 7 of the Communications (Telecommunication and Broadcasting) (Standards and Specification of Cable TV networks) Regulations, 1988.
977. Section 4 of the Torts [New Version] Ordinance.
978. Section 5(a) of the Torts [New Version] Ordinance.

any lawsuit besides liability, if the network operator has acted according to a certain statute, no liability is imposed.[979] Nevertheless, in negligence lawsuits, even if the network operator has acted according to a certain statute, this defence is inapplicable, unless the network operator has proven that the act was not negligent (i.e., a reasonable network operator would have been acting similarly).[980]

If the particular wrongdoer within the network operator is a public servant or any governmental entity (i.e., when the network operator is a government unit, and there are several governmental units in Israel that function as network operators), liability may be imposed only if the civil wrong has been committed intentionally or indifferently (i.e., the higher level of recklessness).[981] Consequently, if the plaintiff could have proven negligence of the public servant or of the governmental entity, but not more than negligence, no liability is imposed. In fact, this establishes an immunity for public servants and governmental units as network operators from civil lawsuits on the ground of negligence.

When there are at least two defendants within one lawsuit regarding the same tort or civil wrong (two network operators or one network operator and one service provider), they would share the liability between them 'together and separately'.[982] That means that both of them are responsible for the whole damage, and the internal division of the responsibility between them is not the plaintiff's concern. Nevertheless, the court may determine the division between them. This arrangement is also applicable for the accessories, inciters, solicitors, advisors, and other accomplices.[983] Of course, the accomplice's liability does not replace the perpetrator's, but it is additional.[984]

The network operator as an employer may have vicarious liability for the negligent conduct of the employees. The conditions for vicarious liability are the confirmation of the network operator to the employee's conduct and the commission of the conduct within the employment.[985] For this purpose, any of the employee's activities in favour of the network operator is considered commission of the conduct within the employment, even if the activity has been performed negligently (towards the network operator).[986] However, the conduct may be either act or omission. The required fault in the civil wrong that has actually occurred through the agent would be attributed to the network operator as principal.[987] Of course, the network operator's liability does not replace the employee's, but it is additional.[988]

Nevertheless, the network operator is exempt from liability if the conduct has not been committed by one of the employees, but by a person who was authorized by an employee without the explicit or implicit consent of the network operator.[989] In

979. Section 5(b) of the Torts [New Version] Ordinance.
980. Section 6 of the Torts [New Version] Ordinance.
981. Section 7A and 7B of the Torts [New Version] Ordinance.
982. Section 11 of the Torts [New Version] Ordinance.
983. Section 12 of the Torts [New Version] Ordinance.
984. Section 16 of the Torts [New Version] Ordinance.
985. Section 13(a)(1) and 13(a)(2) of the Torts (New Version] Ordinance.
986. Section 13(b) of the Torts [New Version] Ordinance.
987. Section 17 of the Torts [New Version] Ordinance.
988. Section 16 of the Torts [New Version] Ordinance.
989. Section 13(a)(2)(a) of the Torts [New Version] Ordinance.

addition, if the network operator has consented, but neither the network operator nor the employee could have chosen any other person (e.g., when the person is a corporation who has an absolute monopoly over the relevant services required for the standard activity of the network operator), both the network operator and the employee are exempt from liability.[990] As aforesaid, in Israel, several corporations are monopolies as network operators (e.g., HOT corporation as cable TV network operator).[991] Thus, the opportunity to choose affects the liability.

In contractual relations between the parties, the contract itself is not an adequate ground for imposition of liability for any civil wrong, unless the contract is deliberately meant to authorize one of the parties to commit the civil wrong on behalf of the other.[992] Nevertheless, the contract may be an adequate ground for imposition of liability on the relevant civil wrong if the choice of the counterparty was negligent (e.g., network operator who negligently chooses service provider),[993] if the damage has occurred due to intervention in the counterparty's conduct,[994] if the party permitted (*ex ante*) or ratified (*ex post*) the civil wrong,[995] if the party is personally liable due to the law,[996] or if the object of the contract is itself civil wrong.[997]

In general, in the ICT area, when there are agency relations between the parties, whether contractual or not (e.g., semi-contractual relations or fiduciary relations), the principal is liable for the agent's conduct.[998] Occasionally, network operators in Israel function as principals and service providers as agents. The required fault in the civil wrong that has actually occurred through the agent would be attributed to the principal.[999] Of course, the principal's liability does not replace the agent's, but it is additional.[1000]

In case of death of the plaintiff, all rights of the dead are reserved for the dead's estate.[1001] Any insolvent plaintiff has all rights to submit any lawsuit for any tort, and insolvency itself is neither defence nor barrier from submission of lawsuits.[1002] However, the right for remedies for any tort is personal and may not be assigned or transferred, unless explicitly permitted by the law.[1003]

The doctrine of contributory negligence has been accepted in Israeli tort law. Accordingly, if the damage has been caused solely by the plaintiff, the network operator is exempt from liability.[1004] If the damage has been caused by the network operator, who was driven to act this way by the plaintiff (intentionally or not), the

990. Section 13(a)(2)(b) of the Torts [New Version] Ordinance.
991. Above at s. [IV]: Monopolies at Part I.
992. Section 15 of the Torts [New Version] Ordinance.
993. Section 15(1) of the Torts [New Version] Ordinance.
994. Section 15(2) of the Torts [New Version] Ordinance.
995. Section 15(3) of the Torts [New Version] Ordinance.
996. Section 15(4) of the Torts [New Version] Ordinance.
997. Section 15(5) of the Torts [New Version] Ordinance.
998. Section 14 of the Torts [New Version] Ordinance.
999. Section 17 of the Torts [New Version] Ordinance.
1000. Section 16 of the Torts [New Version] Ordinance.
1001. Section 19(a) of the Torts [New Version] Ordinance.
1002. Section 21 of the Torts [New Version] Ordinance.
1003. Section 22 of the Torts [New Version] Ordinance.
1004. Section 64 of the Torts [New Version] Ordinance.

court is authorized to consider lower rate of remedies or even exemption for the network operator from remedies, dependent on the involvement of the plaintiff in the factual process that resulted in the particular damage (e.g., sabotage of the plaintiff in the network operator's infrastructure).[1005]

If the plaintiff has negligently contributed to the occurrence of the damage, the court is required to reduce the rate of remedies in favour of the plaintiff to the network operator's contribution to the occurrence of the damage.[1006] For example, if the plaintiff misused ICT equipment supplied by the network operator, but that equipment was defective regardless of the plaintiff's behaviour, it is more likely that the network operator is not considered liable for the whole damage. Thus, if the court is convinced that the plaintiff contributory liability is estimated by 20% of the damage, the network operator is regarded as liable for 80% of the damage, and the remedies in favour of the plaintiff are reduced accordingly.

Sometimes the civil wrong is considered a criminal offence. In such cases, the lawsuit regarding the civil wrong is not affected by any of the criminal proceedings and is not affected if no criminal proceedings have been taken.[1007] Nevertheless, the court may order the parties to notify the police on the facts that might form a criminal offence.

However, the Israeli evidence law regards the judgment in criminal proceedings for the same facts admissible in civil proceedings,[1008] and that may ease the plaintiff the burden of proof. In addition, the victim of any criminal offence may submit a civil lawsuit to the criminal court who has convicted the network operator,[1009] and the court would function as if it were a civil court (i.e., authorized to grant any civil remedy in favour of the plaintiff).

Any civil lawsuit is required to specify explicitly what is the requested remedy, regardless of the legal cause for the lawsuit.[1010] This requirement is relevant to any civil lawsuit. In tort lawsuits, the Israeli court is authorized to grant the plaintiff any remedy within its jurisdiction and subject to any limitation determined explicitly by the law.[1011]

The court is authorized to grant mandatory injunction or prohibitory injunction, whether permanent or temporary.[1012] These injunctions may be given in addition to any other remedy and as sole remedies.[1013] These injunctions do not necessarily derivate from other remedies, but they may be the sole object of the lawsuit. This is significant especially when the major object of the lawsuit is to prevent a future damage, as the damage already been occurred is immaterial. When the court is

1005. Section 65 of the Torts [New Version] Ordinance.
1006. Section 68 of the Torts [New Version] Ordinance.
1007. Section 88 of the Torts [New Version] Ordinance.
1008. Section 42A of the Evidence [New Version] Ordinance, 1971.
1009. Section 77 of the Courts [Combined Version] Act, 1984.
1010. Regulation 10(9) of the Civil Procedure Regulations, 2018.
1011. Section 71 of the Torts [New Version] Ordinance.
1012. Section 72 of the Torts [New Version] Ordinance.
1013. Section 71 of the Torts [New Version] Ordinance.

authorized to grant injunctions in favour of the parties by other provisions of the law (e.g., by the Civil Procedure Regulations, 2018), the above provisions do not negate this authorization.[1014]

Temporary injunction is an injunction that is valid until the judgment is given. When the plaintiff has reasonable causes to believe that the network operator might change the situation or the evidence so that the judgment would not be enforceable, temporary injunction to remain the situation as it is is required. However, the court is authorized to grant a temporary injunction, only if the court is convinced that a real legal question occurs within the lawsuit, it is most probable that the plaintiff would win the case and justice would be prevented unless the injunction is granted.[1015]

Nevertheless, the court has to consider hypothetically the balance of damages between the plaintiff and the network operator as a result of granting the injunction. Thus, if, as a result of granting the injunction in favour of the plaintiff, the network operator would probably be exposed to major damages, whereas the claimed damages by the plaintiff are relatively small and may be evaluated in certain sum of money, the court may refuse to grant the injunction, and it is authorized to grant other remedies in favour of the plaintiff, whether claimed or not.[1016]

However, the common remedy in civil lawsuits on the ground of tort law against network operators is damages. Damages are, basically, payment of money as compensation. The court is authorized to grant damages in favour of the plaintiff in addition to other remedies and as sole remedy.[1017] Under the 2018 regulations of civil procedure, the plaintiff is required to describe in detail the damage that the compensation is related to.[1018]

The general objective of the damages is to compensate for the damage, and not to enrich the plaintiff. Therefore, the court is limited within the scope of the damage when calculating the damages. Moreover, damages for the same damage are granted only once, regardless of the identity of the plaintiff.[1019] Thus, if the network operator has already compensated one plaintiff for a certain damage at full, i.e., the payment is equivalent to the total damage, the network operator is not required to compensate any other party in any further lawsuit for the same damage.

Social security payment which is paid as a result of commission of civil wrong of the network operator is reduced from the total sum of damages paid by the plaintiff's employer.[1020] For example, if an employee suffers from non-ionizing radiation harm estimated 100, the Israeli social security institute determines 1% of functional disability and social security payment of 2 per annum, the employee is 62 years old, and the retirement age in Israel is 67, the employer is required to pay 90.[1021]

1014. Section 75 of the Torts [New Version] Ordinance.
1015. Section 73 of the Torts [New Version] Ordinance.
1016. Section 74 of the Torts [New Version] Ordinance.
1017. Section 76 of the Torts [New Version] Ordinance.
1018. Regulation 10(9) of the Civil Procedure Regulations, 2018.
1019. Section 77(a) of the Torts [New Version] Ordinance.
1020. Section 82 of the Torts [New Version] Ordinance.
1021. math-figure $100 - 2\ (67 - 62) = 90$.

However, any payment due to any insurance contract that is paid for any damage is *not* reduced from the damages payment granted by the court.[1022] For example, ICT infrastructure has been overheated due to the network operator's malfunction or negligence and caused damage to the plaintiff's apartment. However, the apartment is insured by a contract for any damage, including such damage. When the court calculates the damages that the network operator is required to pay in favour of the plaintiff, the payment that has been paid by the insurance company due to the contract is not reduced from the payment that the network operator is required to pay as damages.

Lawsuits for death cases in the ICT area are rare in Israel, and most of them are related to labour law (e.g., an employee dies while at work for a network operator as a result of the network operator's conduct). Nevertheless, certain legal provisions are relevant in this issue. The plaintiffs are the dead's successors or estate and any other person who was financially dependent on the dead, and they are granted damages for the death and for any bodily harm involved.[1023]

In addition, the successors and any other person who was financially dependent on the dead may sue for any future loss caused by the death.[1024] That includes the relative loss of future earnings and any reasonable costs caused by the death (e.g., the funeral costs). Nevertheless, that does not include any payment due to insurance contract (e.g., life insurance or pension) or payment for the time of the grief, which are paid in addition.[1025]

If some network operators acted as accomplices, the plaintiff may sue all of them within the same lawsuit, and all of them altogether would be required to pay the plaintiff the total sum of payment.[1026] However, if one of the accomplices has paid the damages, and the other accomplices have not, a lawsuit by the paying accomplice may be submitted against the other accomplices for their share (i.e., indemnity lawsuit).[1027] The shares may be determined by the court due to the personal contribution to the damage or due to their actual function within the damage (e.g., perpetrators, joint-perpetrators, inciters, accessories, or advisors).[1028]

If the plaintiff is a corporation, and the lawsuit relates to the network operator's liability, the plaintiff is not granted any payment for damages, unless actually proven the damages.[1029] As many legal provisions in the ICT law and consumption law grant plaintiffs payments in lawsuits without any proof of damages, this legal provision towards corporations is very significant. However, it relates to corporations as plaintiffs and not as network operators (which all of them are corporations in Israel). Thus, if a network operator corporation is sued by a physical person, and the law grants payment for damages without any proof of damages, the network operator is required to pay.

1022. Section 86 of the Torts [New Version] Ordinance.
1023. Section 78 of the Torts [New Version] Ordinance.
1024. Section 80 of the Torts [New Version] Ordinance.
1025. Section 81 of the Torts [New Version] Ordinance.
1026. Section 83 of the Torts [New Version] Ordinance.
1027. Section 84(a) of the Torts [New Version] Ordinance.
1028. Section 84(b) of the Torts [New Version] Ordinance.
1029. Section 10 of the Torts [New Version] Ordinance.

When there are at least two network operators within one lawsuit regarding the same tort or civil wrong, they would share the responsibility for the remedies between them 'together and separately'.[1030] That means that both of them are responsible for all of the damages, and the internal division of the responsibility between them towards the remedies is not the plaintiff's concern. Nevertheless, the court may determine the division between them. This arrangement is applicable also for the accessories, inciters, solicitors, advisors, and other accomplices.[1031]

1030. Section 11 of the Torts [New Version] Ordinance.
1031. Section 12 of the Torts [New Version] Ordinance.

Chapter 3. Liability of Service Providers

122. A service provider in Israel is a licensee (the state is the licensor) who establishes and manages ICT services within the Israeli territory. Some of the service providers in Israel function as network operators as well, but not all of them. Major service providers in Israel which are also network operators are Bezeq (landline telephony and Internet services), HOT (cable TV, landline telephony, and Internet services), Pelephone (cellular services), and Cellcom (cellular services). Major service providers which are *not* network operators are 012 (international calls and Internet services) and Rami Levi (cellular services based on Pelephone cellular network).

§1. General Legal Framework and the Applicable Law

123. Service providers usually have a dual system of legal relationships. One aspect of these relationships is contractual, and it relates to the service providers and the users of the service, whether they are other service providers or private consumers. Within this aspect, the users of the services function as clients who 'consume' the services. This aspect of legal relationships has been discussed above.[1032] The other aspect of these relationships is non-contractual. This aspect is discussed in this chapter.

The non-contractual aspect of the legal relationships of service providers may relate to the service providers and the users of the services or third parties. Both users and third parties might be damaged by any use of the services, malfunctioning of the services, unprofessional operating of the services, or unlawful operating of the services. For example, malfunctioning of cellular services might cause severe damages to the users of the services as a result of the loss of useful, and perhaps the only, communication channel.

In addition, the service provider may be liable for the third-party's content. The service provider may be held liable for the third party's content, mostly in cases where the customer has asked not to be provided with such contents. For example, a customer of HOT has sued HOT for erotic content in certain channels (the channels are independent, and HOT functions only as a service provider). The court approved the lawsuit and granted the plaintiff NIS 30,000 (approximately EUR 7,000).[1033]

Another example: a customer of HOT has sued HOT for invading his privacy, as one of the channels broadcasted by HOT showed his picture from the past, although HOT has functioned just as a service provider, and it was not involved in this channel's content. The lawsuit has been dismissed, as the content was considered 'news'.[1034]

The legal ground for all these lawsuits is generally the law of torts. Although several particular civil wrongs have been enacted to protect the users and third parties

1032. Above at Chapter 7: Network Services at Part III.
1033. Civ. App. Req. (Haifa) 3232/08 *HOT v. Isakov* (23 Jun. 2008).
1034. Civ. Cas. 9866-02-13 (Tel Aviv) *Abu Ajaj v. HOT* (30 Dec. 2015).

and thus contributed to determine the liability of service providers, but in most cases, negligence is the wide and useful legal ground for these lawsuits.

In the context of service providers' liability, basically, there are two relevant basic layers of law. The first layer is the general law of torts, the second layer is particular laws which determine the service providers' liability (through particular torts or immunities) within the ICT law. The interpretation rule between these two layers is *lex specialis derogat generali*. Therefore, legal provisions from the particular laws determining service providers' liability derogate legal provisions from the general law of torts.

Thus, even though in certain cases the general law of torts may determine one service provider as liable, and therefore impose certain remedies, the ICT law may determine that liability is not enough to impose any remedies or that the service provider was not liable at all. As the ICT law, in the context of service providers' liability, functions as the specific law, it derogates the general law of torts, which functions as the general law.

Particular liability laws may relate to certain service providers who may be liable in tort law (e.g., cellular service provider) or to certain situations, in which liability may be involved (e.g., liability for malfunction of the services). As the general law of torts has been enacted in the 1940s, under the rule of the British Mandate, and the relevant provisions of the ICT law were enacted far later, these laws are not always coherent, and the rules of interpretation are required.

Liability in tort law is subject to the Israeli conflict of laws rules, and in particular to the rules of choice-of-law in torts. After sixty years of arguments towards the interpretation of choice-of-law rule in tort,[1035] in 2004, inspired by the European and British rules, the Supreme Court has formulated the Israeli rule by case law. Accordingly, the applicable law on torts is the law of the place of occurrence of the tort (*lex loci delicti commissi*), and only if this law has absolutely no relevance to the case, the applicable law is the law that has the closest and most real connection to the tort.[1036]

If the service provider's liability is through an omission, the place of occurrence of the tort is the place where the duty should have been fulfilled. If that liability is through an act, the place of the occurrence of the tort is the place of its actual commission and not necessarily the place where the damage has occurred or has been discovered (*lex loci delicti commissi* and not *lex loci damni*). The second part of the rule grants the court wide discretion towards the interpretation of the law that has 'the closest and most real connection' to the tort.

The jurisdiction of the Israeli court over service providers' liability in tort cases is not different than its jurisdiction in any other case in torts, and it is determined by the general rules of the Israeli conflict of laws. Accordingly, if the law determines the Israeli court as the authorized forum, if both parties agreed on the court's jurisdiction over the particular case, if the lawsuit's documents have been accepted by

---

1035. *See, e.g.*, Civ. App. 180/51 *Goldcorn v. Wissotzky*, 8(1) PD 262 (1954); Civ. App. 98/67 *Livhar v. Gazit and Shaham*, 21(2) PD 243 (1967); Civ. App. 750/79 *Klausner v. Berkowitz*, 37(4) PD 449 (1983).

1036. Civ. App. 1432/03 *Yinon v. Karan*, 59(1) PD 345 (2004); Civ. Cer. 4655/09 *Scaler v. Ubiner* (25 Oct. 2011).

the defendant or by the defendant's local representative or if the plaintiff was authorized to deliver the lawsuit's documents to the defendant outside Israel, the Israeli court has the jurisdiction over the case.

§2. Liability, Immunities and Remedies

124. There are several civil wrongs which are in common use in the context of service providers. The general tort of fraud is generally used in cases where the service provider claims for certain characteristics, but they turn to be false.[1037] For example, the service provider claims for certain speed of data transportation, but objective examinations do not support that. However, fraud is dependent on the service provider's awareness of the factual data and on the service provider's fraudulent intent (i.e., the service provider's intent to mislead the plaintiff by the false data).

However, the most common civil wrong that is used for the service provider's liability in torts is the tort of infringement of enacted duty.[1038] In both civil and criminal statutes, several duties are imposed directly on service providers. If a certain duty enacted within a certain statute is infringed by the service provider, any person who experienced any damage as a result of the infringement has the right to submit a lawsuit on the ground of infringement of enacted duty. For example, the law prohibits service providers to enable annoying end users with commercial advertisements, unless previously agreed.[1039] If this duty is infringed, a lawsuit against the service provider is submitted on the ground of infringement of enacted duty, regardless a lawsuit against the advertiser.

As a result, the tort of infringement of enacted duty is used to enforce legal duties towards service providers. In this context, the service provider is bound to service the customers with a high quality of service and according to the specific conditions determined in the license which has licensed the service provider's activity.[1040] The minister of communications is responsible for supervising the service providers. If the minister suspects that a service provider operates telecommunication services of low quality, endangers the competition in the specific field of telecommunication, or unable to ensure regular service, the minister may order specific orders to the service provider to meet the requirements. The orders may be given after the service provider would be given a fair chance to explain the act or omission.

Nevertheless, if immediate actions are required, the minister may order the orders without enabling the service provider to explain. Such orders would be compulsory only after two days, and the service provider may comment within these two days. After the orders became compulsory, the service provider must be given a fair chance to explain the act or omission as soon as possible. The orders would be compulsory for up to six months.

1037. Section 63 of the Torts [New Version] Ordinance.
1038. Sections 29–34 of the Torts [New Version] Ordinance.
1039. Section 30A of the Communication (Telecommunication and Broadcasting) Act, 1982.
1040. Section 11 of the Communication (Telecommunication and Broadcasting) Act, 1982.

When a service provider of telephony services disconnects a customer from a phone service for unpaid bills, the service provider must enable the customer the use of the service to call emergency centres operated in Israel for at least two months from the date of disconnection, free of charge.[1041] However, any call to any emergency centre in Israel must be free of charge from any supporting device (e.g., mobile phones and landline telephones). Due to privacy reasons, any calls for emergency centres would not be included in the customer bills, and no information upon them would be given to *any* third party.[1042] Emergency centres in Israel include not only the police, the fire department, and the medical services, but assisting centres for women sexually attacked, mental first aid centres, and other assisting centres as well.[1043]

In times of war or other emergency situations, including communications crisis (i.e., fatal harm to civil communication infrastructure), the minister of communications or the prime minister may license a public unit (e.g., communications unit of the Israeli police or communications unit of the Israeli Defence Forces) to operate telecommunications services as service provider in favour of the civil population in addition to the private service providers who fail to operate these services at full or in high quality.[1044] However, when the emergency situation is over, the license automatically expires.

If no emergency situation has been declared, but the minister of communications realizes that the private service provider fails to operate the telecommunication services due to objective reasons or difficulties, the minister may temporarily license a public unit to operate these services as service provider in favour of the public.[1045] However, public units should be licensed to operate telecommunication services as service providers only in extremely rare circumstances and only as a solution of the last resort.

Any service provider is allowed to determine operative rules for customers, as long as these rules are not contradicted with the law, and that they are certified by the minister of communications.[1046] The minister may demand amendments of the rules in favour of the public, and if the service provider did not amend them within ninety days, the minister may amend them in lieu of the service provider.

Service providers are required to charge the customers fair fares. The minister is allowed to determine maximum fares for any telecommunication service.[1047] However, the competition in the Israeli telecommunication market is considered to be developed enough for not intervening in the market fares. The ongoing trend of the fares in the Israeli market is lowering the fares and guarantee of high quality. For example, in 2019, Internet services of 100 Mb (download) were proposed for NIS

1041. Section 12 of the Communication (Telecommunication and Broadcasting) Act, 1982.
1042. Section 12A of the Communication (Telecommunication and Broadcasting) Act, 1982.
1043. Section 12A(e) of the Communication (Telecommunication and Broadcasting) Act, 1982.
1044. Section 13(b) of the Communication (Telecommunication and Broadcasting) Act, 1982.
1045. Section 13B of the Communication (Telecommunication and Broadcasting) Act, 1982.
1046. Section 14 of the Communication (Telecommunication and Broadcasting) Act, 1982.
1047. Section 15 of the Communication (Telecommunication and Broadcasting) Act, 1982.

15 per month (approximately EUR 3.5 or USD 4), whereas in 2015, these very services were proposed for NIS 30. Debt for any private service provider is considered civil debt, and the service provider may submit a lawsuit against the customers who fail to pay the bills.

Service provider is allowed to build any infrastructure in order to ensure the telecommunication services only if it matches the legal requirement of the ministry of environmental protection.[1048] In spite of the increasing use of mobile phones by Israelis, cellular radiation is not welcome in cities' centres. Therefore, mobile services companies as service providers (including virtual mobile network operators, which actually function as service providers) are challenged to ensure high-quality services without relying on massive infrastructure in cities' centres. The infrastructure may be theirs (if they function as network operators as well) or not. However, any cellular transmitting device (e.g., antenna) is restricted in radiation rates and physical dimensions, for reasons of public health.

Most breaches of the license conditions by service providers are protected through criminal offences.[1049] Regardless of this type of protection, at any time after the license is granted to the service provider, the minister of communications may amend it or abolish it, if the service provider has asked for that, if not all conditions of the license were fulfilled, if the service provider has still not begun to operate the service, if the service provider has stopped the service, if the service provider has begun bankruptcy proceedings, if the quality of the service is insufficient or out of public welfare reasons.[1050] Service providers are also subject to particular standardization regarding the infrastructure and the quality of services.

However, service provider's liability in tort law is subject to a minimum damage proven by the plaintiff, and the mere proof of all elements of the tort is not enough in order to determine liability.[1051] This resembles the general defence of *de minimis* in criminal law, as the minimum damage is presumed to have social interest. Many lawsuits submitted by consumers against service providers are declined for this reason, even though liability has been proven, especially if fair compensation has been offered before the lawsuit has been submitted.

If the plaintiff has been exposed to the malfunction or negligence of the service provider knowingly or willingly, the plaintiff's right to any remedy is reduced or nullified.[1052] However, if the lawsuit is based on infringement of any legal duty (i.e., determined by a particular statute), this is not a defence for the service provider. In any lawsuit besides liability, if the service provider has acted according to a certain statute, no liability is imposed.[1053] Nevertheless, in negligence lawsuits, even if the service provider has acted according to a certain statute, this defence is inapplicable, unless the service provider has proven that the act was not negligent (i.e., a reasonable service provider would have been acting similarly).[1054]

1048. Section 27B of the Communication (Telecommunication and Broadcasting) Act, 1982.
1049. Chapter 7 of the Communication (Telecommunication and Broadcasting) Act, 1982.
1050. Section 6 of the Communication (Telecommunication and Broadcasting) Act, 1982.
1051. Section 4 of the Torts [New Version] Ordinance.
1052. Section 5(a) of the Torts [New Version] Ordinance.
1053. Section 5(b) of the Torts [New Version] Ordinance.
1054. Section 6 of the Torts [New Version] Ordinance.

If the particular wrongdoer within the service provider is a public servant or any governmental entity (i.e., when the service provider is a government unit, and there are several governmental units in Israel which function as service providers), liability may be imposed only if the civil wrong has been committed intentionally or indifferently (i.e., the higher level of recklessness).[1055] Consequently, if the plaintiff could have proven negligence of the public servant or of the governmental entity, but not more than negligence, no liability is imposed. In fact, this establishes an immunity for public servants and governmental units as service providers from civil lawsuits on the ground of negligence.

When there are at least two defendants within one lawsuit regarding the same tort or civil wrong (two service providers or one service provider and one network operator), they would share the liability between them 'together and separately'.[1056] That means that both of them are responsible for the whole damage, and the internal division of the responsibility between them is not the plaintiff's concern. Nevertheless, the court may determine the division between them. This arrangement is also applicable for the accessories, inciters, solicitors, advisors, and other accomplices.[1057] Of course, the accomplice's liability does not replace the perpetrator's, but it is additional.[1058]

The service provider as an employer may have vicarious liability for the negligent conduct of the employees. The conditions for vicarious liability are the confirmation of the service provider to the employee's conduct and the commission of the conduct within the employment.[1059] For this purpose, any of the employee's activities in favour of the service provider is considered commission of the conduct within the employment, even if the activity has been performed negligently (towards the service provider).[1060] However, the conduct may be either act or omission. The required fault in the civil wrong that has actually occurred through the agent would be attributed to the service provider as principal.[1061] Of course, the service provider's liability does not replace the employee's, but it is additional.[1062]

Nevertheless, the service provider is exempt from liability if the conduct has not been committed by one of the employees, but by a person who was authorized by an employee without the explicit or implicit consent of the service provider.[1063] In addition, if the service provider has consented, but neither the service provider nor the employee could have chosen any other person (e.g., when the person is a corporation who has a monopoly over the relevant services required for the standard activity of the service provider), both the service provider and the employee are

1055. Section 7A and 7B of the Torts [New Version] Ordinance.
1056. Section 11 of the Torts [New Version] Ordinance.
1057. Section 12 of the Torts [New Version] Ordinance.
1058. Section 16 of the Torts [New Version] Ordinance.
1059. Section 13(a)(1) and 13(a)(2) of the Torts [New Version] Ordinance.
1060. Section 13(b) of the Torts [New Version] Ordinance.
1061. Section 17 of the Torts [New Version] Ordinance.
1062. Section 16 of the Torts [New Version] Ordinance.
1063. Section 13(a)(2)(a) of the Torts [New Version] Ordinance.

exempt from liability.[1064] As aforesaid, in Israel, several corporations are monopolies as service providers (e.g., HOT corporation as cable TV service provider).[1065] Thus, the opportunity to choose affects the liability.

In contractual relations between the parties, the contract itself is not an adequate ground for imposition of liability for any civil wrong, unless the contract is deliberately meant to authorize one of the parties to commit the civil wrong on behalf of the other.[1066] Nevertheless, the contract may be an adequate ground for imposition of liability on the relevant civil wrong if the choice of the counterparty was negligent (e.g., service provider who negligently chooses network operator with low-quality infrastructure),[1067] if the damage has occurred due to intervention in the counterparty's conduct,[1068] if the party permitted (*ex ante*) or ratified (*ex post*) the civil wrong,[1069] if the party is personally liable due to the law,[1070] or if the object of the contract is itself civil wrong.[1071]

In general, in the ICT area, when there are agency relations between the parties, whether contractual or not (e.g., semi-contractual relations or fiduciary relations), the principal is liable for the agent's conduct.[1072] Occasionally, service providers in Israel function as principals and service providers as agents. The required fault in the civil wrong that has actually occurred through the agent would be attributed to the principal.[1073] Of course, the principal's liability does not replace the agent's, but it is additional.[1074]

In case of death of the plaintiff, all rights of the dead are reserved for the dead's estate.[1075] Any insolvent plaintiff has all rights to submit any lawsuit for any tort, and insolvency itself is neither defence nor barrier from submission of lawsuits.[1076] However, the right for remedies for any tort is personal and may not be assigned or transferred, unless explicitly permitted by the law.[1077]

The doctrine of contributory negligence has been accepted in Israeli tort law. Accordingly, if the damage has been caused solely by the plaintiff, the service provider is exempt from liability.[1078] If the damage has been caused by the service provider, who was driven to act this way by the plaintiff (intentionally or not), the court is authorized to consider lower rate of remedies or even exemption for the service

1064. Section 13(a)(2)(b) of the Torts [New Version] Ordinance.
1065. Above at s. [IV]: Monopolies at Part I.
1066. Section 15 of the Torts [New Version] Ordinance.
1067. Section 15(1) of the Torts [New Version] Ordinance.
1068. Section 15(2) of the Torts [New Version] Ordinance.
1069. Section 15(3) of the Torts [New Version] Ordinance.
1070. Section 15(4) of the Torts [New Version] Ordinance.
1071. Section 15(5) of the Torts [New Version] Ordinance.
1072. Section 14 of the Torts [New Version] Ordinance.
1073. Section 17 of the Torts [New Version] Ordinance.
1074. Section 16 of the Torts [New Version] Ordinance.
1075. Section 19(a) of the Torts [New Version] Ordinance.
1076. Section 21 of the Torts [New Version] Ordinance.
1077. Section 22 of the Torts [New Version] Ordinance.
1078. Section 64 of the Torts [New Version] Ordinance.

provider from remedies, dependent on the involvement of the plaintiff in the factual process that resulted in the particular damage (e.g., sabotage of the plaintiff in the service provider's infrastructure).[1079]

If the plaintiff has negligently contributed to the occurrence of the damage, the court is required to reduce the rate of remedies in favour of the plaintiff to the service provider's contribution to the occurrence of the damage.[1080] For example, if the plaintiff misused ICT equipment supplied by the service provider, but that equipment was defective regardless of the plaintiff's behaviour, it is more likely that the service provider is not considered liable for the whole damage. Thus, if the court is convinced that the plaintiff's contributory liability is estimated by 10% of the damage, the service provider is regarded as liable for 90% of the damage, and the remedies in favour of the plaintiff are reduced accordingly.

Sometimes the civil wrong is considered a criminal offence. In such cases, the lawsuit regarding the civil wrong is not affected by any of the criminal proceedings and is not affected if no criminal proceedings have been taken.[1081] Nevertheless, the court may order the parties to notify the police on the facts that might form a criminal offence.

However, the Israeli evidence law regards admissible in civil proceedings the judgment in criminal proceedings for the same facts,[1082] and that may ease the plaintiff the burden of proof. In addition, the victim of any criminal offence may submit a civil lawsuit to the criminal court who has convicted the service provider,[1083] and the court would function as if it were a civil court (i.e., authorized to grant any civil remedy in favour of the plaintiff).

Any civil lawsuit is required to specify explicitly what is the requested remedy, regardless of the legal cause for the lawsuit.[1084] This requirement is relevant to any civil lawsuit. In tort lawsuits, the Israeli court is authorized to grant the plaintiff any remedy within its jurisdiction and subject to any limitation determined explicitly by the law.[1085]

The court is authorized to grant mandatory injunction or prohibitory injunction, whether permanent or temporary.[1086] These injunctions may be given in addition to any other remedy and as sole remedies.[1087] These injunctions do not necessarily derivate from other remedies, but they may be the sole objects of the lawsuit. This is significant especially when the major object of the lawsuit is to prevent a future damage, as the damage already been occurred is immaterial. When the court is authorized to grant injunctions in favour of the parties by other provisions of the law (e.g., by the Civil Procedure Regulations, 2018), the above provisions do not negate this authorization.[1088]

1079. Section 65 of the Torts [New Version] Ordinance.
1080. Section 68 of the Torts [New Version] Ordinance.
1081. Section 88 of the Torts [New Version] Ordinance.
1082. Section 42A of the Evidence [New Version] Ordinance, 1971.
1083. Section 77 of the Courts [Combined Version] Act, 1984.
1084. Regulation 10(9) of the Civil Procedure Regulations, 2018.
1085. Section 71 of the Torts [New Version] Ordinance.
1086. Section 72 of the Torts [New Version] Ordinance.
1087. Section 71 of the Torts [New Version] Ordinance.
1088. Section 75 of the Torts [New Version] Ordinance.

Temporary injunction is an injunction that is valid until the judgment is given. When the plaintiff has reasonable causes to believe that the service provider might change the situation or the evidence so that the judgment would not be enforceable, temporary injunction to remain the situation as it is is required. However, the court is authorized to grant a temporary injunction, only if the court is convinced that a real legal question occurs within the lawsuit, it is most probable that the plaintiff would win the case and justice would be prevented unless the injunction is granted.[1089]

Nevertheless, the court has to consider hypothetically the balance of damages between the plaintiff and the service provider as a result of granting the injunction. Thus, if, as a result of granting the injunction in favour of the plaintiff, the service provider would probably be exposed to major damages, whereas the claimed damages by the plaintiff are relatively small and may be evaluated in certain sum of money, the court may refuse to grant the injunction, and it is authorized to grant other remedies in favour of the plaintiff, whether claimed or not.[1090]

However, the common remedy in civil lawsuits on the ground of tort law against service providers is damages. Damages are, basically, payment of money as compensation. The court is authorized to grant damages in favour of the plaintiff in addition to other remedies and as sole remedy.[1091] Under the 2018 regulations of civil procedure, the plaintiff is required to describe in detail the damage that the compensation is related to.[1092]

The general objective of the damages is to compensate for the damage, and not to enrich the plaintiff. Therefore, the court is limited within the scope of the damage when calculating the damages. Moreover, damages for the same damage are granted only once, regardless of the identity of the plaintiff.[1093] Thus, if the service provider has already compensated one plaintiff for a certain damage at full, i.e., the payment is equivalent to the total damage, the service provider is not required to compensate any other party in any further lawsuit for the same damage.

Social security payment which is paid as a result of commission of civil wrong of the service provider is reduced from the total sum of damages paid by the plaintiff's employer.[1094] For example, if an employee suffers from non-ionizing radiation harm estimated 100, the Israeli social security institute determines 3% of functional disability and social security payment of 3 per annum, the employee is 60 years old, and the retirement age in Israel is 67, the employer is required to pay 79.[1095]

However, any payment due to any insurance contract that is paid for any damage is *not* reduced from the damages payment granted by the court.[1096] For example, ICT infrastructure has been overheated due to the service provider's malfunction or negligence, and caused damage to the plaintiff's apartment. However, the apartment is insured by a contract for any damage, including such damage. When the court

1089. Section 73 of the Torts [New Version] Ordinance.
1090. Section 74 of the Torts [New Version] Ordinance.
1091. Section 76 of the Torts [New Version] Ordinance.
1092. Regulation 10(9) of the Civil Procedure Regulations, 2018.
1093. Section 77(a) of the Torts [New Version] Ordinance.
1094. Section 82 of the Torts [New Version] Ordinance.
1095. $100 - 3 (67 - 60) = 79$.
1096. Section 86 of the Torts [New Version] Ordinance.

calculates the damages that the service provider is required to pay in favour of the plaintiff, the payment that has been paid by the insurance company due to the contract is not reduced from the payment that the service provider is required to pay as damages.

Lawsuits for death cases in the ICT area are rare in Israel, and most of them are related to labour law (e.g., an employee dies while at work for service provider as a result of the service provider's conduct). Nevertheless, certain legal provisions are relevant in this issue. The plaintiffs are the dead's successors or estate and any other person who was financially dependent on the dead, and they are granted damages for the death and for any bodily harm involved.[1097]

In addition, the successors and any other person who was financially dependent on the dead may sue for any future loss caused by the death.[1098] That includes the relative loss of future earnings and any reasonable costs caused by the death (e.g., the funeral costs). Nevertheless, that does not include any payment due to insurance contract (e.g., life insurance or pension) or payment for the time of the grief, which is paid in addition.[1099]

If some service providers acted as accomplices, the plaintiff might sue all of them within the same lawsuit, and all of them altogether would be required to pay the plaintiff the total sum of payment.[1100] However, if one of the accomplices has paid the damages, and the other accomplices have not, a lawsuit by the paying accomplice may be submitted against the other accomplices for their share (i.e., indemnity lawsuit).[1101] The shares may be determined by the court due to the personal contribution to the damage or due to their actual function within the damage (e.g., perpetrators, joint-perpetrators, inciters, accessories, or advisors).[1102]

If the plaintiff is a corporation, and the lawsuit relates to the service provider's liability, the plaintiff is not granted any payment for damages, unless actually proven the damages.[1103] As many legal provisions in the ICT law and consumption law grant plaintiffs payments in lawsuits without any proof of damages, this legal provision towards corporations is very significant. However, it relates to corporations as plaintiffs and not as service providers (all of them are corporations in Israel). Thus, if a service provider corporation is sued by a physical person, and the law grants payment for damages without any proof of damages, the service provider is required to pay.

When there are at least two service providers within one lawsuit regarding the same tort or civil wrong, they would share the responsibility for the remedies between them 'together and separately'.[1104] That means that both of them are responsible for all of the damages, and the internal division of the responsibility

---

1097. Section 78 of the Torts [New Version] Ordinance.
1098. Section 80 of the Torts [New Version] Ordinance.
1099. Section 81 of the Torts [New Version] Ordinance.
1100. Section 83 of the Torts [New Version] Ordinance.
1101. Section 84(a) of the Torts [New Version] Ordinance.
1102. Section 84(b) of the Torts [New Version] Ordinance.
1103. Section 10 of the Torts [New Version] Ordinance.
1104. Section 11 of the Torts [New Version] Ordinance.

between them towards the remedies is not the plaintiff's concern. Nevertheless, the court may determine the division between them. This arrangement is applicable also for the accessories, inciters, solicitors, advisors, and other accomplices.[1105]

1105. Section 12 of the Torts [New Version] Ordinance.

Chapter 4. Product Liability

125. Traditionally, product liability has two major legal aspects. The first is contractual, and the second is non-contractual. If the product is of low quality or not satisfactory in contrast to the promised product within the agreement, it may be considered as breach of contract. These issues have been discussed above,[1106] and they are regulated by the law of contracts and the consumption law. However, product liability includes more issues beyond the contractual. For example, bodily injury occurred due to reasonable use of the product. These issues are generally not covered by the contractual aspect, and they are discussed in this chapter.

§1. General Legal Framework and the Applicable Law

126. In general, product liability issues, which are *not* covered by the contractual legal relations between the parties, are regulated through the law of torts. In most cases, the lawsuit against the product's manufacturer on the ground of negligence or other relevant civil wrong. These lawsuits may require the plaintiff to prove the facts under uneasy burden of proof. The continuous experience revealed that most plaintiffs are having difficulties in proving the manufacturer's liability under the general law of torts.

Therefore, the Israeli legislator has followed the American legislator and some European legislators, and has enacted in 1980, a particular statute that reduces the burden of proof for the plaintiff into the level of strict liability (of the manufacturer), as long as the lawsuit relates to bodily injury occurred in Israel, but also reduces the rate of damages that may be paid as compensation.[1107] All other lawsuits regarding defected products or products liability in general are regulated through the general law of torts. The legislator has also enacted particular civil wrongs specified to product liability within the ICT area, but all of them are subject to the general law of torts.

Consequently, there are three basic layers of the law relating to product liability within ICT area. The first layer is the general law of torts, the second layer is the particular product liability law (regarding bodily injury), and the third layer is the ICT law (creating particular civil wrongs). The interpretation rule between these three layers is *lex specialis derogat generali*. Therefore, legal provisions from ICT law and legal provisions from particular product liability law derogate legal provisions from the general law of torts. Nevertheless, unless explicitly determined, the specific layers are interpreted through the general law of torts.[1108]

Thus, even though in certain cases the general law of torts may determine one person as liable, and therefore impose certain remedies, the ICT law may determine that the general product liability is not enough to impose any remedies or that the

1106. Above at Part III.
1107. The Liability for Defected Products Act, 1980.
1108. *See*, *e.g.*, s. 8 of the Liability for Defected Products Act, 1980.

person was not liable at all. As the ICT law in the context of product liability functions as specific law, it derogates the general law of torts, which functions as the general law.

Particular product liability laws may relate to certain persons who may be liable (e.g., mobile phones manufacturers) or to certain situations in which product liability may be involved (e.g., liability for mobile phones' explosion). As the general law of torts has been enacted in the 1940s, under the rule of the British Mandate, and the relevant provisions of the ICT law were enacted not before the 1990s, these laws are not always coherent, and the rules of interpretation are required.

Product liability is subject to the Israeli conflict of laws rules, and in particular to the rules of choice-of-law in torts. After sixty years of arguments towards the interpretation of choice-of-law rule in tort,[1109] in 2004, inspired by the European and British rules, the Supreme Court has formulated the Israeli rule by case law. Accordingly, the applicable law on torts is the law of the place of occurrence of the tort (*lex loci delicti commissi*), and only if this law has absolutely no relevance to the case, the applicable law is the law which has the closest and most real connection to the tort.[1110]

If product liability is through an omission, the place of occurrence of the tort is the place where the duty should have been fulfilled. If product liability is through an act, the place of the occurrence of the tort is the place of its actual commission and not necessarily the place where the damage has occurred or has been discovered (*lex loci delicti commissi* and not *lex loci damni*). The second part of the rule grants the court wide discretion towards the interpretation of the law that has 'the closest and most real connection' to the tort.

However, some of the product liability cases in the ICT context are related to bodily injury. In these cases, the applicable law may be different. The applicable law in cases of bodily injury under tort law, which involve an element of product liability, is still the law of the place of occurrence of the tort (*lex loci delicti commissi*), but this place is the very place where the bodily injury has occurred (*lex loci damni*). Only if this law has absolutely no relevance to the case, the applicable law is the law which has the closest and most real connection to the bodily injury.

In addition, some of the product liability cases in the ICT context are related to IP torts, i.e., torts which are defined within the IP law and involve an element of product liability. In these cases, the applicable law may be also different. The applicable law in IP torts which involve an element of product liability is still the law of the place of occurrence of the tort (*lex loci delicti commissi*), but this place is the very place where the IP is protected (*lex loci protectionis*). Only if this law has absolutely no relevance to the case, the applicable law is the law which has the closest and most real connection to the IP tort.

The jurisdiction of the Israeli court over product liability cases in the ICT context is not different than its jurisdiction in any other case in torts, and it is determined by

1109. *See, e.g.*, Civ. App. 180/51 *Goldcorn v. Wissotzky*, 8(1) PD 262 (1954); Civ. App. 98/67 *Livhar v. Gazit and Shaham*, 21(2) PD 243 (1967); Civ. App. 750/79 *Klausner v. Berkowitz*, 37(4) PD 449 (1983).

1110. Civ. App. 1432/03 *Yinon v. Karan*, 59(1) PD 345 (2004); Civ. Cer. 4655/09 *Scaler v. Ubiner* (25 Oct. 2011).

the general rules of the Israeli conflict of laws. Accordingly, if the law determines the Israeli court as the authorized forum, if both parties agreed on the court's jurisdiction over the particular case, if the lawsuit's documents have been accepted by the defendant or by the defendant's local representative or if the plaintiff was authorized to deliver the lawsuit's documents to the defendant outside Israel, the Israeli court has the jurisdiction over the case.

§2. Liability, Immunities and Remedies

127. Due the general legal framework towards products liability, two types of lawsuit should be distinguished. The first is bodily injury lawsuits with product liability elements, and the second is other lawsuits with product liability elements. The liability, immunities, and remedies in relation to both types of lawsuits are discussed below.

I. Bodily Injury Lawsuits with Product Liability Elements

128. For bodily injury lawsuits with product liability elements, a manufacturer is defined as the manufacturer of the product, the importer of the product, the product provider in case of unknown manufacturer or importer, or any person in which may be considered manufacturer in any reasonable person's objective point of view (e.g., if the logo of that person is printed on the product and the product is original).[1111] Bodily injury is defined as death, disease, bodily harm, bodily deformation, and any mental or cognitive damage,[1112] but only if it occurred in Israel.[1113] If the bodily injury has occurred outside Israel, the general law of torts is applicable.

Defected product is defined as any product that, due to any defect, may cause bodily injury or that using the product requires certain warnings or certain special instructions, but they were not given prior to the use of the product, although no defect in the product is detected.[1114] If the court has only circumstantial evidence, the product is presumed to be defected, if the reasonable conclusion out of the evidence is that the product was defected.[1115]

A manufacturer is liable for any bodily injury caused by defected product regardless of the question of fault, unless a relevant defence is applicable.[1116] This type of liability of the manufacturer is compatible with strict liability. If the bodily injury has been caused by certain defect component of the product, both the manufacturer of the component and the manufacturer of the product are liable.[1117]

1111. The definition of the term 'manufacturer' in section 1 of the Liability for Defected Products Act, 1980.
1112. The definition of the term 'bodily injury' in section 1 of the Liability for Defected Products Act, 1980.
1113. Section 9(b) of the Liability for Defected Products Act, 1980.
1114. Section 3(a) of the Liability for Defected Products Act, 1980.
1115. Section 3(b) of the Liability for Defected Products Act, 1980.
1116. Section 2(a) of the Liability for Defected Products Act, 1980.
1117. Section 2(b) of the Liability for Defected Products Act, 1980.

The manufacturer has the right to plead six defences, and no other defence may be heard within the court. The first defence may be relevant only when the defendant is the product provider in case of unknown manufacturer or importer. According to the first defence, if the defendant has notified the plaintiff, within a reasonable time after required by the plaintiff, details of how to locate the manufacturer or the importer, the product provider is not liable for the bodily injury.[1118]

The second defence is when the defect in the product has been created when the product was already released by the manufacturer. Moreover, if the manufacturer has proven in court that the product has passed safety examinations before it was released, the manufacturer is exempt from liability.[1119] The third defence is when according to the scientific and technological developments that were known at the time the product was released by the manufacturer, the manufacturer could not have known that the product safety level was unsatisfactory.[1120]

The fourth defence is when the product was released not by the manufacturer or without the manufacturer's consent, and the manufacturer has taken all reasonable measures to prevent the product's release and to warn any potential users from using that product.[1121] The fifth defence is when the plaintiff was aware of the danger using the product, but still has used it willingly.[1122] Nevertheless, the fifth defence is inapplicable if the plaintiff is under the age of 12.[1123]

The sixth defence is when the plaintiff has acted within *severe* negligence using the product. In general, when the plaintiff has used the product negligently, the manufacturer is not exempt from liability. However, severe negligence of the plaintiff while using the product may reduce the rate of damages in favour of the plaintiff due to the court's discretion.[1124] This defence is not meant to exempt the manufacturer, but only to reduce the rate of compensation. Nevertheless, the sixth defence is inapplicable if the plaintiff is under the age of 12.[1125]

If the bodily injury has caused loss of earning or loss of earning ability, any income beyond three times the average salary is not calculated.[1126] The average salary in Israel is approximately NIS 11,000 (approximately EUR 2,700). In addition, damages for mental damage would not exceed NIS 310,000 (approximately EUR 75,000).[1127]

If the bodily injury has caused death, the plaintiffs are generally the dead's successors or estate and any other person who was financially dependent on the dead, and they are granted damages for the death and for any bodily harm involved.[1128] In addition, the successors and any other person who was financially dependent on the

1118. Section 2(c) of the Liability for Defected Products Act, 1980.
1119. Section 4(a)(1) of the Liability for Defected Products Act, 1980.
1120. Section 4(a)(2) of the Liability for Defected Products Act, 1980.
1121. Section 4(a)(3) of the Liability for Defected Products Act, 1980.
1122. Section 4(a)(4) of the Liability for Defected Products Act, 1980.
1123. Section 4(c)(1) of the Liability for Defected Products Act, 1980.
1124. Section 4(b) of the Liability for Defected Products Act, 1980.
1125. Section 4(c)(2) of the Liability for Defected Products Act, 1980.
1126. Section 5(a) of the Liability for Defected Products Act, 1980.
1127. Section 5(b) of the Liability for Defected Products Act, 1980.
1128. Section 78 of the Torts [New Version] Ordinance.

dead may sue for any future loss caused by the death.[1129] That includes the relative loss of future earnings and any reasonable costs caused by the death (e.g., the funeral costs). Nevertheless, that does not include any payment due to insurance contract (e.g., life insurance or pension) or payment for the time of the grief, which is paid in addition.[1130]

The substantive obsolescence of lawsuit for bodily injury with product liability element is three years,[1131] and the procedural obsolescence is ten years from the end of the year that the particular product has actually been released from the manufacturer.[1132] Any contradicting clause in any contract between the parties is nullified, and the legislation provisions in this issue derogate such contractual clauses.[1133] On any other matter within such a lawsuit, the general law of torts is applicable.[1134]

II. Other Lawsuits with Product Liability Elements

129. If the lawsuit is not bodily injury lawsuit with product liability elements or if the lawsuit relates to bodily injury, occurred outside Israel, with product liability elements, such lawsuits are subject to the general law of torts. Whereas, in most cases, the relations between the customer and the product provider are generally contractual, in most cases, the relations between the customer and the product's manufacturer are not contractual.

There are several civil wrongs which are in common use in the context of product liability. The general tort of fraud is generally used in cases where the manufacturer claims for certain characteristics of the product, but they turn to be false.[1135] For example, the manufacturer claims for certain rate of radiation radiated from the cellular device (SAR), but objective examinations show much higher rates. However, fraud is dependent on the manufacturer's awareness of the factual data and on the manufacturer's fraudulent intent (i.e., the manufacturer's intent to mislead the plaintiff by the false data).

However, the most common civil wrongs that are used for the manufacturer's liability in torts are the torts of negligence and infringement of enacted duty.[1136] Negligence has been discussed above.[1137] As to infringement of enacted duty, in both civil and criminal statutes, several duties are imposed directly on manufacturers. If a certain duty enacted within a certain statute is infringed by the manufacturer, any person who experienced any damage as a result of the infringement has the right to submit a lawsuit on the ground of infringement of enacted duty. For example, the law prohibits manufacturers of cellular devices, if the radiation rate is beyond certain rate. If this duty is infringed, a lawsuit against the manufacturer is

1129. Section 80 of the Torts [New Version] Ordinance.
1130. Section 81 of the Torts [New Version] Ordinance.
1131. Section 6(a) of the Liability for Defected Products Act, 1980.
1132. Section 6(b) of the Liability for Defected Products Act, 1980.
1133. Section 7 of the Liability for Defected Products Act, 1980.
1134. Sections 8 and 10 of the Liability for Defected Products Act, 1980.
1135. Section 63 of the Torts [New Version] Ordinance.
1136. Sections 29–34 of the Torts [New Version] Ordinance.
1137. Above at Chapter 1: Negligence (at this part).

submitted on the ground of infringement of enacted duty, regardless of a lawsuit against the importer or the merchant who sold the device to the customer.

As a result, the tort of infringement of enacted duty is used to enforce legal duties towards manufacturers. However, product liability in tort law is subject to a minimum damage proven by the plaintiff, and the mere proof of all elements of the tort is not enough in order to determine liability.[1138] This resembles the general defence of *de minimis* in criminal law, as the minimum damage is presumed to have social interest. Many lawsuits submitted by consumers against manufacturers are declined for this reason, even though liability has been proven, especially if fair compensation has been offered before the lawsuit has been submitted.

If the plaintiff has been exposed to the negligence or other misbehave of the manufacturer knowingly or willingly, the plaintiff's right to any remedy is reduced or nullified.[1139] However, if the lawsuit is based on infringement of any legal duty (i.e., determined by a particular statute), this is not a defence for the manufacturer. In any lawsuit besides negligence, if the manufacturer has acted according to a certain statute, no product liability is imposed.[1140] Nevertheless, in negligence lawsuits, even if the manufacturer has acted according to a certain statute, this defence is inapplicable, unless the manufacturer has proven that the act was not negligent (i.e., a reasonable person would have been acting similarly).[1141]

If the particular wrongdoer is a public servant or any governmental entity in the ICT area manufacturing ICT products (there are several manufacturers which are governmental units), product liability may be imposed only if the civil wrong has been committed intentionally or indifferently (i.e., the higher level of recklessness).[1142] Consequently, if the plaintiff could have proven negligence of the public servant or of the governmental entity, but not more than negligence, no product liability is imposed. In fact, this establishes an immunity for public servants and governmental entities in the ICT area from product liability for negligence.

When there are at least two defendants within one lawsuit regarding the same tort or civil wrong (e.g., the manufacturer and the product provider), they would share the liability for the product between them 'together and separately'.[1143] That means that both of them are responsible for the whole damage, and the internal division of the responsibility between them is not the plaintiff's concern. Nevertheless, the court may determine the division between them. This arrangement is applicable also for the accessories, inciters, solicitors, advisors, and other accomplices.[1144] Of course, the accomplice's liability for the product does not replace the perpetrator's, but it is additional.[1145]

The employer may have vicarious liability for the product for the conduct of the employee. The conditions for vicarious liability for the product are the confirmation of the employer to the employee's conduct and the commission of the conduct

1138. Section 4 of the Torts [New Version] Ordinance.
1139. Section 5(a) of the Torts [New Version] Ordinance.
1140. Section 5(b) of the Torts [New Version] Ordinance.
1141. Section 6 of the Torts [New Version] Ordinance.
1142. Section 7A and 7B of the Torts [New Version] Ordinance.
1143. Section 11 of the Torts [New Version] Ordinance.
1144. Section 12 of the Torts [New Version] Ordinance.
1145. Section 16 of the Torts [New Version] Ordinance.

within the employment.[1146] For this purpose, any of the employee's activities in favour of the employer is considered commission of the conduct within the employment, even if the activity has been performed negligently (towards the employer).[1147] However, the conduct may be either act or omission. The required fault in the civil wrong that has actually occurred through the agent would be attributed to the principal.[1148] Of course, the employer's liability for the product does not replace the employee's, but it is additional.[1149]

Nevertheless, the employer is exempt from liability for the product if the conduct has not been committed by one of the employees, but by a person who was authorized by an employee without the explicit or implicit consent of the employer.[1150] In addition, if the employer has consented, but neither the employer nor the employee could have chosen any other person (e.g., when the person is a corporation who has a monopoly over the relevant product), both the employer and the employee are exempt from liability for the product.[1151] As aforesaid, in the Israeli ICT market, several corporations are monopolies in relation to certain products.[1152] Thus, the opportunity to choose affects the liability for the product.

In contractual relations between the parties, the contract itself is not an adequate ground for imposition of liability for the product for any civil wrong, unless the contract is deliberately meant to authorize one of the parties to commit the civil wrong on behalf of the other.[1153] Nevertheless, the contract may be an adequate ground for imposition of liability for the product on the relevant civil wrong if the choice of the counterparty was negligent,[1154] if the damage has occurred due to intervention in the counterparty's conduct,[1155] if the party permitted (*ex ante*) or ratified (*ex post*) the civil wrong,[1156] if the party is personally liable due to the law,[1157] or if the object of the contract is itself civil wrong.[1158]

In general, in the ICT area, when there are agency relations between the parties, whether contractual or not (e.g., semi-contractual relations or fiduciary relations), the principal is liable for the agent's conduct.[1159] The required fault in the civil wrong that has actually occurred through the agent would be attributed to the principal.[1160] Of course, the principal's liability for the product does not replace the agent's, but it is additional.[1161]

1146. Section 13(a)(1) and 13(a)(2) of the Torts [New Version] Ordinance.
1147. Section 13(b) of the Torts [New Version] Ordinance.
1148. Section 17 of the Torts [New Version] Ordinance.
1149. Section 16 of the Torts [New Version] Ordinance.
1150. Section 13(a)(2)(a) of the Torts [New Version] Ordinance.
1151. Section 13(a)(2)(b) of the Torts [New Version] Ordinance.
1152. Above at s. [IV]: Monopolies at Part I.
1153. Section 15 of the Torts [New Version] Ordinance.
1154. Section 15(1) of the Torts [New Version] Ordinance.
1155. Section 15(2) of the Torts [New Version] Ordinance.
1156. Section 15(3) of the Torts [New Version] Ordinance.
1157. Section 15(4) of the Torts [New Version] Ordinance.
1158. Section 15(5) of the Torts [New Version] Ordinance.
1159. Section 14 of the Torts [New Version] Ordinance.
1160. Section 17 of the Torts [New Version] Ordinance.
1161. Section 16 of the Torts [New Version] Ordinance.

In case of death of the plaintiff or of the manufacturer, all rights of the dead are reserved for the dead's estate.[1162] Death itself does not form any exemption from liability for the product. Nevertheless, if the dead person is the manufacturer, and the conduct is considered criminal offence as well, no criminal legal proceedings are allowed.[1163] If the dead person was an insolvent manufacturer, the above legal arrangement is not different.[1164] Any insolvent plaintiff has all rights to submit any lawsuit for any tort, and insolvency itself is neither defence nor barrier from submission of lawsuits.[1165] However, the right for remedies for any tort is personal and may not be assigned, unless explicitly permitted by the law.[1166]

The doctrine of contributory negligence has been accepted in Israeli tort law. Accordingly, if the damage has been caused solely by the plaintiff, the manufacturer is exempt from liability for the product.[1167] If the damage has been caused by the manufacturer, who was driven to act this way by the plaintiff (intentionally or not), the court is authorized to consider lower rate of remedies or even exemption for the manufacturer from remedies, dependent on the involvement of the plaintiff in the factual process that resulted in the particular damage.[1168]

If the plaintiff has negligently contributed to the occurrence of the damage, the court is required to reduce the rate of remedies in favour of the plaintiff to the manufacturer's contribution to the occurrence of the damage.[1169] For example, if the plaintiff misused ICT product, but that product was defective regardless of the plaintiff's behaviour, it is more likely that the manufacturer is not considered liable for the whole damage. Thus, if the court is convinced that the plaintiff contributory negligence is estimated by 15% of the damage, the manufacturer is regarded as liable for 85% of the damage, and the remedies in favour of the plaintiff are reduced accordingly.

Sometimes the civil wrong is considered a criminal offence. Negligence, for example, is one of the mental element requirements within the Israeli substantive criminal law, and a few dozens of offences may be committed under negligence. In such cases, the lawsuit regarding the civil wrong is not affected by any of the criminal proceedings and is not affected if no criminal proceedings have been taken.[1170] Nevertheless, the court may order the parties to notify the police on the facts that might form a criminal offence.

However, the Israeli evidence law regards admissible in civil proceedings the judgment in criminal proceedings for the same facts,[1171] and that may ease the plaintiff the burden of proof. In addition, the victim of any criminal offence may submit

1162. Section 19(a) of the Torts [New Version] Ordinance.
1163. Section 236 of the Criminal Justice [Combined Version] Act, 1982.
1164. Section 20 of the Torts [New Version] Ordinance.
1165. Section 21 of the Torts [New Version] Ordinance.
1166. Section 22 of the Torts [New Version] Ordinance.
1167. Section 64 of the Torts [New Version] Ordinance.
1168. Section 65 of the Torts [New Version] Ordinance.
1169. Section 68 of the Torts [New Version] Ordinance.
1170. Section 88 of the Torts [New Version] Ordinance.
1171. Section 42A of the Evidence [New Version] Ordinance, 1971.

a civil lawsuit to the criminal court who has convicted the manufacturer,[1172] and the court would function as if it were a civil court (i.e., authorized to grant any civil remedy in favour of the plaintiff).

Any civil lawsuit is required to specify explicitly what is the requested remedy, regardless of the legal cause for the lawsuit.[1173] This requirement is relevant to any civil lawsuit, including lawsuits for negligence. In tort lawsuits, the Israeli court is authorized to grant the plaintiff any remedy within its jurisdiction and subject to any limitation determined explicitly by the law.[1174]

The court is authorized to grant mandatory injunction or prohibitory injunction, whether permanent or temporary.[1175] These injunctions may be given in addition to any other remedy and as sole remedies.[1176] These injunctions do not necessarily derivate from other remedies, but they may be the sole objects of the lawsuit. This is significant especially when the major object of the lawsuit is to prevent a future damage, as the damage already been occurred is immaterial. When the court is authorized to grant injunctions in favour of the parties by other provisions of the law (e.g., by the Civil Procedure Regulations, 2018), the above provisions do not negate this authorization.[1177]

Temporary injunction is an injunction which is valid until the judgment is given. When the plaintiff has reasonable causes to believe that the manufacturer might change the situation or the evidence so that the judgment would not be enforceable, temporary injunction to remain the situation as it is, is required. However, the court is authorized to grant a temporary injunction, only if the court is convinced that a real legal question occurs within the lawsuit, it is most probable that the plaintiff would win the case and justice would be prevented unless the injunction is granted.[1178]

Nevertheless, the court has to consider hypothetically the balance of damages between the plaintiff and the manufacturer as a result of granting the injunction. Thus, if, as a result of granting the injunction in favour of the plaintiff, the manufacturer would probably be exposed to major damages, whereas the claimed damages by the plaintiff are relatively small and may be evaluated in certain sum of money, the court may refuse to grant the injunction, and it is authorized to grant other remedies in favour of the plaintiff, whether claimed or not.[1179]

However, the common remedy in negligence lawsuits is damages. Damages for product liability are, basically, payment of money as compensation. The court is authorized to grant damages in favour of the plaintiff in addition to other remedies and as sole remedy.[1180] Under the 2018 regulations of civil procedure, the plaintiff is required to describe in detail the damage that the compensation is related to.[1181]

1172. Section 77 of the Courts [Combined Version] Act, 1984.
1173. Regulation 10(9) of the Civil Procedure Regulations, 2018.
1174. Section 71 of the Torts [New Version] Ordinance.
1175. Section 72 of the Torts [New Version] Ordinance.
1176. Section 71 of the Torts [New Version] Ordinance.
1177. Section 75 of the Torts [New Version] Ordinance.
1178. Section 73 of the Torts [New Version] Ordinance.
1179. Section 74 of the Torts [New Version] Ordinance.
1180. Section 76 of the Torts [New Version] Ordinance.
1181. Regulation 10(9) of the Civil Procedure Regulations, 2018.

The general objective of the damages is to compensate for the damage, and not to enrich the plaintiff. Therefore, the court is limited within the scope of the damage when calculating the damages. Moreover, damages for the same damage are granted only once, regardless of the identity of the plaintiff.[1182] Thus, if the manufacturer has already compensated one plaintiff for a certain damage at full, i.e., the payment is equivalent to the total damage, the manufacturer is not required to compensate any other party in any further lawsuit for the same damage.

Social security payment which is paid as a result of negligence of the manufacturer is reduced from the total sum of damages paid by the employer.[1183] For example, if an employee suffers from any harm estimated 100, the Israeli social security institute determines 2% of functional disability and social security payment of 2 per annum, the employee is 60 years old, and the retirement age in Israel is 67, the employer is required to pay 86.[1184]

However, any payment due to any insurance contract that is paid for any damage is *not* reduced from the damages payment granted by the court.[1185] For example, ICT product has been overheated due to the manufacturer's negligence, and caused damage to the plaintiff's apartment. However, the apartment is insured by a contract for any damage, including such damage. When the court calculates the damages that the manufacturer is required to pay in favour of the plaintiff, the payment that has been paid by the insurance company due to the contract is not reduced from the payment that the manufacturer is required to pay as damages.

Lawsuits for death cases in the ICT area are rare in Israel, and most of them are related to labour law (e.g., an employee dies while at work for ICT company as a result of the company's negligence). Nevertheless, certain legal provisions are relevant in this issue. The plaintiffs are the dead's successors or estate and any other person who was financially dependent on the dead, and they are granted damages for the death and for any bodily harm involved.[1186]

In addition, the successors and any other person who was financially dependent on the dead may sue for any future loss caused by the death.[1187] That includes the relative loss of future earnings and any reasonable costs caused by the death (e.g., the funeral costs). Nevertheless, that does not include any payment due to insurance contract (e.g., life insurance or pension) or payment for the time of the grief, which is paid in addition.[1188]

If the manufacturers acted as accomplices, the plaintiff might sue all of them within the same lawsuit, and all of them altogether would be required to pay the plaintiff the total sum of payment.[1189] However, if one of the accomplices has paid the damages, and the other accomplices have not, a lawsuit by the paying accomplice may be submitted against the other accomplices for their share (i.e., indemnity

---

1182. Section 77(a) of the Torts [New Version] Ordinance.
1183. Section 82 of the Torts [New Version] Ordinance.
1184. $100 - 2\ (67 - 60) = 86$.
1185. Section 86 of the Torts [New Version] Ordinance.
1186. Section 78 of the Torts [New Version] Ordinance.
1187. Section 80 of the Torts [New Version] Ordinance.
1188. Section 81 of the Torts [New Version] Ordinance.
1189. Section 83 of the Torts [New Version] Ordinance.

lawsuit).[1190] The shares may be determined by the court due to the personal contribution to the damage or due to their actual function within the damage (e.g., perpetrators, joint-perpetrators, inciters, accessories, or advisors).[1191]

If the plaintiff is a corporation, and the lawsuit relates to the ICT product liability, the corporation is not granted any payment for damages, unless actually proven the damages.[1192] As many legal provisions in the ICT law and consumption law grant plaintiffs payments in lawsuits without any proof of damages, this legal provision towards corporations is very significant. However, it relates to corporations as plaintiffs and not as manufacturers. Thus, if a corporation is sued by a physical person, and the law grants payment for damages without any proof of damages, the corporation is required to pay.

1190. Section 84(a) of the Torts [New Version] Ordinance.
1191. Section 84(b) of the Torts [New Version] Ordinance.
1192. Section 10 of the Torts [New Version] Ordinance.

Part VI. Privacy Protection

130. Privacy protection within the context of ICT law may be divided into two main issues. One issue relates to personal data processing, and it focuses on personal database regulation. The other issue relates to protection of telecommunications privacy. Israel is not a Member State in the European Union; therefore, the GDPR (General Data Protection Regulation) is not applicable directly in Israel, but the EU has officially recognized Israel as having adequate protection for personal data permitting cross-border transfers.[1193] These issues are discussed below.

1193. (2011/61/EU). *See*: https://eur-lex.europa.eu/LexUriServ/LexUriServ.do?uri=OJ:L:2011:027:0039:0042:EN:PDF (accessed 23 Jul. 2021).

Chapter 1. Regulation of Personal Data Processing

131. The regulation of personal data processing in Israel is focused on the personal data within databases. The very possession of personal data within any database is considered as invasion of privacy. As the use of databases containing personal data increases, the need for regulation towards privacy protection increases as well. In general, there are no particular principles or requirements for personal data processing besides those which concern privacy protection (described below) and those which concern technical standardization of computer communications. In this issue, there are four major layers of law: privacy protection in databases, direct mailing, data transfer among governmental units, and data security. These layers are discussed below.

§1. Privacy Protection in Databases

132. In the context of privacy protection, 'database' is defined as any collection of data, stored in any type of media, and intended for computer processing.[1194] Nevertheless, if the collection of the data is intended for personal use without any profit or it includes no data besides names, addresses, and communications (e.g., e-mails or telephone numbers), it is not considered database. For example, the contacts list in any mobile phone is not considered database if it includes only the above details.

However, 'data' is defined in this context as factual information towards a private person, including identity information, personality information, personal and family status, economic information, medical information, social information, professional details, the person's opinions, and the person's beliefs.[1195]

Any database must be registered in the database registry supervised by the ministry of justice, if the database contains the data on at least 10,000 persons, if it contains personal data (identity information, economical information, medical information, the person's opinions, or the person's beliefs), if the data has not arrived at the database by the object persons or due to their consent, if the database is possessed by any governmental unit or if the database is intended to be used for direct mailing,[1196] unless the data has already been published due to any legal provision or has been open and accessible for the public.[1197]

No person is allowed to possess or manage any database that is required to be registered and has not been registered yet.[1198] If registered, the database may be

1194. The definition of the term 'database' in s. 7 of the Privacy Protection Act, 1981.
1195. The definition of the term 'data' in s. 7 of the Privacy Protection Act, 1981.
1196. Section 8(c) of the Privacy Protection Act, 1981.
1197. Section 8(d) of the Privacy Protection Act, 1981.
1198. Section 8(a) of the Privacy Protection Act, 1981.

used only for the purposes declared at the time of registry.[1199] The legal duty to register the database is imposed on any person who possesses it or manages it, but registration is required to be once. Thus, once the database has been registered, the use of the information included within the database is legal, and there is no necessary to register it over again per any use.

For registration of the database, an application is submitted to the registrar of databases within the ministry of justice.[1200] The application is required to include the identity details of the database owners, possessors, and managers; the purposes of the database; the purposes of the use of the database; the information included within the database; details on exporting the data outside Israel; and details on receiving information from any governmental unit.[1201] The database's owner, possessor, or manager has the legal duty to update any of the above details by a direct application to the registrar.[1202]

Within ninety days after the application has been submitted, the registrar is required to register the database, unless the database is illegal, the database is intended for illegal purposes or the information included in the database has been received or collected unlawfully.[1203] However, the registrar may add other purposes than noted within the application or change the purposes, if the new purposes are more compatible with the actual activity of the database.[1204] Refuse to register the database or any change in the database's purposes require fair notice and fair chance to plead against the refusal or the change.[1205]

The registrar should be qualified at least as a judge of the Magistrates' Court.[1206] The registrar is authorized to use inspection powers, and an inspection unit is subject to the registrar. Accordingly, the registrar is authorized to enter any place, to confiscate documents and files, to search at any place, question any person, and demand documents and other evidence from any person.[1207] If after the database is registered, an infringement of any legal provision is occurred, the registrar is authorized to suspend the validity of registration of the database.[1208] However, an application to delete any database from the registry requires reasonable proofs that the information has been completely deleted.[1209]

1199. Section 8(b) of the Privacy Protection Act, 1981.
1200. Section 9(a) of the Privacy Protection Act, 1981.
1201. Section 9(b) of the Privacy Protection Act, 1981.
1202. Section 9(d) of the Privacy Protection Act, 1981.
1203. Section 10(a)(1) of the Privacy Protection Act, 1981.
1204. Section 10(a)(2) of the Privacy Protection Act, 1981.
1205. Section 10(a)(3) of the Privacy Protection Act, 1981.
1206. The definition of the term 'registrar' in s. 7 of the Privacy Protection Act, 1981.
1207. Section 10(e1) of the Privacy Protection Act, 1981.
1208. Section 10(f) of the Privacy Protection Act, 1981.
1209. Section 10(b3) of the Privacy Protection Act, 1981.

The registry of databases is required to be open and accessible to the public.[1210] The registry is accessible via the ministry of justice website and may be downloaded for free, with no password or any other identification process.[1211] In addition, the ministry of justice enables an online search within the registry.[1212] The registry is required to include the identity details of the database owners, possessors, and managers; the purposes of the database; the purposes of the use of the database; the information included within the database; details on exporting the data outside Israel; and details on receiving information from any governmental unit.[1213]

Any application to any private person by the database's manager to deliver personal information must be followed by a detailed notification that includes the purposes of collecting the information, whether that person has legal duty to deliver the information, and to whom the information is intended to be transferred and the reasons for the transfer.[1214] After the personal data of any person has been registered, that person has the right to read the information,[1215] either in Hebrew, English, or Arabic.[1216] If the demand to disclose the information within the registry is refused, a lawsuit may be submitted to the court for a mandatory injunction to order the database's manager to disclose the personal data according to the court's order.[1217] A special procedure for this type of lawsuits has been regulated.[1218]

Any person has the right to demand to correct any wrong information within the database.[1219] If the person is not Israeli, the right is also to delete the information from the database.[1220] If the database's manager refuses to correct the information, a notification on the refusal should be sent to the person.[1221] If the demand to correct the information within the registry is refused, a lawsuit may be submitted to the court for a mandatory injunction to order the database's manager to change the registry according to the court's order.[1222] A special procedure for this type of lawsuits has been regulated.[1223]

The database's owner, the database's possessors, and the database's manager have the legal duty to secure the data.[1224] Data security is discussed below in detail.[1225] In general, data security is expressed by limitation of access to the database. If the

---

1210. Section 12(a) of the Privacy Protection Act, 1981.
1211. *See*: https://data.gov.il/dataset/pinkas/resource/fd56bf5b-7918-4906-99e4-b0e5102ae268 (accessed 23 Jul. 2021).
1212. *See*: https://www.justice.gov.il/Units/ilita/subjects/HaganatHapratiyut/actions/Pages/Eyun.aspx (accessed 23 Jul. 2021).
1213. Section 12(b) of the Privacy Protection Act, 1981.
1214. Section 11 of the Privacy Protection Act, 1981.
1215. Section 13(a) of the Privacy Protection Act, 1981.
1216. Section 13(b) of the Privacy Protection Act, 1981.
1217. Section 15 of the Privacy Protection Act, 1981.
1218. The Privacy Protection (Conditions For Personal Data Disclosure and Procedures) Regulations, 1981.
1219. Section 14(a) of the Privacy Protection Act, 1981.
1220. *Ibid.*
1221. Section 14(c) of the Privacy Protection Act, 1981.
1222. Section 15 of the Privacy Protection Act, 1981.
1223. The Privacy Protection (Conditions For Personal Data Disclosure and Procedures) Regulations, 1981.
1224. Section 17 of the Privacy Protection Act, 1981.
1225. Below at §4: Data Security at this part.

database possessor is a bank or government unit, or possesses more than four databases, a data security officer in charge should be appointed with an appropriate professional qualification to secure the data.[1226]

During the COVID-19 pandemic, the Israeli government used private information taken out from the cellular phones to detect quarantined inhabitants and to warn their environment. This usage of private information was defined as part of emergency measures taken in order to reduce the probability of being infected by the virus.

However, although most Israeli inhabitants considered these measures as reasonable, these measures were heavily criticized, until eventually abolished in April 2021.

§2. Direct Mailing

133. One of the most common uses of databases is direct mailing for commercial purposes. 'Direct mailing' is defined as any personal address to any person, which is based on the presence of that person's information in a database.[1227] The personal address may be through any type of communication, including postal mail, facsimile, e-mail, and telephone calls.[1228] Sometimes direct mailing may be useful for both parties, but in most cases, this is a heavy burden for the addressee. Accordingly, direct mailing has been regulated through privacy law in Israel in 1996.

The database used for direct mailing must be registered, and one of its declared purposes must be direct mailing.[1229] The possessor and the manager of such database are required to have the exact source of the database, the time of the data collection, and to whom this data has been transferred from that source.[1230]

Any address to any person within direct mailing is required to include a clear notification that this is direct mailing, the number of the database's registry, a notification on the right to be deleted from the database and the exact way to request deletion, and the identity of the database's owner.[1231] Any addressee has the right that all personal data would be deleted from the database.[1232] In addition, any addressee has the right to prohibit any transfer of personal information from that database to any third party, for a determined period of time or permanently.[1233]

If so requested, the database's owner has the duty to act accordingly and notify the addressee within thirty days that the request has been accepted.[1234] If no such

1226. Section 17B of the Privacy Protection Act, 1981.
1227. The definition of the term 'direct mailing' in s. 17C of the Privacy Protection Act, 1981.
1228. The definition of the term 'address' in s. 17C of the Privacy Protection Act, 1981.
1229. Section 17D of the Privacy Protection Act, 1981.
1230. Section 17E of the Privacy Protection Act, 1981.
1231. Section 17F(a) of the Privacy Protection Act, 1981.
1232. Section 17F(b) of the Privacy Protection Act, 1981.
1233. Section 17F(c) of the Privacy Protection Act, 1981.
1234. Section 17F(d) of the Privacy Protection Act, 1981.

notification has been received by the addressee, the addressee has the right to submit a lawsuit to the court and request for a mandatory injunction to order the database's owner to act accordingly.[1235] These rights of the addressee are granted and transferred to the addressee's relatives in case of the addressee's death.[1236] Accordingly, the addressee's relatives may request the deletion of the addressee's information from the direct mailing database.

These legal provisions have been expanded to all types of personal data possessed by any person, if used for the purpose of direct mailing.[1237] However, governmental units are presumed to act not for commercial purposes; therefore, governmental units are allowed to use direct mailing if necessary or efficient, and they are not subject to the above legal provisions.[1238]

§3. Personal Data Transfer

I. Personal Data Transfer from Governmental Units

134. Governmental units collect personal data of citizens since ancient times. Sometimes it is used in order to improve their services, but the danger of misuse of the data does not disappear. Therefore, the Israeli legislator attempted to reduce these dangers by regulating the personal data transfer from governmental units through privacy law in 1985.

In general, any transfer of personal data from or by any governmental unit is prohibited, unless the individual person has consented to it, unless the data was published lawfully, or unless the public had a legal access to the data.[1239] The personal data in this context contains *any* information relating to the individual person.[1240] The definition of governmental unit in this context includes also domestic authorities and any public entity, besides the state's institutes of all powers (legislature, executive, and judiciary).[1241]

However, personal data transfer among governmental units is not prohibited in general, unless prohibited by a particular provision of law or if the data transfer is considered immoral in the particular context.[1242] For example, the ministry of interior transfers personal data of Israeli citizens to the central election committee a few weeks before the general elections to the Knesset, in order to enable the committee to address the citizens to vote and notify the citizens of their democratic rights to vote.

Transfer of personal data among governmental units requires registry of the data transfer within the database registry,[1243] discussed above.[1244] The governmental unit

1235. Section 17F(e) of the Privacy Protection Act, 1981.
1236. Section 17F(f) of the Privacy Protection Act, 1981.
1237. Section 17G of the Privacy Protection Act, 1981.
1238. Section 17H of the Privacy Protection Act, 1981.
1239. Section 23B(a) of the Privacy Protection Act, 1981.
1240. Section 23A of the Privacy Protection Act, 1981.
1241. The definition of the term 'governmental unit' in s. 23 of the Privacy Protection Act, 1981.
1242. Section 23C of the Privacy Protection Act, 1981.
1243. Section 23D(a), 23D(b) and 23D(c) of the Privacy Protection Act, 1981.

which has received the information is prohibited from making any use of the data, unless the use is specifically determined by the law.[1245] The secrecy of the personal data must be kept by the receiving governmental unit as if the data has been collected directly by the receiving unit.[1246]

In addition, hospitals (public and private) have been defined as governmental units in the context of receiving information, and the information includes the healthcare condition of the patient, and for any person accepted for treatment also date of birth, country of birth, parents' country of birth, and immigration birth. If the hospital is a university hospital, the information includes also the patient's name, address, ID number, and sex.[1247]

Health Maintenance Organizations (HMOs) are also defined as governmental units in this context of receiving information, and the information includes the individual's date of birth, country of birth, parents' country of birth, immigration date, sex, address, lists of information from the National Security Institute, and details on a car accident (if treatment due to car accident is required).[1248]

Universities are also defined as governmental units in this context of receiving information for any research, and the information includes individual's name, address, ID number, date of birth, sex, country of origin, and immigration date.[1249] IDF handicaps organization is also defined as a governmental unit in this context of receiving information for the welfare of the handicaps, and the information includes the handicap's name, address, ID number, date of birth, type of disabilities, and date of disabilities.[1250]

Other organizations are accepted occasionally as governmental units due to their public activities. These organizations include Yad Labanim (for the memory of soldiers killed within the defence of Israel),[1251] national labour organizations,[1252] the

---

1244. Above at §1: Privacy Protection in Databases at this chapter.
1245. Section 23D(d) of the Privacy Protection Act, 1981.
1246. Section 23D(e) of the Privacy Protection Act, 1981.
1247. Regulation 1(1) of the Privacy Protection (Governmental Units' Determination) Regulations, 1986.
1248. Regulation 1(2) of the Privacy Protection (Governmental Units' Determination) Regulations, 1986.
1249. Regulation 1(3) of the Privacy Protection (Governmental Units' Determination) Regulations, 1986.
1250. Regulation 1(4) of the Privacy Protection (Governmental Units' Determination) Regulations, 1986.
1251. Regulation 1(5) of the Privacy Protection (Governmental Units' Determination) Regulations, 1986.
1252. Regulation 1(6) of the Privacy Protection (Governmental Units' Determination) Regulations, 1986.

Jewish Agency,[1253] the World Zionist Organization,[1254] the public servants organizations,[1255] Anti-Fraud in Insurance Organization,[1256] and Bezeq (for ensuring discounts to certain populations).[1257]

The procedure of personal data transfer between two governmental units has been regulated by the ministry of justice. Accordingly, the general manager of each governmental unit appoints an internal committee to manage the personal data transfer.[1258] The committee is responsible to ensure that the data security measures of both governmental units are compatible with the information and these measures match between the units.[1259]

The personal data transfer is required to be managed and monitored through an official protocol, and the registrar should be notified for any personal data transfer.[1260] The protocol may be amended by the committees of both governmental units in order to ensure higher level of privacy protection.[1261] Any list or record of information is required to include a warning that the information is protected by law, and transfer of the information is unlawful.[1262]

II. Personal Data Transfer Outside Israel

135. Personal data transfer outside Israel has been regulated in order to maintain the privacy protection. The major principle in this context is reciprocity. Accordingly, personal data transfer by individuals or by governmental units to any person outside Israel is subject to the condition, the data security level by the law of the foreign state is not less than the data security level granted by Israeli law.[1263]

The required level of data security must include legal processing of the information, the information is used for the declared purpose alone, the information is update and accurate, any individual included within the database has the right to

1253. Regulation 1(7) of the Privacy Protection (Governmental Units' Determination) Regulations, 1986.
1254. *Ibid.*
1255. Regulation 1(8) of the Privacy Protection (Governmental Units' Determination) Regulations, 1986.
1256. Regulation 1(10) of the Privacy Protection (Governmental Units' Determination) Regulations, 1986.
1257. Regulation 1(12) of the Privacy Protection (Governmental Units' Determination) Regulations, 1986.
1258. Regulation 3A(a) of the Privacy Protection (Possession of Data and Data Transfer among Governmental Units) Regulations, 1986.
1259. Regulation 4 of the Privacy Protection (Possession of Data and Data Transfer among Governmental Units) Regulations, 1986.
1260. Regulation 7 of the Privacy Protection (Possession of Data and Data Transfer among Governmental Units) Regulations, 1986.
1261. Regulation 5 of the Privacy Protection (Possession of Data and Data Transfer among Governmental Units) Regulations, 1986.
1262. Regulation 11 of the Privacy Protection (Possession of Data and Data Transfer among Governmental Units) Regulations, 1986.
1263. Regulation 1 of the Privacy Protection (Information Transfer Outside Israel) Regulations, 2001.

update the information, the information is disclosed for any individual included within the database, and reasonable measures of data security are taken.[1264]

However, reciprocity and the above conditions are not required in several types of cases. Thus, personal data transfer outside Israel regardless of the above conditions is allowed if the individual included within the database has consented,[1265] if the personal data transfer is required for the individual's safety and the individual's consent is unreachable,[1266] if the receiving person is a corporation controlled by the transferring person,[1267] or if the information is transferred to a person who has been committed to the above conditions.[1268]

Personal data transfer outside Israel regardless of the above conditions is also allowed if the information has already been published lawfully,[1269] if the information is accessible to any person lawfully,[1270] if the personal data transfer is required for the safety of the public,[1271] if the personal data transfer is required by the law,[1272] if the personal data transfer is to a state subject to the GDPR,[1273] or if the information is transferred to a state that the registrar has declared it has an adequate private protection standards.[1274]

Nevertheless, any personal data transfer outside Israel requires the transferring person (individual or governmental unit) to ensure that the information receiver is committed, in written document, that the information receiver *actually* takes all necessary measures to ensure privacy protection, and that the information is not transferred to anyone else, inside that state or outside it.[1275] In the legal process between Israel and the foreign state (e.g., extradition), both states may determine other conditions for the personal data transfer.[1276]

1264. *Ibid.*
1265. Regulation 2(1) of the Privacy Protection (Information Transfer Outside Israel) Regulations, 2001.
1266. Regulation 2(2) of the Privacy Protection (Information Transfer Outside Israel) Regulations, 2001.
1267. Regulation 2(3) of the Privacy Protection (Information Transfer Outside Israel) Regulations, 2001.
1268. Regulation 2(4) of the Privacy Protection (Information Transfer Outside Israel) Regulations, 2001.
1269. Regulation 2(5) of the Privacy Protection (Information Transfer Outside Israel) Regulations, 2001.
1270. *Ibid.*
1271. Regulation 2(6) of the Privacy Protection (Information Transfer Outside Israel) Regulations, 2001.
1272. Regulation 2(7) of the Privacy Protection (Information Transfer Outside Israel) Regulations, 2001.
1273. Regulation 2(8)(1) of the Privacy Protection (Information Transfer Outside Israel) Regulations, 2001.
1274. Regulation 2(8)(3) of the Privacy Protection (Information Transfer Outside Israel) Regulations, 2001.
1275. Regulation 3 of the Privacy Protection (Information Transfer Outside Israel) Regulations, 2001.
1276. Regulation 4 of the Privacy Protection (Information Transfer Outside Israel) Regulations, 2001.

§4. DATA SECURITY

136. Data security in the context of privacy protection has been re-regulated in 2018,[1277] in order to make databases in Israel compatible with the modern cyber threats. Israel is being attacked on a daily basis by pro-Arab hostile hackers in order to weaken the Israeli economy, defence, and social life. This situation required Israel to develop adequate solutions within the field of data security. Israeli developments are shared with Israel's allies for their cyber protection. Accordingly, the National Cyber Security Authority has been established in order to manage these solutions.

I. Categories of Databases

137. In the context of privacy protection regarding data security, all databases have been categorized into four main categories. The first category is databases managed by an individual.[1278] The individual may also be a corporation controlled by an individual, but only the individual and no more than two other individuals are authorized to use the database. This category does not include databases whose purpose is to collect personal data for commercial purposes or for transfer it for commercial purposes, databases which include personal data of at least 10,000 persons or databases which include personal data that is subject to secrecy duties by law (e.g., personal data of an advocate's clients).

The second category is databases of basic data security level. This category is the default category, and it is defined in contrast to the other three categories.[1279] Accordingly, databases of basic data security levels are all databases, which are not within the first, the third, or the fourth categories.

The third category consists of databases of medium data security level.[1280] This category includes databases whose main purpose is to collect personal data for commercial purposes (including direct mailing), databases owned by governmental units, and databases which contain personal life details, healthcare details, mental health details, genetic information, political opinions details, religious beliefs details, criminal record details, communications details in criminal context,[1281] biometric data, financial information, or personal consumption habits.

However, the third category does not include databases managed by individuals, databases which include facial photographs only which are used for the management of the business only, or databases that the number of persons who have direct access to the personal data is not higher than ten.

1277. Actually, the regulations were enacted in 2017, but they were validated in 8 May 2018.

1278. The definition of the term 'database managed by an individual' in regulation 1 of the Privacy Protection (Data Security) Regulations, 2017.

1279. The definition of the term 'databases requiring basic data security level' in in regulation 1 of the Privacy Protection (Data Security) Regulations, 2017.

1280. The definition of the term 'databases requiring medium data security level' in in regulation 1 of the Privacy Protection (Data Security) Regulations, 2017.

1281. *See* below at s. [III]: Telecommunications Data Powers at Part VII.

The fourth category consists of databases of higher data security level.[1282] This category includes databases whose main purpose is to collect personal data for commercial purposes (including direct mailing) of at least 100,000 persons and databases relating to at least 100,000 persons, and which contain personal life details, healthcare details, mental health details, genetic information, political opinions details, religious beliefs details, criminal record details, communications details in criminal context, biometric data, financial information, or personal consumption habits.

In addition, the fourth category includes databases that the number of persons who have direct access to the personal data is over 100, and which contain personal life details, healthcare details, mental health details, genetic information, political opinions details, religious beliefs details, criminal record details, communications details in criminal context, biometric data, financial information, or personal consumption habits.

II. Data Security Measures and Procedures

138. Any owner of any database (from all four categories) is required to define within a definitions document a general description of the collecting personal data activities, a general description of the use of the personal data, the purposes of the use of the personal data, the types of personal data included within the database, details on transfer of the personal data outside Israel (purposes, use, countries, transfer methods, and the receiver's identity), a general description of data processing through third parties, a general description of the risks and dangers to the data security and the measures taken to solve them and the identities of the database's owner, possessors, and data security officer.[1283]

The database's owner is required to update the definitions document whenever a change has been done within one of the above details. The update must be finished by the end of the calendar year of which the change has occurred.[1284] In addition, the database's owner is required to check the quantity of personal data possessed by the database, and if there really is a need in all of it.[1285] If the database possessor is a bank or government unit, or possesses more than four databases, a data security officer in charge should be appointed with an appropriate professional qualification to secure the data.[1286]

The data security officer is directly subordinated to the database's manager or to a senior director who is directly subordinated to the database's manager.[1287] The officer is required to prepare a security protocol and inspection programme for the confirmation of the database's owner.[1288] It is prohibited that the officer would fulfil

---

1282. The definition of the term 'databases requiring higher data security level' in in regulation 1 of the Privacy Protection (Data Security) Regulations, 2017.
1283. Regulation 2(a) of the Privacy Protection (Data Security) Regulations, 2017.
1284. Regulation 2(b) of the Privacy Protection (Data Security) Regulations, 2017.
1285. Regulation 2(c) of the Privacy Protection (Data Security) Regulations, 2017.
1286. Section 17B of the Privacy Protection Act, 1981.
1287. Regulation 3(1) of the Privacy Protection (Data Security) Regulations, 2017.
1288. Regulation 3(2) and 3(3) of the Privacy Protection (Data Security) Regulations, 2017.

any other office within the organization that may create any conflict of interests between the offices.[1289] For this purpose, the database's owner must allocate adequate resources.[1290]

It is the database's owner responsibility to determine a security protocol due to the definitions document, and this protocol is binding for any person who has any access to the database.[1291] However, in order to maintain a higher level of security, the database's owner is required not to expose details from the security protocol unless absolutely necessary for the database's use and management.[1292]

Security protocols are required to include necessary details, including the physical and environmental security of the database's physical location,[1293] the list of accesses to the database,[1294] the computing systems of data security and the ways to operate them,[1295] instructions for the persons who have access to the database towards data security,[1296] risks and dangers that the database is exposed to,[1297] instructions in cases of data security failure,[1298] and instructions towards the use of portable devices within the database.[1299]

If the database is of the third or fourth categories (medium or higher data security levels), the security protocols are required to include, in addition, the identification and verification measures for the access to the database,[1300] the inspection activities towards the database's security,[1301] instructions for periodic security examinations and inspections,[1302] instructions towards backup of personal data,[1303] and instructions towards development activities within the database including definition of the access of the developers.[1304]

The database's owner is required to examine annually if the security protocol requires amendments or updates, especially if significant changes have been made within the database's computing systems or within the computing processes,[1305] and especially if new technological risks have occurred that might be relevant to the database.[1306] If several databases are owned by the same person (individual or corporation), the same security protocol may be used for all of them as long as the databases are of the same data security level.[1307]

1289. Regulation 3(4) of the Privacy Protection (Data Security) Regulations, 2017.
1290. Regulation 3(6) of the Privacy Protection (Data Security) Regulations, 2017.
1291. Regulation 4(a) of the Privacy Protection (Data Security) Regulations, 2017.
1292. Regulation 4(b) of the Privacy Protection (Data Security) Regulations, 2017.
1293. Regulation 4(c)(1) of the Privacy Protection (Data Security) Regulations, 2017.
1294. Regulation 4(c)(2) of the Privacy Protection (Data Security) Regulations, 2017.
1295. Regulation 4(c)(3) of the Privacy Protection (Data Security) Regulations, 2017.
1296. Regulation 4(c)(4) of the Privacy Protection (Data Security) Regulations, 2017.
1297. Regulation 4(c)(5) of the Privacy Protection (Data Security) Regulations, 2017.
1298. Regulation 4(c)(6) of the Privacy Protection (Data Security) Regulations, 2017.
1299. Regulation 4(c)(7) of the Privacy Protection (Data Security) Regulations, 2017.
1300. Regulation 4(d)(1) of the Privacy Protection (Data Security) Regulations, 2017.
1301. Regulation 4(d)(2) of the Privacy Protection (Data Security) Regulations, 2017.
1302. Regulation 4(d)(3) of the Privacy Protection (Data Security) Regulations, 2017.
1303. Regulation 4(d)(4) of the Privacy Protection (Data Security) Regulations, 2017.
1304. Regulation 4(d)(5) of the Privacy Protection (Data Security) Regulations, 2017.
1305. Regulation 4(e)(1) of the Privacy Protection (Data Security) Regulations, 2017.
1306. Regulation 4(e)(2) of the Privacy Protection (Data Security) Regulations, 2017.
1307. Regulation 4(f) of the Privacy Protection (Data Security) Regulations, 2017.

The database's owner is required to possess an updated document of the database's structure and systems, including hardware components; software for the use, maintenance, support, monitoring, and security of the database; software used for communications; the network's schemes; and the date of the last update of the document.[1308] The document is required to be accessible only to the persons needing this information to fulfil their functions within the organization.[1309]

If the database is of the fourth category (higher data security level), the database's owner is responsible for making risks surveys at least once in eighteen months, in order to detect any required changes within the security systems and to update the above document of the database's structure and systems.[1310] These risks surveys are required to include attempts to access the system in order to detect security failures.[1311]

All hardware of the database is required to be kept in safe places, which prevents unauthorized access to it, in accordance with the level of privacy included within the database.[1312] If the database is of the third or fourth categories (medium or higher data security levels), the database's owner is required to monitor any access to the above safe places.[1313]

Data security affects manpower considerations. Accordingly, the database's owner is required to check the potential employee's background in order to verify that they may be trusted to access the database within their employment.[1314] After being hired, the employee would be given specific and accurate instructions towards any sensitive information regarding the database.[1315] If the database is of the third or fourth categories (medium or higher data security levels), the database's owner is required to perform professional appointments regarding these instructions with all employees, at least once in two years.[1316]

Accesses to the database should be managed by the database's owner, and the access is given to any employee only in accordance with the definition of the employee's function.[1317] An update list of all accesses is required to be kept by the database's owner, and it should include the names of the employees and the exact access given.[1318] After the employment is over, the employee's access is required to be cancelled.[1319]

The database's owner is required to take all necessary measures in order to ensure that no unauthorized access to the database would occur.[1320] However, if the database is of the third or fourth categories (medium or higher data security levels), the identification of the accessing employee should be based on physical measure

1308. Regulation 5(a) of the Privacy Protection (Data Security) Regulations, 2017.
1309. Regulation 5(b) of the Privacy Protection (Data Security) Regulations, 2017.
1310. Regulation 5(c) of the Privacy Protection (Data Security) Regulations, 2017.
1311. Regulation 5(d) of the Privacy Protection (Data Security) Regulations, 2017.
1312. Regulation 6(a) of the Privacy Protection (Data Security) Regulations, 2017.
1313. Regulation 6(b) of the Privacy Protection (Data Security) Regulations, 2017.
1314. Regulation 7(a) of the Privacy Protection (Data Security) Regulations, 2017.
1315. Regulation 7(b) of the Privacy Protection (Data Security) Regulations, 2017.
1316. Regulation 7(c) of the Privacy Protection (Data Security) Regulations, 2017.
1317. Regulation 8(a) of the Privacy Protection (Data Security) Regulations, 2017.
1318. Regulation 8(b) of the Privacy Protection (Data Security) Regulations, 2017.
1319. Regulation 9(c) of the Privacy Protection (Data Security) Regulations, 2017.
1320. Regulation 9(a) of the Privacy Protection (Data Security) Regulations, 2017.

exclusively controlled by the employee (e.g., fingerprints). In addition, the data security protocol is required to include instructions towards the passwords (i.e., how many letters, from what type, changing password frequency, etc.), the disconnection from the database after a certain period of time of inactivity, and operative instructions towards errors or problems.[1321]

If the database is of the third or fourth categories (medium or higher data security levels), a monitoring system is required for any access to the database, including the identity details of any person who has accessed the database, the date and time of any access, and the personal data which has been accessed.[1322] These details should be saved for at least twenty-four months,[1323] and any change within the definitions of the monitoring system would be automatically notified to the persons who are responsible for its function.

The database's owner is responsible for the detection and monitoring of any security failure or accident. The documentation and monitoring are required to be automatic, if possible.[1324] The data security protocol is required to include clear instructions in case of security failure, including cancellation of access to the database, if necessary.[1325] If the database is of the third category (medium data security level), the database's owner is required to appoint a meeting with the relevant employees to discuss the security failures, at least once a year, and if the database is of the fourth category (higher data security level), at least once in three months.[1326]

The database's owner is required to restrict the connectivity of portable devices to the database in accordance with the data security level of the database, and use reasonable protection measures to protect the data copied to such devices, including encryption methods.[1327] All hardware and software used with the database must be updated occasionally under the direct responsibility of the database's owner.[1328]

The database is not allowed to be connected to the Internet or to any other public network, unless the database is using adequate protecting measures from unauthorized access into the database and from any other known malware.[1329] Any data transfer through the Internet or through any other public network must be encrypted,[1330] and requires at least two identification measures.[1331] If the database is of the third or fourth categories (medium or higher data security levels), at least one of the identification measures must be physical.

Outsourcing of any service regarding the database is allowed only after verification of the creditability of the outsourced entity regarding data security, and clear determination of the outsourced entity's functions, access, service, duties, and

---

1321. Regulation 9(b) of the Privacy Protection (Data Security) Regulations, 2017.
1322. Regulation 10(a) of the Privacy Protection (Data Security) Regulations, 2017.
1323. Regulation 10(d) of the Privacy Protection (Data Security) Regulations, 2017.
1324. Regulation 11(a) of the Privacy Protection (Data Security) Regulations, 2017.
1325. Regulation 11(b) of the Privacy Protection (Data Security) Regulations, 2017.
1326. Regulation 11(c) of the Privacy Protection (Data Security) Regulations, 2017.
1327. Regulation 12 of the Privacy Protection (Data Security) Regulations, 2017.
1328. Regulation 13(c) of the Privacy Protection (Data Security) Regulations, 2017.
1329. Regulation 14(a) of the Privacy Protection (Data Security) Regulations, 2017.
1330. Regulation 14(b) of the Privacy Protection (Data Security) Regulations, 2017.
1331. Regulation 14(c) of the Privacy Protection (Data Security) Regulations, 2017.

responsibility.[1332] The database's owner is not released from responsibility in this case, and there must be performed actions of inspection, detection, and monitoring.[1333]

If the database is of the third or fourth categories (medium or higher data security levels), the database's owner is required to organize external or internal inspection on all data security issues, at least once in twenty-four months, by a qualified person.[1334] A report at the end of the inspection is required to make the required changes in order to be compatible with the regulations.

All of the above duties imposed on the database's owner are imposed on the database's manager as well, and these duties, besides those relating to the definitions documents and the outsourcing, are imposed on the database's possessor as well.[1335] However, the registrar is authorized to exempt the database's owner, manager or possessors from some of the duties, if convinced that they are unnecessary regarding the relevant use of the database and the number of persons who has access to the database.[1336]

The registrar is also authorized to order that if the database stands within an official standard of database security, it is considered as fulfilling the above regulations. However, official standard in this context relates to a standard determined by the Israeli Standards Institute,[1337] and international standard recognized by the Israeli Standards Institute, or any other standard recognized officially by the registrar.[1338]

1332. Regulation 15(a)(1) and 15(a)(2) of the Privacy Protection (Data Security) Regulations, 2017.
1333. Regulation 15(a)(4) of the Privacy Protection (Data Security) Regulations, 2017.
1334. Regulation 16(a) of the Privacy Protection (Data Security) Regulations, 2017.
1335. Regulation 19(a) of the Privacy Protection (Data Security) Regulations, 2017.
1336. Regulation 20(a) of the Privacy Protection (Data Security) Regulations, 2017.
1337. For the Israeli Standards Institute *see* above at Chapter 4: Legal Status of Standardization at Part I.
1338. Regulation 20(b) of the Privacy Protection (Data Security) Regulations, 2017. IS 27000 is an example for such standard determined by the Israeli Standards Institute from 2018, available in English. *See* https://portal.sii.org.il/heb/standardization/teken/?tid=c3c678e0-8126-429f-930e-8dc21f25c1ab (accessed 23 Jul. 2021).

Chapter 2. Protection of Telecommunications Privacy

139. Protection of telecommunications privacy is generally regulated through the procedural law of courts, the privacy protection law, and the anti-defamation law. When the protection of privacy is required within any legal proceedings, the procedural law of courts is relevant and functions as specific law. In other cases, the privacy protection law is the relevant law, unless the publication is defamatory, and the anti-defamation law becomes relevant. These three aspects of protection of telecommunications privacy is discussed below.

§1. Privacy in Legal Proceedings

140. In both criminal and non-criminal legal proceedings in Israel, publicity is considered as the individual's right in order to ensure justice.[1339] When justice is not seen in public, the courts may act arbitrarily; therefore, the individual is kept by the law from giving up this right. As a result, the general rule is that all legal proceedings are open to the public, and any person is authorized to enter the law court within any sessions.[1340] This includes the press as well.

However, the court may order to limit audience presence at the law court (*in camera*) in a certain session, all of it or part of it, if a certain interest requires protection and it is considered in higher position. These interests are not under the court's discretion, but determined explicitly by the law, and they include the privacy protection of a minor in legal proceedings,[1341] the privacy protection of a mentally retarded person,[1342] the privacy protection of a victim of sexual offence,[1343] the privacy protection of a victim of violence by a family member,[1344] privacy protection of a victim of slavery, human trafficking or sexual slavery offences,[1345] and protection of commercial secrets.[1346]

The court may also consider to limit audience presence at the law court (*in camera*) in certain situations of public security, national security,[1347] protecting interests

1339. *See* Gabriel Hallevy, *Theory of Criminal Justice* vol. II 589–596 (Bursi Publishing House 2011); Gabriel Hallevy, *Theory of Civil Procedure* vol. III 109–118 (Bursi Publishing House 2019).
1340. Section 68(a) of the Courts [Combined Version] Act, 1984. *See* Civ. App. Req. 1386/14 *Innes-King v. Itonut Zahav Ltd.* (12 May 2014).
1341. Section 68(b)(4) of the Courts [Combined Version] Act, 1984.
1342. *Ibid., See* HCJ 2098/91 *Anon. v. Social Service*, 45(3) PD 217 (1991).
1343. Section 68(b)(5) of the Courts [Combined Version] Act, 1984.
1344. Section 68(b)(13) of the Courts [Combined Version] Act, 1984.
1345. Section 68(b)(9) of the Courts [Combined Version] Act, 1984.
1346. Section 68(b)(8) of the Courts [Combined Version] Act, 1984. *See* Civ. App. Req. 8362/17 *Delek Motors v. State* (4 Jan. 2018); Civ. App. 2800/97 *Lipson v. Gehl*, 53(3) PD 714 (1999).
1347. Section 68(b)(1) of the Courts [Combined Version] Act, 1984.

of Israeli foreign affairs,[1348] protection of morals,[1349] and protection of witnesses.[1350] The court generally uses judicial discretion within these situations and avoids limitations. If necessary, part of the session is limited, and it is rare that all session is limited for audience presence.

A different question is the question of publications within any media or by the press. Of course, if the court session is without any audience (*in camera*), no press is allowed to be present at the law court, and no publication is allowed as well.[1351] If the session is open for the public, the general rule is that the press is allowed to publish a fair report on it. However, this does not include photography, and photographing anyone within the law court or publishing it require the court's consent.[1352] This prohibition is intended for privacy protection interests.

If one of the parties is a minor, no publications towards the minor's trial (criminal trial or not) are allowed.[1353] Publications are neither allowed when the object is a plaintiff who sued for bodily harm (unless the plaintiff has consented),[1354] or a suspect in commission of any criminal offence (for the first forty-eight hours from the first interrogation,[1355] or that the publication might interfere the interrogation).[1356] These prohibitions are intended for privacy protection interests, and they are considered criminal offences of up to six months imprisonment.[1357]

If the court has prohibited publication in favour of the individual's privacy, any person (including the press) may submit the court a request to cancel the prohibitory injunction.[1358] For the cancellation of the prohibition, the court has to be convinced that the interest to enable publication is stronger than the interest of the individual's privacy, and that the damage to the individual's privacy from publication is lower than the damage to the public from the prohibition to publish. The court's decision may be appealed within seven days.[1359]

Israeli law accepts other reasons than privacy protection for the prohibition of publications (e.g., *sub judice* in criminal trials),[1360] but privacy protection is the major reason in Israel for prohibition of publication of court's sessions. In 2002, it was suggested that court sessions would be broadcasted in a certain TV channel ('Court TV'), but the judges have consistently refused. However, the Knesset broadcasts all discussions that take place within the main hall.

1348. Section 68(b)(2) of the Courts [Combined Version] Act, 1984.
1349. Section 68(b)(3) of the Courts [Combined Version] Act, 1984.
1350. Section 68(b)(7) of the Courts [Combined Version] Act, 1984.
1351. Section 70(a) of the Courts [Combined Version] Act, 1984. *See* Cri. App. 5114/97 *Sulimani v. State*, 55(2) PD 721 (2001).
1352. Section 70(b) of the Courts [Combined Version] Act, 1984. *See* Cri. Req. 4275/07 *Israel Broadcasting Authority v. State* (17 Sep. 2007).
1353. Section 70(c) of the Courts [Combined Version] Act, 1984. *See* Cri. Req. 11793/05 *Israeli News Corporation v. State* (5 Apr. 2006).
1354. Section 70(c1) of the Courts [Combined Version] Act, 1984.
1355. Section 70(d1) of the Courts [Combined Version] Act, 1984.
1356. Section 70(e) of the Courts [Combined Version] Act, 1984.
1357. Section 70(f) of the Courts [Combined Version] Act, 1984.
1358. Section 70C(a) of the Courts [Combined Version] Act, 1984.
1359. Section 70D of the Courts [Combined Version] Act, 1984.
1360. Section 71 of the Courts [Combined Version] Act, 1984.

§2. General Privacy Protection

141. The main protection of telecommunications privacy outside legal proceedings is through the privacy protection law. The general rule is that the individual's privacy is protected, unless the individual has explicitly consented otherwise.[1361] However, the definition of 'privacy' in this context may vary. Privacy in this context is defined through the definition of invasion into privacy. Thus, as long as a certain act is not considered invading into the individual's privacy, it is allowed. Invasion into privacy is considered identical whether it is made by any governmental unit or by individuals. Nevertheless, as to invasion into privacy by a governmental unit, it is regulated by the wiretapping law as well, as discussed below.[1362]

Within the context of telecommunications privacy, invasion into the individual's privacy is defined as any detection of the individual that may be disturbing (e.g., by paparazzi reporters),[1363] unlawful wiretapping,[1364] publication of the individual's photo when not in public,[1365] publication of the individual's humiliating photo when in public,[1366] publication of a bodily injured individual's photo at the time when the injury occurred and that the publication may be embarrassing,[1367] or publication of a mentally injured individual's photo at the time when the injury occurred and that the publication may be embarrassing,[1368]

Invasion into the individual's privacy is defined as publication of any of the individual's letter which was not intended to be published (unless the letter is 15 years old or it has historical value),[1369] profitable publication of the individual's name, photo, or voice,[1370] publication of any news item on the private life of any individual not in its original context,[1371] publication of any fact of individual's private life, sexual behaviour or healthcare condition, when not in public,[1372] or publication of the individual's dead body, unless the dead has consented, 15 years have passed since the death or at least one of the dead's close relatives (i.e., spouse, children, parents, or brothers) have consented.[1373]

The above types of invasion to the individual's privacy may also be prohibited within other laws (e.g., wiretapping is prohibited under certain circumstances regardless of the invasion to the individual's privacy),[1374] and other legal measures and other legal proceedings may be taken in addition. However, the privacy protection is not dependent on consequences of the other legal proceedings as it is defined separately.

1361. Section 1 of the Privacy Protection Act, 1981.
1362. Below at s. [II]: Wiretapping Powers at Part VII.
1363. Section 2(1) of the Privacy Protection Act, 1981.
1364. Section 2(2) of the Privacy Protection Act, 1981.
1365. Section 2(3) of the Privacy Protection Act, 1981.
1366. Section 2(4) of the Privacy Protection Act, 1981.
1367. Section 2(4A) of the Privacy Protection Act, 1981.
1368. *Ibid.*
1369. Section 2(5) of the Privacy Protection Act, 1981.
1370. Section 2(6) of the Privacy Protection Act, 1981.
1371. Section 2(9) of the Privacy Protection Act, 1981.
1372. Section 2(11) of the Privacy Protection Act, 1981.
1373. Section 2A(a) of the Privacy Protection Act, 1981.
1374. According to s. 2 of the Wiretapping Act, 1979.

Publication in this context is defined not only through telecommunication media, but by any expression (verbal, written, painted, oral, by motion, etc.), as long as it has been intended to other addressees (including one addressee) besides the individual.[1375] However, in this context of privacy protection, only physical persons (not corporations) are considered individuals that their privacy might be invaded.[1376] Corporations' privacy is not considered invaded within the above categories.

Invasion into privacy is considered both civil wrong in tort law and criminal offence of up to five years imprisonment.[1377] As civil wrong, the court is authorized to grant the individual remedy of damages without any proof of any actual damage of up to approximately NIS 60,000 (approximately EUR 15,000).[1378] If the court has convicted any person for the above privacy protection offence, the court is also authorized to grant the individual remedy of damages without any proof of any actual damage of up to approximately NIS 60,000.[1379]

If the invasion into privacy was through a publication in a newspaper (including digital newspaper), both civil and criminal liability for the invasion are related to the person who made it to be published (e.g., the reporter), to the newspaper's editor and to any person who has decided on the publication. Civil liability is also related to the newspaper's publisher.[1380] However, if the newspaper's editor has taken reasonable measures in order to prevent the particular invasion into the individual's privacy, the editor is not criminally liable.[1381] The editor's civil liability remains unchanged.

In addition, if the newspaper is not digital, but printed, the printing entity (e.g., printing house) of the newspaper and its distributor are held liable both in criminal law and civil law for the invasion into the individual's privacy, unless they did not know, or had no duty to know by law, that the newspaper contains any invasion into anyone's privacy.[1382]

The obsolescence for submission of civil lawsuit regarding invasion into privacy is two years,[1383] whereas the obsolescence for submission of indictment regarding invasion into privacy is five years.[1384] However, liability for invasion into the individual's privacy, both in civil and criminal proceedings, is subject to a minimum damage proven by the plaintiff or the prosecutor, and the mere proof of the invasion is not enough in order to determine liability.[1385] This resembles the general defence of *de minimis* in criminal law, as the minimum damage is presumed to have social interest.

1375. Section 2 of the Defamation Prohibition Act, 1965, which is applicable through the definition of the term 'publication' in s. 3 of the Privacy Protection Act, 1981.
1376. Section 3 of the Privacy Protection Act, 1981.
1377. Sections 4 and 5 of the Privacy Protection Act, 1981.
1378. Section 29A(b) of the Privacy Protection Act, 1981.
1379. Section 29A(a) of the Privacy Protection Act, 1981.
1380. Section 30(a) of the Privacy Protection Act, 1981.
1381. Section 30(b) of the Privacy Protection Act, 1981.
1382. Section 31 of the Privacy Protection Act, 1981.
1383. Section 26 of the Privacy Protection Act, 1981.
1384. Section 9 of the Criminal Justice [Combined Version] Act, 1982.
1385. Section 6 of the Privacy Protection Act, 1981 together with s. 34R of the Israeli Penal Code, 1977 and with s. 4 of the Torts [New Version] Ordinance.

In any criminal or civil proceedings towards the invasion of privacy, the defendant may plead several defences. One defence is the defence of protected publications.[1386] Protected publications are official publications of acts of the state's powers (legislature, executive, and judiciary),[1387] or any other official publications of any authority in Israel.[1388] The defence of authorized act relates to publications or other types of invasion into privacy, that the defendant was explicitly authorized to commit.[1389]

If the defendant did not know about the invasion into the individual's privacy, had no legal duty to know about the invasion, had legal duty to invade the individual's privacy, invaded into the individual's privacy in order to protect legitimate interest, invaded into the individual's privacy within lawful professional occupation, accidently invaded into the individual's privacy, invaded into the individual's privacy through legitimate criticism or invaded into the individual's privacy through submission of complaint to the police, it may be considered defence,[1390] if the invasion into the individual's privacy has not exceeded reasonability within the particular circumstances of the case.[1391]

If the defendant pleads a defence, the burden of proof is balance of probabilities, both in criminal and civil proceedings, and the counterparty (the prosecutor or the plaintiff) has the right to refute the defence through separate evidence within a separate part of the trial.[1392] However, if the defendant fails to prove any of the above defences, but proves that the invasion into the individual's privacy was nothing rather than repetition of previous publication, that no purpose to harm existed, or that an appropriate apology has been published, the court may consider that when determining the punishment or the damages.[1393]

Any evidence that has been acquired through invasion of the individual's privacy is inadmissible at any legal proceedings (not necessarily in proceedings when the individual is party), unless the individual has explicitly consented or the court has justified the admissibility of the evidence in the case after considering special circumstances.[1394]

§3. Defamatory Publications

142. When the invasion into the individual's privacy includes defamatory publication, supplementary legal provisions may apply. These legal provisions are from the defamation prohibition law. In general, these legal provisions apply *in addition* to the legal provisions from the privacy protection law. Thus, a person may be

1386. Section 18(1) of the Privacy Protection Act, 1981.
1387. Section 13(1)–(3), (5) of the Defamation Prohibition Act, 1965.
1388. Section 13(2)–(4), (6)–(11) of the Defamation Prohibition Act, 1965.
1389. Section 19 of the Privacy Protection Act, 1981.
1390. Section 18(2) of the Privacy Protection Act, 1981.
1391. Section 20(a) of the Privacy Protection Act, 1981.
1392. Section 21 of the Privacy Protection Act, 1981.
1393. Section 22 of the Privacy Protection Act, 1981.
1394. Section 32 of the Privacy Protection Act, 1981.

indicted or sued for the same act, both through privacy protection law and defamation prohibition law, but the punishment in criminal proceedings is one punishment for all offences.[1395]

Defamation is defined as anything that its *publication* might humiliate any person, might present any person as an object for hatred or mockery, might cause any person any financial or social loss or might present any person in any humiliating manner regarding the person's origin, religion, age, sex, gender or disability (physical, mental or cognitive).[1396] Unlike the privacy protection law, the defamation prohibition law protects corporations as well as physical persons.[1397] However, in civil proceedings, damages in favour of the corporation are dependent on proof of actual damage caused by the defamatory publication.

Publication in this context is defined not only through telecommunication media, but by any expression (verbal, written, painted, oral, by motion, etc.), as long as it has been intended to other addressees (including one addressee) besides the victim of the defamation.[1398] The publication may be explicit or implicit, full or partial, and it is still considered publication in this context.[1399] The victim person is not required to be alive at the time of publication, and the victim's relatives may sue instead of the victim.[1400]

Defamatory publication, with a specific intent to cause damage, published to at least two addressees is considered criminal offence of up to one-year imprisonment.[1401] Although the general prosecution in Israel is authorized to prosecute for defamatory publications, no charges are submitted due to the attorney general's guidelines of 2006 to minimize the intervention in defamatory publications.[1402] However, the victim may prosecute (in criminal proceedings) the defendant within private criminal complaint.[1403] In addition, defamatory publication which has been published to at least two addressees is considered civil wrong under the law of torts.[1404]

When the defamatory publication is within any media, both civil and criminal liability for the publication are related to the person who made it to be published (e.g., the reporter), to the media's editor (e.g., the editor of the blog published with a particular website) and to any person who has decided on the publication. Civil

---

1395. Section 186 of the Criminal Justice [Combined Version] Act, 1982.
1396. Section 1 of the Defamation Prohibition Act, 1965.
1397. *Ibid.*
1398. Section 2 of the Defamation Prohibition Act, 1965. *See, e.g.*, Civ.Cas. (Tel-Aviv) 154328/02 *Koren v. Kofman* (15 May 2003).
1399. Section 3 of the Defamation Prohibition Act, 1965.
1400. Section 5 of the Defamation Prohibition Act, 1965.
1401. Section 6 of the Defamation Prohibition Act, 1965.
1402. Attorney General's Guidelines, 4.1107 (2006).
1403. Section 8 of the Defamation Prohibition Act, 1965. *See* Gabriel Hallevy, *The Private Prosecution and Criminal Justice*, 9 OAC L. Rev. 381 (2011).
1404. Section 7 of the Defamation Prohibition Act, 1965.

liability is also related to the media's publisher, broadcaster, or executive manager.[1405] However, if the media's editor has taken reasonable measures in order to prevent the defamatory publication, the editor is not criminally liable.[1406] The editor's civil liability remains unchanged.

In addition, if the media is a newspaper which is not digital, but printed, the printing entity (e.g., printing house) of the newspaper and its distributor are held liable both in criminal law and civil law for the defamatory publication, unless they did not know, or had no duty to know by law, that the newspaper contains any defamatory publication.[1407]

In any criminal or civil proceedings towards the defamatory publication, the defendant may plead several defences. One defence is the defence of protected publication.[1408] Protected publications are official publications of acts of the state's powers (legislature, executive and judiciary),[1409] or any other official publications of any authority in Israel.[1410] The defence of authorized act relates to defamatory publications, that the defendant was explicitly authorized to publish.[1411]

A very significant defence in case of defamatory publication is the defence of truthful publication ('truth I spoke'). This defence requires two elements: the factual details of the publications are completely true and the publication raises public interest.[1412] This defence has been used in Israeli legal history to cope with complicated issues that have been brought to the Israeli court. One of the most significant example was the function of Jewish leadership in Europe within the holocaust during the Second World War.[1413]

If the defendant did not know about the defamatory publication, had no legal duty to know about it, had legal duty to publish it, or published it in order to protect legitimate interest, it may be considered defence in any criminal or civil proceedings for defamatory publication,[1414] if the defendant has acted in good faith (bona fide). However, if the person who is the object of defamation has requested the media's editor, broadcaster, executive manager, or the person who decided on the publication, that reasonable denial or correction would be published, and the request was refused, they are not allowed to plead any defence of good faith.[1415]

When a telecommunication media publishes that a criminal interrogation has been opened against an individual, that an individual was criminally charged or that an individual has been convicted within a criminal trial, and after the publication the legal situation of the individual has been changed favourably (i.e., the interrogation ended up with no evidence, the individual was exonerated or an appeal on

---

1405. Section 11(a) of the Defamation Prohibition Act, 1965.
1406. Section 11(b) of the Defamation Prohibition Act, 1965.
1407. Section 12 of the Defamation Prohibition Act, 1965.
1408. Section 13 of the Defamation Prohibition Act, 1965.
1409. Section 13(1)–(3), (5) of the Defamation Prohibition Act, 1965.
1410. Section 13(2)–(4), (6)–(8) and (10)–(11) of the Defamation Prohibition Act, 1965.
1411. Section 13(9) of the Defamation Prohibition Act, 1965.
1412. Section 14 of the Defamation Prohibition Act, 1965.
1413. *See, e.g.*, Cri. Cas. (Jerusalem) 124/53 *Attorney General v. Gruenwald* (22 Jun. 1955); Cri. App. 232/55 *Attorney General v. Gruenwald,* 12(3) PD 2017 (1958).
1414. Section 15(1)–(3) of the Defamation Prohibition Act, 1965.
1415. Section 17 of the Defamation Prohibition Act, 1965.

the conviction has been accepted in favour of the convicted), that media has to publish the update within the same framework of the first publication, if the individual has asked for it in writing.[1416]

Expressing legitimate opinion may also be considered defence in any criminal or civil proceedings for defamatory publication, if the defendant has acted in good faith (bona fide). This defence includes opinion on the public function (e.g., judicial) of the person; on the person's behaviour as a party in legal proceedings; on any creation in literature, science, or art; or on the person's functioning as subject to the defendant if factually justified.[1417]

If the defamatory publication has been broadcasted on TV or on radio, within live broadcast that has not been recorded in advance, and the defendant did not know, and could have not known, on any intent to publish any defamation, it is considered defence, if the defendant is the media's publisher, broadcaster, or executive manager.[1418] If the publication was nothing but news delivery to the editor of the media in order to examine the possibility of publication, it is considered defence.[1419] If the publication is a fair coverage or report on a public matter or on a matter accessible to the public, it is considered defence as well.[1420]

Any defence is rejected if the publication was not true and the defendant did not believe it was true, if the publication was not true and the defendant has not taken any reasonable measures to verify its content or if the defendant has intended to cause damage that exceeds the inevitable damage caused in order to defend the relevant interests.[1421]

If the defendant pleads a defence, the burden of proof is balance of probabilities, both in criminal and civil proceedings, and the counterparty (the prosecutor or the plaintiff) has the right to refute the defence through separate evidence within a separate part of the trial.[1422] However, the defendant has the duty to prove that the publication has not exceeded reasonability under particular circumstances.[1423]

If the defendant has been convicted in criminal trial for defamatory publication, the court may impose, in addition to the punishment, damages in favour of the victim without proof of actual damage, of up to approximately NIS 70,000 (approximately EUR 17,000) per publication.[1424] In civil lawsuits for defamatory publications, the court may impose damages in favour of the victim without proof of actual damage, of up to approximately NIS 70,000 per publication,[1425] and if the publication was specifically intended to cause damage, up to approximately NIS 140,000 per publication.[1426]

1416. Section 25A(a) and 25A(b) of the Defamation Prohibition Act, 1965.
1417. Section 15(4)–(7) of the Defamation Prohibition Act, 1965.
1418. Section 15(12) of the Defamation Prohibition Act, 1965.
1419. Section 15(11) of the Defamation Prohibition Act, 1965.
1420. Section 15(9) of the Defamation Prohibition Act, 1965.
1421. Section 16(b) of the Defamation Prohibition Act, 1965.
1422. Section 18 of the Defamation Prohibition Act, 1965.
1423. Section 16(a) of the Defamation Prohibition Act, 1965.
1424. Section 7A(a) of the Defamation Prohibition Act, 1965.
1425. Section 7A(b) of the Defamation Prohibition Act, 1965.
1426. Section 7A(c) of the Defamation Prohibition Act, 1965.

In addition to any punishment or remedy in both criminal or civil proceedings, the court may grant any prohibitory injunction or mandatory injunction in order to prevent the continuance of defamation,[1427] e.g., confiscation of the publications, publication of an apology, removal of any content from any website or publication of denial as to the defamatory publication's content. If the defendant has confessed at some of the defamatory publications, the court may impose such injunction at once, before the judgment is given.[1428]

In any criminal or civil proceedings relating defamatory publication, even if the defendant has failed to prove any evidence, the court may consider some mitigating circumstances regarding the punishment or the damages. The mitigating circumstances may be considered if the defendant was sincerely convinced that the publication was true, if the defendant did not intend to cause any harm, if the defamatory publication was nothing but a repetition notifying the identity of the origin or if the defendant has apologized for the publication, corrected it, denied it or taken reasonable measures to stop its distribution.[1429]

1427. Section 9 of the Defamation Prohibition Act, 1965.
1428. Section 10 of the Defamation Prohibition Act, 1965.
1429. Section 19 of the Defamation Prohibition Act, 1965.

Part VII. Computer-Related Crime

143. One of the most significant aspects of cyber law is the criminal law aspect. This aspect relates both to substantive criminal law and criminal procedure. In general, the basic principles of criminal law have not been amended due to the cyber law, but small amendments and adaptations of particular legal provisions have been embraced. These aspects of cyber law are discussed below.

Chapter 1. General Legal Development

§1. Incorporation of Cyber Law into Criminal Law

144. Until 1995 no legal change has been embraced into the Israeli criminal law towards the cyber law aspects of computer-related delinquency. These aspects include regulation of the delinquency itself and legal measures to detect that delinquency. Traditional criminal law has been applied to cope with the growing phenomenon of computer-related delinquency.

The first significant change was accepted in 1995. The ministry of justice asked for experts opinions in order to embrace cyber law insights into criminal law. This initiative has been motivated by the growing part of the use of computer in daily life and industry, the fact that computer systems activity was not regulated at all in Israeli law, and by the higher rates of computer delinquency since the 1990s whereas the Israeli courts experienced difficulties in the implementation of the basic principles of criminal law when discussing this type of delinquency.[1430]

In addition, the use of computing systems to commit offences required the development of legal provisions that would enable the law enforcement authorities to detect this type of delinquency, whether the Internet or other networks are used or not. Of course, derivative adaptations were required to the law of evidence and the criminal procedure. For example, is printed document from the computer database admissible as an evidence of the information stored in the computer's hardware? Is reading one's e-mail is wiretapping? Is digital document is considered to be a 'document'? etc.

As a result, in July 1995, the Knesset has enacted the Computers Act, 1995. This legislation has regulated a general framework of the use of computers within the commission of offences. Within this act new offences have been defined, and amendments within the law of evidence and criminal justice were embraced. The Computers Act, 1995 was the first step towards the regulation of cyber offences under criminal law. This act has also created parallel civil wrongs, but the major development held by this act was in the aspect of criminal law.

Since 1995 and on, the legal development within the substantive criminal law was focused on the definition of new offences from time to time, but the general part of criminal law was not changed. As to criminal procedure and evidence law, the legal development is focused on adaptation of traditional procedures and terms into the new realm of cyber offences. For example, the police search powers had to be developed into search within computing systems.

Thus, incorporation of cyber law within the Israeli criminal law is focused on the definition of new offences and adaptation of the criminal procedures. However, the evolution of artificial intelligence (AI) technology poses new challenges, and Israeli criminal law is still left behind. Consequently, these challenges may be coped with only through the existing principles of criminal law, as discussed below.[1431]

1430. *See* the Computers Law Bill, 1994.
1431. Below at §2: Cyber Delinquency Involving Artificial Intelligence Technology.

§2. Detection and Law Enforcement

145. Although Israeli legislation since 1995, as to criminal procedure and evidence law, is focused on adaptation of traditional procedures and terms into the new realm of cyber offences, the legislation itself does not suffice to cope with cyber delinquency. An efficient struggle against cyber delinquency requires qualified professionals that are able to track and detect cyber delinquency and enforce the law using sophisticated and advanced technological measures. This requirement has been increased as the cyber delinquency from outside Israel towards Israeli websites has been increased.

In 2012, the ministry of public security had stated that cyber delinquency is no less than strategic threat on Israel. Israel is a target for cyber-attacks of many pro-Arab and anti-Semitic organizations, and part of the public security in Israel is the safety of the cyberspace. Consequently, Israel has developed sophisticated measures to defend itself from cyber delinquency. Part of these measures is developed in the IDF, part in the Israeli hi-tech industry and part in the Israeli police.

In April 2016, Israel had joined the Budapest Convention on Cybercrime, and it was ratified in September 2016. In general, the Budapest convention is the first international covenant that addresses Internet and computer delinquency by harmonizing national and domestic laws, improving investigative techniques, and increasing cooperation among nations. It was drawn up by the Council of Europe, with the active participation of the Council of Europe's observer states Canada, Japan, Philippines, South Africa, and the US.

However, cyber delinquency which is not related to national security is treated by the Israeli police. Consequently, the National Cyber Unit (NCU) was established in 2014 under the Israeli police. The cyber delinquency that is treated by NCU is that which is targeted to damage local economy, essential infrastructure, and financial institutes, and in addition, sexual cyber delinquency (e.g., paedophile networks) and other offences using cyber space as framework (e.g., drug dealing using the web).

The NCU has been authorized to collect information (intelligence), to investigate, and to develop technological solutions to the operational requirements of investigations due to the Israeli legal requirements. As international cyber delinquency has increased, the NCU had to develop the framework with other cyber units around the world in order to share the Israeli advanced technology with them and in order to share intelligence.

For example, ransom malwares are considered to require international cooperation, and such cooperation is in favour of all cooperating states. As a result, Israel has joined the 'nomoreransom' international enterprise, and NCU has established in April 2017 assisting measures in a special website.[1432] This website contains about 40 measures to decode the ransom malware, open to all applicants (Israelis or not), free of charge, and available 24/7.

1432. *See* http://www.nomoreransom.gov.il/default.aspx (accessed 23 Jul. 2021).

The NCU offers other services available 24/7 for any applicant (Israeli or not) within fishing frauds (i.e., 'fishing' personal details of the victims, and these details are used to break into their bank accounts, etc.), carding frauds (i.e., stealing credit cards details from financial institutes) and other frauds.

Chapter 2. Application of Substantive Criminal Law in the Area of ICT

146. The application of substantive criminal law in the area of ICT in Israel is focused on definition of particular offences, as aforesaid.[1433] However, when artificial technology is involved in cyber delinquency (e.g., fraud in the stock exchange market committed by or through AI software), the applicability of the general part is required as well. These two aspects of the substantive criminal law application in the area of ICT are discussed below.

§1. Particular Cyber Offences

147. The two main sets of particular cyber offences are from the computer law and telecommunications law. In other cases, the traditional particular offences function as the framework for criminal liability. For example, when an offender steals the victim's credit card details ('carding' fraud), there is no necessary with a special particular offence, but the traditional particular offence of theft is applicable. The above two main sets of particular cyber offences are intended to cover more easily cyber offences, which are not easily covered by traditional particular offences. These two sets of particular offences are discussed below.

I. Computer Offences

148. Computer offences were enacted in Israel in 1995 for the first time. Until then, the Israeli courts have used traditional particular offences, but these offences did not cover all computer offences easily. The main term for the definition of computer offences is obviously the 'computer'. A computer is defined as any device, in which using software, it processes data arithmetically or logically, except for calculators.[1434] The calculator is defined as a device that is capable of nothing but arithmetical calculations.[1435] Consequently, not only PCs or working stations are considered computers, but many other devices as well, including smartphones, car-engine computers (installed in modern cars), smart TVs, and tablets.

As the computer offences are focused on the data stored within the computer hardware, the law divides this data into two categories: software and other data. Software is defined as a set of instructions readable by a computer, that is intended to cause the computer to function in general or in certain way.[1436] The instructions are encoded electronically, electrochemically, electro-optically, or in any other way in a portable device or within the computer itself. As a result, both operating systems and other applications are considered 'software'.

1433. *See* above at §1: Incorporation of Cyber Law into Criminal Law.
1434. The definition of the term 'computer' in section 1 of the Computers Act, 1995.
1435. The definition of the term 'assisting computer' in section 1 of the Computers Act, 1995.
1436. The definition of the term 'software' in section 1 of the Computers Act, 1995.

Other data, in this context, is defined as signals, information, terms, or instructions, which are not 'software', readable by a computer, stored in the computer or in any other device, and are not intended to be used only by a calculator.[1437] For example, the data which operates the computer's camera is considered 'software', but the picture photographed by that camera operated by the software is not 'software', but other data.

Using these terms, the Israeli computer law defines five main particular sets of offences, which are intended to regulate computer offences. These particular offences are computer's interruption offences, false data offences, unlawful access offence, unlawful instrumental access offence, and software offences. These offences are discussed below.

Computer's interruption offences are two offences. The first offence relates to any disruption within the regular activity of the computer or to any interruption to use any computer.[1438] The second offence relates to deletion of any data, including software, within any computer, to cause any change or disruption within the data or to interrupt the use of the data.[1439] Thus, the first offence relates to the computer, whereas the second relates to the data. These are criminal offences of up to five years imprisonment.

The ultimate defence in these offences is the authorized acts defence. Accordingly, if the perpetrator was authorized to act this way (e.g., the owner of a PC formats it, and as a result, deletes most of the data stored within the computer's hardware), no criminal liability is imposed. These offences do not require a component of consequences within their factual element requirement ('conduct offences'). These offences require *mens rea* within the mental element requirement; therefore, negligent conduct does not suffice to impose criminal liability for these offences.

False data offences are two offences. False data is defined as any deceptive data, i.e., any data that might deceive any reasonable person, in the context that it is used.[1440] The false data may be formed in any way, including any output. The term 'output' is defined as any data, signs, terms or instructions that are produced, in any way, by a computer.[1441] For example, printed documents, digital pictures or digital sounds generated by a computer are considered output.

The first offence relates to data that is not software, and it includes transferring of any false data, storing any false data within the computer's hardware, or committing any act which is resulted from false data or false output.[1442] The second offence relates to software, and it includes composing software, transferring software, or storing software in a computer, that the result of these acts would be false data or false output.[1443] Operating the computer with such software may also be considered within the second offence. These are criminal offences of up to five years imprisonment.

1437. The definition of the term 'data' in section 1 of the Computers Act, 1995.
1438. Section 2(1) of the Computers Act, 1995.
1439. Section 2(2) of the Computers Act, 1995.
1440. The definition of the term 'false data' in s. 3(b) of the Computers Act, 1995.
1441. The definition of the term 'output' in s. 1 of the Computers Act, 1995.
1442. Section 3(a)(1) of the Computers Act, 1995.
1443. Section 3(a)(2) of the Computers Act, 1995.

The ultimate defence in these offences is authorized acts, as self-deception is not considered deception in the context of criminal law. Accordingly, if the perpetrator was authorized to act this way (e.g., the owner of a PC knowingly uses false data), no criminal liability is imposed. These offences do not require a component of consequences within their factual element requirement ('conduct offences'). These offences require specific intent (i.e., a purpose to create false data or false output) within the mental element requirement,[1444] therefore, mere knowledge or awareness would not suffice, and of course negligent conduct would not suffice to impose criminal liability for these offences.

Unlawful access offence is the basic offence in the Israeli criminal law that was designed to cope with hackers. There are additional offences that may be relevant (e.g., privacy protection offences),[1445] directly or indirectly, but this is the basic and direct framework to cope with hackers. Accordingly, any unauthorized access to software or to any other data stored in a computer is considered criminal offence of up to three years imprisonment.[1446]

The 'access' required within this offence is defined as any act of login into the computer, whether using communication with the computer or physically, but not wiretapping.[1447] Wiretapping has been excluded from this offence as wiretapping is defined separately as a particular defence, which is not limited to use of computers. The wiretapping offence is considered more severe, as the punishment is up to five years imprisonment.[1448]

The ultimate defence in this offence is the authorized act's defence. Accordingly, if the perpetrator was authorized to act this way (e.g., the owner of a PC turns it on and logins with the relevant username), no criminal liability is imposed. This offence does not require a component of consequences within its factual element requirement ('conduct offences'). This offence requires *mens rea* within the mental element requirement; therefore, negligent conduct does not suffice to impose criminal liability for this offence.[1449]

Unlawful instrumental access offence is an extension of the previous basic offence (unlawful access offence) in cases where the unlawful access has been used just to commit another offence. Thus, within this offence, the access to the computer's data was instrumental in order to commit another offence. For example, a hacker achieves an access to the victim's PC knowingly that the victim stores all passwords in a certain file. The hacker copies the file and uses one of the passwords to transfer money into a third-party's bank account.

In this example, the offender has used the unlawful access to the victim's PC instrumentally in order to commit another offence of theft. This type of activity is considered more severe than the basic unlawful access to a computer's data. Therefore, the unlawful instrumental access offence is considered criminal offence of up

1444. *See* Cri. App. Req. 10342/08 *Alice v. State* (18 Feb. 2009); Cri. Req. 6661/08 *Hamidalov v. State* (10 Sep. 2008); Cri. Req. 6623/08 *Hilf v. State* (4 Aug. 2008).
1445. *See* above at Part VI: Privacy Protection.
1446. Section 4 of the Computers Act, 1995.
1447. The definition of the term 'access' in s. 4 of the Computers Act, 1995.
1448. Section 2 of the Wiretapping Act, 1979.
1449. *See* Cri. App. Req. 10259/09 *Anon. v. State* (1 Jun. 2010); Cri. App. Req. 1721/12 *Irashi v. State* (30 Mar. 2014).

to five years imprisonment.[1450] Of course, the other offence is not assimilated within this offence (e.g., the theft in the above example is not assimilated within the unlawful instrumental access offence), and the offender is indicted for both offences.

The ultimate defence in this offence is the authorized acts defence, which relates to both unlawful access to the computer's data and the offence that was intended to be committed using that access. Accordingly, if the perpetrator was authorized to act this way, no criminal liability is imposed. This offence does not require a component of consequences within its factual element requirement ('conduct offence'). Therefore, the other offence is not required to be actually committed.

This factual element requirement is completed by a higher level of mental element, as this offence requires specific intent (i.e., a purpose to commit the other offence) within the mental element requirement.[1451] Consequently, in order to impose criminal liability for this offence, the prosecution has to prove that computer's data has been actually accessed by the offender, and that the offender has intended to use this information to commit another offence, whether the other offence has been actually committed or not. Of course, mere knowledge or awareness would not suffice, and of course negligent conduct would not suffice to impose criminal liability for this offence.

Software offences are designed to cope with malwares (known in public as 'computer viruses'), and due to the technological developments of malwares, these offences were re-enacted in 2012. There are three software offences. The first offence is the basic core offence which relates to composing the malware, and the two other offences relate to its distribution.

The first offence is the core offence of the struggle in malwares. This offence relates to the composition of a software that is capable of performing certain activities with an intent to perform this activities unlawfully.[1452] These activities include the disruption of the regular operation of the computer, disruption to use the computer,[1453] deletion of computer's data, change of the computer's data, disruption of the use of computer's data,[1454] activities resulting with false data,[1455] unlawful access to the computer's data, instrumentally or not,[1456] wiretapping,[1457] or invasion into privacy.[1458]

In fact, these are the basic activities related to common malwares. However, the very composition of any malware is not considered itself an offence, but only when it is intended to be used unlawfully. For example, during a course in computer sciences, the instructor presents the students a malware for scientific purposes. The instructor has composed it for scientific purposes within that course, and this is not

1450. Section 5 of the Computers Act, 1995.
1451. *See* Cri. App. 9893/06 *Alon-Laufer v. State* (31 Dec. 2007); Cri. App. Req. 10259/09 *Anon. v. State* (1 Jun. 2010); Cri. Req. 1677/17 *Abu-Aza v. State* (13 Mar. 2017).
1452. Section 6(a) of the Computers Act, 1995.
1453. Section 6(a)(1) of the Computers Act, 1995.
1454. Section 6(a)(2) of the Computers Act, 1995.
1455. Section 6(a)(3) of the Computers Act, 1995.
1456. Section 6(a)(4) of the Computers Act, 1995.
1457. Section 6(a)(5) of the Computers Act, 1995.
1458. Section 6(a)(6) of the Computers Act, 1995.

an unlawful purpose. Therefore, in this example no criminal offence has been committed. The maximum punishment for this core offence is three years imprisonment.

The factual element requirement in this offence consists of the composition of the malware, and the success of the malware to perform the above activities is not required. Therefore, this offence does not require any component of consequences within its factual element requirement. However, this factual element requirement is completed by a higher level of mental element, as this offence requires specific intent (i.e., a purpose that the above activities would be performed unlawfully) within the mental element requirement.[1459]

Consequently, in order to impose criminal liability for this offence, the prosecution has to prove that the offender has actually composed a malware, and that the malware was not composed in good faith, but with a purpose to cause *unlawfully* disruption of the regular operation of the computer, disruption to use the computer, deletion of computer's data, change of the computer's data, disruption of the use of computer's data, activities resulting with false data, unlawful access to the computer's data, instrumentally or not, wiretapping, or invasion into privacy. Of course, mere knowledge or awareness would not suffice, and of course negligent conduct would not suffice to impose criminal liability for this offence.

The second and third offences within the software offences relate to the distribution of malwares. The second offence relates to any distribution of access code (e.g., password) to a malware that is intended to perform unlawfully disruption of the regular operation of the computer, disruption to use the computer, deletion of computer's data, change of the computer's data, disruption of the use of computer's data, activities resulting with false data, unlawful access to the computer's data, instrumentally or not, wiretapping, or invasion into privacy.[1460]

Not only distribution is included within this offence, but also any offer to the public of such access code, transfer to anyone of such access code, and installation at any computer of such access code. Any of these activities is considered criminal offence of up to three years imprisonment.

The factual element requirement in this offence consists of the above activities of distribution, offering, transfer, and installation of the access code, and the success of the malware to perform the above activities is not required. Therefore, this offence does not require any component of consequences within its factual element requirement. However, this factual element requirement is completed by a higher level of mental element, as this offence requires specific intent (i.e., a purpose that the above activities would be performed unlawfully) within the mental element requirement.

Consequently, in order to impose criminal liability for this offence, the prosecution has to prove that the offender has actually distributed, offered, transferred, or installed an access code to malware, and that it was not done in good faith, but with a purpose to cause *unlawfully* disruption of the regular operation of the computer, disruption to use the computer, deletion of computer's data, change of the computer's data, disruption of the use of computer's data, activities resulting with false

---

1459. *See* Cri. Req. 9883/04 *Sternberg v. State* (5 Nov. 2004).
1460. Section 6(b) of the Computers Act, 1995.

data, unlawful access to the computer's data, instrumentally or not, wiretapping, or invasion into privacy. Of course, mere knowledge or awareness would not suffice, and of course negligent conduct would not suffice to impose criminal liability for this offence.

The third offence relates to any distribution of malware or device containing malware that is intended to perform unlawfully disruption of the regular operation of the computer, disruption to use the computer, deletion of computer's data, change of the computer's data, disruption of the use of computer's data, activities resulting with false data, unlawful access to the computer's data, instrumentally or not, wiretapping, or invasion into privacy.[1461] Not only distribution is included within this offence, but also any offer to the public of such malware or device, transfer to anyone of such malware or device, and installation at any computer of such malware or device. Any of these activities is considered a criminal offence of up to five years imprisonment.

The factual element requirement in this offence consists of the above activities of distribution, offering, transfer, and installation of the malware or device, and the success of the malware to perform the above activities is not required. Therefore, this offence does not require any component of consequences within its factual element requirement. However, this factual element requirement is completed by a higher level of mental element, as this offence requires specific intent (i.e., a purpose that the above activities would be performed unlawfully) within the mental element requirement.

Consequently, in order to impose criminal liability for this offence, the prosecution has to prove that the offender has actually distributed, offered, transferred, or installed malware or device containing malware, and that it was not done in good faith, but with a purpose to cause *unlawfully* disruption of the regular operation of the computer, disruption to use the computer, deletion of computer's data, change of the computer's data, disruption of the use of computer's data, activities resulting with false data, unlawful access to the computer's data, instrumentally or not, wiretapping, or invasion into privacy. Of course, mere knowledge or awareness would not suffice, and of course negligent conduct would not suffice to impose criminal liability for this offence.

II. Telecommunications Offences Using Computer Systems

149. Telecommunication activity is defined in Israeli law as transmitting, transferring, or receiving any sign, voice, or information using wires or not using wires, electronically, optically, or using any electromagnetic system.[1462] By law, all telecommunication activities are under the responsibility of the state, but the state has

1461. Section 6(c) of the Computers Act, 1995.

1462. The definition of 'Telecommunication' in s. 1 of the Communication (Telecommunication and Broadcasting) Act, 1982.

the right to grant licenses to activate telecommunication services to other entities.[1463] As a result, no person is allowed to activate telecommunication services unless licensed to do so by the state.[1464]

Most telecommunication services are activated using computer systems. Thus, activating telecommunication services without license is considered a criminal offence of up to three years imprisonment.[1465] In addition, the court is authorized to order confiscation of the computer systems used for the telecommunication services and the telecommunication device itself.[1466] For this purpose, search authorizations of the police and the ministry of communications' employees were broadened in this context.[1467]

Nevertheless, a few telecommunication activities are allowed to be activated without any license from the state. These activities include self-transmission on a private territory, manufacturing telecommunication devices, operating traffic lights, electronic data processing, and some other activities.[1468]

The telecommunications law is the legal framework in Israel in coping with the phenomenon of bullying and harassment within the Internet. Bullying and harassment were not invented with the Internet, and they are not unique to the Internet. Long ago people were bullying and harassing other people using telecommunications devices, namely the telephone. As technology advanced, bullying and harassment found new ways of expression, but their content and purpose were not actually changed.

The bullying and harassment using the Internet are known as 'Cyberbullying' and 'Cyber-harassment'. Cyberbullying and cyber-harassment are also known as 'online bullying'. Sometimes they include 'shaming', sometimes much beyond that. It has become increasingly common, especially among teenagers. Cyberbullying is when someone, typically teens, bully or harass others on social media websites. Harmful bullying behaviour may include posting rumours, threats, sexual remarks, a victims' personal information, or pejorative labels (i.e., hate speech). Bullying or harassment can be identified by repeated behaviour and an intent to cause harm. Victims may have lower self-esteem, increased suicidal ideation, and a variety of emotional responses, including being scared, frustrated, angry, and depressed.

The Israeli telecommunications law does not distinguish between the different forms of bullying and harassment, as long as they are committed through any telecommunications devices. Therefore, any use of *any* telecommunications device in a manner that might unlawfully scare, harm, harass, or annoy is considered criminal offence of up to three years imprisonment.[1469]

This offence's factual element requirement is adequately wide to include and cover the phenomenon of cyberstalking and cyber-trolling (known also as 'Internet

1463. Section 2(a) of the Communication (Telecommunication and Broadcasting) Act, 1982.
1464. Section 2(b) of the Communication (Telecommunication and Broadcasting) Act, 1982.
1465. Section 28(a) of the Communication (Telecommunication and Broadcasting) Act, 1982.
1466. Section 28(b) of the Communication (Telecommunication and Broadcasting) Act, 1982.
1467. Section 28A of the Communication (Telecommunication and Broadcasting) Act, 1982.
1468. Section 3 of the Communication (Telecommunication and Broadcasting) Act, 1982.
1469. Section 30 of the Communication (Telecommunication and Broadcasting) Act, 1982. *See* Cri. Ret. 4609/06 *Rot v. State* (29 Apr. 2007).

trolling') as well. In general, cyberstalking is the use of the Internet or other electronic means to stalk or harass through stalking an individual, group, or organization. It may also include false accusations and defamation, but not necessarily. It may also include monitoring, identity theft, threats, vandalism, solicitation for sex, or gathering information that may be used to threaten, embarrass, or harass. Cyberstalking is often accompanied by offline stalking.

Internet trolls intentionally try to provoke or offend others in order to elicit a reaction. Trolls and cyberbullies do not always have the same goals. Some trolls engage in cyberbullying, whereas others may be engaged in comparatively harmless mischief. A troll may be disruptive either for their own amusement or because they are genuinely a combative person. As aforesaid, both cyberstalking and cyber-trolling are covered within this offence.

Although commercial advertisements while using the Internet may be annoying, the telecommunications law includes a separate offence for using any telecommunications form (including, but not only, the Internet) to annoy individuals with commercial advertisements.[1470] Accordingly, any advertiser is not allowed to advertise anything directly without the consent of the end user.[1471] However, passive or indirect advertisement is not criminal offence.

For example, if the advertiser sends a commercial advertisement to an e-mail address of an individual without previous consent, it is considered criminal offence, but an advertising banner in a website is allowed. Nevertheless, if the advertiser has advertised directly anything, but enabled the end user (the addressee of the advertisement) to refuse the acceptance of further advertisements or to remove the end user's details from the relevant list (e.g., to remove the end user's e-mail address from the mailing list), it is not considered criminal offence.[1472]

In addition, if the addressee has delivered the mailing details to the advertiser while purchasing products or services, physically or virtually, the advertiser has notified explicitly that these details would be used for sending advertising materials, and the addressee has not objected, the direct advertising is not considered criminal offence.[1473] However, the addressee should have an opportunity at any time to cancel the consent.

Misleading advertisements using the Internet are considered criminal offence, whether the advertisements are direct or not.[1474] The advertiser is required to check that all details are correct and updated within any advertisement. In addition, the advertiser is required to add the word 'advertisement' (or similar word) at the head of the advertisement (i.e., as part of the e-mail subject or title, if advertising through e-mail), the advertiser's name, address, and 'remove' opportunity.[1475] Infringement of at least one of these duties is considered criminal offence of up to NIS 75,300 fine (approximately EUR 18,000), and it is also considered civil wrong.

The telecommunications law includes offences regarding the computer's infrastructure as well. Any end-equipment (i.e., telecommunication device) connected to

1470. Section 30A(f)(1) of the Communication (Telecommunication and Broadcasting) Act, 1982.
1471. Section 30A(b) of the Communication (Telecommunication and Broadcasting) Act, 1982.
1472. Section 30A(c)(2) of the Communication (Telecommunication and Broadcasting) Act, 1982.
1473. Section 30A(c)(1) of the Communication (Telecommunication and Broadcasting) Act, 1982.
1474. Section 30A(f)(2) of the Communication (Telecommunication and Broadcasting) Act, 1982.
1475. Section 30A(e)(1) of the Communication (Telecommunication and Broadcasting) Act, 1982.

the computing telecommunications infrastructure is required to be compatible with it, for not causing any damage to it, otherwise it is considered a criminal offence of up to NIS 226,000 fine (approximately EUR 55,000).[1476] If the device is a computer or a portable device which contains malware intended to damage the infrastructure through connection with it, it is a separate offence in addition to the computer offence that may be relevant as well.

§2. Cyber Delinquency Involving AI Technology

150. Israel is using AI technology for various utilities in governmental functions (e.g., police robots), in hospitals (e.g., AI surgeons), industry, and other spheres of life. However, using AI technology sometimes involves commission of criminal offences. The question of the criminal liability in offences involving AI system has been introduced to the world for the first time by Professor Hallevy.[1477]

The involvement of AI systems in cyber delinquency is increasing, but not only in cyber delinquency. Autonomous cars cause death and injury, AI systems commit frauds in the stock exchanges, AI systems commit IP offences in various fields, and there are many more examples. Within cyber delinquency, AI systems are used to analyse the addressees for spam or other telecommunications offences, to write advanced malware codes, to analyse the victim's defences, if any, to analyse the network characteristics, and so on.

As no particular legislation on this issue, Hallevy's three models for the criminal liability in cases involving AI systems have been the basis for any further solution. The models have been described in detail in the book *When Robots Kill* (2013),[1478] and since many parts of these models have been embraced worldwide, and translated to many languages, including Turkish and Chinese.[1479] Basically, within the current definitions of criminal law, there are three basic models of criminal liability, dependent on the particular type of AI technology used. Below is described the applicability of these models in Israel. For further applicability in other countries, legal materials have been published.[1480]

1476. Sections 35 and 36A(a) of the Communication (Telecommunication and Broadcasting) Act, 1982.

1477. *See*, *e.g.*, Gabriel Hallevy, *The Criminal Liability of Artificial Intelligence Entities – from Science Fiction to Legal Social Control*, 4 Akron Intell. Prop. J. 171 (2009).

1478. Gabriel Hallevy, *When Robots Kill – Artificial Intelligence under Criminal Law* (UPNE 2013).

1479. Gabriel Hallevy, *Yapay Zekaya Sahip Varlıkların Cezai Sorumluluğu - Bilim Kurgudan Yasal Toplumsal Denetime* (Çeviren: Müslüm Fincan), 24 Küresel Bakış Çeviri Hukuk Dergisi, 111 (2018); Gabriel Hallevy 人工智能实体的刑事责任 (Translation: 赵增田 译, 同济大学) 同济大学 (Tongji University).

1480. *See*, *e.g.*, in Europe: Gabriel Hallevy, *Liability for Crimes Involving Artificial Intelligence Systems* (Springer International Publishing 2015).

I. The Relevant General Requirements for the Imposition of Criminal Liability

151. The basic question of criminal law is the question of criminal liability, i.e., whether the specific entity (human or corporation) bears a criminal liability for a specific offence committed at a specific point in time and space. In order to impose a criminal liability upon a person, there are two main elements that should be existed. The first is the external element or factual element, i.e., conduct committed by the offender (*actus reus*), and the other is the internal element or mental element, i.e., knowledge or general intention towards the factual element (*mens rea*). If one of them is missing, no criminal liability might be imposed.

The conduct requirement might be expressed by acts or omissions.[1481] Sometimes some more external ingredients are required in addition to the conduct, such as specific results of the conduct and specific circumstances the conduct was done under. The core of the external element remains the conduct.[1482] The internal element has some levels of mental requirements. The highest level is expressed by knowledge, and sometimes it is accompanied with a requirement of intention or specific intention.[1483] Lower levels are expressed by negligence[1484] (lack of knowledge in conditions a reasonable person could have known) or even lower by strict liability offences.[1485]

No other qualifications are required in order to impose criminal liability. Further qualifications or capabilities are not required in order to impose criminal liability, not from humans nor from any other kind of entity, including corporations and AI entities. An entity might possess further capabilities, but in order to impose criminal liability, the existence of the external element and the internal element required in the specific offence is quite enough. A spider is capable of acting, but it has no capability of formulating the mental element requirements; therefore, a spider bite bears no criminal liability. Even when a parrot repeats words it hears, it has no capability of formulating the mental element required for libel.

In order to impose criminal liability upon any kind of entity, these requirements should be proved as existed in the specific entity. When it is proved that a person committed the relevant conduct accompanied with relevant knowledge or intention, the person is criminally liable due to the specific offence. The relevant question towards the criminal liability of AI entities is how these entities might formulate these relevant requirements of criminal liability. It is possible to enable the imposition of criminal liability upon AI entities in three models of liability: the Perpetration-by-Another liability model; the Natural Probable Consequence liability model; and the Direct Liability model. These three possible models are introduced hereinafter in relation to Israeli law.

1481. Section 18(b) of the Israeli Penal Code, 1977.
1482. Section 18(a) of the Israeli Penal Code, 1977.
1483. Section 20(a) of the Israeli Penal Code, 1977.
1484. Section 21 of the Israeli Penal Code, 1977.
1485. Section 22 of the Israeli Penal Code, 1977.

II. The Perpetration-by-Another Liability Model

152. The first model does not consider any human feature of the AI entity. The AI entity is considered as an innocent agent. Accordingly, due to that legal point of view, a machine is a machine, and never human. However, one cannot ignore the capabilities of an AI entity, as mentioned above. Due to this model, these capabilities are not enough in order to regard the AI entity as a perpetrator of an offence. These capabilities might resemble the parallel capabilities of a mentally limited person, such as a child, a mentally incompetent, or a person who lacks a criminal state of mind to engage the conduct.

Legally, when an offence is committed by an innocent agent, as where a person causes a child, a mentally incompetent, or a person who lacks a criminal state of mind to engage the conduct, that person is criminally liable as a perpetrator-by-another.[1486] In such cases, the intermediary is regarded as a mere instrument, even though it is a sophisticated instrument, and the originating actor (the perpetrator-by-another) is the real perpetrator as a principal in the first degree. That perpetrator-by-another is accountable for the conduct of the innocent agent, and the perpetrator liability is determined on the basis of that conduct and the perpetrator-by-another own mental state.

The derivative question is who the perpetrator-by-another is. There are two possible persons who are entitled to become the perpetrators-by-another. The first is the programmer of the AI software and the second is the user, or the edge user. The programmer of the AI software might design the program in order to commit offences by the AI entity. For example, the programmer designs a software of a robot operating. The robot is intended to be placed in a factory, and its software is designed to burn the factory at night while no person is there. The robot has committed the arson, but the programmer is considered as the perpetrator.

The second person who might be considered as the perpetrator-by-another is the user of the AI entity. The user did not program the software, but he uses the AI entity, including its software, for its own benefit. For example, the user purchases a servant-robot, which is designed to execute any order given by its master. The specific user is identified by the robot as that master, and the master orders the robot to assault an invader to the house. The robot executes the order exactly as it has been ordered. This is not different than a master who orders his dog to attack a passing-by person. The robot has committed an assault, but the user is considered as the perpetrator.

In both possible possibilities, the factual commission of the specific offence has been done by the AI entity. The programmer or the user did not commit any conduct which is defined in the specific offence definition; therefore, no external element of the specific offence has been existed in them. The perpetration-by-another liability model considers the conduct committed by the AI entity as if it is the programmer's or the user's. The legal basis for that is the instrumental usage of the AI

1486. Section 29(c) of the Israeli Penal Code, 1977.

entity as an innocent agent. No mental feature required for the imposition of criminal liability is attributed to the AI entity.[1487]

When the programmers or the users use the AI entity instrumentally, the commission of the conduct by the AI entity is attributed to them. The internal element required in the specific offence already exists in their mind. The programmer intends to the commission of the arson, and the user intends to the commission of the assault, even though the factual commission of these offences is done through a robot, which is an AI entity. The instrumental usage of an innocent agent is considered as the own perpetration of the user.

This liability model does not attribute any mental capability, or any human mental capability, to the AI entity. According to this model, there is no legal difference between an AI entity and a screwdriver or an animal. When a burglar uses a screwdriver in order to open up a window, he uses the screwdriver instrumentally, and the screwdriver is not criminally liable. The screwdriver 'action' is, in fact, the burglar's. This is the same legal situation when using an animal instrumentally. An assault committed by a dog due to its master's order is, in fact, an assault committed by the master.

That kind of a legal model might be suitable for two kinds of situations. The first situation is a usage of an AI entity to commit an offence with no usage of its advanced capabilities. The second situation is a usage of a very old version AI entity, which lacks the modern advanced capabilities of the modern AI entities. In both situations, the usage of the AI entity is an instrumental usage. Still it is a usage of an AI entity, due to the capabilities to execute an order to commit an offence. A screwdriver cannot execute such an order, a dog can. A dog cannot execute complicated orders, an AI entity can.[1488]

The perpetration-by-another liability model is not suitable when the AI entity has decided to commit an offence due to the experience or knowledge it has gained by itself. This model is not suitable when the software of the AI entity was not designed in order to commit the specific offence, but still it has been committed by the AI entity. Even when the specific AI entity functions not as an innocent agent, but as a semi-innocent agent,[1489] this model is not suitable.

However, the perpetration-by-another liability model might be suitable when an instrumental usage of the AI entity was done by the programmer or by the user, and there was no usage of the AI entity advanced capabilities. The legal result of applying this model is that the programmers or the users are fully criminally liable for the specific offence committed, and the AI entity has no criminal liability at all.

1487. The AI entity is used as an instrument and not as a participant, although it uses its features of processing information. *See, e.g.*, George R. Cross & Cary G. Debessonet, *An Artificial Intelligence Application in the Law: CCLIPS, A Computer Program That Processes Legal Information*, 1 High Tech. L. J. 329 (1986).

1488. Gabriel Hallevy, *When Robots Kill – Artificial Intelligence under Criminal Law* 22–25 (UPNE 2013).

1489. Section 29(c)(3) of the Israeli Penal Code, 1977.

III. The Natural Probable Consequence Liability Model

153. The second model of criminal liability assumes a deep involvement of the programmers or the users in the AI entity's daily activities, but they did not plan to commit any offence through the AI entity. However, during the execution of its daily missions, the AI entity commits an offence. The programmers or the users did not know about the commission of the offence until it has already been done, they did not plan any commission of any offence, and they did not participated in any part of the commission of that specific offence.

Such a situation might be demonstrated by a design of an AI robot or software which is developed to function as an automatic pilot. The AI entity is programmed to protect the mission as part of the mission of flying the plane. During the flight the human pilot activates the automatic pilot which is the AI entity, and the program is initialized. When the automatic pilot is activated, the human pilot sees a storm coming closer to the plane and tries to abort the mission and return back. The AI entity understands the human pilot acts as a threat upon the mission and acts in order to eliminate that threat. It might cut of the air supply to the pilot or activate the ejection seat, etc. As a result, the human pilot is killed by the AI entity acts.

Of course, the programmer did not intend to kill anyone, especially not the human pilot, but still the human pilot is killed out of the AI entity acts, and these acts were done according to the program. Another example is AI software, which is designed to detect threats from the Internet and protect a computer system from these threats. A few days after the software is activated, it figures out that the best way to detect such threats by entering to websites which it defines as dangerous and destroying any software which is recognized as a threat. When the software does that, it commits a computer offence, although the programmer did not intend the AI entity to do so.

In these cases, the first model is not legally suitable. The first model assumes a plan of the programmers or the users to commit an offence through the AI entity by using some of its capabilities instrumentally. This is not the legal situation in these cases. In these cases, the programmers or the users did not know about the commission of the offence, they did not plan it, and they did not intend to do that using the AI entity. For such cases, the second model might create a suitable legal response. This model is based upon the ability of the programmers or the users to foresee the forthcoming commission of the offence.

According to the second model, a person might be held accountable for an offence, since that offence is a natural and probable consequence of that person's conduct. Originally, the natural probable consequence liability is used to impose criminal liability upon accomplices, that one of them has committed an offence which was not planned by them all and which was not part of the conspiracy. The established rule stated by courts and commentators is that accomplice liability extends to acts of the perpetrator which were a 'natural and probable consequence',[1490] of a criminal scheme the accomplice encouraged or aided.[1491] The

1490. Section 34A(a) of the Israeli Penal Code, 1977.

1491. Section 34A(a)(2) of the Israeli Penal Code, 1977.

natural probable consequence liability has been widely accepted in accomplice liability statutes and recodifications, including in Israel.[1492]

The natural probable consequence liability seems to be legally suitable for the situations an AI entity committed an offence while the programmer or user did not know about it, intended it, or participated in it. The natural probable consequence liability model requires the programmer or the user to be in a mental state of negligence, not more. The programmers or users are not require to know about any forthcoming commission of any offence as a result of their activity, but such a commission is a natural probable consequence of their activity.

A negligent person, in a criminal context, is a person who does not know about the offence, but a reasonable person could have known about it, since the specific offence is a natural probable consequence of that person's conduct.[1493] The programmers or users of an AI entity, who could have known about the probable possibility of the forthcoming commission of the specific offence, are criminally liable for the specific offence even though they did not actually know about it. This is, however, the very legal basis for the criminal liability in negligence cases. Negligence is in fact an awareness omission, or a knowledge omission.[1494] The negligent person omitted knowledge, not acts.

The natural probable consequence liability model would permit liability to be predicated upon negligence even when the crime involved requires a different state of mind.[1495] Such is not legally legitimate as to one who has personally committed the offence. It is considered legally legitimate as to a person who has not been the physical perpetrator of the offence, but has been one of its intellectual reasons. Reasonable programmers or users could have foreseen the offence, and therefore prevent it from being committed by the AI entity.

However, the legal results of applying the natural probable consequence liability model upon the programmer or the user are different in two different types of factual cases. The first type of cases is when the programmers or users were negligent as to the commission of the offence while programming or using the AI entity with no criminal intent to commit any offence. The second type of cases is when the programmers or users programmed or used the AI entity knowingly and wilfully in order to commit one offence through the AI entity, but the AI entity swerved the plan and committed another offence in addition to the planned offence or instead of it.

The first type of case is a pure case of negligence. The programmers or users acted or omitted negligently; therefore, there is no reason why not to hold them accountable for a negligence offence, if there is such an offence in the specific legal system. Thus, as to the above example, where a programmer of an automatic pilot negligently programmed it to defend its mission with no restrictions on human life taking, the programmer is negligent as to the homicide of the human pilot. As a result, if there is a specific offence of a negligent homicide in that legal system, this is the most severe offence the programmer might be accountable to, not manslaughter nor murder that requires knowledge or intent.

1492. Section 34A of the Israeli Penal Code, 1977.
1493. Section 34A(a)(2) of the Israeli Penal Code, 1977.
1494. Section 21 of the Israeli Penal Code, 1977.
1495. Section 34A(a) of the Israeli Penal Code, 1977.

The second type of cases resembles the basic idea of the natural probable consequence liability in accomplice liability. The dangerousness of the very association or conspiracy in purpose to commit an offence is the legal reason for the more severe accountability to be imposed upon the conspiracy members. For example, a programmer programs an AI entity to commit a violent robbery in a bank, but the programmer does not program the AI entity to kill anyone. During the execution of the violent robbery, the AI entity kills one of the people that were present at the bank and resisted the robbery. In such cases, criminal negligence liability alone is not enough. The dangerousness of such a situation might not be expressed in negligence alone.

As a result, according to the natural probable consequence liability model, when the programmers or users programmed or used the AI entity knowingly and wilfully in order to commit one offence through the AI entity, but the AI entity swerved the plan and committed another offence in addition to the planed offence or instead of it, the programmers or users shall be accountable for the offence itself as if it had been committed knowingly and wilfully. In the above example of the robbery, the programmer shall be criminally accountable for the robbery (if committed) and for the killing as an offence of manslaughter,[1496] or murder, which require knowledge and intent.[1497]

Still remains the question, what is the criminal liability of the AI entity itself when the natural probable consequence liability model is applied. In fact, there are two possible results. If the AI entity acted as an innocent agent for not knowing anything about the criminal prohibition, it is not criminally accountable for the offence it has committed. In such situations, the AI entity functions no differently than the functions of the AI entity under the first model (the perpetration-by-another liability model). But, if the AI entity did not function as an innocent agent, in addition to the criminal liability of the programmer or the user due to the natural probable consequence liability model, the AI entity shall be criminally liable for the specific offence directly. A direct liability model of the AI entity is the core of the third model as described hereinafter.

IV. The Direct Liability Model

154. The third model does not assume any dependence of the AI entity in a specific programmer or user. The third model focuses on the AI entity itself. As discussed above, criminal liability for a specific offence is mainly combined out of the external element and the internal element of that offence.[1498] Any person, that both elements of the specific offence are attributed to, is held criminally accountable for that specific offence. No other qualifications are required in order to impose criminal liability. A person might possess further capabilities, but in order to impose criminal liability, the existence of the external element and the internal element required in the specific offence is quite enough.

1496. Section 298 of the Israeli Penal Code, 1977.
1497. Section 300(a)(2) of the Israeli Penal Code, 1977.
1498. Above at s. [I]: The Relevant General Requirements for the Imposition of Criminal Liability.

In order to impose criminal liability upon any kind of entity, these requirements should be proved as existing in the specific entity. When it is proved that a person committed the relevant conduct accompanied with relevant knowledge or intention, the person is criminally liable due to the specific offence. The relevant question towards the criminal liability of AI entities is how these entities might formulate these relevant requirements of criminal liability. Are AI entities different than human persons in this context?

An AI algorithm might have very many features and qualifications, which might be much better than those of an average human. But, no such features or qualifications are required in order to impose criminal liability. When a human or corporation formulated both the external element and the internal element, a criminal liability is imposed. If an AI entity has the capability to formulate both external element and internal element, and in fact, it really formulates it, there is nothing to prevent the criminal liability from being imposed upon that AI entity.

Generally, the performance of the external element of the offence is easily attributed to the AI entity. As long as the AI entity controls a mechanical or other mechanism to move its moving parts, any act might be considered as performed by the AI entity. Thus, when an AI robot activates its electric or hydraulic arm and moves it, it might be considered as an act, if the specific offence requires such an act. For example, in the specific offence of assault, such as an electric or hydraulic movement of an AI robot, that hits a person standing nearby, is considered as a fulfilment of the external element of the assault offence.

When the offence might be committed by an omission, it is even simpler. Under an omission requirement, the AI entity is not required to act at all. The very inaction is the legal basis for the omission, as long as there was a duty to act. If a duty to act is imposed upon the AI entity, and it does not act, the external element requirement of the specific offence is fulfilled by way of an omission.

The attribution of the internal element of the offence to the AI entity is the real legal problem in most cases. The attribution of the mental element differs from one AI technology to other. Most cognitive capabilities developed in the modern AI technology are immaterial for the question of the criminal liability imposition. Creativity is a human feature that humans do share with some animals, but creativity is not required in order to impose criminal liability. Even the most uncreative persons are criminally liable. All mental requirements that are required in order to impose criminal liability are knowledge, intent, negligence, etc., as required in the specific offence and under the general theory of criminal law.

Knowledge is defined as sensory reception of factual data and their understanding.[1499] Most AI systems are well equipped for such a reception. Sensory receptors of sights, voices, physical contacts, touches, etc. are not rare in most AI systems. These receptors transfer the factual data received to the central processing units that analyse them. The analysis process is a process which is parallel to human understanding. The human brain understands the data received by eyes, ears, hands, etc.

1499. Gabriel Hallevy, *Theory of Criminal Law* vol. II 69–76 (2009).

by analysing that data. Advanced AI algorithms are trying to imitate the human brain understanding process. These processes are not so different.[1500]

A requirement of a specific intent is the strongest requirement of the internal element.[1501] A specific intent is the existence of a purpose or an aim that a factual event will occur. The specific intent which is required in murder is a purpose or an aim that a certain person will be dead. As a result of the existence of such an intent, the perpetrator of the offence commits the offence, i.e., performs the external element of the specific offence. This situation is not unique to humans. An AI entity might be programmed to have a purpose or an aim and to take actions in order to achieve that purpose. This is a specific intent.

One might assert that humans do have feelings which cannot be imitated by AI software, even the most advanced software. Such feelings are love, affection, hatred, jealousy, etc. That might be correct in relation to the technology of the beginning of the twenty-first century. In spite of that, such feelings are most rarely required in specific offence. Most specific offences are satisfied with knowledge about the existence of the external element. Few offences require a specific intent requirement in addition to knowledge. Almost all other offences are satisfied with much less than that (negligence, recklessness, strict liability). Perhaps in very few specific offences that do require certain feelings (e.g., crimes of racism out of hatred through the net), it is not legally legitimate to impose criminal liability upon AI entity which has no such feelings, but in any other specific offences, it is not a barrier.

If a person established both external element and internal element of a specific offence, the person is criminally liable. Therefore, why should an AI entity that established all elements of an offence be exempt from criminal liability? One might argue that some parts of human population are exempt from criminal liability although both external and internal elements are established. Such parts of the population are infants and mental ills.

Infancy does exempt from criminal liability due to a specific order in criminal law.[1502] The social rationale of infancy defence is to protect the infants from the harmful consequences of the criminal process and let them be socially handled in other social frames. Are there such frames for AI entities? The original legal rationale of infancy defence was the incapability of an infant to understand the fault reflected out of the infant's conduct (*doli incapax*). Later an infant could have been criminally liable if the presumption of mental incapability was rebutted by proof of an ability to distinguish between good and evil. Could that be similarly asserted upon AI entities? Most of the AI algorithms are capable of analysing permitted and forbidden.

Mentally ills are presumed to lack the fault element of the specific offence due to their mental illness (*doli incapax*).[1503] That illness defects the mental capabilities to

1500. Daniel C. Dennett, *Evolution, Error, and Intentionality*, The Foundations of Artificial Intelligence 190 (Derek Partridge and Yorick Wilks eds., 2006); B. Chandraswkaran, *What Kind of Information Processing Is Intelligence?*, The Foundations of Artificial Intelligence 14 (Derek Partridge and Yorick Wilks eds., 2006).
1501. Section 90A(2) of the Israeli Penal Code, 1977.
1502. Section 34F of the Israeli Penal Code, 1977.
1503. Section 34H of the Israeli Penal Code, 1977.

distinguish good and evil (cognitive capabilities)[1504] and to control internal impulses.[1505] When an AI algorithm functions properly there is no reason for not using all of its capabilities to process an analysis of the factual data received through its receptors. However, it is an interesting legal question whether a defence of insanity might be attributed to a malfunctioning AI algorithm, which its internal capabilities are defected as a result of that malfunction.

When an AI entity establishes all elements of a specific offence, both external and internal, there is no reason to prevent an imposition of criminal liability upon it to that offence. The AI entity criminal liability does not replace the criminal liability of the programmers or the users, if criminal liability is imposed on the programmers and users by any other legal path. Criminal liability is not to be divided, but to be added. The criminal liability of the AI entity is imposed in addition to the criminal liability of the human programmer or user.

However, the criminal liability of the AI entity is not depended on the criminal liability of the programmer or user of that AI entity. As a result, if the specific AI entity was programmed or used by another AI entity, the criminal liability of the programmed or used AI entity is not influenced by that fact. The programmed or used AI entity shall be criminally accountable to the specific offence due to the direct liability model, unless it is an innocent agent. In addition, the programmer or user AI entity shall be criminally accountable for that very offence due to one of the three liability models, according to the specific role of it. The chain of criminal liability might go on if there are more involved entities, human entities, or AI entities.

There is no reason to eliminate a criminal liability of an AI entity or a human entity, which is based upon complicity between them. An AI entity and human entity might cooperate as joint-perpetrators, as accessories and abettors, etc., and the relevant criminal liability might be imposed on them accordingly. Since the factual and mental capabilities of an AI entity are sufficient to impose criminal liability upon it, if these capabilities are satisfying the legal requirements of the joint-perpetrator, the accessories and abettors, etc., the relevant criminal liability as joint-perpetrator, as accessories and abettors, etc., should be imposed whether it is an AI entity or a human entity.

Not only positive factual and mental elements might be attributed to the AI entity. All relevant negative fault elements are attributable to AI entities. Most of these elements are expressed by the general defences in criminal law, e.g., self-defence, necessity, duress, intoxication, etc. For some of these defences (justifications), there is no material difference between humans or AI entities, since they relate to a specific situation (in rem) regardless what the offender specific identity is. For example, an AI entity that serves under the local police forces is given an order to arrest a person illegally. If the order given is not manifestly illegal, the executer of the order is not criminally liable.[1506] In that case, there is no difference whether the executer is human or AI entity.

1504. Section 34H(1) of the Israeli Penal Code, 1977.
1505. Section 34H(2) of the Israeli Penal Code, 1977.
1506. Section 34M of the Israeli Penal Code, 1977.

For other defences (excuses and exempts) some application adjustments should be done. For example, intoxication defence is applied when the offender is under the physical influence of intoxicating matter (e.g., alcohol, drugs). The influence of alcohol on AI entity is minor, at most, but the influence of an electronic virus that has been infecting the operating system of the AI entity might be considered parallel to the influence of intoxicating matters on humans. Some other influences might be considered as parallel to insanity, loss of control, etc.

It might be summed up that the criminal liability of an AI entity according to the direct liability model is not different than the relevant criminal liability of a human. In some cases, there should be some adjustments, but substantively it is the very same criminal liability which is founded upon the same elements and examined in the same ways.

V. Coordination of the Three Liability Models

155. The three liability models described above are not alternative models. These models might be applied coordinately in order to create a full image of criminal liability in the specific context of AI entity involvement. Each of the three models does not negate any of the rest of them. Thus, applying the second model is possible as a single model for the specific situation and is possible as one part of a combination of two of the legal models or of all three of them.

When the AI entity plays a role of an innocent agent in the perpetration of the specific offence, and the programmer is the only person who directs that perpetration, the application of the perpetration-by-another model (first liability model) is the most appropriate legal model for that situation. In that very situation, when the programmer is itself an AI entity (when an AI entity programs another AI entity to commit a specific offence), the direct liability model (third liability model) is most appropriate to be applied as to the criminal liability of the AI entity programmer. The third liability model in that situation is applied in addition to the first liability model, and not instead. Thus, in such situations, the AI entity programmer shall be criminally liable due to a combination of the perpetration-by-another liability model and the direct liability model.

When the AI entity plays a role of the physical perpetrator of the specific offence, but that very offence was not planned to be perpetrated, the natural probable consequence liability model might be appropriate to be applied. The programmer might be considered as negligent if no offence was deliberately planned to be perpetrated, or the programmer might be considered as fully accountable for that specific offence if another offence was deliberately planned, and the specific offence was perpetrated not as part of the criminal scheme. Nevertheless, when the programmer is not human, the direct liability model is necessary to be applied in addition to the simultaneous application of the natural probable consequence liability model. So is the situation when the physical perpetrator is human, and the planner is an AI entity.

Coordination of all three liability models creates an opaque net of criminal liability. The combined and coordinated application of these three models reveals a new legal situation in the specific context of AI entities and criminal law. As a result, when AI entities and human entities are involved, directly or indirectly, in a perpetration of a specific offence, it would be much more difficult to evade criminal liability. The social benefit of such a legal policy is of a very high value. All entities, human, legal, or AI, are subordinated to the criminal law. If the clearest purpose of the imposition of criminal liability is the application of the legal social control in the specific society, then the coordinated application of all three models is necessary in the very context of AI entities involvement.

VI. General Punishment Adjustment Considerations

156. Let us assume an AI entity is criminally liable. Let us assume it is indicted, tried, and convicted. After the conviction, the court should sentence that AI entity. If the most appropriate punishment in the specific circumstances is one-year of imprisonment, for example, how can such a punishment be carried out by an AI entity? How can a capital penalty be carried out by an AI entity? How can an AI entity carry out a probation or even a fine? Where there is no body to arrest (especially in cases of an AI software that was not applied to a physical body, such as a robot), what is the practical meaning of imprisonment? Where no bank account is available for the sentenced AI entity, what is the practical meaning of fine?

Similar legal problems were raised when the criminal liability of corporation was recognized.[1507] Some asked how any of the legitimate penalties executed upon human could be applicable upon corporations. The answer was simple and legally applicable. When a punishment might be executed by a corporation as it is executed by human, it would be imposed without any change. Such is the fine penalty, in which the money is paid by the corporation the same way a human pay the fine and the same way a corporation pays its bills in a civil context. However, when the physical execution of a punishment by a corporation cannot be done the same way as by humans, an adjustment is required. So the legal situation is towards AI entities.

The punishment adjustment considerations examine the theoretical foundations of any applied punishment. These considerations are applied in a similar path and contain three stages. Each stage might be described by a question: (1) What is the basic nature of the specific penalty for a human? (2) How is that nature expressed in AI entities? (3) What practical actions may achieve the same effects of the nature of the specific penalty when they are imposed on an AI entity?

The most significant advantage of these punishment adjustment considerations is that the nature of the specific punishments remains identical when imposed upon humans and AI entities. This path of punishment adjustment considerations is demonstrated hereinafter in some of the punishments used in modern societies: capital penalty, imprisonment, suspended imprisonment, community service, and fine.

1507. Gerard E. Lynch, *The Role of Criminal Law in Policing Corporate Misconduct*, 60 Law and Contemp. Probs. 23 (1997); Richard Gruner, *To Let the Punishment Fit the Organization: Sanctioning Corporate Offenders Through Corporate Probation*, 16 Am. J. Crim. L. 1 (1988); Steven Walt & William S. Laufer, *Why Personhood Doesn't Matter: Corporate Criminal Liability and Sanctions*, 18 Am. J. Crim. L. 263 (1991); John C. Coffee, Jr., *'No Soul to Damn: No Body to Kick': An Unscandalised Inquiry Into the Problem of Corporate Punishment*, 79 Mich. L. Rev. 386 (1981).

Capital penalty is considered the most severe punishment for a human, and there is no consensus towards its constitutionality in different jurisdictions and in Israel. The capital penalty has the most significant value of incapacitation in relation to recidivism, since the offender is incapable of committing any further offence while being dead. The nature of capital penalty for a human is deprivation of human life. The 'life' of an AI entity is its independent existence as an entity. Sometimes it has a physical appearance (e.g., as a robot), sometimes it has not and only an abstract appearance exists (e.g., as a software installed on a computer system or on a server in a network).

Considering the significant value of incapacitation of the capital penalty, the practical action that may achieve the same effects of the nature of the capital penalty when imposed on an AI entity is to delete the AI software which controls the AI entity. After the delete action, the AI entity is incapacitated from committing any further offences. The delete abolishes the independent existence of the AI entity and functions as a death penalty for it.

Imprisonment is one of the most popular punishments imposed in severe offences in Israel.[1508] The nature of imprisonment penalty for a human is deprivation of human liberty and imposition of severe limitations on human free behaviour, freedom of movements and freedom of managing the personal life. The 'liberty' or 'freedom' of an AI entity includes the freedom to act as an AI entity in the relevant area. For example an AI entity in a medical service has the freedom to participate in surgeries; an AI entity in a factory has the freedom to manufacture, etc.

Considering that nature of the imprisonment penalty, the practical action that may achieve the same effects of the nature of the imprisonment when imposed on an AI entity is to get the AI entity out of use for a determinate period. During that period, no action which is related to the AI entity's freedom is allowed, and thus its freedom or liberty is restricted.

Suspended imprisonment is a very popular intermediate sanction in Israel for increasing the deterrent effect upon the offender with no use of an actual imprisonment.[1509] The nature of suspended imprisonment for a human is the actual threat of imprisonment if the human commits a specific offence or a type of specific offences. If the human commits such an offence, an imprisonment punishment would be imposed for the first offence besides the punishment imposed for the second. As a result the human person is deterred from committing another offence and become a recidivist offender.

Practically, suspended imprisonment is imposed only in the legal records. No physical action is taken when suspended imprisonment is imposed. As a result, there is no difference in imposition of a suspended imprisonment upon human entities and upon AI entities. The statutory criminal records of the state does not distinguish suspended imprisonment which is related to human persons, corporations, or AI entities, as long as the relevant entity may be identified specifically and accurately.

Community service is a very popular intermediate sanction in Israel with no use of an actual imprisonment.[1510] In most legal systems, the community service is a

1508. Sections 41–48 of the Israeli Penal Code, 1977.
1509. Sections 52–60 of the Israeli Penal Code, 1977.
1510. Sections 82–86A of the Israeli Penal Code, 1977.

substitute for actual imprisonment for short periods. In some legal systems, the community service is imposed together with probation for the offender to 'pay a price' for the damages caused by the specific offence. The nature of community service for a human is a compulsory contribution of labour to the community. An AI entity might be applied as a worker in very many areas.

When an AI entity works in a factory, its work is done for the benefit of the factory owners or for the benefits of the other workers in order to ease and facilitate their professional tasks. The same way an AI entity is working for the benefit of private persons, it may work for the benefit of community. When the work for the benefit of the community is imposed on the AI entity as a compulsory contribution of labour to the community, it may be considered as a community service. Thus, the nature of the community service remains identical when imposed upon humans and AI entities.

Fine is the most popular intermediate sanction in Israel with no use of an actual imprisonment.[1511] The nature of fine for a human is deprivation of the human from some of its property, whether the property is money (fine) or other property (forfeiture). When a person does not pay the fine, or has not enough property to pay the fine, substitute penalties are imposed upon the person, especially imprisonment.[1512] The imposition of a fine upon a corporation is identical to the imposition of a fine upon a person, since both persons and corporations do have property and bank accounts, so the payment of a fine is identical whether the paying entity is human or legal.

However, most AI entities have no money or property of their own, nor have they any bank accounts. If the AI entity does have its own property or money, the imposition of a fine upon it would be identical to the imposition of a fine upon humans or corporations. If not, for most humans and corporations property is gained through labour.[1513] Within the fine penalty, the property, which is a result of labour, is transferred to the state. That labour might be transferred to the state whether it has been paid in a property form or it has been paid directly as labour. As a result, a fine of an AI entity might be collected as money or property and as labour for the benefit of the community. When the fine is collected as a labour for the benefit of the community, it is not different than the community service described above.

Thus, most common punishments are applicable for AI entities. The imposition of the specific penalties on AI entities does not negate the nature of these penalties in comparison to their imposition upon humans. Of course, some general punishment adjustment considerations are required in order to apply these penalties, but still the nature of these penalties remains identical concerning humans and AI entities.

1511. Sections 61–71 of the Israeli Penal Code, 1977.
1512. Section 71 of the Israeli Penal Code, 1977.
1513. John Locke, *Two Treatises of Government* (1689).

Chapter 3. Application of Criminal Procedure Law in the Area of ICT

157. The application of Israeli criminal procedure law in the area of ICT is within almost all stages of the criminal process, but focused mostly on the crime detection and evidentiary questions. For example, when a search within the computer's hard disk is required for the investigation of sexual offence (e.g., paedophile sexual matter), the criminal procedure should include a reasonable protocol for that, in order to prevent unnecessary damage, but still fulfil the investigation's destiny. The application of the criminal procedure law within the area of ICT may be divided into criminal process issues and evidentiary issues.

§1. Criminal Process Issues

158. As technology has been used by offenders, it has also been used by the law enforcement authorities, especially within the area of ICT. For example, in order to detect computer offences, it is required, in general, to check the suspect's computer and search within its hardware. Sometimes the use of criminal procedure within the area of ICT is indirect. For example, tracking the suspect's exact place may require use of ICT devices within the criminal procedure. The main criminal process issues in the area of ICT are discussed below.

I. Search and Confiscation Powers

159. Computer offences are generally perpetrated through computers, and computers are used not only for the perpetration of computer offences. Therefore, search and confiscation powers are required in most cases to acquire the required evidence.[1514] However, search within a computer and the computer's confiscation may be problematic in various aspects (e.g., invasion into the suspect's privacy or damaging the computer's hardware or software). As a result, particular legal provisions have been enacted accordingly.

Search within any computer requires a warrant from the court, which contains particular instructions towards the commission of the search and the purpose of the search.[1515] Such warrant may be considered by the court only if the search is necessary to ensure the availability of the relevant evidence,[1516] if the court is convinced that the computer is used for the commission of an offence or to store evidence unlawfully,[1517] or if the court is convinced that an offence is committed against the computer's possessor using the computer.[1518]

1514. For search and confiscation powers in general in Israeli law *see* Gabriel Hallevy, *Theory of Criminal Justice* vol. II 305–379 (Bursi Publishing House 2011).
1515. Section 23A(b) of the Criminal Justice (Arrest and Search) [New Version] Ordinance, 1969.
1516. Section 23(1) of the Criminal Justice (Arrest and Search) [New Version] Ordinance, 1969.
1517. Section 23(2) of the Criminal Justice (Arrest and Search) [New Version] Ordinance, 1969.
1518. Section 23(3) of the Criminal Justice (Arrest and Search) [New Version] Ordinance, 1969.

The search within the computer includes the production of any output accordingly, and the search is required to be performed by a professional technician.[1519] This is required in order to prevent unnecessary damage to the computer and in order to prevent any damage to the evidence reliability. An output of data-related communication between computers (e.g., printed e-mail document) is not considered wiretapping in this context.[1520]

The search itself requires at least two witnesses who are not policemen, in order to ensure objectivity and neutrality, and all actions of the search must be recorded within a protocol.[1521] The search is required to be careful, especially towards the suspect's privacy.[1522] The presence of the computer's possessor is allowed, but if suspected to conceal anything, the police is authorized to expand the search accordingly.[1523] By the end of the search, the computer's possessor is asked to sign on the protocol as an evidence for its true content, and so are the two witnesses.[1524]

If during the search the suspicions were verified, it might be required to confiscate the computer or parts of it. If the computer is not used for professional purposes (e.g., PC used at home by an individual), the police may confiscate the computer if the suspicions were indeed verified.[1525] If the computer's hardware is not the evidence and is not required for the presentation of the evidence, the police is required to return the computer to its possessor no later than thirty days after the confiscation, unless the court determined explicitly a longer term.[1526]

However, if the computer is used for professional purposes (e.g., a computer in a business), confiscation is allowed only due to the court's warrant.[1527] If the court's warrant has been given without the computer's possessor's presence, it would be valid for forty-eight hours, and after that it would be reviewed in court with the computer's possessor's presence.[1528]

After the computer's confiscation (whether the computer is used for professional purposes or not), the computer's possessor may request to copy the computer's content. If so has been requested, the police is required to enable the necessary acts within four days from the submission of the request.[1529] The police may request the court to extend this term beyond four days, but the police must indicate a justified reason for the extension.

Copying the computer's content would be within the police station and by a professional technician,[1530] but not by the computer's possessor, in order to prevent

---

1519. Section 23A(a) of the Criminal Justice (Arrest and Search) [New Version] Ordinance, 1969.
1520. Section 23A(c) of the Criminal Justice (Arrest and Search) [New Version] Ordinance, 1969.
1521. Section 26(a) of the Criminal Justice (Arrest and Search) [New Version] Ordinance, 1969.
1522. Section 26(b) of the Criminal Justice (Arrest and Search) [New Version] Ordinance, 1969.
1523. Sections 28–29 of the Criminal Justice (Arrest and Search) [New Version] Ordinance, 1969.
1524. Section 27 of the Criminal Justice (Arrest and Search) [New Version] Ordinance, 1969.
1525. Section 32(a) of the Criminal Justice (Arrest and Search) [New Version] Ordinance, 1969.
1526. Section 32(b1) of the Criminal Justice (Arrest and Search) [New Version] Ordinance, 1969.
1527. Section 32(b) of the Criminal Justice (Arrest and Search) [New Version] Ordinance, 1969.
1528. *Ibid.*
1529. Section 32A(a) of the Criminal Justice (Arrest and Search) [New Version] Ordinance, 1969.
1530. Section 32A(c) of the Criminal Justice (Arrest and Search) [New Version] Ordinance, 1969.

deletion of evidence. All actions performed within the search and confiscation powers may be supervised and judicially reviewed by the court, if the computer's possessor submits a relevant request to the court.[1531]

II. Wiretapping Powers

160. In some of the computer-related offences, it is necessary to use wiretapping powers in order to detect the offences and the offenders.[1532] For example, anonymous defamation through the Internet or anonymous cyberbullying may require the use of wiretapping powers. Wiretapping is defined as 'listening' without the consent of any of the participants within the telecommunications message.[1533] 'Listening' is defined as absorbing, recording, or copying any telecommunications message using a device.[1534]

Originally, in 1979, the wiretapping law was focused on telephone conversations, but as telecommunications technology made some advance, the wiretapping law was adapted accordingly. Thus, using any device to read a telecommunications message, such as e-mail, SMS, WhatsApp message, etc., without the consent of any of the participants (i.e., the sender or one of the addressees), is considered wiretapping. Of course, the traditional listening to telephone calls without the participants consent is still considered wiretapping.

Wiretapping itself is considered criminal offence of up to five years imprisonment, unless the wiretapping was authorized officially.[1535] Moreover, the very use of the content of any message absorbed through wiretapping is considered criminal offence of up to five years imprisonment,[1536] and so is the installation of any device used for wiretapping.[1537] However, wiretapping may be authorized under certain circumstances in the criminal context or the national security context.

In the criminal context, the president of any District Court may authorize wiretapping, if requested by the police, after being convinced that it is required to discover, detect, investigate or prevent a felony, and that the invasion into privacy under these circumstances is reasonable.[1538] In Israel, felony is defined as any offence that the maximum punishment determined within it is more than three years imprisonment.[1539] Thus, not all offences in Israeli law may be subject to wiretapping.

The court may consider the police's request ex parte. If the wiretapping has been authorized by the court, the warrant is valid for no more than three months, but it

---

1531. *See* Gabriel Hallevy, *Theory of Criminal Justice* vol. II 362–379 (Bursi Publishing House 2011).
1532. For wiretapping powers in general in Israeli law *see* Gabriel Hallevy, *Theory of Criminal Justice* vol. II 440–456 (Bursi Publishing House 2011).
1533. The definition of the term 'wiretapping' in section 1 of the Wiretapping Act, 1979.
1534. The definition of the term 'listening' in section 1 of the Wiretapping Act, 1979.
1535. Section 2(a) of the Wiretapping Act, 1979.
1536. Section 2(b) of the Wiretapping Act, 1979.
1537. Section 2(c) of the Wiretapping Act, 1979.
1538. Section 6(a) of the Wiretapping Act, 1979. *See* Cri. App. 10532/09 *Smahdan v. State* (5 Aug. 2010); HCJ 5207/04 *Apple v. Attorney General* (20 May 2010).
1539. Section 24(1) of the Israeli Penal Code, 1977.

may be renewed if new circumstances have occurred.[1540] The warrant is required to include the specific details of the wiretapping, including the telecommunications device used for the wiretapping.[1541] If the court has not authorized the request, the attorney general may submit an appeal to the president of the Supreme Court.[1542]

However, the procedure within the District Court may not match the police needs in emergency situations. Consequently, in emergency situations, if there is not enough time to submit a request to the District Court, the general commissioner of the police is authorized to permit wiretapping for no more than forty-eight hours.[1543] If permitted, the wiretapping authorization is reported immediately to the attorney general, who may cancel the authorization.[1544] Within this period of forty-eight hours, the police is required to submit a request to the District Court, as forty-eight hours suffice for the court's decision.

In the national security context, a minister is authorized to permit wiretapping, if the commander of any of the national security authorities has requested so in writing.[1545] The minister is required to consider the invasion into privacy and the national security considerations, and only if reasonable balance between them leads to permit the wiretapping, the minister is authorized to do so.

The permit is required to include the specific details of the wiretapping, including the telecommunications device used for the wiretapping.[1546] The permit is valid for no more than three months, and it may be renewed, if new circumstances have occurred.[1547] The minister is required to report the government all the permits given, but if the minister is the minister of defence, an immediate report to the prime minister is delivered.[1548] In addition, any minister is required to report to the Knesset annually on the permits given in the passing year.

III. Telecommunications Data Powers

161. As wiretapping powers invade intensively into the individual's privacy, as the content of the telecommunications message is wiretapped, there was a necessary in criminal procedure for lesser powers, that would be legislated and exercised in less severe cases. Most of the computer-related offences are not considered felonies; therefore, they may not be subject to wiretapping. Accordingly, the law has evolved in 2007 into telecommunications data which does not contain the telecommunications content, and created new criminal justice powers.[1549]

1540. Section 6(e) of the Wiretapping Act, 1979.
1541. Section 6(d) of the Wiretapping Act, 1979.
1542. Section 6(c) of the Wiretapping Act, 1979.
1543. Section 7(a) of the Wiretapping Act, 1979.
1544. Section 7(b) of the Wiretapping Act, 1979.
1545. Section 4(a) of the Wiretapping Act, 1979.
1546. Section 4(b) of the Wiretapping Act, 1979.
1547. Section 4(c) of the Wiretapping Act, 1979.
1548. Section 4(d) of the Wiretapping Act, 1979.
1549. For telecommunications data powers in general in Israeli law *see* Gabriel Hallevy, *Theory of Criminal Justice* vol. II 423–439 (Bursi Publishing House 2011).

Telecommunications data in this context includes location data (the location of the device), service-type data (the type of telecommunications services used within the particular device) and data-transfer data (type of telecommunications message, the time of transmission or reception, length of the message, etc.), but not the content of the telecommunications message.[1550] The use of telecommunications powers is considered less invading into the individual's privacy in comparison to wiretapping powers; therefore, it is permitted more easily.

In fact, wiretapping is the combination of telecommunications data with the content of the message. Telecommunications data may be very helpful in the detection of computer-related offences, especially when the offences are not felonies, and therefore not subject to wiretapping law. In most cases, telecommunications data functions as circumstantial evidence for the commission of the computer-related offence, but sometimes it is the direct evidence.

For example, if a person texts 5 text messages (e.g., SMS) within 3 minutes from the mobile phone to the victim's mobile phone, and the victim does not respond, that may be considered a circumstantial evidence for harassment, even though the content of these text messages is unknown to the court. Similarly, if a business sends an e-mail simultaneously to 15,000 e-mail addresses, it may be considered a circumstantial evidence for the commission of some offences relating to advertising materials.[1551]

As a direct evidence, telecommunications data may be relevant when the communications act is itself prohibited, not necessarily in computer-related offences. For example, a husband is ordered by the court not to contact his wife in any way. Such an order is very common in family violence cases and not necessarily in computer-related offences. The telecommunications data that the husband did send his wife a text message is, itself, a direct evidence for the relevant offence (e.g., infringement of judicial warrant).

There is no doubt that telecommunications data powers involve invasion into the individual's privacy, but when the content of the message is excluded from these powers, the invasion is considered lesser in comparison to wiretapping, as aforesaid. As a result, the judicial mechanism involved in these powers is lesser in comparison to wiretapping powers.

Any police officer may submit the Magistrates' Court a request to exercise the telecommunications data powers.[1552] The relevant Magistrates' Court is chosen by the police due to its distance from the police station or from the place where the offence has been committed or about to be committed. The request is for a judicial warrant, which orders a telecommunications licensee to deliver telecommunications data to the police.

The request is required to include detailed explanation for the necessary telecommunications data, which is for the purposes of saving life, protecting human life,

1550. The definition of the term 'telecommunications data' in section 1 of the Criminal Justice (Telecommunications Powers) Act, 2007.

1551. *See* above at s. [II]: Telecommunications Offences using Computer Systems.

1552. Section 2(a) of the Criminal Justice (Telecommunications Powers) Act, 2007.

detection of offences, prevention of offences, detection of offenders, or lawful confiscation of property.[1553] The court is required to consider the invasion into privacy involved, and only if the invasion is proportional and reasonable, the court is authorized to accept the request. However, if the telecommunications data is related to a commercial business, the police is required to indicate how that business is *directly* involved within the offence (e.g., as an accomplice).[1554]

If the court is convinced that the above conditions are fulfilled, it may summon any person, that the decision may affect, to be heard. The court does not have to consider the police's request ex parte, as the telecommunications data is possessed by a third party and the judicial warrant is addressed to that third party. The court is authorized to order the third party (telecommunications licensee) to deliver the relevant telecommunications data to the police. The judicial warrant is valid for no more than thirty days.[1555]

However, the procedure within the magistrate's court may not match the police needs in emergency situations. Consequently, in emergency situations, if there is not enough time to submit a request to the magistrate's court, a police officer, in the rank of chief superintendent from the investigations and intelligence department who has been authorized by the police general commissioner, is authorized to order the telecommunications licensee to deliver the relevant telecommunications data to the police.[1556]

However, that police officer is authorized to do so, only if the relevant offence is a felony (in Israel, felony is defined as any offence that the maximum punishment determined within it is more than three years imprisonment),[1557] and the order is valid for no more than twenty-four hours.[1558] Within this period of twenty-four hours, the police is required to submit a request to the Magistrates' Court, as twenty-four hours suffice for the court's decision. The police officer is required to report to a superior police officer on any order that has been given in emergency situations.[1559]

During the COVID-19 pandemic, the Israeli government used private information taken out from the cellular phones to detect quarantined inhabitants and to warn their environment. This usage of private information was defined as part of emergency measures taken in order to reduce the probability of being infected by the virus.

Although most Israeli inhabitants considered these measures as reasonable, these measures were heavily criticized, until eventually abolished in April 2021.

1553. Section 3(a) of the Criminal Justice (Telecommunications Powers) Act, 2007.
1554. Section 3(b) of the Criminal Justice (Telecommunications Powers) Act, 2007.
1555. Section 3(j) of the Criminal Justice (Telecommunications Powers) Act, 2007.
1556. Section 4(a) of the Criminal Justice (Telecommunications Powers) Act, 2007.
1557. Section 24(1) of the Israeli Penal Code, 1977.
1558. Section 4(b) of the Criminal Justice (Telecommunications Powers) Act, 2007.
1559. Section 4(d) of the Criminal Justice (Telecommunications Powers) Act, 2007.

IV. Arrests Powers and Electronically Inspected Arrests

162. Computer-related offences are subject to the general arrests powers of the police.[1560] These powers are usually exercised when there is a suspicion that the offender would probably destroy evidence, and any access of the offender to any computer, including mobile phone, endangers the investigation. Therefore, most computer-related offences are investigated within concealed measures at the beginning, and only when the investigation begins the overt stages, the offender's arrest may be required.

As computer-related offences' investigation requires confiscation (or, at least, search) of the computer, and these powers require judicial warrant, in order to arrest the suspect for the investigation, the police generally submits a request of arrest together with the request of search and confiscation.[1561] The request is submitted to the Magistrates' Court,[1562] with all necessary materials to justify the arrest.[1563]

If there is a reasonable suspicion that the suspect has committed the offence, the court is required to check whether at least one of three alternative conditions is fulfilled. The first alternative is that if the suspect is not arrested, it is most likely that the investigation is interrupted or evidence is destroyed.[1564] The second alternative is that the suspect endangers an individual's security, the public security, or the national security.[1565] The third alternative is that there are some investigation procedures that may not be executed unless the suspect is arrested.[1566]

However, before ordering the suspect's arrest, the court is required to consider an alternative to the arrest that would harm the suspect's freedom at a lesser level.[1567] One of these alternatives is electronically inspected arrest, which does not require the suspect to be held in the police station or in any public detention. Accordingly, the court may determine that the suspect would be present at certain place or would not come closer than a certain distance to a certain place. If the purpose is to make the suspect be far from certain computer, this alternative may be relevant.

In order to detect the suspect's location 24/7, the suspect within electronically inspected arrest is required to carry 24/7 a locator device that transmits its location to the police.[1568] If the electronically inspected arrest conditions are infringed, the

1560. For arrests powers in general in Israeli law *see* Gabriel Hallevy, *Theory of Criminal Justice* vol. II 37–304 (Bursi Publishing House 2011).
1561. Search and confiscation powers have been discussed above at s. [I]: Search and Confiscation Powers.
1562. Section 2 of the Criminal Justice (Arrests Powers) Act, 1996.
1563. Section 12 of the Criminal Justice (Arrests Powers) Act, 1996.
1564. Section 13(a)(1) of the Criminal Justice (Arrests Powers) Act, 1996. *See* Cri. Req. 7529/99 *Ben Ami v. State* (3 Nov. 1999).
1565. Section 13(a)(2) of the Criminal Justice (Arrests Powers) Act, 1996.
1566. Section 13(a)(3) of the Criminal Justice (Arrests Powers) Act, 1996. *See* Cri. Req. 5492/98 *Bronson v. State*, 52(4) PD 116 (1998).
1567. Section 13(b) of the Criminal Justice (Arrests Powers) Act, 1996. *See* Cri. Req. 6350/97 *Rosenstein v. State* (29 Oct. 1997); Cri. Req. 4822/97 *State v. Ben Ari*, 51(3) PD 809 (1997).
1568. Section 22D of the Criminal Justice (Arrests Powers) Act, 1996.

suspect is returned to the traditional arrest (behind the bars).[1569] However, all types of arrests that are within the suspect's investigation are limited to thirty days at the most.[1570]

In more rare cases, there is a necessary to arrest the defendant (previously the 'suspect'), after being indicted, for the whole period of the trial. If there is an apparent evidence that the defendant has committed the offence,[1571] the court is required to check whether at least one of three alternative conditions are fulfilled.[1572] The first alternative is that if the defendant is not arrested, it is most likely that the defendant would interrupt the trial, intimidate witnesses or damage evidence.[1573] The second alternative is that the defendant endangers an individual's security, the public security, or the national security.[1574] The third alternative is that the offence is severe within its circumstances.[1575]

Within this type of arrest, the court is required to consider an alternative to the arrest that would harm the defendant's freedom at a lesser level.[1576] One of these alternatives is electronically inspected arrest, which does not require the defendant to be held in the police station or in any public detention. Accordingly, the court may determine that the defendant would be present at certain place or would not come closer than a certain distance to a certain place as long as the trial continues. If the electronically inspected arrest conditions are infringed, the defendant is returned to the traditional arrest (behind the bars).[1577]

However, all types of arrests of the defendant (after being indicted) are limited to nine months at the most, whereas electronically inspected arrest is limited to eighteen months at the most.[1578] After this period is passed, the defendant is released from the arrest, and the trial continues. Therefore, the prosecution generally makes efforts to finish the trial before that period is passed.

V. Telephone Number Blocking Powers

163. In recent years, typical offences are committed through mobile smartphones. Smartphones are defined 'computers',[1579] therefore, these offences are computer-related offences. These offences are committed while concealment of the

1569. Section 22H of the Criminal Justice (Arrests Powers) Act, 1996.
1570. Section 17(b) of the Criminal Justice (Arrests Powers) Act, 1996.
1571. Section 21(b) of the Criminal Justice (Arrests Powers) Act, 1996. *See* Cri. Req. 1648/11 *Avitan v. State* (7 Mar. 2011); Cri. Req. 1734/11 *Zaban v. State* (10 Mar. 2011).
1572. *See* Cri. Req. 1464/06 *State v. Nashef* (21 Feb. 2006); Cri. Req. 8482/00 *Hamza v. State* (3 Dec. 2000).
1573. Section 21(a)(1)(a) of the Criminal Justice (Arrests Powers) Act, 1996.
1574. Section 21(a)(1)(b) of the Criminal Justice (Arrests Powers) Act, 1996. *See* Cri. App. 9613/04 *Ben Simon v. State* (4 Sep. 2006).
1575. Section 21(a)(1)(c) of the Criminal Justice (Arrests Powers) Act, 1996. *See* Cri. Req. 8003/03 *Abu Juda v. State* (9 Sep. 2003); Cri. Req. 3856/03 *Ihab v. State* (5 May 2003).
1576. Section 13(b) of the Criminal Justice (Arrests Powers) Act, 1996.
1577. Section 22H of the Criminal Justice (Arrests Powers) Act, 1996.
1578. Section 61 of the Criminal Justice (Arrests Powers) Act, 1996.
1579. The definition of the term 'computer' in section 1 of the Computers Act, 1995.

perpetrator's identity in various ways. One of these ways is through using a smartphone with no registered owner or possessor (e.g., using a pre-paid telephone line). That makes the offender's detection become uneasy, and the prevention of offences becomes very difficult.

Sometimes these offences are telecommunications offences, but often these offences relate to human trafficking, to prostitution services, and to drug dealing, especially with children. As a result, in 2018, new criminal justice powers were enacted and authorized the police and the court to order on blocking the telephone number for any incoming or outgoing services (e.g., calls or SMS). Thus the telecommunications infrastructure for the commission of the offence is removed.

The law distinguishes between administrative decree and judicial warrant. Accordingly, if based on evidence, there is a suspicion that a telephone number is published in order to commit an offence of drugs, prostitution, or human trafficking, a police officer in the rank of commander suspects is authorized to order the telecommunications licensee to block the telephone number to any incoming or outgoing telecommunications services. This is an administrative decree, and it is valid for no more than thirty days.[1580]

At least twenty-four hours before the administrative decree is given, the telephone number possessor or owner is given a notification and a chance to plead in this issue.[1581] The notification is required to include a telephone number for connection that would be available at least twelve hours a day. After at least twenty-four hours, the administrative decree is executed. The telephone number possessor or owner may submit an appeal on the administrative decree to the Magistrates' Court as long as the decree is valid.[1582]

If an administrative decree has been given in relation to a certain telephone number, another administrative decree may be given only once in two years.[1583] Therefore, in order to maintain the certain telephone number blocked, it is necessary to submit the court a request for a judicial warrant.

A prosecutor may submit a request to the Magistrates' Court to order to block a telephone number, and the court is authorized to grant such a judicial warrant, if convinced that it is necessary to the prevention of the relevant offences. The judicial warrant is valid for no more than sixty days, and the court may renew it for not more than sixty days.[1584] The sixty days term is intended to enable the prosecutor to indict the telephone number possessor or owner in the relevant offences.

After the telephone number possessor or owner is indicted, the prosecutor may submit (together with the indictment) a request to the Magistrates' Court to order to

1580. Section 2(a) of the Telephone Number Blocking for Prevention of the Commission of Offences Act, 2018.
1581. Section 2(b) of the Telephone Number Blocking for Prevention of the Commission of Offences Act, 2018.
1582. Section 2(e) of the Telephone Number Blocking for Prevention of the Commission of Offences Act, 2018.
1583. Section 2(f) of the Telephone Number Blocking for Prevention of the Commission of Offences Act, 2018.
1584. Section 3(a) of the Telephone Number Blocking for Prevention of the Commission of Offences Act, 2018.

block a telephone number until the end of the trial.[1585] If the criminal trial has been resulted in a conviction of the telephone number possessor or owner, the court may renew that order for another term of no more than five years from the day of judgment. It is assumed that after five years of blocking, the particular number is no longer relevant for the previous offences. However, if the number is used for new offences (of the same type, or not), new administrative decrees or judicial warrants may be used.

At any point, the telephone number possessor or owner may request to reconsider the judicial warrant or the administrative decree. The court is required to reconsider these measures, if convinced by evidence that circumstances have changed.[1586] Any of the court's decisions, all along the criminal process, may be appealed within thirty days.[1587]

The addressee of both the administrative decree and the judicial warrant is the telecommunications licensee. After the decree or order is received by the licensee, it must implement it immediately, and no later than twenty-four hours from its reception.[1588] Although the telecommunications licensee has a standing within the court, and may request the cancellation or amendment of the decree or of the order, it is not likely for it to do so, as the telecommunications licensee is a third party who has no interest in the case.

VI. Extradition Powers in Computer-Related Offences

164. As technology advanced and the Internet became more available, accessible, useful and in use, many computer-related offences became more international. For example, a hacker from one country uses the Internet to enter a computer located in another country. However, although cyberspace is generally not limited through the country's boundaries or any political international boundaries, the jurisdiction of courts within the criminal process is. As a result, the extradition powers may be required as part of the international cooperation between the countries.[1589]

For example, in 2017, an eighteen years old Israeli hacker has entered several sensitive computer in the US. The American FBI asked the Israeli authorities to arrest him and extradite him to the US for a trial. Although the computer offences were actually committed while being at his father apartment in Israel, these offences are indictable in the US. Extradition powers are exercised occasionally in Israel, and as international cooperation between countries has increased, so has the use of extradition powers. Accordingly, the Israeli extradition law was reformed in 2001.

1585. Section 3(b) of the Telephone Number Blocking for Prevention of the Commission of Offences Act, 2018.
1586. Section 3(d) of the Telephone Number Blocking for Prevention of the Commission of Offences Act, 2018.
1587. Section 3(e) of the Telephone Number Blocking for Prevention of the Commission of Offences Act, 2018.
1588. Section 6 of the Telephone Number Blocking for Prevention of the Commission of Offences Act, 2018.
1589. For extradition powers in general in Israeli law *see* Gabriel Hallevy, *Theory of Criminal Justice* vol. II 380–419 (Bursi Publishing House 2011).

Extradition powers may be exercised only towards 'extradition offences'. These offences are defined as any offence of maximum punishment in Israel of at least one-year imprisonment.[1590] This definition covers most computer-related offences. If the offender is Israeli, the extradition should be requested only for judging the offender, but for the punishment, the convicted offender is transferred back to Israel. The requesting country is required to guarantee that as a condition for extradition, unless the offender has preferred to stay outside Israel for the punishment period.[1591]

Exercising the extradition powers requires a bilateral covenant between Israel and the requesting country, that all conditions of the covenant are fulfilled, and reciprocity between the countries towards exercising the extradition powers.[1592] If these conditions are a priori fulfilled, the minister of justice delivers the foreign country's request to the District Court of Jerusalem to determine whether the offender may be extradited.[1593] The court should also examine whether there is an adequate evidence for indictment under the Israeli standard.[1594]

Within the court, the offender may plead several defences to prevent the extradition. These defences include discrimination by the foreign state on grounds of origin or religion as the basis for the extradition request,[1595] political offence (i.e., the request is not justified for criminal law reasons, and the offender is persecuted on political ground),[1596] res judicata,[1597] obsolescence according to Israeli law,[1598] amnesty or pardon in the requesting country,[1599] local public policy (i.e., the extradition is contradicted with the local public policy),[1600] and a few more defences.

The District Court's decision whether the offender may be extradited may be appealed by both parties to the Supreme Court within thirty days.[1601] If thirty days have passed and no appeal has been submitted, the decision is considered final, and it is transferred to the ministry of justice for implementation.[1602] Both the Israeli ministry of justice and the foreign ministry of justice are required to determine the terms for the actual transfer of the offender to the requesting country's authorities. If the offender's arrest is required, the District Court may order accordingly until the offender is actually transferred,[1603] and the Israeli criminal procedure towards arrests is applied.

1590. Section 2(a) of the Extradition Act, 1954.
1591. Section 1A(a) of the Extradition Act, 1954.
1592. Section 2A of the Extradition Act, 1954. *See* Cri. App. 3234/10 *Anon. v. Attorney General* (16 Jan. 2011).
1593. Section 3(a) of the Extradition Act, 1954.
1594. Section 9 of the Extradition Act, 1954.
1595. Section 2B(a)(2) of the Extradition Act, 1954.
1596. Section 2B(a)(1) of the Extradition Act, 1954.
1597. Sections 2B(a)(4)–(5) of the Extradition Act, 1954.
1598. Section 2B(a)(6) of the Extradition Act, 1954. *See* Cri. App. 2144/08 *Mondrovich v. State* (14 Jan. 2010).
1599. Section 2B(a)(7) of the Extradition Act, 1954.
1600. Section 2B(a)(8) of the Extradition Act, 1954. *See* Cri. App. 4333/10 *Lavi v. State* (13 Feb. 2011).
1601. Section 13 of the Extradition Act, 1954.
1602. Section 14 of the Extradition Act, 1954.
1603. Section 15 of the Extradition Act, 1954.

VII. Juvenile Judging and Sentencing in Computer-Related Offences

165. Advanced technology is accessible not only for professionals within their profession, but for all population, and for children and teenagers as well. In fact, the age for hi-tech devices to be relevant and useful in Israel is gradually decreasing. One of the results of this phenomenon is that juvenile delinquency includes computer-related offences in increasing rates. Juvenile delinquency in this area includes not only cyberbullying and cyber-harassment, but also involvement in frauds. Many of the prominent hackers in Israel are teenagers.

The common cyberbullying is when someone, typically teens, bully or harass others on social media websites. Harmful bullying behaviour may include posting rumours, threats, sexual remarks, a victims' personal information, or pejorative labels (i.e., hate speech). Bullying or harassment can be identified by repeated behaviour and an intent to harm. Victims may have lower self-esteem, increased suicidal ideation, and a variety of emotional responses, including being scared, frustrated, angry, and depressed.

Some of the juvenile computer-related offences may be treated out of the criminal justice system (i.e., through educational and social welfare systems). It is inevitable when the offender is under the age of 12, which is the age for criminal liability in Israel.[1604] However, most offenders are above 12 years old and beneath 18, which is the age of legal maturity in Israel. Many of these juvenile delinquency cases are treated by the Juvenile Court System that became specialized in juvenile computer-related offences.

The Juvenile Court System includes two instances: Magistrates' Juvenile Court and District Juvenile Court.[1605] The judges in this system are qualified not only in juvenile law and criminal law, but also in social work, education, and psychology. Juvenile offenders are interrogated separately by special investigators in the police or in the cyber units of the police.[1606] Arrests powers are exercised only as the last resort. So are exercised other criminal justice powers towards juvenile offenders.

The obsolescence for any computer-related offence committed by juvenile offender is one year.[1607] If indicted, the juvenile offender has all procedural rights of an adult offender, and some additional rights for the protection of the offender. For example, the legal proceedings in the juvenile court system are *in camera*, in order to protect the offender's privacy.[1608] At the verdict, the court may exonerate the offender or determine that the offence has been committed by the offender, but the court may not convict the offender at this stage.[1609]

If the court has determined that the offender has committed the offence, the offender is sent to the Juvenile Probation Service to be examined. The Juvenile Probation Service's report is submitted to the court together with other reports and

1604. Section 34F of the Israeli Penal Code, 1977.
1605. Section 2 of the Juvenile (Trialing, Sentencing and Treatment Methods) Act, 1971.
1606. Section 9A of the Juvenile (Trialing, Sentencing and Treatment Methods) Act, 1971.
1607. Section 14 of the Juvenile (Trialing, Sentencing and Treatment Methods) Act, 1971.
1608. Section 9 of the Juvenile (Trialing, Sentencing and Treatment Methods) Act, 1971. *See* Cri. Req. 1700/01 *Anon. v. State* (29 Mar. 2001); Cri. Req. 508/07 *Frank v. State* (21 Jan. 2007).
1609. Section 21 of the Juvenile (Trialing, Sentencing and Treatment Methods) Act, 1971.

examinations required for the final decision in the case.[1610] At the end of this process, the court may decide one of three optional decisions. The first optional decision is to exempt the offender from any punishment or treatment.[1611] This decision is required when the personal circumstances of the juvenile offender require no additional treatment for being rehabilitated.

The second optional decision is to order a particular treatment method without the conviction of the offender.[1612] Treatment methods may include staying away from computers (including mobile smartphones), probation under the supervision of the juvenile probation service, limitations on the juvenile's behaviour, imposition of a duty to compensate the victim, and imposition of duties on the juvenile's parents to be involved in the rehabilitation process of the juvenile.[1613]

The third optional decision is to convict and sentence the offender.[1614] This optional decision is considered as the last resort, and only if there is no effective treatment method in the particular circumstances of the offence and of the offender, conviction and sentencing may be considered. Not all punishments may be imposed on juvenile convicted offenders. The main purpose of the punishment is required to be rehabilitation and not retribution.[1615] The very conviction is considered as part of the punishment, as the offender's criminal record may affect the future.

Imprisonment is possible, but only in a special juvenile prison, and for a short term, and only if the offender is at least 14 years old, and only as the last resort.[1616] The parents may be involved within the offender's rehabilitation,[1617] but in computer-related offences it is rare. In most computer-related offences in which the offender is convicted, the court imposes probation orders with public service within the community using the technological knowledge of the offender.

Eight years after the conviction the juvenile offender's criminal record is deleted (in comparison to seventeen years, if the offender is an adult).[1618] If the offender was under 16 years old when the offence has committed, the criminal record is deleted after six years.[1619] This enables the juvenile to rehabilitate within the community, acquire profession and integrate within the local hi-tech industry.

1610. Section 22 of the Juvenile (Trialing, Sentencing and Treatment Methods) Act, 1971.

1611. Section 24(3) of the Juvenile (Trialing, Sentencing and Treatment Methods) Act, 1971. *See* Cri. App. Req. 1666/05 *Stabski v. State* (24 Mar. 2004).

1612. Section 24(2) of the Juvenile (Trialing, Sentencing and Treatment Methods) Act, 1971. *See* Cri. App. 4092/07 *Anon. v. State* (17 Oct. 2007); Cri. App. Req. 10006/06 *Anon. v. State* (6 Dec. 2006).

1613. Section 26 of the Juvenile (Trialing, Sentencing and Treatment Methods) Act, 1971.

1614. Section 24(1) of the Juvenile (Trialing, Sentencing and Treatment Methods) Act, 1971. *See* Cri. App. 7211/04 *State v. Anon.* (13 Mar. 2006); Cri. App. 9262/03 *Anon. v. State*, 58(4) PD 869 (2004).

1615. For the general considerations of punishment and sentencing *see* Gabriel Hallevy, *The Right to Be Punished: Modern Doctrinal Sentencing* 57–102 (Springer-Verlag 2013).

1616. Section 25(a) of the Juvenile (Trialing, Sentencing and Treatment Methods) Act, 1971.

1617. Section 29 of the Juvenile (Trialing, Sentencing and Treatment Methods) Act, 1971.

1618. Sections 14(b) and 16(b) of the Criminal Record and Rehabilitation Act, 1981.

1619. *Ibid.*

VIII. Plea Bargains in Computer-Related Offences

166. About 85%–95% of the criminal cases in Israel are resulted in plea bargains. The Israeli criminal justice system is adversary; therefore, plea bargains are allowed, and even motivated and encouraged by the court. Within this 'deal' between the offender and the prosecution, the offender is required to confess the commission of the offence, and the prosecution reduces the number of charges and their severity. As to the punishment, it is under judicial jurisdiction, but the prosecution may undertake to request for a mitigating punishment.

In computer-related offences, one of the major problems is to collect the adequate evidence for conviction, especially when the offender has acted alone. Therefore, within many investigations of computer-related offences, without the cooperation of the offender, it is not likely to solve the case. This problem is also typical to white-collar crimes. As technology advances, so are the offenders' methods to commit the offences and conceal them from the law enforcement authorities.

As a result, in 2012, the Israeli legislator has formally expanded the plea bargaining framework into the stage of investigation, with the opportunity of closing the case without the offender's conviction. Accordingly, a prosecutor may offer an offender, who is suspected in the commission of computer-related offences of maximum punishment of no more than three years imprisonment, to confess the commission of the offence. In return, the prosecutor closes the case without any conviction, and the offender is not indicted in court.[1620]

In addition, the prosecutor may impose several duties on the offender in favour of the community, regarding the general considerations of punishment and sentencing in Israel.[1621] These duties may include payment to the state's treasury,[1622] payment of compensation to the victim,[1623] the offender's commitment not to commit any offence in the future,[1624] the offender's commitment to cooperate with the probation service,[1625] and the offender's consent to stay away from computers to a certain period of time.[1626]

The offender is allowed to read all the materials held by the prosecution prior to the settlement,[1627] and if agreed on the settlement's terms, the settlement would be explicit, in writing, and formed as an agreement between the prosecution and the offender.[1628] If not agreed, the prosecutor may continue the ordinary criminal procedure that may result in indictment in court or in closing the case without any

1620. Section 67B of the Criminal Justice [Combined Version] Act, 1982.
1621. For the general considerations of punishment and sentencing *see* Gabriel Hallevy, *The Right to Be Punished: Modern Doctrinal Sentencing* 57–102 (Springer-Verlag 2013).
1622. Section 67C(a)(1) of the Criminal Justice [Combined Version] Act, 1982.
1623. Section 67C(a)(2) of the Criminal Justice [Combined Version] Act, 1982.
1624. Section 67C(a)(3) of the Criminal Justice [Combined Version] Act, 1982.
1625. Section 67C(a)(4) of the Criminal Justice [Combined Version] Act, 1982.
1626. Section 67C(a)(5) of the Criminal Justice [Combined Version] Act, 1982.
1627. Section 67D of the Criminal Justice [Combined Version] Act, 1982.
1628. Section 67E of the Criminal Justice [Combined Version] Act, 1982.

settlement.[1629] The settlements details are published within the prosecution's website, but without identification details of the offender or the victim.[1630]

However, most plea bargains in computer-related offences are done *after* the offender is indicted in court. After the prosecution statement is read for the offender, the court may discuss it with both parties not formally.[1631] Within this discussion, the court may examine whether the optimal and most efficient solution for both parties is plea bargaining. In most cases, both parties agree, and under the court's supervision, plea bargaining is formed.

If the parties do not agree, the criminal proceedings would continue. However, at any point, both parties may present the court an agreement between them that reflects plea bargaining. The court's jurisdiction and discretion are not limited by this agreement, and it may reject it for reasons of public policy. Nevertheless, in most cases, the court accepts the agreement, since the agreement reflects the balance between the parties' interests due to the evidence.

If the particular computer-related offence has victims, although they have no formal standing within the criminal process, they may object the agreement. The victims are allowed to submit a statement towards the agreement to the prosecution, if the offence is cyberbullying or cyber-harassment which involves sexual content or violence.[1632] The prosecution's discretion is not limited by this statement, but the victims may apply to the high court of justice against the agreement, if it is in contrast to the public policy. However, as aforesaid, the agreement is not rejected by the court.

§2. Evidentiary Issues

167. Several evidentiary issues have been affected by the application of criminal procedure law in the area of ICT. Traditional evidence was required to evolve and be compatible with computer-related offences. Moreover, within the commission of traditional offences (e.g., theft or fraud), technological measures were used by the offenders, and the law of evidence was required to develop legal measures to cope with the new types of evidence. The main evidentiary issues in the area of ICT are discussed below.

I. The Documentary Evidence

168. The documentary evidence is considered the major type of evidence in criminal proceedings towards computer-related offences. Although in most cases the

---

1629. Section 67G of the Criminal Justice [Combined Version] Act, 1982.
1630. Section 67H of the Criminal Justice [Combined Version] Act, 1982.
1631. Section 143A of the Criminal Justice [Combined Version] Act, 1982.
1632. Section 17 of the Victims' Rights Act, 2001. *See* Cri. App. 2153/02 *Idelberg v. State* (7 Dec. 2006); HCJ 2477/07 *Anon. v. State* (27 May 2007).

documentary evidence is circumstantial evidence, the interpretation of the documentary evidence within computer-related offences makes it close to direct evidence. This is very significant in computer-related offences, where no direct witnesses testify in the trial. Most witnesses in these criminal trials are professionals or experts who simply interpret the evidence to the court.

The basic definition within the documentary evidence is the definition of the term 'document'. When traditionally defined, the term 'document' referred to paper-made documents, but as technology advanced, this definition was required to evolve, so it may include voice records, electronic documents, or digital files. Document is defined as anything in which information of any description is recorded.[1633]

As a result, the above definition has been interpreted as embracing not only paper-made documents, but also voice records and computer files, as long as they record information of any kind.[1634] Therefore, computer files which contain the information related to the offence were admissible as documents in Israel, and the court was authorized to determine the factual infrastructure of the case due to the information contained in these files.

Nevertheless, one of the conditions for the admissibility of the documentary evidence is being primary evidence and not secondary evidence. This condition refers to the admissibility of the original document and not of a copy. However, in digital documents, the question is what the original is. Any output is a copy of the information stored in the computer, and the information stored in the computer must be formed in any way to be accessible as an evidence.

The definition of the term 'copy' in relation to a document is anything onto which information recorded in the document has been copied, by whether means and whether directly or indirectly. This definition covers any output of the computer's data. However, as the 'original' document in this context is inaccessible, the relevant English Common Law rule has been embraced in Israel, and the copy may be submitted as if it were the original.[1635] Thus, any of the computer's output may be submitted to the court as the 'original' document.

For example, in cyberbullying offences, a screenshot of the mobile smartphone is considered original document, in malware offences, a print of the software instructions (i.e., the malware code) is considered original document, and in cyber-harassment offences, a print of the e-mail content is considered original document. These original documents may have been achieved using the search and confiscation powers discussed above,[1636] or the wiretapping discussed above.[1637]

However, in most of the legal proceedings in regard to computer-related offences, the documentary evidence requires identification of the responsible person, beyond

1633. *See, e.g.*, Cri. App. 3974/92 *Azulai v. State*, 47(2) PD 565 (1993); Gabriel Hallevy, *Theory of the Law of Evidence* vol. III 435–437 (Bursi Publishing House 2013).

1634. *See, e.g.*, Cri. App. 312/67 *Mordechai v. Attorney General,* 22(2) PD 63 (1968); Cri. App. 24/73 *Meisel v. State*, 27(2) PD 421 (1973); Cri. App. 331/88 *Haluba v. State*, 44(4) PD 141 (1990).

1635. *See, e.g.*, Cri. App. 595/79 *Alkurd v. State,* 34(3) PD 35 (1980).

1636. Above at s. [I]: Search and Confiscation Powers.

1637. Above at s. [II]: Wiretapping Powers.

its authentication. For example, if a bullying SMS has been received into the victim's mobile smartphone, it still requires an evidence that the offender is responsible for sending it to the victim. The same requirement rises anytime when telecommunications data is transferred from one device to another.

One of the methods of such identification is within an evidence of signature. In general, signature is any information that identifies a certain person with the content of certain document. However, signature is not always required by the law, and rarely a certain type of signature on the document is required. For example, valid bank cheques require hand signature by Israeli law.

Digital documents transferred from one device to another device may generally be identified with the device, but not necessarily with a certain person. For example, A brakes into B's mobile smartphone and sends into C's mobile smartphone a WhatsApp bullying message, as if the sender were B. The signature in this situation, if any, is of B's device, but not of B as an individual. The signature may be a circumstantial evidence for B sending the message, but not more.

Some advance in this area has been made through the use of electronic signature, but this has not solved the problem completely when computer-related offences are committed using impersonation. The electronic signature is defined as a signature, which is an electronic information or sign, that is attached or linked to any electronic message.[1638] The electronic signature itself is not software, but electronic information or electronic sign(s), although the signature may be produced using a typical software.

There are two particular types of electronic signatures that may be admissible under Israeli law as evidence in this context. The first type is the *secured electronic signature*. This type of electronic signature requires the fulfilment of four conditions. It should be unique to the signing person, it enables identification of the signing person, it is produced using a measure that is solely controlled by the signing person, and it enables to track any change made in the electronic message *after* being signed electronically.[1639]

The second type of electronic signatures is the *certified electronic signature*. The certified electronic signature is a secured electronic signature that has been certified by a certifying agent.[1640] The certification is towards the measure that produces the electronic signature is actually controlled by the person who seems to be signing on the electronic message.

If the law requires signed document, an electronic signature may fulfil this requirement if the electronic signature is a *certified* electronic signature.[1641] Nevertheless, if the electronic signature is not certified, but it fulfils the purposes of the particular law requiring signature (i.e., the signature fulfils the purpose of the particular signature's requirement), it may suffice.[1642]

1638. *See* the definition of the term 'electronic signature' in section 1 of the Electronic Signature Act, 2001.

1639. *See* the definition of the term 'secured electronic signature' in section 1 of the Electronic Signature Act, 2001.

1640. *See* the definition of the term 'certified electronic signature' in section 1 of the Electronic Signature Act, 2001.

1641. Section 2(a)(1) of the Electronic Signature Act, 2001.

1642. Section 2(a)(2) of the Electronic Signature Act, 2001.

The general rule in Israeli law of evidence is that in any legal proceeding, any signature is not inadmissible just because it is electronic signature,[1643] unless specifically determined otherwise. However, the admissibility of the electronic signature does not necessarily reflect its reliability. In addition, secured electronic signature is admissible in any legal proceedings as an evidence that the electronic message has not been changed after it has been signed and that the message has been signed with an electronic signature produced using a measure that is solely controlled by the signing person.[1644] If the electronic signature is certified, it is also an admissible evidence that the electronic message has actually been signed by the person who controls the measure.[1645]

A party to a contract who wishes to use any electronic message of the counterparty, signed electronically and related to the contract (e.g., cancellation notification), has the duty to prove that the counterparty did sign (electronically) the message. Nevertheless, if the electronic signature is certified, it is presumed so, and the counterparty has the duty to refute it.[1646]

An output of any electronic message which is singed by a certified electronic signature is not considered a copy but the original document, in any legal proceedings.[1647] Nevertheless, such an output is considered a copy and not the original document, if the message is an official judgment, a banknote, a promissory note, a physical share deed, or a report from the real estate registry.[1648]

II. Institutional Records

169. Institutional records are very useful in criminal trials towards computer-related offences which are committed by institutes in business context. These records enable reliable detection of the offence in most cases. In fact, the institutional records are an expansion of the former bankers' books, which were embraced from the English Common Law into Israeli law. The expansion was made in 1995 through the enactment of the computer law provisions for the first time in Israel.

Institutional record is defined as any document, including an output of computer data, which has been formed by an institute during the institute's ordinary activity.[1649] 'Institute', in this context, is defined as the state, domestic authority, any business, or anyone who provides *any* service to the public.[1650] As all types of business are covered by the definition of institute, the institutional record becomes very useful in computer-related offences committed in any business context. For

1643. Section 3(a) of the Electronic Signature Act, 2001.
1644. Sections 3(b)(1) and 3(b)(2) of the Electronic Signature Act, 2001.
1645. Section 3(b)(3) of the Electronic Signature Act, 2001.
1646. Section 3A of the Electronic Signature Act, 2001.
1647. Section 6(a) of the Electronic Signature Act, 2001.
1648. Section 6(b) of the Electronic Signature Act, 2001.
1649. The definition of the term 'institutional record' in s. 35 of the Evidence [New Version] Ordinance, 1971. *See* Cri. App. 8899/06 *Armin v. State* (29 Jul. 2007); Cri. App. Req. 9908/08 *Galagal v. State* (23 Feb. 2009).
1650. The definition of the term 'institute' in s. 35 of the Evidence [New Version] Ordinance, 1971.

example, spam e-mails with commercial content, spyware used by competitors, unlawful direct mailing, or unlawful database for commercial purposes.

Nevertheless, data from the police or from the prosecution authorities is not considered institutional record, if the data is related to the particular criminal case.[1651] The reason is that this data requires higher level of reliability in criminal proceedings, and there are particular rules from the law of evidence regulating the admissibility of this data. For example, a confession of the suspect during the police interrogation is subject to the confession rule,[1652] and may not be submitted to the court as an admissible evidence for being institutional record.

The rationale behind the institutional records approach in Israeli evidence law is that institutions use their own records; therefore, the content of these records is presumed to be reliable. Accordingly, an institutional record is considered admissible in any legal proceedings if two basic conditions are fulfilled, and if the institutional record is a computer output, if additional third and fourth conditions are fulfilled as well.

The first basic condition is that the institute ordinarily uses the types of documents in which the particular institutional record is.[1653] The second basic condition is that the method of collecting and storing the data within the document is reliable.[1654] These two basic conditions are required in regard to all institutional records, and their purpose is to ensure the reliability of the data included within the institutional records.

However, if the institutional record is a computer output, two more conditions are required to be fulfilled. The third condition (the additional first condition) is that the production of the output is reliable, regardless of the method of collecting and storing the data.[1655] For example, if the output is a printed document, according to the third condition, the printing method is required to be reliable, i.e., no data has been lost during the printing.

The fourth condition (the additional second condition) is that the institute ordinarily takes reasonable protection measures from malwares.[1656] The reasonability of the measures and the required level of protection is determined due to the relevant data within the output. As sensitive the data is, the higher level of protection is required. For example, bank data that contains the individual's financial information requires a high level of protection, whereas for most small businesses, a simple anti-virus software may suffice. As the output of institutional record is considered the original, the date of the data contained within the institutional record is presumed to be the date of the data contained within the output.[1657]

The admissibility of the institutional record does not replace any admissibility rule in the Israeli evidence law regarding the data, and if the data is inadmissible due to any rule in evidence law, it is inadmissible as institutional record.[1658] For

1651. Section 36(c) of the Evidence [New Version] Ordinance, 1971.
1652. Section 12 of the Evidence [New Version] Ordinance, 1971.
1653. Section 36(a)(1) of the Evidence [New Version] Ordinance, 1971.
1654. Section 36(a)(2) of the Evidence [New Version] Ordinance, 1971.
1655. Section 36(a)(3)(a) of the Evidence [New Version] Ordinance, 1971.
1656. Section 36(a)(3)(b) of the Evidence [New Version] Ordinance, 1971.
1657. Section 36(b) of the Evidence [New Version] Ordinance, 1971.
1658. Section 39B(a) of the Evidence [New Version] Ordinance, 1971.

example, if the data is considered hearsay, and it is inadmissible due to the Israeli hearsay rule, it is still inadmissible as institutional record.

Moreover, the admissibility of the institutional record does not change the procedure regarding submission of documentary evidence. Thus, when the institutional record is submitted to the court by any competent witness, the counterparty has the right to cross-examine the witness, as if the witness were any other witness.[1659] Sometimes, the cross-examination is the only effective way to find out the fulfilment of all of the above conditions.

III. Judicial Notice

170. As technology advanced, new terminology has entered into the courts. This terminology is inevitable in computer-related offences. Some of the terms are in common use, some are not. It is not likely to be involved in criminal proceedings towards computer-related offences without using at least some of the terms of hardware, software, malware, code, cyber, algorithm, spam, anti-virus, topography, chip, or AI.

These, and many other terms, are professional terms from the area of computer science. According to the opinion rule in Israeli law of evidence (embraced from the English Common Law), professional evidence requires expert testimony. However, in order to ease some of the obvious, but professional, facts, the judicial notice doctrine has also been embraced from the English Common Law to Israeli law of evidence.[1660]

According to the judicial notice doctrine, as interpreted in Israel, a party is exempt from proving any fact, and the fact is presumed to be within the court's knowledge, if the fact is of general knowledge and it is within the knowledge of a reasonable person.[1661] The question is, of course, whether professional terms used in computer-related offences criminal proceedings are covered within the judicial notice doctrine, or they require proof and explanation by experts.

The general trend in Israeli society is to be open-minded to hi-tech and advanced technology from a very young age. As a result, the reasonable Israeli person knows and uses most of the professional terms used in computer science. The court does not stay behind, and the ongoing trend in Israeli criminal proceedings towards computer-related offences is that these professional terms are covered by the judicial notice doctrine, and they require no expert testimony.

However, complicated processes involved within the commission of the computer-related offences, new malware methods, original cyber-crimes, etc., in most cases, are considered requiring expert testimony. The expert may be nominated by the court for the certain case, but in general, the expert is testifying on behalf of the parties.

1659. Section 36(d) of the Evidence [New Version] Ordinance, 1971.

1660. *See, e.g.*, Cri. App. 4675/97 *Rozov v. State*, 53(4) PD 337 (1999); Cri. App. 621/88 *Peiler v. State*, 47(3) 112 (1993); Civ. Serv. App. 3871/96 *Ravid v. Commissioner of the Civil Service*, 50(3) PD 272 (1996).

1661. *Ibid.*

Conclusions

171. Israel has made significant steps in high technology, computer science, and cyber since its establishment in 1948. Israel's development of cutting-edge technologies in software, communications and the life sciences has evoked comparisons with Silicon Valley. Israel ranks tenth in the Bloomberg Innovation Index, and is first in the world in expenditure on research and development as a percentage of GDP. Israel boasts 140 scientists, technicians, and engineers per 10,000 employees, the highest number in the world (in comparison, the same is 85 for the US).

One of the most growing markets in Israel since the 1990s is the communications technology market. The catalyst for this growth was both the entrance of the Internet for private and commercial use and the mobile phones. Israeli corporations are active in developing conventional and mobile phone infrastructure overseas, as well as operating and maintaining them. In addition to developing basic infrastructure, Israeli companies have also entered high-tech niche markets. Systems developed in Israel can increase the capacity of digital satellite and fibre optic cable telecommunications links by five times.

E-services are the most growing e-commerce market in Israel. Most Israelis prefer to manage their daily life through the Internet rather than through human interactions. For example, banking services in Israel are rarely given by bankers face-to-face. Since the 1990s, most Israelis preferred banking services through the telephone, and since the beginning of the new millennium, most Israelis prefer their banking services through the Internet. That allowed the banks in Israel to reduce manpower in customer services into minimum, but it has also motivated them to find sophisticated solutions for security of the data and accessibility of the banking services in the Internet.

The services on the Internet are widely spread among Israelis, both as consumers and as business. Most Israelis find the services on the Internet much more comfortable for them than face-to-face or telephone services. As of 2021, most of the daily services are consumed in Israel through the Internet, and that includes banking services, other financial services (pension, for example), tourism services, insurance services, transportation services (order train, bus or taxi, for example), information services, food services, health services (mostly medical doctors who advise their patients through video-conferences applications) leisure services, and many more. Many international companies which service Israelis keep operating a website in Hebrew, knowing the Israelis prefer using it. Alitalia, Iberia, and Crowne Plaza are examples in the tourism area.

However, Israeli law has made progress in much smaller steps. Some ICT areas are not fully covered by the law, some technologies are not covered at all by Israeli law, although they are already in use in Israel for several years. In most cases, traditional legal spheres are used to locate solutions to legal problems from the ICT area. Some progress has indeed done, but in very small steps, as aforesaid, within the regulation of the ICT market, within the protection of IP in the ICT sector, within ICT contracts, within electronic transactions, within non-contractual liability, within privacy protection, and within computer-related delinquency.

Today, the major challenge is the regulation of AI technology. This technology challenges both current cyber law and criminal law, and the usage of it is increasing daily. Following the regulation of AI technology are, of course, the super intelligence (SI) and post-biology.

Selected Bibliography

Jack L. Arnold, *Church History (1073-1517)* (1999).

Haim Hillel Ben Sason, *Israel History in Middle Ages* (Dvir 1972).

Oded Bustenay, *The History of Israel During the First Temple Period* vol. I (2nd ed., Open University Press 2007).

Oded Bustenay, *The History of Israel During the First Temple Period* vol. II (2nd ed., Open University Press 2007).

Oded Bustenay, *The History of Israel During the First Temple Period* vol. III (2nd ed., Open University Press 2007).

Oded Bustenay, *The History of Israel During the First Temple Period* vol. IV (2nd ed., Open University Press 2007).

B. Chandraswkaran, *What Kind of Information Processing Is Intelligence?*, The Foundations of Artificial Intelligence 14 (Derek Partridge and Yorick Wilks eds., 2006).

John C. Coffee, Jr., *'No Soul to Damn: No Body to Kick': An Unscandalised Inquiry into the Problem of Corporate Punishment*, 79 Michigan Law Review 386 (1981).

George R. Cross and Cary G. Debessonet, *An Artificial Intelligence Application in the Law: CCLIPS, A Computer Program that Processes Legal Information*, 1 High Technology Law Journal 329 (1986).

Daniel C. Dennett, *Evolution, Error, and Intentionality*, The Foundations of Artificial Intelligence 190 (Derek Partridge and Yorick Wilks eds., 2006).

Shmuel Etinger, *Israel History in the New Age* (Dvir 1969).

Richard Gruner, *To Let the Punishment Fit the Organization: Sanctioning Corporate Offenders Through Corporate Probation*, 16 American Journal of Criminal Law 1 (1988).

Gabriel Hallevy, *Liability for Crimes Involving Artificial Intelligence Systems* (Springer International Publishing 2015).

Gabriel Hallevy, *The Right to Be Punished: Modern Doctrinal Sentencing* (Springer-Verlag 2013).

Gabriel Hallevy, *Theory of Civil Procedure* vol. III (Bursi Publishing House 2019).

Gabriel Hallevy, *Theory of Criminal Justice* vol. II (Bursi Publishing House 2011).

Gabriel Hallevy, *Theory of Criminal Law* vol. II (2009).

Gabriel Hallevy, *Theory of the Conflict of Laws* vol. I (Bursi Publishing House 2014).

Gabriel Hallevy, *Theory of the Conflict of Laws* vol. II (Bursi Publishing House 2014).

Selected Bibliography

Gabriel Hallevy, *Theory of the Law of Evidence* vol. III (Bursi Publishing House 2013).

Gabriel Hallevy, *When Robots Kill – Artificial Intelligence under Criminal Law* (UPNE 2013).

Gabriel Hallevy, *Is ADR (Alternative Dispute Resolution) Philosophy Relevant to Criminal Justice? – Plea Bargains as Mediation Process Between the Accused and the Prosecution*, 6 Original Law Review 1 (2009).

Gabriel Hallevy, *The Criminal Liability of Artificial Intelligence Entities – from Science Fiction to Legal Social Control*, 4 Akron Intellectual Property Journal 171 (2009).

Gabriel Hallevy, *The Private Prosecution and Criminal Justice*, 9 OAC Law Review 381 (2011).

Gabriel Hallevy, *Therapeutic Victim-Offender Mediation Within the Criminal Justice Process – Sharpening the Evaluation of Personal Potential for Rehabilitation while Righting Wrongs under the Alternative-Dispute-Resolution (ADR) Philosoph*y, 16 Harvard Negotiation Law Review 65 (2011).

Gabriel Hallevy, *Yapay Zekaya Sahip Varlıkların Cezai Sorumluluğu - Bilim Kurgudan Yasal Toplumsal Denetime* (Çeviren: Müslüm Fincan), 24 Küresel Bakış Çeviri Hukuk Dergisi, 111 (2018).

Gabriel Hallevy 人工智能实体的刑事责任 赵增田 译, 同济大学) 同济大学 (Tongji University).

Jenny Lebl, *Haj Amin and Berlin* (1996).

Gerard E. Lynch, *The Role of Criminal Law in Policing Corporate Misconduct*, 60 Law and Contemporary Problems 23 (1997).

Mordechai Naor and Dan Giladi, *Eretz Israel in the 20th Century* (Ministry of Defence Press, 1990).

Uriel Rappaport, *A History of Israel in the Period of the Second Temple* (3rd ed., Amichai 1984).

Uriel Rappaport, *From Cyrus to Alexander: The Jews under Persian Rule* (Open University Press 2004).

Gabriela Shalev, *Government Contracts: The Law and the Judge*, 11 Iyunei Mishpat 201 (1986).

Dana Vinkler, *Making an Israeli Television - Discussions Prior to the Establishment of Television in Israel, 1948-1968* (2006).

Steven Walt and William S. Laufer, *Why Personhood Doesn't Matter: Corporate Criminal Liability and Sanctions*, 18 American Journal of Criminal Justice 263 (1991).

Other Sources

Attorney General's Guidelines, 4.1107 (2006).

Computers Law Bill, 1994.

Table of Cases

Table of Legislation

Table of Legislation

Table of Legislation

Index

The numbers here refer to paragraph numbers.

Index

Index

Index